Multilingualism, Discourse and Ethnography

Routledge Critical Studies in Multilingualism

EDITED BY MARILYN MARTIN-JONES, *MOSAIC Centre for Research on Multilingualism, University of Birmingham*

1 **Language in Late Capitalism**
Pride and Profit
*Edited by Alexandre Duchêne
and Monica Heller*

2. **Language Mixing and Code-Switching in Writing**
Approaches to Mixed-Language
Written Discourse
*Edited by Mark Sebba, Shahrzad
Mahootian and Carla Jonsson*

3. **Multilingualism, Discourse,
and Ethnography**
*Edited by Sheena Gardner
and Marilyn Martin-Jones*

Multilingualism, Discourse and Ethnography

Sheena Gardner and
Marilyn Martin-Jones

Routledge
Taylor & Francis Group

NEW YORK LONDON

First published 2012
by Routledge
711 Third Avenue, New York, NY 10017

Simultaneously published in the UK
by Routledge
2 Park Square, Milton Park, Abingdon, Oxfordshire OX14 4RN

First issued in paperback 2014

*Routledge is an imprint of the Taylor & Francis Group,
an informa business*

Library of Congress Cataloging-in-Publication Data
Gardner, Sheena.
   Multilingualism, discourse and ethnography / Sheena Gardner and
Marilyn Martin-Jones.
      p. cm. — (Routledge Critical Studies in Multilingualism; 2)
   Includes bibliographical references and index.
   1.   Multilingualism.   2.   Discourse analysis.   I. Martin-Jones,
Marilyn.   II. Title.
   P115.G38 2011
   306.44'6—dc22
   2011035268

ISBN: 978-0-415-87494-6 (hbk)
ISBN: 978-1-138-79298-2 (pbk)

Typeset in Sabon
by IBT Global.

Contents

Acknowledgements   ix

Introduction: Multilingualism, Discourse and Ethnography   1
MARILYN MARTIN-JONES AND SHEENA GARDNER

PART I
Linking Local Practices to Wider Social Processes

Introduction   19
LI WEI

1   Rethinking Sociolinguistic Ethnography:
    From Community and Identity to Process and Practice   24
    MONICA HELLER

2   Sociolinguistic Perspectives on Language
    and Multilingualism in Institutions   34
    MELISSA G. MOYER

3   Unpicking Agency in Sociolinguistic Research with Migrants   47
    DAVID BLOCK

PART II
Researching Identities and Identities in Research Practice

Introduction   63
MARILYN MARTIN-JONES

4   Pontian Greek Adolescents: The Negotiation of
    Identities in an Urban Context in Northern Greece   67
    ELENI MARIOU

5 Negotiation of Identities across Times and Spaces   82
   ADRIAN BLACKLEDGE AND ANGELA CREESE

6 Authenticity, Legitimacy and Power:
   Critical Ethnography and Identity Politics   95
   FRANCES GIAMPAPA

PART III
Taking Account of Trajectories:
Multilingualism across Social Spaces

   Introduction   111
   MONICA HELLER

7 Cultural Geography and the
   Retheorisation of Sociolinguistic Space   114
   MIKE BAYNHAM

8 Diaspora Youth, Ancestral Languages and
   English as 'Translation' in Multilingual Space   131
   GILL CRESSEY

PART IV
Visual and Semiotic Perspectives on Multilingualism

   Introduction   145
   MARK SEBBA

9 Material Ethnographies of Multilingualism: Linguistic
   Landscapes in the Township of Khayelitsha   149
   CHRISTOPHER STROUD AND SIBONILE MPENDUKANA

10 Experiences and Expressions of Multilingualism:
   Visual Ethnography and Discourse Analysis in
   Research with Sámi Children   163
   SARI PIETIKÄINEN

11 Ethnographic Perspectives on Multilingual Computer-Mediated
    Discourse: Insights from Finnish Football Forums on the Web   179
    SAMU KYTÖLÄ AND JANNIS ANDROUTSOPOULOS

12 Multilingual Nation Online? Possibilities and
    Constraints on the BBC Voices Website   197
    BETHAN L. DAVIES, TOMMASO M. MILANI AND WILL TURNER

PART V
Interpreting Voices from the Classroom

Introduction   217
CHARMIAN KENNER

13 English as an Additional Language
    Policy-Rendered Theory and Classroom Interaction   222
    CONSTANT LEUNG

14 Young Learner Perspectives through
    Researcher-Initiated Role Play   241
    AIZAN YAACOB AND SHEENA GARDNER

15 Doing Ethnography in Multilingual Schools: Shifting
    Research Positioning in Response to Dialogic Methods   256
    CARLA JONSSON

16 Ideologies and Issues of Access in Multilingual
    School Ethnography: A French Example   269
    FLORENCE BONACINA

PART VI
Building Researcher-Researched Relationships

Introduction   285
ANGELA CREESE

17 The Advantages of Research in Familiar Locales, Viewed
from the Perspectives of Researcher and Researched:
Reflections on Ethnographic Fieldwork in Mozambique   288
FELICIANO CHIMBUTANE

18 A Critical Linguistic Ethnographic Approach to
Language Disabilities in Multilingual Families   305
DEIRDRE MARTIN

19 "Part of the Puzzle": The Retrospective Interview as
Reflexive Practice in Collaborative Ethnographic Research   319
GABRIELE BUDACH

20 Collaborative Practice, Linguistic Anthropological
Enquiry and the Mediation between Researcher
and Practitioner Discourses   334
ALEXANDRA JAFFE

Contributors   353
Index   357

Acknowledgements

As the title *Multilingualism, Discourse, and Ethnography* suggests, this edited collection brings together researchers with overlapping and mutually invigorating interests. This confluence would not have been possible without the support which we here acknowledge with deep gratitude.

At the heart of the volume is the work of MOSAIC, the Centre for Research on Multilingualism at the University of Birmingham, which was launched in April 2008 in a seminar attended by, amongst others, those whose chapters are included in this volume. This event brought together researchers from around the world, integrating those with research reputations in different aspects of research on multilingualism, discourse and ethnography with newcomers to this dynamic, expanding arena. We are grateful to all who made the launch a success and particularly to those whose contributions have been carefully written up for this volume. By including short introductions as well as full chapters, we aim to convey something of the interaction around the research themes sparked in the 2008 launch.

The launch enjoyed financial support from the British Academy and the Research Committee of the School of Education, University of Birmingham. Here we would also recognise the organisational support from Jacqui Wootton, Events coordinator for the School of Education, from Lily Ilič, Secretary for the Department of Language, Discourse and Society whose efficiency with contracts and file management was invaluable, and from Dr Gaye Houghton, a recent graduate from the doctoral programme, whose assistance with the editing of final manuscript drafts contributed hugely to the polished appearance of the final volume.

This volume is one in the *Critical Studies in Multilingualism* series, an idea proposed by Marilyn Martin-Jones and supported through the initial strategic negotiations by Louisa Semlyen of Routledge, UK, and then formally by Erica Wetter of Routledge, New York. Latterly, Felisa Salvago-Keyes's cool head and capable hands have steered the manuscript to print. We are highly appreciative of all at Routledge for their patience and professional support.

Sheena Gardner and Marilyn Martin-Jones
MOSAIC Centre for Research on Multilingualism
University of Birmingham

Introduction
Multilingualism, Discourse and Ethnography

Marilyn Martin-Jones and Sheena Gardner

Over the last two decades, sociolinguistic research on multilingualism has been transformed. Two broad processes of change have been at work: firstly, there has been a broad epistemological shift to a critical and ethnographic approach, one that has reflected and contributed to the wider turn, across the social sciences, towards critical and poststructuralist perspectives on social life. Secondly, over the last ten years or so, there has been an intense focus on the social, cultural and linguistic changes ushered in by globalisation, by transnational population flows, by the advent of new communication technologies, by the changes taking place in the political and economic landscape of different regions of the world. These changes have had major implications for the ways in which we conceptualise the relationship between language and society and the multilingual realities of the contemporary era. A new sociolinguistics of multilingualism is now being forged: one that takes account of the new communicative order and the particular cultural conditions of our times, while retaining a central concern with the processes involved in the construction of social difference and social inequality.

The contributors to this volume have been at the forefront of these epistemological shifts in sociolinguistic research on multilingualism. They write here about the conceptual and methodological challenges posed by these shifts and by the profound social, cultural and linguistic changes that we have witnessed in the late modern era. We also learn about the innovative ways in which they have addressed some of these challenges. In addition, the reflexivity of recent interpretive and ethnographic research in the social sciences is evident here. There is ample reflection across the chapters of the volume on the role of researchers as socially-situated actors, with their own biographies and subjectivities, within the research process and on the fluid and negotiated nature of the researcher-researched relationships that are formed in and out of the field. The chapters are based on research in diverse research sites—in local lifeworlds, in diasporic spaces, in institutional worlds such as education and the media and in virtual worlds. They illustrate some of the key ways in which the field of multilingualism has been transformed over the last twenty years or so and they reveal the distance that we have all travelled. Our aim, as editors of this volume, has been to represent the range and depth of current research which combines discursive and ethnographic perspectives on multilingualism. In this introduction to the volume, we provide a brief genealogy of the shifts in thinking about multilingualism that have taken place in sociolinguistics and linguistic anthropology and we outline some of the new directions that are being taken. We also indicate how the volume has been organised.

MULTILINGUALISM AND DISCOURSE: EPISTEMOLOGICAL SHIFTS

From Meaning in Interaction to the Workings of Symbolic Power

For almost half a century, sociolinguists, anthropologists and Hallidayan linguists worked away at countering the structuralist preoccupation with language as a decontextualised system of forms, arguing instead for a focus on the study of "communicative practices" (Hanks, 1996) and on language "as a social semiotic" (Halliday, 1978). From the late 1960s onwards, we saw the emergence of new strands of research on interaction and on the situated practices of meaning-making in spoken discourse. Reflecting the wider influence of social constructionism, social identities and relationships came to be seen as constructed, reproduced, negotiated or even recast in the communicative cycles of day-to-day life. Within this new frame, there was more scope for characterising speaker agency. Many of those involved in this turn towards interaction were themselves involved in linguistic and anthropological research in multilingual settings (e.g. Hymes, 1972; Erickson, 1975; Gumperz, 1982; LePage and Tabouret-Keller, 1985). Within the field of multilingualism, different strands of research on language in interaction emerged, including Hymesian ethnography of communication, conversation analysis and microethnography. These different strands were drawn together in particularly productive ways in the work of John Gumperz (1982) and combined with insights from Goffman's (1967) approach to interaction analysis. Gumperz (1982) was committed to working towards a "sociolinguistic analysis" which would "yield new insights into the workings of social process" (1982: 7). However, in this and other research in the tradition of interactional sociolinguistics, the focus remained primarily on the lived texture and dynamics of everyday communication, in local lifeworlds or institutional worlds (e.g. classrooms, law courts or medical settings).

By the end of the 1980s, interest had turned, in sociolinguistic and linguistic anthropological circles, to the new epistemological spaces opened up by developments in social theory, notably the turn towards poststructuralism, postmodernism and critical theory. Within the field of multilingualism, three linguistic anthropologists (Gal, 1989; Heller, 1992, 1995,

1999; Woolard, 1985, 1989) were the first to lay the foundations for a critical, ethnographic sociolinguistics, by engaging with key conceptual advances in poststructuralist theory, notably those in the work of Bourdieu (1977, 1991). These scholars were seeking ways of linking their detailed ethnographic accounts of language ideologies and interactional practices, in different local sites, with their analyses of institutional and historical processes, with wider discourses about language and identity and with specific political and economic conditions.

From these foundations, a distinct tradition of critical, ethnographic and discourse analytic research on multilingualism gradually emerged and is still being consolidated and fine-tuned today, as several chapters in this volume show. Research has been conducted in different cultural and historical contexts and in different social spaces (e.g. Heller, 1999; Heller and Martin-Jones, 2001; Pavlenko and Blackledge, 2004; Baynham and Da Fina, 2005; Luk and Lin, 2007; Kanno, 2008; Blackledge and Creese, 2010; Martín Rojo, 2010; McCarty, 2011). This research has incorporated critical reflexivity (Pennycook, 2001), while aiming to reveal links between local practices (multilingual or monolingual) and wider social and ideological processes, either by investigating the ways in which language is bound up with social categorisation and stratification (Heller, 1999, 2011) or by researching the ways in which identities are constructed, negotiated or contested in different multilingual settings (Pavlenko and Blackledge, 2004).

Imagined Communities and Language Ideologies

The influence of poststructuralist and postmodern thought was also evident in the writing on language ideology that flourished in the 1990s (e.g. Gal and Woolard, 1995; Schieffelin, Woolard and Kroskrity, 1998; Blommaert, 1999). The research addressed the central question of "how linguistic units came to be linked to social units" (Gal and Irvine, 1995: 970), how people in different settings come to be constructed as a community, how languages are tied to whole populations in a particular polity. This strand of work in sociolinguistics and linguistic anthropology provided a trenchant critique of grand narratives and modernist assumptions about the links between languages and nation-states. It had a significant historical dimension and involved tracing the discursive threads involved in the construction of nationhood in primarily unitary and essentialised terms, in different historical contexts, from nineteenth century Europe (e.g. Grillo, 1989; Rindler Schjerve, 2003) to the language revitalisation and minority rights movements of the twentieth century (e.g. Urla, 1993; Jaffe, 1999; Pujolar, 2001; Heller, 2011) and to postcolonial contexts (e.g. Errington, 1998; Stroud, 1999). This work on language ideology and nationhood has been characterised by considerable reflexivity and has thrown light on the role of linguists and anthropologists, over time, in these discursive and ideological processes. As nation-states came to be defined as linguistically and homogeneous entities, bilingualism and multilingualism emerged as 'problems' for this essentialising project. As Heller (2007: 5) has aptly observed: "[B]ilingualism . . . had to be explained and evaluated" in the social science disciplines emerging in the late nineteenth and early twentieth century.

We see similar traces of poststructuralist and postmodern thinking in recent writing about language (e.g. Makoni and Pennycook, 2007; Heller, 2007; Errington, 2008; Pennycook, 2010). For example, Makoni and Pennycook (2007: 2) argue that the notion that languages are discrete, bounded entities and "countable institutions" is a social construct. As in the case of the one-language-one-nation ideology discussed above, they call for critical, historical research which unpacks the discursive processes involved in the classification, naming and invention of languages. They refer to this project as the "disinvention" of languages. Given the creativity and hybridity emerging in urban popular culture, in minority group vernaculars and in mediated communication, there is growing consensus that it is more useful to talk about linguistic resources than languages. This shift in thinking echoes Hymes' (1996) call for a focus on ways of speaking and on "varieties, modalities, styles and genres, ways of using language as a resource" (1996: 70).

Heller (2007) captures this broad epistemological shift in the field of multilingualism and sets out a new agenda for research of a critical and ethnographic nature. She argues that we need to "move discussion of bilingualism away from a focus on the whole bounded units of code and community, and towards a more processual and materialist approach which privileges language as social practice, speakers as social actors and boundaries as products of social action" (2007: 1).

MULTILINGUALISM IN A GLOBAL ERA

The last decade of the twentieth century and the first decade of the twenty-first century saw a surge of interest in globalisation. In the sociological and anthropological literature of this period, there was a veritable feast of commentary and analysis on the changing social and cultural conditions of the late modern age (e.g. Harvey, 1989; Appadurai, 1996; Castells, 2000; Hannerz, 1996). In an early collection of papers on sociolinguistics and globalisation, Coupland (2003) noted that sociolinguists were "late getting to the party". However, in recent years significant sociolinguistic contributions have been made, through empirical work and theory-building, to the characterisation of the political, economic and cultural conditions of late modernity and to identification of the ways in which language practices and ideologies organise and legitimise these conditions.

As we know from the sociological and anthropological literature, globalisation is complex and multi-faceted and it is also not a linear process. Dynamic tensions operate between local and global. There are tropes that recur in the general social science literature and some of these have been picked up in recent writing in sociolinguistics. They have provided starting points for posing new kinds of question, for creating new research foci and identifying new objects of study. One recurring trope is that of mobility or flow. Sociolinguists have picked up the notion of mobility in a number of ways. For example, Heller (2007) argues that we need to turn our gaze away "from stability to mobility" (2011: 5–6) and focus on the development of trajectories over time. She specifically mentions the trajectories of social actors and of linguistic and material resources and recommends that we should focus on the ways in which these trajectories do or do not intersect. Blommaert (2010) calls for a "sociolinguistics of mobile resources", one which takes into account the diverse material and symbolic ties that get established across global networks (e.g. transnational diaspora). He argues that we need a sociolinguistic analysis that represents linguistic and semiotic phenomena as being located and distributed across scales, from global to local, and specifically, one that interrogates the links between scales (for further discussion of the notion of scales, see Collins, Slembrouck and Baynham, 2009). At the same time, Pennycook (2010) reminds us that globalisation should not only be understood in terms of global movement from above but also as locally generated mobilities. Tracking such mobilities, through networks and trajectories, is what presents the greatest challenge to sociolinguists, including those of us who are researching multilingualism. Sociolinguistics has traditionally conceptualised language practices as being spatially located (see, Chapter 7 by Baynham in this volume, for a historical account of this tendency) but language practices have not yet been studied as part of temporal *and* spatial trajectories.

In an early contribution, Appadurai (1996) identified different facets of globalisation in terms of rapidly changing '-scapes'. In the sections that follow, we focus on just three of these: his ethnoscapes, his technoscapes and his mediascapes. Technoscapes and mediascapes are discussed in just one section. Sociolinguists working on multilingualism and multilingual literacy, including several contributors to this book, have begun to explore all three of these areas of globalisation and their implications for our understanding of language in late modernity.

New Ethnoscapes, New Multilingual Realities

There has been a distinct intensification of transnational population flows in the last two decades and this has brought about far-reaching changes of a social and demographic nature and the creation of new ethnoscapes. We focus here on recent research related to transnational labour migration and to the movement of refugees, because it provides the wider context for several chapters in this volume. New and increasingly diverse patterns of migration have given rise to much greater population diversity in countries that have become key migration destinations. This social and demographic phenomenon is now referred to as "superdiversity" (Vertovec, 2007). In his research on the changing patterns of migration to the UK, Vertovec (2007: 1024) has pointed out that these patterns are characterised by "dynamic interplay of variables among an increased number of new, small and scattered, multiple origin, transnationally connected, socio-economically differentiated and legally stratified immigrants who have arrived over the last decade". Whereas there has been considerable debate in anthropology, migration studies and sociology about the new social and demographic aspects of superdiversity, sociolinguists are only now beginning to consider the ramifications of superdiversity for our understanding of multilingualism (e.g. Blommaert and Rampton, forthcoming). The concept of superdiversity has been formulated to capture the increasingly differentiated composition, social positioning and trajectories of different groups of migrant origin in the twenty-first century and, as Martin-Jones, Blackledge and Creese (2012) have put it, "the meshing and interweaving of diversities" in which not only 'ethnicity' (or country of origin) but also other social categories, like class, gender, disability or generation, intersect (e.g. Menard-Warwick, 2009; Martin, Chapter 18, this volume).

The implications of these new patterns of mobility and settlement (and sometimes further migration) for the study of multilingualism are myriad. As Blommaert (2010) has observed, the networks of contemporary urban neighbourhoods are often organised as both local and translocal, real as well as virtual. He argues that these new diasporic lines of connectedness are bound to shape the development of communicative repertoires and language and literacy practices. There is empirical work to be done, along the lines of some of the chapters in this volume. As yet, we know rather little about the processes of change in the communicative repertoires and language practices of those who have been caught up in the ever-diversifying population flows of the last couple of decades. There are a few guiding lights. Take, for example, the detailed critical, ethnographic work done by literacy scholars and sociolinguists like Lam (2006), Bailey (2007), Lytra (2007) and Blackledge and Creese (2010). A further dimension of complexity lies in the now well-documented phenomenon of the emergence of vernaculars and hybridised ways of speaking in multilingual, urban neighbourhoods, across generations of settlement (e.g. Sebba, 1993; Rampton, 1995). Thus, sociolinguistic superdiversity encompasses linguistic resources transplanted in the process of transnational migration, local vernaculars and localised ways of speaking.

New Technoscapes and Mediascapes: Multilingual Literacy and Multimodality

With the advent of new digital technologies and with the globalised spread of new technoscapes and mediascapes, there have, of course, been major changes in the communicative order. The pace of communication has quickened and the time-space compression of contemporary social life has made it possible to build and sustain translocal relationships over distance (e.g. within diasporic spaces), through the use of new media and the internet. In the new communicative landscape of the twenty-first century, we read, write and use texts in ways that are substantially different from those of only a few decades ago. There has been considerable diversification of communication media, digital artefacts (e.g. new software) and textual resources (e.g. new genres, such as blogs and tweets). Screen literacy has created affordances for combining multiple modes of semiosis (e.g. colour, image or sound) with text, so that meaning-making practices are now more multimodal and integrated in nature (Kress, 2003), although, inevitably, access to the new digital technologies of literacy is unevenly distributed. Moreover, as Androutsopoulos (2007) has shown us, computer-mediated communication is becoming increasingly multilingual.

A range of research avenues are now being opened up with regard to multilingual literacy and multimodality in computer-based communication. These include the investigation of the creative and nuanced ways in which young people draw on the linguistic resources and semiotic modes available to them as they negotiate virtual identities and relationships, both locally and globally, across diasporic spaces (e.g. McGinnis, Goodstein-Stolzenberg and Saliani, 2007; Lam and Rosario-Ramos, 2009). It also includes studies of multiple language use in specific online communities of practice (e.g. the football forums discussed in this volume by Kytölä and Androtsopoulos). In addition, it includes research into the use of different scripts in online communication (e.g. Warschauer, El Said and Zohry, 2002; Lee, 2007). Studies of multilingualism in the media are now gathering pace, although the early focus was primarily on multilingualism in advertising (e.g. Piller, 2003; Kelly Holmes, 2005).

Androutsopoulos (2007) surveys the range of studies of multilingualism in other media, including research on language mixing in popular music (e.g. African hip-hop, Algerian *rai* and Bollywood sound tracks), studies of bilingual host-caller radio talk and niche fashion magazines. He concludes that "linguistic diversity is gaining an unprecedented visibility in the mediascapes of the late twentieth and early twenty-first century" (2007: 207). He sees this as being due to the creation of diasporic 'communities' with their own public sphere and to the "changing conditions of media production and consumption" (2007: 208). He also notes that "access to media production is becoming more accessible to marginalized social groups" (ibid.). The net effect of this public visibility of multilingualism is that multilingual practices are also seeping into the dominant, globalising media (as we see in Chapter 12 by Davies et al., in this volume).

As we have indicated, research into multilingualism in mediated discourse, in these different spaces within the current communicative landscape, is more advanced in some areas than in others. Moreover, as Sebba (forthcoming) has noted, these different forms of communication pose considerable methodological and analytic challenges for the sociolinguist, especially in the case of online, digital literacy in multilingual settings. The situated practices of blending linguistic and orthographic resources in written discourse, on page and on screen, are new and also subject to rapid change and refashioning, particularly among young people in their local and translocal networks. We need a body of comparative work, in different multilingual settings, to build a deeper understanding of the significance of these processes of linguistic change.

Global Changes in Political Economy, New Discourses and Practices

Underpinning the changes taking place in the different -scapes of contemporary life is the transformation of the global political and economic order. In the last two decades or so, we have witnessed a broad shift from a world in which nation-states regulated markets to one in which state control over capital has been eroded in the face of rapid expansion of capitalism and the globalisation of economic activity. This major change in the world order has been accompanied by a decline in industrial capitalism, in the countries of the global north and west, and by the development of a tertiary sector which services global networks of production and consumption and which facilitates modes of production which are increasingly digitally mediated. One consequence of these global economic changes is the emergence of the now all-too-familiar neo-liberal political conditions in which the role of the nation-state in regulating the private sector has been greatly diminished and, instead, it has taken on the role of facilitator of globalised capitalism.

Duchêne and Heller (2011) have argued that, in these new political and economic conditions, language and communication have taken on a new prominence and that we have seen the creation of new sites of discursive production outside of or indirectly related to state control. These include supra-national agencies, non-governmental organisations (NGOs), the private sector or religion. Heller (2011) has done extended ethnographic work, over the best part of a decade, in French Canada, documenting the way in which these new political and economic conditions have spawned new discourses. She writes about a discursive shift, in that context, from a former 'discourse of rights' to a 'discourse of profit', and shows that the role of the Canadian state has changed from that of 'protector' of the rights of French speakers as Canadian citizens to that of acting as facilitator for the production and circulation of material and symbolic products associated, in some way, with French Canada: products which range from Canadian cheeses with bilingual branding sold in street markets in France, or French Canadian cultural products, such as exhibitions related to cultural heritage. The commodification of identity, in different domains—in tourism, in advertising or in the mass media—is giving rise to different multilingual practices in different settings, with their own local particularities. For example, Stroud and Mpendukana (Chapter 9, this volume) illustrate for us the ways in which globalised discourses of consumption and consumer identities are resemioticised through the use of multilingual and multimodal resources within the linguistic landscape of a South African township.

Another significant aspect of the role of language in the new globalised economy is the rise of language industries. As da Silva et al. (2007: 187) have noted: "Today, language is still being used in the process of selling products (as a communicational tool) but more importantly, it has become a product itself (that is, a marketable resource)". Language industries provide a whole range of services, from translation and interpreting to private language teaching, outsourced work for publishers, bilingual website design or research and development work by NGOs focussing on language policy or planning. Such industries are becoming more prominent in today's globalised multilingual world with its premium on the rapid circulation of information. The language entrepreneurs who work in such industries, particularly those involved in translation, tend to represent languages as discrete, bounded systems and language forms as appropriate or inappropriate. This ideological stance is due to their investment in this particular kind of economic activity.

One particular language industry that has been given close scrutiny by sociolinguists who are researching multilingualism is that of call centres. This research builds on and extends the insights of Cameron (2001). The first empirical work in bilingual call centres was carried out in Canada (e.g. Roy, 2003). What emerges clearly from this work is the construction of bilingualism as a commodifiable skill within this sector of the service economy. At the same time, communicative practices are highly regulated and, as da Silva et al. (2007: 190) point out, "bilingual workers need to be well versed in the particular cultural/context vocabulary relevant to the clients' needs and 'caring' styles of communication are expected. Not surprisingly, in the Canadian context, this is a highly gendered sector of the economy.

Moyer (Chapter 2, this volume) draws our attention to the new tendency to outsource call centre operations using English to countries in the global south where English graduates move into the "word-force" in this sector at lower rates of pay. Here, we see global asymmetries being constructed in the exploitation of language 'skills'.

NEW OBJECTS OF STUDY, NEW RESEARCH LENSES

In the sections above, we have charted some of the ways in which the changing conditions of our times have obliged us to ask new questions and have revealed the inadequacy of traditional conceptual frameworks for the study of the new multilingual realities of contemporary life. As new objects of study are being identified, new research lenses are being honed. The chapters in this volume provide a rich range of examples of the new conceptual and methodological directions that are being taken in research in our field and of the new reflexivity evident in this research.

As we have shown, one of the discursive tropes that recur in transdisciplinary research on globalisation is that of mobility and, indexing a postructuralist and postmodern stance, the term is generally used in the plural—as 'mobilities'—along with cognate terms such as flows or circulations. As we have also shown, terms such as these have served as compass points for sociolinguists who are endeavouring to identify the ways in which language is bound up with the processes of change at work in contemporary society. The notion of 'trajectory' (e.g. Heller, 2011; Duchêne and Heller, 2011) is being used as a means of grasping the flows of people, resources (linguistic and material), texts and discourses that traverse today's world and as a means of capturing the intersecting dimensions of time and space. However, trajectories are not seen as linear pathways or as equivalent in nature. As Duchêne and Heller (2011) put it: "[T]he landscape is uneven, unbounded and fluid, and . . . social actors occupy different (and differently advantageous) positions with respect to access to the resources that circulate across it)".

The adoption of new conceptual compass points such as the notion of trajectories (Heller, 2011) or mobile resources (Blommaert, 2010) implies methodological innovation, new ethnographic approaches and new ways of interpreting and analysing texts. Marcus (1995) and Hannerz (2003) provide us with useful starting points with their explicit rationales for doing multi-sited ethnography. This approach allows us to track the circulation of social actors, resources, texts or discourses across different social spaces and identify the links between the practices observable in different sites, real and virtual. At the same time, longitudinal or historical perspectives allow us to capture the temporal dimension and the ways in which trajectories develop over time. This is a dimension that was largely overlooked in the sociolinguistics of the latter half of the twentieth century, with its synchronic focus.

Whereas the notion of trajectories is foregrounded in the chapters in Part III of this book, in other chapters we see the trajectories of particular social actors. For example, in the chapter by Budach, we encounter teachers with transnational trajectories; in the chapter by Mariou, we read about the cross-generational trajectories of people moving from Russia and Georgia to Greece. We also see trajectories of discourses, including discourses of consumption (Stroud and Mpendukana), policy discourses (Leung, Chimbutane) and discourses about multilingualism circulating rapidly in real time in the virtual spaces of football forums (Kytölä and Androutsopoulos).

Last, but not least, the chapters in this volume remind us of the significance of the linguistic and semiotic resources we draw on in our own research practice and of the ways in which multilingualism and 'translation' shapes our experiences and sense-making as ethnographers in and out of the field. Over half of the contributors to this volume are researchers who use languages other than English in their research in the field, while writing in English here (and using other languages, at other times, to teach and to write). Moreover, in several chapters, we see research collaboration across language boundaries (e.g. Yaacob and Gardner; Kytölä and Androutsopoulos; Stroud and Mpendukana). We also have examples of team ethnography (Blackledge and Creese; Moyer), with different voices being brought into play and given expression in the research process. And, in addition, we even see the evaluation of the 'authenticity' of the (Italian-Canadian) voice of a researcher (Giampapa) by research participants.

ORGANISATION AND CONTENT OF THE BOOK

The book has been organised into six parts. Each part focuses on a different area of research on multilingualism in which conceptual and methodological challenges are being addressed. Each opens with a brief introduction which reflects on the themes emerging from the individual chapters and on the thematic resonances across chapters. Part I, 'Linking Local Practices to Wider Social Processes' (with an Introduction by Li Wei), focuses on the global processes of political, economic and social change that are reshaping contemporary life and considers how these processes oblige us to rethink the ways in which we understand the relationship between language and society (Heller; Moyer) and structure and agency (Block).

Part II, 'Researching Identities and Identities in Research Practice' (with an Introduction by Marilyn Martin-Jones), demonstrates how critical ethnographic research on multilingualism provides a way of seeing the detail of everyday discourse practices *and* the ways in which these practices are embedded in and shaped by wider historical and ideological processes. The focus in the three chapters in this part is on the construction of identities, and all three chapters take a temporal and spatial perspective in their analyses of the ideologies and practices they document.

In Part III, 'Taking Account of Trajectories: Multilingualism across Social Spaces' (with an Introduction by Monica Heller), the discussion of time and space widens out to incorporate transdisciplinary perspectives, from geography, migration studies, sociolinguistics and cultural studies. The research presented here (especially that by Baynham) demonstrates the conceptual and methodological advantages that accrue from reconceptualising the notion of sociolinguistic space and from understanding the value of narrative (Cressey) in building accounts of the trajectories of social actors and the ways in which they make places into social spaces.

Part IV, 'Developing Visual and Semiotic Perspectives on Multilingualism' (with an Introduction by Mark Sebba), addresses conceptual and methodological issues that arise in the study of multilingualism within the technoscapes and mediascapes of the twenty-first century. Here, new objects of study are identified and new research methods are explored (e.g. Pietikainen). The authors present and discuss examples of new lines of enquiry and reflect on the value and/or constraints of different approaches to data gathering and data analysis.

Part V, 'Interpreting Voices from the Classroom' (with an Introduction by Charmian Kenner), turns our attention to ethnographic and discourse analytic research in multilingual classroom settings. The authors of the four chapters here offer reflections on different stages of the research process (Leung; Yaacob and Gardner; Jonsson; Bonacina) and on the interface between research, language policy and pedagogy.

Part VI, 'Building Researcher-Researched Relationships' (with an Introduction by Angela Creese), demonstrates, in illuminating detail, the importance of reflexivity in critical, ethnographic research. In these four final chapters, we see the ways in which the authors have grappled with and committed to the building of democratic and dialogic relationships in the field.

The book provides a rare space for reflection on critical ethnographic research in multilingual settings. It does not set out definitive solutions to the conceptual and methodological issues that arise in research on multilingualism in the social conditions of our times. Instead, it foregrounds these issues and engages with them. Our use of the present participle in each of the section sub-headings (*Linking, Researching, Taking Account Of, Developing, Interpreting* and *Building*) reflects the fact that the ideas that we have considered here are still working their way through the field. We hope that the volume will have resonances for those who are addressing similar issues in their own research.

REFERENCES

Androutsopoulos, J. 2007. Bilingualism in the mass media and on the internet. In *Bilingualism: A Social Approach*, ed. M. Heller, 207–30. Basingstoke, Hampshire: Palgrave Macmillan.

Appadurai, A. 1996. *Modernity at Large: Cultural Dimensions of Globalization*. Minneapolis: University of Minnesota Press.

Bailey, B. 2007. Heteroglossia and boundaries. In *Bilingualism: A Social Approach*, ed. M. Heller, 257–74. Basingstoke, Hampshire: Palgrave Macmillan.

Baynham, M. and A. Da Fina (eds) 2005. *Dislocations/Relocations: Narratives of Displacement*. Manchester: St Jerome.

Blackledge, A. and Creese, A. 2010. *Multilingualism: A Critical Perspective*. London: Continuum.

Blommaert, J. (ed.) 1999. *Language Ideological Debates*. Berlin: Mouton de Gruyter.

———. 2010. *The Sociolinguistics of Globalization*. Cambridge: Cambridge University Press.

Blommaert, J. and Rampton, B. Forthcoming. Language and superdiversity. *Diversities*.

Bourdieu, P. 1977. *Outline of a Theory of Practice*. Cambridge: Cambridge University Press.

———. 1991. *Language and Symbolic Power*. Cambridge, MA: Harvard University Press.

Cameron, D. 2001. *Good to Talk?* London: Sage.

Castells, M. 2000. *The Information Age: Economy, Society and Culture*. Oxford: Blackwell.

Collins, J., Slembrouck, S. and Baynham, M. (eds) 2009. *Globalization and Language in Contact*. London: Continuum, 1–16.

Coupland, N. (ed.) 2003. Sociolinguistics and globalization (thematic issue). *Journal of Sociolinguistics*,7(4).

da Silva, E., McLaughlin, M. and Richards, M. 2007. Bilingualism and the globalized new economy: the commodification of language and identity. In *Bilingualism: A Social Approach*, ed. M. Heller, 183–206. Basingstoke, Hampshire: Palgrave Macmillan.

Duchêne, A. and Heller, M. 2011. *Language in Late Capitalism: Pride and Profit*. London and New York: Routledge.

Erickson, F. 1975. Gatekeeping and the melting pot: interaction in counselling encounters. *Harvard Educational Review* 45: 44–70.

Errington, J. J. 1998. *Shifting Languages: Interaction and Identity in Javanese Indonesia*. Cambridge: Cambridge University Press.

———. 2008. *Linguistics in a Colonial World: A Story of Language, Meaning and Power*. Oxford: Blackwell.

Gal, S. 1989. Language and political economy. *Annual Review of Anthropology* 18: 345–67.

Gal, S. and Irvine, J. 1995. The boundaries of languages and disciplines: how ideologies construct difference. *Social Research* 62(4): 967–1001.

Gal, S. and Woolard, K. A. 1995. Constructing languages and publics: authority and representation. *Pragmatics* 5: 155–66.

Goffman, E. 1967. *Interaction Ritual*. Harmondsworth: Penguin.

Grillo, R. 1989. *Dominant Languages: Language and Hierarchy in Britain and France*. Cambridge: Cambridge University Press.

Gumperz, J. J. 1982. *Discourse Strategies*. Cambridge: Cambridge University Press.

Halliday, M. A. K. 1978. *Language as a Social Semiotic*. London: Edward Arnold.

Hanks, W. F. 1996. *Language and Communicative Practices*. Boulder, CO: Westview Press.

Hannerz, U. 1996. *Transnational Connections*. London and New York: Routledge.

———. 2003. On being there . . . and there . . . and there! Reflections on multi-sited ethnography. *Ethnography* 4(2): 201–16.

Harvey, D. 1989. *The Condition of Post-Modernity*. Oxford: Blackwell.

Heller, M. 1992. The politics of codeswitching and language choice. *Journal of Multilingual and Multicultural Development* 3: 1–13.

———. 1995. Language choice, social institutions and symbolic domination. *Language in Society* 24(3): 373–405.

———. 1999. *Linguistic Minorities and Modernity*. London: Longman.

———. (ed.) 2007. *Bilingualism: A Social Approach*. Basingstoke, Hampshire: Palgrave Macmillan.

———. 2011. *Paths to Post-Nationalism: A Critical Ethnography of Language and Identity*. Oxford: Oxford University Press.

Heller, M. and Martin-Jones, M. (eds) 2001. *Voices of Authority: Education and Linguistic Difference*. Westport, CT: Ablex.

Hymes, D. 1972. Models of the interaction of language and social life. In *Directions in Sociolinguistics: The Ethnography of Communication*, ed. J. J. Gumperz and D. Hymes, 35–71. New York: Holt, Rinehart and Winston.

———. 1996. *Ethnography, Linguistics, Narrative Inequality: Towards an Understanding of Voice*. London: Taylor and Francis.

Jaffe, A. 1999. *Ideologies in Action: Language Politics on Corsica*. Berlin: Mouton de Gruyter.

Kanno, Y. 2008. *Language and Education in Japan: Unequal Access to Bilingualism,* Basingstoke, Hampshire: Palgrave Macmillan.

Kelly Holmes, H. 2005. *Advertising as Multilingual Communication*. Basingstoke, Hampshire: Palgrave Macmillan.

Kress, G. 2003. *Literacy in the New Media Age*. London and New York: Routledge.

Lam, E. 2006. Re-envisioning language, literacy and the immigrant subject in new mediascapes. *Pedagogies: An International Journal* 1(3): 171–95.

Lam, E. and Rosario-Ramos, E. 2009. Multilingual literacies in transnational digital mediated contexts: an exploratory study of immigrant teens in the United States. *Language and Education* 23(2): 171–90.

Lee, C. K.-M. 2007. Affordances and text-making practices in online instant messaging. *Written Communication* 24(3): 223–49.

LePage, R. and Tabouret-Keller, A. 1985. *Acts of Identity*. Cambridge: Cambridge University Press.

Luk, J. C. M. and Lin, A. M. Y. 2007. *Classroom Interactions as Cross-Cultural Encounters*. Mahwah, NJ: Lawrence Erlbaum.

Lytra, V. 2007. *Play Frames and Social Identities*. Amsterdam: John Benjamins.

Marcus, G. 1995. Ethnography in/of the world system: the emergence of multi-sited ethnography. *Annual Review of Anthropology* 24: 95–117.

Makoni, S. and Pennycook, A. (eds) 2007. *Disinventing and Reconstituting Languages*. Clevedon: Multilingual Matters.

Martin-Jones, M., Blackledge, A. and Creese, A. 2012. (eds) *The Routledge Handbook of Multilingualism*. London and New York: Routledge, 1–29.

Martín Rojo, L. 2010. *Constructing Inequality in Multilingual Classrooms*. Berlin: Mouton de Gruyter.

McCarty, T. L. (ed.) 2011. *Ethnography of Language Policy*. London and New York: Routledge.

McGinnis, T., Goodstein-Stolzenberg, A. and Saliani, E. C. 2007. indnpride: online spaces of transnational youth as sites of creativity and sophisticated literacy and identity work. *Linguistics and Education* 18(3 & 4): 305–24.

Menard-Warwick, J. 2009. *Gendered Identities and Immigrant Language Learning*. Bristol: Multilingual Matters.

Pavlenko, A. and Blackledge, A. 2004. Introduction: new theoretical approaches to the study of negotiation of identities in multilingual contexts. In *Negotiation of Identities in Multilingual Contexts*, ed. A. Pavlenko and A. Blackledge, 1–33. Clevedon,: Multilingual Matters.

Pennycook, A. 2001. *Critical Applied Linguistics*. Mahwah, NJ: Lawrence Erlbaum.

———. 2010. *Language as a Local Practice*. London and New York: Routledge.

Piller, I. 2003. Advertising as a site of language contact. *Annual Review of Applied Linguistics* 23: 170–83.

Pujolar, J. 2001. *Gender, Heteroglossia and Power: A Sociolinguistic Study of Youth Culture*. Berlin: Mouton de Gruyter.

Rampton, B. 1995. *Crossing: Language and Ethnicity among Adolescents*. London: Longman.

Rindler Schjerve, R. (ed.) 2003. *Diglossia and Power: Language Policies and Practice in the 19th Century Habsburg Empire*. Berlin: Mouton de Gruyter.

Roy, S. 2003. Bilingualism and standardization in a Canadian call center: challenges for a linguistic minority community. In *Language Socialization in Multilingual Societies*, ed. R. Bayley and S. Schecter, 269–87. Clevedon: Multilingual Matters.

Schieffelin, B. B., Woolard, K. A. and Kroskrity, P. V. (eds) 1998. *Language Ideologies: Practice and Theory*. Oxford: Oxford University Press.

Sebba, M. 1993. *London Jamaican*. London: Longman.

———. Forthcoming. Introduction. In *Language Mixing and Code-Switching in Writing: Approaches to Mixed Language Written Discourse*, ed. M. Sebba, S. Mahootian and C. Jonsson. London and New York: Routledge.

Stroud, C. 1999. Portuguese as ideology and politics in Mozambique: semiotic (re) constructions of a post-colony. In *Language Ideological Debates*, ed. J. Blommaert, 343–80. Berlin: Mouton de Gruyter.

Urla, J. 1993. Cultural politics in an age of statistics: numbers, nations, and the making of a Basque identity. *American Ethnologist* 20(1): 818–43.

Vertovec, S. 2007. Super-diversity and its implications. *Ethnic and Racial Studies*, 30(6): 1024–54.

Warschauer, M., El Said, G. R. and Zohry, A. 2002. Language choice online: globalization and identity in Egypt. *Journal of Computer-Mediated Communication* 7(4). doi: 10.1111/j.1083-6101.2002.tb00157.x

Woolard, K. A. 1985. Language variation and cultural hegemony: towards an integration of sociolinguistics and social theory. *American Ethnologist* 12: 38–48.

———. 1989. *Double Talk: Bilingualism and the Politics of Ethnicity in Catalonia*. Stanford, CA: Stanford University Press.

Part I

Linking Local Practices to Wider Social Processes

Introduction

Li Wei

In 1980, Joshua Fishman, a father figure in the field of sociolinguistics and multilingualism, argued in a review article that, whereas considerable progress had been made in what he termed "micro analysis" where "variation theory, discourse analysis, speech act theory, pragmatics, and ethnomethodological concerns and sensitivities have pretty much become modern day orthodoxies" (1980: 161), hardly any attention had been paid to making connections with sociology or with socio-cultural theory more generally; "none at all, indeed, except for the ethnomethodological corner thereof", Fishman claimed. He further stated, "If we look for linkages between macro-sociolinguistic efforts and the parent disciplines, the situation is even less heartening, because not only are such links exceedingly few and far between, but nothing approaching schools of thought or elaborated points of view are discernible. That being the case the likelihood of productive theoretical linkages between micro- and macro-sociolinguistic endeavours is rather remote for the foreseeable future" (1980: 161).

On the surface, things have certainly changed since the publication of Fishman's article. At least in the field of multilingualism research, there are many more frequent mentions of sociologists and socio-cultural theorists such as Pierre Bourdieu, Benedict Anderson, and Stuart Hall. Even Anthony Giddens, Michel Foucault, Edward Said, and Homi Bhabha get an occasional reference. Concepts such as cultural capital, symbolic dominance, and hegemony are now part of the discourse of many sociolinguists. Yet, methodologically, advances in integrating investigation of social processes at a global level and the interpretation of everyday practices at a local level into a coherent, critical analysis have been rather limited. In fact, there are now signs of a polarization between those sociolinguists who talk about ideology, power and social structures in abstract, purely theoretical terms, making occasional and superficial references to language policies, language attitudes, and community relations, and those who continue to focus on detailed documentation and description of what multilingual individuals and communities do on a daily basis. Sometimes, not a single example from naturally occurring social interaction is found in the publications by the former group of researchers, whereas the latter group produce pages after pages of transcripts with descriptions of the local context but no critical engagement with social or sociological theories.

The situation is unlikely to change in any fundamental way, unless we can overcome conceptual dichotomies such as micro-macro, event-structure, agency-social structure or even cause-effect. Take language and migration for example. It is often assumed that migration is a large-scale socio-demographic process and it impacts on many aspects of individuals' social life including language. But there are plenty of cases where language is the cause or motivation for migration. People decide to leave one place for another because their language is no longer acceptable to others in the locality or because they identify more with a different community who would accept their language. Of course, such beliefs and attitudes towards various languages are tied to other historical and socio-cultural processes. Religion, for instance, may play a role. The key point here is that different processes are nested in one another. The so-called micro-macro distinction is a relative notion, just as power and agency are also relative notions. There are always higher and lower levels at which agency and structure operate. Sociolinguists, especially those working on multilingualism, perhaps need to shift their gaze to the nested relationships between these different processes at work in social life and the mutual effects they have on each other.

One area in which there has been considerable conceptual and methodological innovation of late is in the study of translocal and transnational multilingualism, but this research is still at an early stage and we lack a comparative dimension. Linguistic ethnographers have done an excellent job in providing some fascinating documentation of local practices including systematic and detailed descriptions of variation in local practices. They have often done so with equally detailed and fascinating discussion of the immediate socio-cultural and political contexts. But a fuller understanding of the wider social processes and the interconnections between local practices and wider processes of social change cannot be gained without comparative analyses. It is particularly interesting to note that recent research into language and globalisation tends to be done at a local level, building on the case study tradition. The value of such case studies notwithstanding, we cannot appreciate the complex interrelationships between language and globalisation without examining the differential impact that globalisation has had in different communities and without comparing the distinct responses to globalisation within these communities.

The chapters in the first part of this book address head-on a number of the issues that I have raised here and provide illuminating examples of the ways in which local practices in multilingual settings are linked to wider social processes and to political and economic change. In Chapter 1, Monica Heller argues that we need to "let go of" the sociolinguistic dichotomy between macro and micro perspectives and challenge the long-held belief that different aspects of social life "can be discretely assigned to different orders of experience and organisation" (p. 26). Her own concern is with the ways in which social difference and social inequality are constructed in the particular social and historical context of French Canada. In her chapter, she traces her own trajectory as a researcher working in that context, showing how, over two decades, she sustained a focus on the politics of language in Canada and on the ways in which different varieties of French and English were drawn upon and assigned value by different social actors in different institutional settings: in French-language minority schools and in public and private sector workplaces. During this phase of her work, she notes that she came to see these institutions as key sites for the "discursive construction of ideologies of language, identity and nation and of social categories" (p. 27) and, at the same time, as sites for the production and distribution of prestigious language resources. She argues that focussing on processes such as social categorisation and on how the distribution and evaluation of language resources is bound up with these processes "enables us to unpack the dynamic between agency and structuration" (p. 31). In the second part of her chapter, Monica Heller then goes on to show how, with the far-reaching changes ushered in by globalisation, she turned her research gaze away from individual institutions to the wider political and economic arena and began to focus on the specific ways in which these changes were being played out in French-speaking areas of Northeastern Canada. Here, she writes about the new patterns of labour migration that are emerging, especially in the wake of crises in industries that have, historically, sustained local populations of French speakers. These new migrations (e.g. to the new oil and gas fields of Northwestern Canada) have sociolinguistic consequences and French/English bilingualism has taken on new meanings associated with new mobilities. Heller also writes of the growing importance of bilingualism as a resource in the rapidly expanding new economy (e.g. in call centres, tourism or the new media). In this chapter, and in much of her recent work (e.g. Heller, 2007, 2011), she reminds us of the need to do a fundamental rethink of our approaches to research on multilingualism so as to take account of the new political and economic conditions of the global era.

In Chapter 2, Melissa Moyer provides a useful overview of the productive ways in which conceptual frameworks from other social sciences have recently been taken up by sociolinguists researching multilingualism. She focuses on conceptual frameworks and lines of enquiry developed in research related to different aspects of globalisation (e.g. the new economy, the advent of new technologies and contemporary mobilities and population flows), in research on the new work order and in recent writing on language ideology. Drawing on interactional and textual data gathered as part of a wider research project in Barcelona, she demonstrates that sociolinguists can open up a window on the wider social processes of concern to other social scientists precisely by studying the detail of everyday interactions in multilingual settings, provided that they ask different kinds of questions and move beyond a preoccupation with language as cultural practice or with variation within the language system. Like Heller, she sees the debate about macro and micro levels of analysis as belonging to an earlier moment in the history of sociolinguistics, prior to its current openness to social theory. Moyer calls for the adoption of a critical sociolinguistic perspective in research on multilingualism; one that addresses the unprecedented changes taking place around us in today's globalised society and the increasing asymmetries of power created by these changes. She highlights, in particular, the need to understand the increasing construction of language as a commodity within the new economy; the increasing regimentation of language within the service economy and in new workplaces such as call centres, where communication is key; the role of language as a resource for gaining access to different institutional spaces and to particular kinds of material resources and the ways in which language ideologies are taken up and reproduced in everyday language practices in local settings. These aspects of language in contemporary social life take different forms in different cultural and institutional contexts; multilingualism is being taken up and reshaped in different ways so, as I remarked earlier, comparisons across contexts will further our understanding of the ways in which language is bound up with these social changes.

In Chapter 3, David Block turns his attention to the vexed question of the relationship between agency and social structure. He does this as part of a more general project of reviewing poststructuralist approaches to identity, including research on processes of identification and subject positioning in multilingual settings conducted by sociolinguists and linguistic anthropologists. Block notes that in the sociolinguistic literature on identity, there is a tendency to view agency from an interactionist perspective, as "emergent in social interaction" (p. 49). He therefore turns to recent work in other social sciences where attempts have been made to conceptualise agency in ways that take more account of social structures and the manner in which structures constrain agency. He argues that these sources provide useful pointers as to how we can reconceptualise agency in the current fluid, postmodern, twenty-first century context, whereas early poststructuralist thought (e.g. the work of Bourdieu) was constrained by the fact that it was "still firmly anchored in modernity" (p. 51), when societies were characterised by greater stability and continuity.

All three of the authors contributing to this first part of the book offer valuable pointers as to how we might refashion our research lenses so that we can take better account of the ways in which multilingualism is being reshaped in different contexts in the current global era. Their lines of argument are firmly grounded in recent social theory. Thirty years on from Fishman's review article, we are beginning to develop a more robust social component for sociolinguistic studies of multilingualism.

REFERENCES

Fishman, J. 1980. Theoretical issues and problems in the sociolinguistic enterprise. *Annual Review of Applied Linguistics* 1: 161–67.

Heller, M. 2007. Bilingualism as ideology and practice. In M. Heller (ed.) *Bilingualism: A Social Approach*, ed. M. Heller, 1–22. Basingstoke, Hampshire: Palgrave Macmillan.

———. 2011. *Paths to Post-Nationalism: A Critical Ethnography of Language and Identity*. Oxford: Oxford University Press.

1 Rethinking Sociolinguistic Ethnography
From Community and Identity to Process and Practice

Monica Heller

METHODS, QUESTIONS AND WHAT WE SEE

I need to begin by insisting that I cannot write a chapter about methods as though methods were technical skills. I see them as practices of enquiry, shaped by the questions we ask, and by what we experience. This is, then, more in the way of an account of why I have been doing what I have been doing lately, my methods evolving as my questions emerge, and as I find myself wanting to account for things I may not have noticed before, or which may not have been around earlier.

I am scarcely alone in trying to make sense out of the kinds of social change we are currently experiencing, and I have certainly been inspired by the efforts of others; I hope therefore that this text may be useful to readers asking questions similar to mine. This is, I think, likely to be particularly true of people asking questions about multilingualism, a field whose very nature points to movement and fragmentation, despite our long-standing attempts to make it sit still.

That is the crux of the matter: the tools we inherited to make sense of multilingualism belong to an era when we were invested, as social scientists, in understanding languages as whole, bounded systems, lined up as neatly as possible with political, cultural and territorial boundaries. Indeed, I think the very idea of "multilingualism" comes out of the ideological complex of the nation-state with its focus on homogeneity (Hobsbawm, 1990; Gal, 2001; Heller, 2007); it is a way to neaten up the mess of multiplicity, to put disorderly matter back "into place" (to use Mary Douglas' felicitous turn of phrase). It became a matter for academic enquiry, a "problem" to be described and regulated, only insofar as it was the opposite of the uniformity that was hegemonically constructed as "normal", and therefore to be asked questions about. We have no courses or textbooks on "monolingualism" (although Peter Nelde used to quip that monolingualism is a curable disease).

But if we follow the enquiry into multilingualism where it takes us, it points constantly in the direction of complexity and change, and the more we find out about it, the more prevalent it seems. There are two ways of looking at the juncture at which we currently find ourselves. One is a notion I take from Thomas Kuhn (1962), that scientific paradigms always generate data that doesn't fit, and that the way we usually deal with such data is to ignore it; claim that it is flawed, impossible or wrong; or just slide it quietly under the table hoping it will go away. Eventually, he says, it piles up, refuses to be ignored, and requires a radical readjustment in descriptive and explanatory paradigms, provoking what he calls a "scientific revolution". It is certainly the case that we have been sitting on ever-increasing mountains of data about "multilingualism" which refuse to go away no matter how outraged people get about such sloppy, careless, disrespectful or dangerous linguistic practices.

It is equally possible, as many scholars of globalisation have argued, that there is something materially different about current social conditions. Specifically, it has been argued that the expansion of capitalism, and of capitalist markets, has made it impossible to regulate markets as easily through the mechanisms of the nation-state, and that therefore we are seeing faster and more numerous forms of circulation of people and of material and symbolic resources (Harvey, 1989; Giddens, 1990; Appadurai, 1996; Castells, 2000). This results in more frequent and more widespread experiences of multilingualism, experiences not as easily contained by the mechanisms heretofore invented. I am inclined to believe that we are experiencing a combination of the two, forcing us to think about, and ask questions about, multilingualism in new ways.

Ethnography is certainly a useful tool in this juncture, both as a way to get some kind of handle on what is happening, and as a way to experiment with helpful modes of enquiry for phenomena we have little experience with. It is useful because it asks us to be in a constant dialectical relationship with our accounts and our explanations; it holds up our questions against what we count as evidence by way of answers, and forces us to reframe those questions if we cannot find answers, or if what we see cannot be made sense of in their terms. But, as anthropology discovered a couple of decades ago already, even ethnography has had to be untied from its nationalist and colonialist moorings (Rabinow and Sullivan, 1979; Clifford and Marcus, 1986), and we are left to invent an ethnography which can cut loose from "cultures" and "communities" and "languages" as objects or systems, in order to grasp at processes of social construction and the practices that constitute them.

This means letting go of the idea of holism, and accepting that all enquiries are necessarily situated and partial; we can follow threads of circulating actors and objects (Appadurai, 1996; Hannerz, 1996, 2003; Bestor, 2001), trace the trajectories of texts (Cicourel, 2002; Briggs, 2007), connect the dots among ideas and cultural practices in a Giddensian web of unforeseeable consequences of social action across time and space (Giddens, 1984), but we cannot expect boundaries beyond those whose construction we can observe, or uniformity beyond that which social actors struggle to create and impose. It also means letting go of the dichotomy between so-called macro and micro (or the macro-meso-micro triad) levels of social life, with their inherent assumptions that social phenomena can be discretely assigned to different orders of experience and organization, rather than being constitutive of social reality, whether immediately apprehensible by an individual or not. It also opens up the possibility that some questions are best addressed by more than one person, in order to have multiple points of entry into complex networks of social relations and social activities, especially as they are strung out over space. It certainly has also proved an advantage to me to be able to follow processes unfolding over time, that is, to bring history into ethnography in the present, not only the past.

I have come to this through my own path, doggedly, some might say stubbornly, trying to understand how social difference and social inequality get constructed in my own social space. What I want to know most broadly is how the construction of social categories (by which I mean socially meaningful, socially deployed categories, such as the ones most salient to us now, like gender, sexuality, race, class, ethnicity, religion) is connected to the construction of social inequality. I want to understand how and why we construct social difference at all, and why it takes the shape it does in specific places, under specific conditions. And most centrally I want to know what difference that social difference makes, in terms of how it constrains people's access to resources (both in the positive sense of what opportunities are opened up, and in the negative sense of what obstacles people find in their way).

What I want to know most specifically is how this plays out around the categorical opposition of French and English in Canadian society. Partly this is a political choice: Canada is where I live. Partly it is an opportunistic one: Canada is a deeply imperfect nation-state, and therefore a revealing political space for understanding the role of, and limits to, that particular political formation in shaping language, culture and identity. Partly it is a methodological-theoretical one: because I live there, it is relatively easier for me to follow changes over time and from multiple perspectives, to follow people and things around, and to have multiple relations through the discursive spaces of interest to me and with the people involved. And partly it is an analytical one: whereas many other kinds of categorisation are relevant to the organisation of difference and inequality in Canada (and beyond, of course), the French-English opposition is in many ways foundational to, or at least constraining for, every other one that may be pertinent to us. The focus is not meant to be exclusive or to claim any political priority; it is a way into a complex web, only parts of which I can explore, and only parts of which I am well-equipped to examine. I depend on others to teach me what I cannot learn on my own.

ORGANISING ENQUIRY

In grand sociolinguistic ethnographic tradition, I began examining these questions by looking at how linguistic resources, typically assigned metadiscursively to different languages (French, English) or linguistic varieties (Canadian English, "bon français", "joual", "français de France, etc.) were mobilised in interaction in institutional settings: between the mid-1970s and the mid-1990s I did fieldwork in a hospital, a large manufacturing company, and a lot of schools, in Ontario and in Quebec. I picked these sites because I had evidence (not hard to come by) that they played important roles in the politics of language in Canada. I came to understand that they needed to be understood both as sites of production and distribution of all kinds of *resources*, including linguistic ones, and as sites of discursive construction of ideologies of language, identity and nation, and of social categories.

The first ethnographic rethinking I needed to do, then, was about how to conceptualise institutional spaces. I had to move away from at some level taking them for granted, and to think instead of institutions as *discursive sites* that are particularly important because of the value of the resources they distribute. But a focus on those spaces as bounded became hard to sustain, as I began to realise how complex were the *trajectories* of those very resources, as well as of the social actors participating in them. These three concepts (*resource*, *discursive space*, *trajectory*) helped me work at understanding the histories and interconnectedness of both the processes of categorisation at work, and of the practices that constitute them.

Just to give one example: making sense of interaction in an out-patient clinic of a large Montreal hospital in the 1970s meant grasping at least something about why the hospital was known as an "English" hospital, and used that language for most of its official business, whereas so many members of its staff (at all levels and in all categories) and so many of its patients spoke English as a language learned relatively late in life, or not at all. Understanding that meant going far beyond the boundaries not only of interactions as they unfolded around (and with) me, but also of the physical space of the hospital itself. It meant understanding something about immigration; something about ideologies of health care; something about ethnolinguistic categories in the organization of work in Montreal; something about gender and class. In other words, it meant understanding the trajectories of the women I worked with, of the doctors and administrators whose work shaped our own, and of the patients; the history of the hospital and of socialised medicine in Quebec; and how "our" hospital (where I had a summer job through the connections of my father, who worked there as a doctor) stood in contradistinction to the French one not more than four city blocks away.

But it was not until I tried to unravel the complexities of one, relatively small, Toronto high school (it only had about 400 students spread over six grades, compared to most urban North American high schools which usually have enrolments of more than a thousand over four grades) that my idea of myself as a lone ethnographer got really shaken up. I had worked as part of a team before, but ultimately had always relied on myself and the data I collected to make sense out of anything. High schools make you choose alignments with students or teachers—it is difficult to be trusted by both to the same extent (I note that Eckert [1989] is very explicit about her refusal to even set foot in the staff room in order to preserve her relationships with, and access to data about, students). By the early 1990s, in any case, I could no longer pass as a high school student; boys especially were polite, but distant. In addition, class, race and gender tensions (played out mainly on the field of popular culture, especially music) made it difficult to be on good terms with everyone; working class students in particular took it badly if too much time was spent with others.

I was able to put together a team of graduate students, gay and straight, male and female, all more or less bilingual (albeit in different ways); at least one of us was at school almost every day for over two years. Our different networks and perspectives allowed for a more complex and dynamic appreciation of what was going on in that school, and how as an institution it could be understood to emerge, every day, out of the convergence of multiple trajectories of social actors, institutions and communicative resources. The core of it became, in our view, the daily management of contradictions between the nationalist ideology of linguistic and cultural uniformity which gave the school its legitimacy in the Canadian political context of the late twentieth century, the multilingual experiences and practices of every last individual involved in the school, and the often conflicting interests in managing or exposing those contradictions on the part of social actors with different social locations, and hence access to different kinds of (differentially-valued) linguistic resources. Class, immigration status, gender and sexuality all informed the social constraints which people differentially either struggled with or were able to profit from.

Broadly speaking, through the twenty years of fieldwork leading to the end of this school(s) ethnography, I witnessed the development of a consistent set of discursive tensions, between an ethnonational idea of language, culture and identity, premised on tight borders and homogeneity within them, and a fragmented, mobile, multiple process in which language was increasingly understood, in fact, as a technical skill and commodifiable resource, and not in terms of identity or authenticity at all. And even authenticity was increasingly commodified and subject to struggles over ownership.

In the school project (see Heller et al., 2006), we made some attempt to understand the sources of and shape of these tensions by following the threads of discursive construction beyond the school; it became clear to us that whereas a lot of discursive construction went on there, the source of value of linguistic and other resources lay elsewhere. We grappled, among other things, with the institutional constraints on the school as part of a large state-funded and state-regulated school system, with its own history in the development of Western liberal democratic nation-states; with the political economy of immigration which explained the presence of the vast majority of students within a time depth of three generations; with the labour mobility increasingly characteristic of the Canadian labour market, and which explained just about everyone else, including the teachers (and me); as well as of course with the always unfolding history of francophone nationalism in Canada. What that taught me was that it was time to move beyond the focus on specific institutional spaces, and to focus on identifying where the value of resources gets defined, and on the linkages and mobility which are the sites of distribution, of individual and collective positioning, and, potentially, of struggle.

SPREADING OUT: ETHNOGRAPHIES
OF DISCURSIVE SHIFTS

What has followed has been an attempt to make up methods which allow me and my collaborators to respond to what we see; the field has driven the methodology. In a long series of projects (see acknowledgements), we have examined the relationship between state policy and funding practices regarding what the Canadian federal government has constructed as "official language minority communities" (that is, populations recognisable in the state's terms as "anglophones" in Quebec and "francophones" everywhere else); the institutions and associations understood to represent, indeed in many ways to constitute, those communities; the workplaces involved in the economic activities central to the discursive reproduction of those communities (or challenges to it), that is, to the reproduction of the categories of "anglophone" and "francophone" and to the value of the linguistic and cultural resources they putatively control; and the involvement of people who are at least potential members of those categories through those institutional, associative and economic spaces.

We have been concerned to understand how the discourse of francophone nationalism gets constituted in a shifting political economic field, one in which the state is shifting its role from that of *protector* to that of *producer*; in which concerns about *rights* and *sovereignty* are replaced by concerns about *services* and *economic development*; in which efforts to reproduce *communities* cede priority to efforts to produce *commodities*; in which *citizens* are increasingly understood as *shareholders*; and in which language is understood less as a *talent* or an essential element of *identity*, and more as a technical *skill*.

This has involved participating (in a variety of guises, not always only as researchers) in the activities of a wide variety of francophone institutions and associations (including, for example, churches, charitable associations, GLBTQ movement groups, credit unions, arts centres, lobbying associations, immigrant settlement groups, health clinics, television and radio stations, among others), and conducting ethnographic work on the collapse of traditional francophone economic activities (mostly related to primary resource extraction in fishing, lumber, mining and agriculture, or in the industrial transformation of their products or in manufacturing more generally), as well as in new economy workplaces where French-English bilingualism and/or francophone identity are key products (in tourism, bio-technology, call centres, translation, new media, the arts, environmental-ism and artisanal production). We have investigated the role of the state in the production and distribution of the resources circulating in those spaces, as it has shifted from a discourse of minority language rights to a discourse of community economic development (da Silva and Heller, 2009). And we have charted the trajectories of objects (with a particular focus on artisa-nal and artistic-cultural products) and of people (with a particular focus on workers displaced from the traditional francophone bastions with their contracting economies, to urban areas across Canada and to the new oil, gas and diamond frontier economies of the Canadian northwest).

In all these cases we still ask, as I did in earlier work: what is at stake in what spaces, and for whom? What kinds of people get to participate, and who gets excluded? Who can (and does) mobilise what kinds of resources, with what results? What kinds of discourses of language, nation and iden-tity are called into play, what do they make sense of, and how? What kinds of understandings of what it means to be francophone (Acadian, Québé-cois, Franco-Ontarian, European, French-Canadian, etc.) do people orient to, or evoke? What sense does it make to be "bilingual"?

To illustrate, I will limit myself to one thread of this set of enquiries, in which we are following people. (See Heller, 2010, 2011, for discussion of a second thread, involving following the circulation of foods authentifiable as "Canadian" on the European market.) We will see that the change we are following is not actually linear, but rather presents itself as a tension in which some ideas of identity and language may be more prevalent than oth-ers for some people, in some places, but where each also serves more and more to constitute the other. Our deep investment in nationalist ideas about language and identity make it difficult to reimagine ourselves, even as we move farther and farther away from living that imagined nation.

Circulating People

In subsequent research, we have taken up the thread of circulating people. The 1992 collapse of the cod fishery in the Atlantic region, long a mainstay of the Acadian communities there, along with more recent crises in forest products and mining industries, has led to an upsurge in well-established patterns of labour migration. This migration is only capturable by the cen-sus when people actually change their permanent address; the many people who migrate temporarily are off the radar. Yet the new frontiers of primary resource extraction depend on the availability of such labour pools in boom periods; companies go so far as to charter cross-Canada flights for east-erner workers as they work shifts of three to six weeks on, followed by one to two weeks off for "home leave". They also contract internationally when that pool has been drained. These are, of course, the first workers to be laid off in the recurrent bust cycles. There are other scenarios as well, involving semi-skilled, skilled and highly educated workers, many of them entering the mobile, multilingual, global economy.

More importantly for my purposes, not only are these scenarios largely off the state-run regulation radar, we know little about how the ethnolinguistic categories structuring Canadian society play out for those actors or in the spaces to which they are tied. What does it mean for a monolingual Acadian ex-fisherman to encounter English-language job training his first day working as a scaffolder in the oil sands, when the only English he knows, as he says, is "yes *pis* no *pis* toaster" ("yes", "no" and "toaster")? Why does he have an Acadian flag on his hard hat? What does it mean for his New Brunswick family and friends for people like him to be gone part of the time, but coming home regularly with increasing knowledge of English and of Western Canada? What does it mean for the young monolingual Québécoise to get her first job as a *"monitrice de langue"* in a French-language minority school in the Northwest Territories, where her French is valued at work, but what she is really after is access to English and to the world beyond Quebec? What does the gas station attendant next to the liquor store make of the "French guys" living in the trailer out back, who have come to fix the bridge this summer?

We approach these questions by trying to identify francophone labour migrants both from the areas they tend to come from (with a particular focus on the human resource rich region of northern New Brunswick) and in the areas they tend to go to (cities, especially Moncton and St. John, in New Brunswick; Montreal; Toronto; and Edmonton, in Alberta; and the primary resource extraction frontier areas of northern Alberta and the Northwest Territories). We then follow what happens to them over the course of a few years, meet with them to the extent possible both where they are from and where they have gone to, and place their experiences in the perspective of what we can find out about the labour market and economic development policies which we expect to help us explain why people do what they do, how valuable (or not) the linguistic resources they can mobilise turn out to be (and for what), and what difference it makes to count as an "Acadian", "a French guy", "un français", a "Québécois", or a "Métis" (as opposed to "Newfies", "northerners", "residents", "Aboriginals" or any of the other categories which seem to structure employment and sociability in those spaces).

A focus on trajectories helps us understand how processes of social categorisation and exclusion work, and why they work the way they do—that is, what is at stake in those modes of social organisation. It helps us move away from looking at people as composed of inherent characteristics, or possessing inalienable traits, and look instead at what they are and are not able to mobilise, as well as why they might want to do so. It helps unpack the dynamic between agency and structuration, by situating multilingualism not as a property of individuals or of groups, or even as a characteristic of spaces, but rather as sets of circulating, constructible and deconstructible resources.

WEBS AND LINKS, SPACES AND TRAJECTORIES, RESOURCES AND ACTORS

Discursive struggles over the meaning of multilingualism such as those I have described here emerge in spaces where the key resources involved are produced, distributed and given value and meaning. The challenge for sociolinguistics is to find ways of describing how resources and actors circulate, constrain what is possible, and how particular social actors creatively navigate those constraints. The methods I have outlined here require loosening up our ideas of ethnography, and recognising in particular that the idea of the bounded and static whole meets its limits in such conditions.

Sociolinguistics has, of course, long worked with the notion of social reality as interactionally produced, and with the idea of identity as having more to do with the construction of social boundaries than with the properties of people or groups. Nonetheless, we are still exploring what it means to put an emphasis on the processes and practices which constitute the making of boundaries (or what I have called elsewhere in this text, categorisation). Perhaps more importantly, we are exploring what it means to understand multilingualism as a set of ideologically-loaded communicative resources, always unequally distributed, on an always uneven playing field.

Contemporary reflexivity (Giddens, 1990) about social organization, and in particular about the nation-state, does not, of course, mean that those discursive complexes are disappearing. The notion of multilingualism remains powerful. But current conditions also require us to take some distance from it, to separate out what people say about it and how they deploy the idea, from what their communicative practices actually may be. Finally, as a site of discursive struggle, the space of "multilingualism" is a particularly revealing site for discovering what people are making of the ideological complex of language-culture-identity-nation-state which has long shaped our lives, and what new ways of organizing ourselves may be emerging.

ACKNOWLEDGEMENTS

The data on which this discussion is based are drawn from a series of research projects funded by the Social Sciences and Humanities Research Council of Canada, the Transcoop Program of the Alexander von Humboldt-Stiftung, the Conseil intenational d'études canadiennes and the Wenner-Gren Foundation for Anthropological Research. I would like to thank the many members of the team who have worked on these projects for all or part of the past twelve years : Gabriel Asselin, Maurice Beaudin, Lindsay Bell, Annette Boudreau, Gabriele Budach, Michelle Daveluy, Gabriella Djerrahian, Lise Dubois, Alexandre Duchêne, Jürgen Erfurt, Philippe Hambye, Emmanuel Kahn, Normand Labrie, Patricia Lamarre, Stéfanie Lamarre, Matthieu Leblanc,

Mélanie LeBlanc, Darryl Leroux, Amal Madibbo, Sonya Malaborza, Claudine Moïse, Mireille McLaughlin, Hubert Noël, Carsten Quell, Mary Richards, Sylvie Roy, Emanuel da Silva, Chantal White, Maia Yarymowich and Natalie Zur Nedden. Peter Auer, Nicolas Béland, Werner Kallmeyer, Luisa Martin Rojo, Melissa Moyer and Joan Pujolar have all been important collaborators in various facets of this endeavour.

REFERENCES

Appadurai, A. 1996. *Modernity at Large: Cultural Dimensions of Globalization.* Minneapolis: University of Minnesota Press.

Bestor, T. 2001. Supply-side sushi: commodity, market, and the global city. *American Anthropologist* 103(1): 76–95.

Briggs, C. (ed.) 2007. Four decades of epistemological revolution: work inspired by Aaron V. Cicourel. *Text & Talk* 27(5–6): 567–760.

Castells, M. 2000. *The Information Age: Economy, Society and Culture* (3 volumes). Oxford: Blackwell.

Cicourel, A. 2002. *Le raisonnement médical.* Paris: Liber.

Clifford, J. and Marcus, G. (ed.) 1986. *Writing Cultures: The Poetics and Politics of Ethnography.* Berkeley and Los Angeles: University of California Press.

da Silva, E. and M. Heller. 2009. From protector to producer: the role of the state in the discursive shift from minority rights to economic development. *Language Policy* 8: 95–116.

Eckert, P. 1989. *Jocks and Burnouts.* New York: Teachers College Press.

Gal, S. 2001. Linguistic theories and national images in nineteenth-century Hungary. In *Languages and Publics: The Making of Authority,* ed. S. Gal and K. Woolard, 30–45. Manchester, UK: St Jerome.

Giddens, A. 1984. *The Constitution of Society.* Berkeley and Los Angeles: University of California Press.

———. 1990. *The Consequences of Modernity.* Berkeley and Los Angeles: University of California Press.

Hannerz, U. 1996. *Transnational Connections: Culture, People, Places.* London, Routledge.

———. 2003. On being there . . . and there . . . and there! Reflections on multi-site ethnography. *Ethnography* 4(2): 201–16.

Harvey, D. 1989. *The Condition of Postmodernity.* Oxford: Blackwell.

Heller, M. (ed.) 2007. *Bilingualism: A Social Approach.* London: Palgrave Macmillan.

———. 2010. A study on transnational spaces. In *Language and Space an international handbook, Vol. 1: Theories and Methods*, ed. P. Auer and J. Schmidt, 724–739. Berlin: Mouton de Gruyter.

Heller, M. with the collaboration of Campbell, M., Dalley, P. and Patrick, D. 2006. *Linguistic Minorities and Modernity: A Sociolinguistic Ethnography* (2nd edition). London: Continuum.

———. 2011 *Paths to Post-Nationalism: A Critical Ethnography of Language and Identity.* Oxford: Oxford University Press.

Hobsbawm, E. 1990. *Nations and Nationalism since 1760.* Cambridge: Cambridge University Press.

Kuhn, T. 1962. *The Structure of Scientific Revolutions.* Chicago: University of Chicago Press.

Rabinow, P. and Sullivan, W. (eds) 1979. *Interpretive Social Science: A Reader.* Berkeley and Los Angeles: University of California Press.

2 Sociolinguistic Perspectives on Language and Multilingualism in Institutions

Melissa G. Moyer

Sociolinguistic research from variationist and ethnographic perspectives is still in many ways oriented to answering certain key questions which are, on the one hand, about variation and change within the language system (Labov, 1972, 2000, 2007) and, on the other hand, about language as a cultural practice that is connected to local productions of meaning and interpretation (Duranti, 1997; Verschueren, 2008). It is also well known that disciplinary agendas in Linguistics—including Sociolinguistics—have not adequately dealt with the connection of language and society. They have not developed adequate theoretical frameworks for going beyond strict correlations of social and contextual factors with language forms, nor with the ways in which interactional and conversational practices construct social and institutional realities. Today, the study of multilingualism provides a domain of enquiry where ideas and concepts from sociology, politics, economics and anthropology provide key references for the sort of knowledge we need to take into account in order to understand the various ways language is connected to complex social processes.

The purpose of this chapter is to discuss how a critical sociolinguistic perspective that takes into account a changing world order brought about by globalisation and the mobility of persons, information and products, is key for understanding the ways language and locally realised multilingual practices are connected to wider social, political and economic processes. Data collected by the CIEN research team,[1] in a multi-sited research project in Catalonia, Spain, are discussed here in connection to the macro-micro theoretical divide in the field of sociolinguistics. I will also consider the way in which the focus on language as form or cultural practice has constrained both the types of question and the sort of knowledge researchers have sought to generate. What has been considered as legitimate data for traditional sociolinguistic analysis is called into question with the data in this chapter. This data is used to illustrate different conceptions of language. Erickson (2004: 175) identifies the micro-macro connection as a major difficulty that consists in reconciling the conduct of talk and general societal processes or, in other words, making links between *voluntarism* (which involves taking local ecologies for the conduct of oral discourse in face-to-face situations as if they were unconnected to ecologies in the wider world) and *determinism* (which involves relying on economic, political and historical analysis to account for the local activity of talk carried out by social actors in a given context.

This chapter takes up data and insights gained from multi-sited ethnographic research carried out in private, public and non-governmental institutions in Catalonia and a call centre in Morocco. Multilingualism is one of the key features that characterises the communication that takes place in the various sites (Moyer, 2011). It explores the manner in which multilingualism gets constructed, as well as the local language practices and linguistic forms, which are part of and a product of wider social processes of a globalised society where people, goods and information are exchanged at speed and over distances previously unknown. The multilingual examples come from a privately owned multinational call centre, a public health clinic and a non-governmental institution (run by a religious body) which is providing language and housing services to newcomers from the developing world who have recently arrived in Catalonia and its metropolitan area in order to find work and better life chances. The examples analysed illustrate how different kinds of information, and data that are not strictly connected to language structure or form, are helpful in building an understanding of the role of language and multilingualism in present day institutions. A focus on the different institutional sites highlights the relevance of multilingualism and the value of (a) language as a *commodity* or as *added value*, (b) language as a key resource for gaining access to valuable *information*, (c) the *regimentation* of language in new work regimes, and finally (d) *ideologies* of language that lead to practices of social inclusion/exclusion. A conception of language not addressed in the present chapter is identity and the way it gets expressed through language. This perspective on language has a long tradition and it has been covered by numerous researchers working in the field of multilingualism (Gumperz, 1982; Heller, 1999; Woolard, 1989, 1998; Moyer, 1998; Blommaert, 2005; and chapters in this volume). A final discussion brings together ideas about how a multi-sited ethnography in various institutional spaces illustrates, from a critical sociolinguistic perspective, the localised ways in which language is being taken up and the way contextual embedding is needed to situate multilingualism within wider social, economic and political processes that are a part of today's globalised world.

LANGUAGE AS A COMMODITY

The commodification of language according to Heller (2010) has become a theme of current sociolinguistic interest because of the ways the new globalised economy is taking up language. In this age, where the exchange of information has become central for establishing and maintaining social and commercial ties, language and multilingual skills play a key role. The expansion of markets beyond the boundaries of nation-states requires the ability to communicate in other languages in order to buy and sell products and services. Information and communication technologies (Sabaté-Dalmau, 2010) are another important dimension upon which the current economy hinges, and these new forms of communication (e.g., the internet, cell phones) provide a practical means for overcoming the constraints of time and space (Appadurai, 1996) and the constraints they traditionally imposed on communication related to expanding global markets. An increasingly service-based economy also places language and communication in the forefront.

The call centre recruitment advertisement in Example 2.1 belongs to a large US company dedicated to providing multinationals and locally based companies from around the world with a wide variety of services. These include specialized information connected to banking and information and communications technology (ICT) as well as the task of selling products such as clothing, electronic devices or travel packages. These services are offered in over thirty languages and hence the need to recruit employees who can offer service in the languages of the companies' clients. Call centres not only make money selling services in different languages, they also provide a workplace where individuals can exchange their multilingual language skills for a job at one of the eighty global centres distributed around twenty-four countries (Urcioli, 2008). It is precisely the exchange of language skills for money or other means of acquiring material resources, such as employment, that imbues them with their economic value.

The commodification of language raises important questions for the sociolinguist concerning issues of power and the economic value of language. Who benefits and how from multilingualism and from the ways it

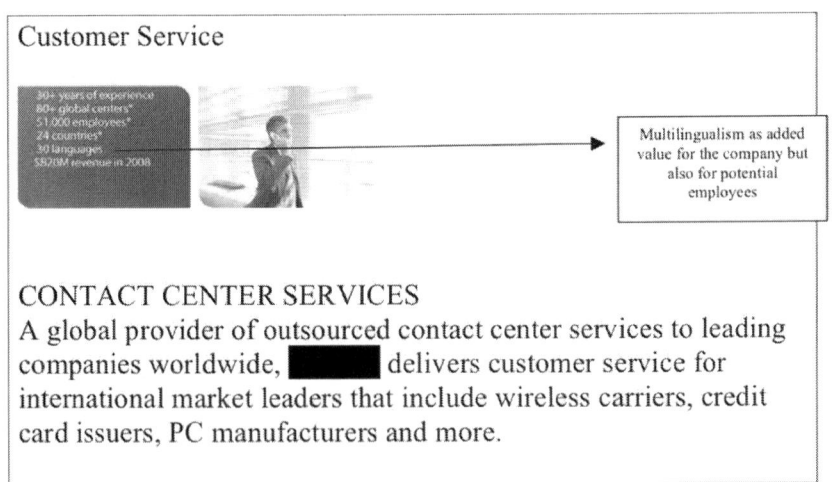

Example 2.1   Online advertisement for call centre recruitment and customer service from a multinational company located in Barcelona; reprinted by permission.

is currently managed in private businesses and institutional settings which are closely connected to local and global relations of power? A feature of many businesses and workplaces in the new service economy is the central role of communication (Cameron, 2000) as well as the need for an increasingly multilingual workforce (Duchêne, 2009) where persons who speak two or more languages are preferred. The role of language as a commodity is supplanting its value and use as a marker of identity, especially in places where linguistic minorities have discovered the economic value of multilingualism and knowledge of English (Heller, 2010).

LANGUAGE AS A RESOURCE FOR ACCESS TO KEY INFORMATION

Access to the information that is needed to live and carry out one's daily activities in a new society is obtained through knowledge of and communication in oral and written varieties of the local language/s. Newcomers need to have a working knowledge of those varieties. It is also important for them to know whom to contact and where, when and how to obtain what they need. As Blommaert (2005: 76–78) points out, seeing language as a resource implies recognition of the fact that there is an unequal access to linguistic and communicative resources that results in differential capacities to accomplish certain functions of expressing and interpreting meanings. Not having access to certain languages, varieties, styles, jargons or genres produces differential access to contextual spaces, and spaces of meaning production and ratification.

For example, migrant populations' access to health depends on their ability to communicate with medical staff and to understand the instructions and the professional knowledge delivered. Language is central to the exchange and the negotiation of information in doctor-patient encounters. Institutions such as a public health clinic—a domain for the implementation of nation welfare programs—must find ways to guarantee patients their rights to health no matter what their country of origin or the languages they speak. One of the ways this is done at a primary health clinic in Barcelona is illustrated in Example 2.2 where access to key information about where a woman must go to get the tests carried out on her baby is explained by the cultural mediator.

Cultural mediators can bridge the language gap and give patients access to health care but, in this example, they take away a patient's agency to negotiate, clarify or contest the doctor's recommended medical treatment. The exchange in lines 1–29 take place in Catalan; the nurse informs the mediator about the doctor's request for a blood test and what the mother needs to do in order to get this test done. Lines 30–49 are in Punjabi; the mediator gives a free translation of the nurse's instructions on where to go to get blood and stool tests done.

Example 2.2[2]   Interaction between nurse and patient at a primary health clinic, assisted by a cultural mediator.

1	*NUR:	vale, la doctora demana anàlisi. Anàlisi de sang.
	%tra:	Ok, the doctor requires tests. A blood test.
2	*MED:	anàlisi de sang?
	%tra:	a blood test?
3	*NUR:	anàlisi de sang i de caca. Els nens tan petits no els punxem
4		nosaltres aquí sinó que els enviem a la vall d´hebrón. Llavors
5		se li ha d´explicar ón és. O sigui, ha d´anar fins a la vall
6		hebrón, un cop sigui allà això és la carretera i el metro, té
7		que anar a Traumatologia.
	%tra:	a blood test and an analysis of stools. We do not put such small children here rather we send them to the Vall d´Hebrón hospital. So, you have to explain where that is. Thus, she has to go to Vall d´Hebrón and once there… that is the road and the subway she has to go to Traumatology.
8	*MED:	// a la sala dels guixos//
	%tra:	To the plaster room
9	*NUR:	//sí, a la sala dels guixos//. O sigui, un cop hagi trobat
10		el departament de traumatologia que està just al davant
11		del edifici aquest tan gran, doncs a la planta baixa
12		que demani per la sala dels guixos i allà ha de portar
13		la petició, perquè si no porta la petició els de la vall
14		d´hebrón no sabrán el que la doctora demana, vale?
	%tra:	Yes, to the plaster room. So, once she has found the department of traumatology which is just in front of of that building which is so tall then it's the ground floor she should ask for the plaster room and she has to turn in the request for a blood test because if she does not bring the request with her the people at Vall d'Hebron will not know which doctor is asking for it, ok?
15	*MED:	// té que anar en dejù?]
	%tra:	is it necessary to refrain from eating before the test?
16	* NUR:	//té que anar en dejù//, de dimarts a divendres, el dia que
17		ella vulgui.
	%tra:	it is necessary to refrain from eating before the test and to go between Tuesday and Friday on the day that is best for her.
18	*MED:	//de dimarts a divendres//
	%tra:	from Tuesday to Friday
19	*NUR:	//exacte, aquí ja ho possa: de dimarts// a divendres, de
20		8:30 a 9:30, no cal trucar abans, no es necessari cita
21		prèvia, dimarts, dimecres, dijous i divendres a partir de
22		les 8:30 fins a les 9:30 es presenti aquí i li treuràn la sang
23		al nen. Ha d´anar en dejù i ha de portar caca. La caca la
24		portarà en aquest potet, no ha de llençar el triptic que hi

(*continued*)

25		ha dintre, sino que ha de agafar una mica de caca amb
26		aquesta cullareta que hi ha aquí i barrejar-ho i elmateix
27		dia que vagi a treure la sang té que portar la caca allà
28		dalt a la vall d'hebrón, vale? I ara li posaré en un sobre,
29		mentres li explicas vaig a buscar un sobre.

%tra: exactly, that's what it says here: from Tuesday to Friday from 830 to 930, there is no need to call first, a previous appointment is unnecessary, Tuesday, Wednesday, Thursday and Friday from 830 to 9- 930 she should go there and they will extract the child's blood. He has to refrain from eating and she should take a sample of the child's stools. the stools can be put in this small jar, she should not throw away the triptych inside but she should take a bit of stool with this little spoon that's here and mix it in and the same day that she goes for the blood extraction she should take the stools up there to the Vall d'Hebron, ok? and I'll give her an envelope, while you explain to her I'll go fetch an envelope.

30	*MED:%tra:	اد ةقبيپ او لَب تَب شک غي اد یوخ اد و چ اب ايج ا ک ىئس طد ا MP
31		بج ىعوت طعاو ظيا تتُب ا بوچ ا ،غيُبَّذ ي تيا ا ،اُب شکغي
32		ىؤاشث د ىيئاو لیيپعو ىؤاشث د ئاو ا پبع ادظيشت بّي يل اُب
33		و ت گج ظک پبع اد و شيہ وکيديک کل تيا،ا چيو قالع ىبپ تُا
34		they say that she has to give the baby a blood test and
35		they have to do a urine test. This test is done somewhere
36		else because he is very small that's why you have to go
37		to the stop on line three to the Vall d'Hebron, Hospital
38		of Vall de Hebron. It is in the mountains look how it is written

39	*PAT:%tra:	ظک جگ ت وؤ؟ Where is it?

40	*MED:	پت ي ہي ُوّو ى ا ا فوُسيي (L.F)
	%tra:	I don't know. I don't have this information.

41	*PAT:	ىو وا اى ا ت ىبپ
	%tra:	it's in the mountains, isn't it?

42	*MED:	ا ل بيخ اش يہ ا ى ا ت ىبپ
	%tra:	I think it is in the mountain.

43	*PAT:	PAT: اد ىئبج ت وشيہ؟
	%tra:	Can you go by metro?

44	*MED:	اُوّب وا،ُب گ ژبج ىعوت وذج توا ذعث وت طا ،ُب بج ى توا ى ج
45		گج طا توا،ُب بج گج ظک ىعوت ک گ يي،دّو اوتو،ُب ع د ز غبک
46		ّذ يل ُش يييغو ىوخ ت
47	%tra:	yes. you need to go there. after you go there you have to
48		show this paper and they will tell you where you need to go so that they can do your blood test, etcetera.

49	*PAT:%tra:	اچب Ok.

Control over the transmission of medical information is left in the hands of the nurse and the cultural mediator whose role, ideally, should be to facilitate the face-to-face interaction between doctor and patient. As Goffman (1967) notes, face-to-face interaction not only allows for agency on the part of participants but it also enables them to collaborate in order to sustain a single common focus of concern. As illustrated by Example 2.2, this does not take place here and not all ways of gaining access to information are equal. This mediated information given to the patient lacks important features that would typically be present in a standard doctor-patient encounter. The dynamic and interactive nature of face-to-face interaction would allow the patient to negotiate the information provided by the doctor, and as we see the patient becomes a passive receiver of the medical information that the mediator transmits to her (Duranti and Goodwin, 1992: 22). Unequal access to health treatment is a reality for patients who do not speak either Catalan or Spanish in spite of the translations provided by the cultural mediator.

THE REGIMENTATION OF LANGUAGE

A third understanding of language that typically emerges in sociolinguistic work concerned with workplace settings has to do with the way language is controlled and regimented. Heller (2010) and Duchêne (2009) argue that one of the outstanding developments of the economy is the new "word-force" that requires jobs where workers are hired for their language skills. Cameron (2000: 56–58) argues that institutional talk and locally managed routines seem increasingly to be giving way to prescribed schedules and formal agendas. A standard script adopted by call centres covers the sequencing, the content and function, and not uncommonly the actual wording or every move the institutional participant makes. In contrast, talk carried out by doctors, therapists, lawyers and business executives has a status that protects them from certain kinds of linguistic regimentation by superiors to which many other workers are now commonly subjected and made accountable.[3]

The development and intensification of linguistic control strategies is the outcome of technological change and the increasing influence of management approaches. This has placed linguistic behaviour as well as other kinds of job behaviour under close scrutiny and surveillance. The locally managed character of interaction is being disrupted by codified and styled forms of talk. Codification and scripts do not eliminate locally managed talk but they create a standard whereby a worker may be held accountable for any deviation.

Example 2.3 is a selection of some of the guidelines used to train employees at a call centre in Morocco. This particular call centre in North Africa represents a US company which has outsourced its calling services from a centre in India that is responsible for producing the instructions and scripts. The availability of an English-language skilled "word-force" made up of recent university graduates in English studies from Morocco makes setting

---

A Selection of Guidelines

* Always ask permission
» (Kindly, Please, Would you…) Never give instructions!
* Always be polite
» Always say "Thanks"!
* Always be corporate
» Use only Professional Corporate Lingo and Style!
* If anyone offers their name, always USE IT!
» This builds credibility and friendship, which in turn builds trust
* Always exude personal power!
 » Never position yourself to be weaker/subordinate!
* Your degree of success/results is directly related to your level of Awareness, Listening & Communication skills!
» Bad agents read scripts only, while great agents have spontaneous conversations
* If you need to repeat something always do so with more personal power, slower, louder & more clearly.
» Never waste conversational time on useless banter!

Example 2.3[4]   Examples of training guidelines for call centre operators.

up a call centre a profitable business. In addition to a script, employees at this company are given a set of guidelines on some of the communicative strategies they need to follow. The prescription of talk in this way at the call centre is also a way of holding employees accountable for their work. Control of employees is exercised by the number of clients an operator successfully manages to gain over a fixed period of time, in addition to the use of cameras and recordings to monitor operators and their language. National boundaries are no longer a barrier for business. Persons who possess the linguistic skills and who speak English can be found all over the world and in places where the minimum wage is lower than in the US and India.

The regulation of talk as illustrated by the above guidelines is intended to maximise efficiency and business for the company. Operators are not free to talk and to negotiate meanings with their interlocutors in the manner of their choosing but rather their interactions are constrained and predetermined, and whenever talk gets personal or off-track strategies are taught in order for operators to get back to the script. This is what Cameron (2000: 123) describes as the "taylorised" work conditions of call centres where language is treated as automated production work similar to the conditions at factories in the era of industrialisation. This new role of language is connected to changes brought about by new technologies, globalisation where economic activity is no longer confined to nation-states and to an increasing service economy where language and multilingual skills have come into the forefront.

LANGUAGE AS IDEOLOGY

Blommaert (2005: 158) understands ideology as a specific set of symbolic representations such as discourses, terms, or arguments that serve a specific purpose and are operated by specific groups or actors recognisable precisely by their usage of such ideas or ways of thinking. Ideology cannot be attributed to one social actor, nor can it be located in one particular site (Foucault, 1972), but rather it embodies an unconscious or implicit set of dispositions that penetrate the whole fabric of societies or communities and results in normalized, naturalized patterns of thought and behavior (Bourdieu, 1977).

An understanding of language use as ideology leads one to ask where precisely to locate ideas and beliefs about language. Woolard (1998: 11–27) and Phillips (1998: 212) show how language structure and form index social meanings and how these meanings are connected to local and global processes of interpretation, but ideology in language can also be found in discourses and in the content where varying degrees of implicitness can be analysed. Ideology provides a link between language and social theory and between the everyday language choices and practices that are shaped by wider social processes and with ever-changing social relations of power and social (in)equality (Erickson, 2004).

Example 2.4 illustrates the thinking of a teacher, who has volunteered for an NGO which is associated with a religious body in a town on the outskirts of Barcelona and which is dedicated to providing shelter and language classes to migrants. In this teacher's discourse, we see revealed a particular view of the social world: migrant (men) will supposedly find jobs in the construction sector which has traditionally been work carried out by Spanish speaking migrants from Southern Spain and, in contrast, Catalan speakers will be those working for the public administration or banks.

The view expressed represents the way that migrants have been typically been positioned in Catalan society in terms of both their social status as well as the language they are expected to speak: migrants are not seen as needing to learn Catalan because they will not be working in a bank. The teacher's way of representing Catalan and Spanish, on the one hand, and the representation of migrants, on the other hand, illustrates the manner in which language comes to index social meanings.

Ideology is also associated with language choices and language forms. Example 2.5 below illustrates how the same teacher undertakes the task of teaching. Not only is Spanish confirmed as the legitimate language of instruction but, also, the ways in which the interaction unfolds and the focus on particular language forms reveal the teacher's views about what counts as useful language to teach and the manner in which it should be taught.

1	*TEA:	+^si hablas catalán en un trabajo ellos ellos no van a trabajar en un banco # eso ya está claro #
2		eso ya lo saben ellos que no trabajarán en un banco.
	%tra:	+^*if you speak Catalan at a job they they are not going to work at a bank# this is*
		already clear # they already know that they won't work at a bank.
3	*RES:	ahem.
4	*TEA:	ellos van a trabajar en la construcción # o: o: yo que sé qué decirte
5		# cosas así # gente donde el 95% habla castellano.
	%tra:	*they are going to work in construction # o:r or I don't know what to tell you # things like this #*
		people where 95% speak Castilian

Example 2.4[5]   Interview with volunteer teacher from an NGO.

1	TEA:	amar qué es? # amar.
	%tra:	to love what is it? # to love.
2	S13:	I don't know.
3	TEA:	do you know? # you don't remember.
	%act:	silence.
4	TEA:	amar # to love.
	%tra:	to love # to love.
5	S13?:	ahhhh # es amar # yeah yeah.
	%tra:	ahhh # it is to love # yeah yeah.
6	TEA:	yo amo # mi padre # yo amo [mi madre]
	%tra:	I love # my father # I love [my mother].
7	S15?:	[xxx].
8	S13:	amá o amó?
	%tra:	amá o amó?
	%com:	the student is asking about the right pronunciation of *amar* since he might be familiar with the Word *amor* [the love].
9	TEA:	no # el amor es the love el amor # pero el verbo es amar # y se dice # yo:
		%tra: no # the love is the love the love # but the verb is to love # and you say # I:
	%act:	TEA writes "yo amo" below "amar" on the board.
10	TEA:	yo amo.
	%tra:	I love.
11	S15:	yo amo.
	%tra:	I love.
12	TEA:	yo amo a? # mi madre.
	%tra:	I love my? # my mother.
13	S15:	yo amo mi madre.
	%tra:	I love my mother.

Example 2.5   Class interaction between teacher and students at an NGO.

The teacher selects the verb paradigm *amar* '*to love*' for instruction. This prototypical example for learning the conjugation of Spanish verbs ending in -*ar* has little to do with the practical communicative knowledge required for migrants to get by in a Catalan town. This raises the question of how an ideological view of language is helpful in the teaching of language to adults of migrant origin as well as for a sociolinguistic analysis of language and migration. Such approaches to teaching have persisted over time, and the meanings they have acquired are indexed in this example. The model this teacher is adopting corresponds to traditional methods for teaching verb conjugations to children in Spanish/Catalan schools. The main goal is to teach grammar rather than the communicative skills that might be useful to adult newcomers who do not speak the local languages. The example the teacher provides to contextualize first person, present indicative in line 12 again shows that such a class is really intended for children (who are supposed to love their mother and father).

CONCEPTIONS OF LANGUAGE

Four conceptions of language have been discussed here: (a) language as a commodity, (b) language as a key resource, (c) language as an object of control, and (d) language as ideology. They provide examples of the sociolinguistic phenomena that current research can address. A critical sociolinguistic perspective guides our research questions towards the ways in which language is connected with the construction of asymmetrical relations of power, with social categorisation and with social processes linked to the definition and construction of nation-state and the workings of the new economy. As has been shown, research on language needs to take account of structure and form (Examples 2.2 and 2.5), but it also involves the investigation of discourses and the way in which ideas and beliefs get conveyed (Example 2.4). At the same time, language also needs to be conceptualised as 'a skill' that becomes objectified as a 'commodity' in activities connected to the new economy (Examples 2.1 and 2.3). The examples I have discussed show how multilingualism is being taken up and reshaped, in different ways in different social, institutional and historical contexts, in an era of economic globalisation and increased mobility. Call centres are businesses that transcend national boundaries by providing multilingual language services, and they carry out business on behalf of private enterprises from around the globe. They are sites of the new economy where the economic value of multilingualism and other language 'skills' is central. Another key feature of our globalised society is the mobility of persons for purposes of work and leisure (Urry, 2007). The linguistic and cultural diversity brought by people from different countries poses a challenge for institutions of the nation-state, such as public health clinics and non-governmental organisations that provide social services to migrants. Communication is at the centre of service provision in these institutions and hence the need to incorporate multilingualism in order to interact with newcomers. However, the construction of multilingualism in these various sites studied is not a neutral process (Moyer, 2010). It is both an interpersonal and an institutional process that gets owned and exercised in ways that (re)produce relations of power and exclusion. Awareness of the way language is taken up by institutions and speakers in the different contexts provides a way of linking up multilingualism in everyday interactions with wider social processes connected to globalization and mobility.

TRANSCRIPTION CONVENTIONS

The transcriptions are carried out using the LIPPS-LIDES (Gardner-Chloros, Moyer and Sebba, 2007) proposals. The conventions listed also appear in the interactions transcribed.

X□Y	speaker X and Y are looking at each other as they talk
[XXX]	utterance unintelligible
text in bold	utterance in Catalan
text in italics	utterance in English
// //	overlapping utterances

#	short pause
:	lengthening of preceding sound
[...]	several turns not included
.	stopping fall in tone
?	rising intonation

NOTES

1. The *Comunicación Intercultural Estrátegias de Negociación* (CIEN) research team is based at the Universitat Autònoma de Barcelona. It has received official recognition and funding from the Catalan research agency SGR2009-1340 and support from the Spanish Ministry of Science and Innovation grant HUM2007-61864 for the project on *The Management of Multilingualism in Private, Public and NGO Institutions*.
2. This piece of data was collected by Dolores Ruíz but it has been transcribed and translated by the author and by Nargus Karim within the context of the CIEN research team project.
3. The language of liberal professions such as doctors and lawyers may also be regimented and homogenised for similar purposes of accountability and quality of services as call centre workers.
4. The examples presented here were obtained by Safae Jabri within the context of the CIEN research team project.
5. The data in both Examples 2.4 and 2.5 were collected by Maria Rosa Garrido within the context of the CIEN research team project.

REFERENCES

Appadurai, A. 1996. *Modernity at Large: Cultural Dimensions of Globalization*. Minneapolis: University of Minnesota Press.

Blommaert, J. 2005. *Discourse*. Cambridge: Cambridge University Press.

Bourdieu, P. 1977. *Outline of a Theory of Practice*. Cambridge: Cambridge University Press.

Cameron, D. 2000. *Good to Talk?* London: Sage.

Duchêne, A. 2009. Marketing, management and performance: multilingualism as commodity in a tourism call centre. *Language Policy* 8: 27–50.

Duranti, A. 1997. *Linguistic Anthropology*. Cambridge: Cambridge University Press.

Duranti, A. and Goodwin, C. 1992. *Rethinking Context*. Cambridge: Cambridge University Press.

Erickson, F. 2004. *Talk and Social Theory*. Cambridge: Polity Press.

Foucault, M. 1972. *The Archaeology of Knowledge*. New York: Pantheon Books.

Gardner-Chloros, P, Moyer, M. and Sebba, M. 2007. Coding and analysing multilingual data: the LIDES project. In *Creating and Digitizing Language Corpora*, ed. J. C. Beal, K. P. Corrigan and Hermann L. Mois, 91–120. Basingstoke: Palgrave Macmillan.

Goffman, E. 1967. *Interaction Ritual: Essays in Face-to-Face Behavior*. Garden City, NY: Doubleday.

Gumperz, J. 1982. *Discourse Strategies*. Cambridge: Cambridge University Press.

Heller, M. 1999. *Linguistic Minorities and Modernity: A Sociolinguistic Ethnography*. London: Longman.

————. 2010. The commodification of language. *Annual Review of Anthropology* 39: 101–14.

Labov, W. 1972. *Sociolinguistic Patterns*. Philadelphia: University of Pennsylvania Press.

————. 2000. *Principles of Linguistic Change. Vol. 2, Social Factors*. Oxford: Blackwell.

————. 2007. Transmission and diffusion. *Language* 83: 344–87.

Moyer, M. 1998. Bilingual conversation strategies in Gibraltar? In *Code-Switching in Conversation*, ed. P. Auer, 215–36. London: Routledge.

————. 2010. The management of multilingualism in public, private and non-governmental institutions. *Sociolinguistic Studies*, 4(2): 267–296.

————. 2011. What multilingualism? Agency and unintended consequences of multilingual practices in a Barcelona health clinic. *Journal of Pragmatics*, 43(5): 1209–1221.

Philips, S. 1998. Languages ideologies in institutions of power. In *Language Ideologies: Practice and Theory*, ed. B. B. Schieffelin, K. A. Woolard and P. V. Kroskrity, 211–25. Oxford: Oxford University Press.

Sabaté-Dalmau, M. 2010. *Voices from a Locutorio: Telecommunications and Migrant Networking*, PhD dissertation. Bellaterra: Universitat Autònoma de Barcelona.

Urcioli, B. 2008. Skills and the selves in the new workplace. American Ethnologist 35(2): 211–28.

Urry, J. 2007. *Mobilities*. Cambridge: Polity Press.

Verschueren, J. 2008. Intercultural communication and the challenges of migration. *Language and Intercultural Communication* 8(1): 21–35.

Woolard, K. A. 1989. *Double Talk*. Stanford: Stanford University Press.

————. 1998. Introduction: language ideology as a field of inquiry? In *Language Ideologies: Practice and Theory*, ed. B. B. Schieffelin, K. A. Woolard and P. V. Kroskrity, 3–50. Oxford: Oxford University Press.

3 Unpicking Agency[1] in Sociolinguistic Research with Migrants

David Block

[Agency is a] controversial topic that has been at the center of discussions of subjectivity for centuries, and one that will never be put
wholly to rest, even as it remains compelling. For in probing agency,
we are, in effect, tackling the fundamental question of responsibility:
in personal action, in aesthetic creation, in inter-persona norms and
social valuations. (Hall, 2004: 5)

In this way, Donald Hall situates agency at the heart of his book-length
discussion of subjectivity. He traces a line of thought ranging from the clas-
sical period (e.g. Plato) to the enlightenment era (Descartes, Kant, Locke) to
the present (Taylor, 1989) in which issues around the autonomy of rational
subjects and their ability to strive for perfection, among other things, have
been the focus of discussion. However, it is agency as part of a more general turn to identity in the social sciences in recent years which is the focus
of this chapter. My aim is to think with the reader about issues around
poststructuralist approaches to identity and current anthropological and
sociological thought about agency, with a view to elaborating a clear way
to understand identity work in context in sociolinguistics and linguistic
anthropology. I first very briefly discuss a poststructuralist approach to
identity, which I see as prevalent in the social sciences today. I then consider
how agency has been conceptualised in recent years, focussing specifically
on recent attempts by two theorists—Sherry Ortner (1989, 2005, 2006)
and Margaret Archer (2007)—to reconcile tensions at the crossroads of
structure and agency. These background discussions lead to a tentative outline of parameters shaping agency as emergent in social practices, which I
then apply a study by Bashir-Ali (2006) to see what we can glean beyond
what the original author gleaned in her analysis.

IDENTITY AND AGENCY

One basic (and big) claim being made here is that in the social sciences
today, and in sociolinguistics and linguistic anthropology in particular, a

good proportion of researchers frame identity as a social process as opposed to a determined and fixed product. The approach to identity that has been adopted for the most part is what I have elsewhere termed 'broadly post-structuralist', where 'structuralism' involves the search for universal and invariant laws of social activity that operate at all levels of human life, and 'poststructuralism' involves a recognition of the limitations of structuralism and an emphasis on the emergent in localised, diverse and variable social activity (Block, 2007). Most work on language and identity inspired in poststructuralism adopts a social constructionist perspective, according to which identity is about the multiple ways in which people position themselves and are positioned, that is, the different subject positions they inhabit or have ascribed to them, within particular social, historical and cultural contexts.

If scholars have generally offered something in the form of a definition when discussing identity (e.g. Benwell and Stokoe, 2006; Block, 2007; Riley, 2007), agency has tended to be a less clearly formulated construct. Comaroff and Comaroff (1997: 37) call it 'that abstraction greatly under-specified, often misused, much fetichized these days by social scientists'. One problem is that authors who use the term seldom provide a clear and unequivocal definition of it, avoiding direct phrasing such as: 'Agency is defined as . . . ' in favour of just getting on with using it. For example, in the index of Bethan Benwell and Liz Stokoe's 2006 book *Discourse and Identity*, the term 'agency' is listed as appearing on twenty-five different pages; however, no definition of the term is provided on any of these pages. Similarly, in *Second Language Identities* (Block, 2007), I list 'agency' in the index as appearing on twelve pages. However, like Benwell and Stokoe, I do not on any of these pages define the term in a direct way.

Among those authors who do actually define agency, some opt for simplicity. For example, in her survey article entitled 'Language and Agency', Laura Ahearn (2001: 112) states early on that '[a]gency refers to the socio-culturally mediated capacity to act'. However, it should be noted that Ahearn subsequently develops an in-depth discussion of the term, conveying to the reader its elusive nature and how difficult it is to define. As if to stress this elusiveness and difficulty, Alessandro Duranti (2004) offers what he calls a 'working definition of agency', which looks as follows:

> Agency is here understood as the property of those entities (i) that have some degree of control over their own behavior, (ii) whose actions in the world affect other entities' (and sometimes their own), and (iii) whose actions are the object of evaluation (e.g. in terms of their responsibility for a given outcome). (Duranti, 2004: 453)

Duranti also discusses agency in terms of its embeddedness in language, that is, what he calls 'agency *in* language', as opposed to 'agency *of* language'. However, in most sociolinguistics literature focusing on identity, agency is framed in terms of human interaction with others against a backdrop of larger social forces.

In their respective approaches to agency, Ahearn and Duranti would appear to be following what Bucholtz and Hall (2005) have called an 'interactionist approach to identity', an approach which situates agency as emergent in social interaction. These authors describe this approach as follows:

> From the perspective of an interactionist approach to identity, the role of agency becomes problematic only when it is conceptualized as located within an individual rational subject who consciously authors his identity without structural constraints. . . . Sociocultural linguists are generally not concerned with calibrating the degree of autonomy or intentionality in any given act; rather, agency is more productively viewed as the accomplishment of social action. (Bucholtz and Hall, 2005: 606)

Whereas this statement makes clear Bucholtz and Hall's rejection of the notion that rational subjects make their way on their own, it nonetheless opens the door to other lines of critique. Sherry Ortner (1989, 2005, 2006) suggests that interactionist approaches often marginalise social structures as constraints on emergent activity. Whereas I do not see in Bucholtz and Hall's work any tendency to ignore social structural constraints, I do see Ortner's point that working at the micro level of social interactionism, one can lose sight of how macro-level social structures impinge on and limit the individual agency of those participating in interactions. Ortner has attempted to reconcile this structure/agency dilemma by formulating what she calls 'Practice Theory', which is based on the assumption that 'culture (in a broad sense) constructs people as particular kinds of social actors, but social actors, through their living, on-the-ground variable practices reproduce or transform—and usually some of each—the culture that made them' (2006: 129).

SHERRY ORTNER'S PRACTICE THEORY

Ortner's starting point is the need to overcome 'oppositions' in social theory in the 1960s and '70s, as presented and argued by practitioners at the time. One such opposition is the age-old issue of whether human beings and their actions are determined by social structures that pre-exist them or whether they are free agents who act on their own behalf and interest and make the world around them with no constraints on their activity. In the sociological and anthropological work foundational to Ortner's thinking—Marx, Durkheim, Levi Strauss—one can see how these two poles are partially reconciled by allowing individuals a degree of agency subject to the overwhelming weight of history, as indicated in the oft-cited quote from Marx:

Men make their own history, but they do not make it just as they please; they do not make it under circumstances chosen by themselves, but under circumstances directly found, given and transmitted from the past. The tradition of all the dead generations weighs like a nightmare on the brain of the living. And just when they seem engaged in revolutionising themselves and things, in creating something entirely new, precisely in such epochs of revolutionary crisis they anxiously conjure up spirits of the past to their service and borrow from them names, slogans and costumes in order to present the new scene of world history in this time-honoured disguise and this borrowed language. (Marx, 1972 [1852]: 437)

More recently, in his work spanning several decades, Pierre Bourdieu navigated the line between determining social structure and individual agency as follows:

It is necessary to abandon all theories which explicitly or implicitly treat practice as a mechanical reaction, directly determined by the antecedent conditions and entirely reducible to the mechanical functioning of pre-established assemblies, "models" or "roles" . . . But rejection of the mechanistic theories in no way implies that, in accordance with another obligatory option, we should bestow on some creative free will the free and wilful power to constitute, on the instant, the meaning of the situation by projecting the ends aiming at its transformation, and that we should reduce the objective intentions and constituted significations of actions and works to the conscious and deliberate intentions of their authors. (Bourdieu, 1977: 73)

In her formulation of Practice Theory, as a model of social activity that includes identity formation (and, by extension, agency), Ortner draws on Bourdieu, as well as other sociologists and social theorists such as Berger and Luckman (1966), Giddens (1979) and de Certeau (1984). However, Ortner believes that there is a need in social theory to work not just at the level of agency but also at the level of subjectivities, which she defines as 'a specifically cultural and historical consciousness' (Ortner, 2005: 34). She explains that her use of the word 'consciousness' is not intended to 'exclude the various unconscious dynamics as seen, for example, in a Freudian unconscious or a Bourdieusian habitus' (Ortner, 2005: 34).

One might well ask which parts of Freud's and Bourdieu's 'unconscious' Ortner would include in her theoretical thinking and which she would reject. The answer to this question is to be found in her discussion of subjectivity:

[S]ubjectivity is always more than those things [i.e., 'the various unconscious dynamics as seen, for example, in a Freudian unconscious or a Bourdieusian habitus'] in two senses. At the individual level, I will assume that, with Giddens, that actors are always at least partially 'knowing subjects', that they have some degree of reflexivity about themselves and their desires, and that they have some 'penetration' into the ways in which they are formed by circumstances. They are, in short, conscious in the conventional psychological sense, something that needs to be emphasized as a complement to, though not a replacement of, Bourdieu's insistence on the inaccessibility to actors of the underlying logic of their practices. (Ortner, 2005: 34)

This statement leads to the question of whether or not one can conserve in one's work an 'insistence on the inaccessibility to actors of the underlying logic of their practices' (Ortner, 2005: 34) while arguing that 'actors are always at least partially "knowing subjects" [with] some degree of reflexivity about themselves and their desires, and that they have some "penetration" into the ways in which they are formed by circumstances' (Ortner, 2005: 34). It is for this reason that it is useful to compare and contrast Ortner's views with those of other scholars, such as Margaret Archer (2000, 2007), who has elaborated a model of how structure and agency interact.

MARGARET ARCHER ON STRUCTURE AND AGENCY

Archer is critical of Bourdieu, and like Ortner she positions him as limited in his approach to agency. First, she questions the timelessness of constructs like habitus, making the point that Bourdieu first developed his theory of practice via his studies of a relatively stable traditional society in North Africa in the 1950s and a 1960s French society still firmly anchored in modernity. For Archer, societies in the early twenty-first century are very different from those studied by sociologists and anthropologists forty and fifty years ago and changes in the object of study necessitate different frameworks. From this perspective, the question seems to be whether or not, and to what extent, Bourdieusian theory helps us to understand the global age characterised by 'time-space compression' (Harvey, 1989), global flows and 'scapes' (Appadurai, 1990), 'hyper-diversity' (Vertovec, 2007) and 'liquid lives' (Bauman, 2005).

Archer's second criticism of Bourdieu—intrinsically linked to the first— is one that has always surrounded use of his thinking. I refer here to how his discussions of structure and practice, and in particular his talk about habitus, seem more at home in discussions of stable societies and collectives, where there is what Archer terms 'contextual continuity' as part and parcel of 'cultural and structural morphostasis'. In other words, as Shilling puts it, 'Bourdieu's formulations are overwhelmingly focused on *continuity* rather than change' (Shilling, 2004: 479; italics in the original). Thus, despite the claims by Bourdieu that habitus embodies not only stable social structure but also a capacity to generate novelty in the face of unanticipated circumstances and experiences, Archer argues that it is only with great difficulty that habitus can account for individual creativity, innovation and change as opposed to continued embeddedness in local social structures, reproduced in the practices engaged in by individuals.

Finally, Archer takes Bourdieu to task for seeming to say that whereas academics can get outside their habitus, thinking beyond the reproduction of social realities again and again, the objects of their analysis cannot do this or can do so only exceptionally. Using Bourdieu's words to great effect, Archer states:

> [E]xalting the habitus also valorises the investigator over the subject because it 'privileges analytical understanding as ineluctably superior to the native understanding of the world' [Bourdieu, 1977 [1972]: 79]. It thus entails the substitution of the third-person accounts for first-person ones [i.e. those of the researcher]. (Archer, 2007: 43)

Nevertheless, despite her criticisms of Bourdieu, Archer is not tempted to follow social theorists who clearly prime agency over social structure. She agrees with scholars such as Giddens (1991, 2000) and Ulrich Beck (Beck and Beck-Gernsheim, 2002) who argue that in the current era of globalisation, we are witnessing in many parts of the world the decline of routinisation, a phenomenon associated with more traditional and static social assemblages. However, she is not willing to sign up to Beck's notion of 'institutionalised individualism', whereby structure and agency are conflated. This conflation is deemed necessary by Beck because in the age of globalisation, traditional socialising structures, such as the nuclear family, the neighbourhood and the school, are eroded as shapers in one's life. Structure thus is redefined in terms of 'self-organisation' and 'self-thematization', in short, the individual project of 'do-it-yourself biographies' (Beck and Beck-Gernsheim, 2002: 23–24).

Instead, Archer attempts to establish a path around Bourdieu and Beck, without losing strong notions of structure and agency along the way. She sees individuals acting according to 'projects', which result from the unique capacity of human beings to reflect on their pasts, presents and futures. Engaging in such project-driven activity, individuals elaborate courses of actions as reactions either to events occurring objectively (i.e. out of reach of their control) in the world or to desires that they feel. So far, Archer's talk of projects looks very similar to Beck's views on individualisation and self-construction. However, unlike Beck, Archer retains the idea that there is social structure. In addition, whereas Beck sees global society in late modernity as 'becoming destructured', Archer sees it as 'undergoing restructuring' (Archer, 2007, 61). Thus, the courses of action that she posits have implications as regards the interrelationship between individuals and their environments, between their internally driven agency and externally driven structure. In particular, Archer emphasises that there are objectively existing social structures, such as groups of people acting in concert, which potentially both constrain and enable individual agency. However, they are not relevant, in a sense, until the individual engages in a project which includes them. Thus, the social structure ever-emergent in an office environment only impacts on an individual's agency when that individual embarks on a project which involves interaction in that environment. And power embodied in the social structure of the office is not experienced by an individual until or unless a part of that individual's life comes into contact with that social structure.

REFRAMING AGENCY

Drawing on what I have examined from selected sources, I now set out to reframe agency, an exercise that will necessarily be partial. The starting point for such an exercise is at the level of practice and the participation in activity mediated by human subjects and abstract and material resources. Thus, whether we are talking about spontaneous exchanges between individuals or an interview between researcher and interviewee, the goal is to examine agency as 'an accomplishment of [situated] social action' (Bucholtz and Hall, 2005: 606) and not just an abstract notion, as in philosophical discussions of free will.

From Ortner's and Archer's work, several conclusions may be drawn. First, it is important to situate any discussion of agency and identity in terms of foundational work in the social sciences (Durkheim, Marx, Lévi-Strauss, Geertz, Goffman and so on). Here I have only made cursory mention of how Ortner and Archer have done this in their work, but I wish to flag this process as important to the development of clear and nuanced discussions of important issues in the social sciences. For it is only by rereading scholars who all too often are 'blackboxed' (Latour, 1987)—that is, cited as practically iconic of particular ideas as opposed to unpacked and scrutinised to see how they actually work for an author at a given place in time—that one can be sure of and confident about one's ideas.

On a more substantive level, I take from Ortner her clearer exposition of practice theory, and in particular her engagement with subjectivity, albeit in a way that differs somewhat from that of Chris Weedon and others working more directly on issues of identity. As we observed above, for Ortner subjectivity is about 'cultural and historical consciousness' (Ortner, 2005: 34), whereas Weedon's subjectivity is framed more in terms of positioning vis-à-vis discursive fields, seen as 'competing ways of giving meaning to the world and of organizing social institutions and process' (Weedon, 1997: 34).

In Archer's work, culture and history are also at the forefront. More critical of Bourdieu, she sees reflexivity as the key link between structure and agency and as a way of accounting not only for continuity and reproduction

of social structures, but also for discontinuities which may be seen as arising out of individual acts of agency. However, by far the most unique element in Archer's theory is her view that whereas social structure exists
independently of individual agency, it is not effective as a shaper of agency
until it is encountered by individuals engaging in activities. Social structure
is thus activated when reflexive beings engage in their life projects, making
it into a mediator of activity. Once activated, a structure serves to shape
activity, facilitating, enabling, hindering, constraining and so on.

Drawing together the previous discussions of identity and subject positioning and Ortner's and Archer's takes on agency, I propose a loose assemblage of four general situating parameters which will help us to understand
both how agency relates to identity and how it is embedded in social structure and everyday practices which in turn are made up of interactions. First,
there is a temporal/historic frame to all acts of agency in subject positioning. Here, there are interactions as situatable within larger life narratives,
which means that we need to consider how acts of agency emerge in terms
of experiences that preceded them and experiences which are anticipated
by them. In doing so, we recognise the embeddedness and inter-dependent
(or intertextual) nature of experiences framed as events in the past and
present. Paralleling Bakhtin (1981), we see how experiences in the present are imbued with the flavours of past experiences. In addition, we take
a marked 'big' historical approach to agency, one that takes us back to
Marx's constraints on agency. In this case, there is recognition of social
processes beyond the awareness of those living them because they are so
big and slow in unfolding (Braudel, 1993; Wallerstein, 2004; Blommaert,
2005). Well-known examples of such big and slow processes include the
rise of capitalism in Europe across centuries or transformations of American societies (north, central, south) via mass immigration. In the current
era, an example is the rise of consumerism as a dominant ideology framing
and shaping so many activities and practices today.

In addition, there is the cultural framing of agency. Here culture is
understood as 'a historically created system of meaning and significance,
or, what comes to the same thing, a system of beliefs and practices in terms
of which a group of human beings understand, regulate and structure their
individual and collective lives' (Parekh, 2000: 143). The issue here is the
extent to which culture is so grounded in the past and current social structures that it determines individuals. Gerd Baumann questions what he terms
the 'essentialist' view of culture whereby '[c]ulture . . . appears as a mold
that shapes lives or, to put it somewhat polemically, as a giant photocopy
machine that keeps turning out identical copies' (Baumann, 1999: 25). He
contrasts this view with the more dynamic and emergent 'processual' view,
whereby '[c]ulture . . . is not so much a photocopy machine as a concert, or
indeed a historically improvised jam session [which] . . . only exists in the
act of being performed, and . . . can never stand still or repeat itself without changing its meaning' (Baumann, 1999: 26). Whereas I find the latter

view somewhat attractive, I tend to heed scholars ranging from Raymond Williams (1977) to Ortner (2006), and in so doing, I tend to see stability in culture even if this stability is an effect as opposed to an essence; that is, it is an impression of stability, created by the continual invocation of certain cultural features—both material and abstract—in the midst of engagement in practices by individuals. These individuals seem to be acting within the confines of something understood as culture but ultimately they are acting on its behalf as they make and remake it via their day-to-day practices.

A third parameter of agency is the way in which all acts of agency involve the assembling of semiotic resources in acts of communication. Following Blommaert (2005), language may be framed as the semiotic resource *par excellence* in interaction. However, we cannot fully analyse and understand interaction without taking into account how language is inflected by accent or style. We also need to take into account other semiotic resources, such as gaze, stance, body movement, dress and even racial phenotype, as all of these dimensions combine with language and each other to make up communicative events. Thus, students who have just joined a class or office workers who have just been hired by a company all find that their acceptance in their new environments—or in Wenger's (1998) terms, their moves from peripheral to more central participation in communities of practice— is dependent on their ability not only to 'talk the talk' but also 'walk the walk'. In other words, they must align all forms of semiotic resources in keeping with their social context in order to make their way as effective players in Bourdieusian fields. Such fields are understood as spaces of social activity with evolving legitimate ways of thinking and acting, in which individuals occupy positions of inferiority, equality and superiority which are dependent on their economic, cultural and social capital in relation to other participants in the social activity (Bourdieu, 1977).

Finally, it is worth mentioning here the importance of physical space and physical positioning which has been brought to the fore by multimodal/ semiotic scholars such as Ron Scollon (e.g. Scollon and Scollon, 2003; Baynham, Chapter 7, this volume). On the one hand, it is worthwhile to place individuals and their practices in macro spaces such as nation-states, cities, neighbourhoods and institutions (e.g. schools). However, it is equally important to consider micro spaces shaping practices, such as rooms and the proxemics of face-to-face interactions.

AN APPLICATION: BASHIR-ALI (2006)

To see how the situatedness of agency plays itself out in day-to-day practices, I examine a recent publication in *TESOL Quarterly* by Khadar Bashir-Ali (2006). In a nine-month study based on interviews and fieldwork, Bashir Ali monitored how Maria, a fifteen-year-old Mexican girl, living in a low-income, predominantly African-American part of a midwestern American city, actively shaped her ongoing identity narrative against a backdrop of spatial, multimodal, temporal/historical and cultural factors. At the time of Bashir-Ali's study, Maria had been living in the US for two and half years. Yet, in this short period of time, she had managed to inhabit an identity based on African-American culture and multimodality and more importantly, seemed to have been accepted by most of her African-American peers. In a school context in which Standard American English was the privileged institutional variety, Maria ignored the norms, practices and discourse of the official school culture and instead opted to affiliate to African-American Vernacular English as resource through which she could construct an African-American identity around the norms, practices and discourses of hip-hop culture. Claiming to be 'Black from ma mama side and Poto Rican from my daddy side' (Bashir-Ali, 2006: 628), she rejected her Spanish speaking Mexican identity, confining her personal history and culture to her home family life and even showing animosity towards them when she was in the school context.

Bashir-Ali conveys Maria's agency in the kinds of activities and events she describes and the language she uses to do so. Thus, Maria is said to 'refuse' to identify with her Mexican past and to 'choose' AAVE as 'she did not see any value in learning SAE' (Bashir-Ali, 2006: 634). In following paragraph, in which Bashir-Ali more or less sums up Maria's situation, we see the image created of a conscious, independent agent making her way in life:

> Maria had a strong desire to be identified as an African-American. She tried everything in her power to adopt and adhere to the linguistic and cultural mannerism of African-American students so that she could, first, pass as one of them, and second, be recognized and enjoy all privileges that come with being with the cool groups at school. Her main objective was to fit in and belong, not to be different. . . . Her academic performance in school was not at all relevant her. (Bashir-Ali, 2006: 635)

And yet, to pretend that Maria was a totally free, rational agent deciding what she wanted to do on her own would be an error (one, I might add, that Bashir-Ali by no means commits). For surrounding Maria was a constellation of historical and cultural phenomena that helped to shape her agency. First, Maria's capacity to act as a free agent both inside and outside school was shaped simultaneously by her personal history as an immigrant, the history of immigration in the US and the history of the neighbourhood where she settled. Being 'different' due to one's past, is surely among the first pieces of baggage that many immigrants work towards losing, and in Maria's case this meant the entire multimodal package made up of Spanish language and Mexican-inflected dress, body movement and so on. Her apparent success in adopting a hip-hop

African-American subjectivity attests to Maria's victory over her personal history and her insertion into the history of her neighbourhood as physical backdrop, imbued in African-American culture. But this success was obviously shaped by these historical factors.

The same applies to the culture of the school versus the African-American culture that she inhabited. In the end, the need to be cool triumphed over the need to achieve in school as she acquiesced to the former while resisting the latter. It would be interesting to imagine a different scenario in which African-American culture was not as prevalent and therefore did not offer an assemblage of resources with which to resist the hegemony of school culture. In this case, would Maria have affiliated more strongly to SAE and inhabited a different multimodal package, i.e. by dressing differently, moving differently and so on? Or, perhaps Maria would have drawn on her Mexican resources more and inhabited the alternative subjectivity of the 'official bilingual'.

In addition, it is interesting to frame Maria's story in terms of how it is physically situated. In her contacts with researchers, she tended to invoke the larger space of her neighbourhood, which was predominately African-American, as the important space in her life. By contrast, she seemed to avoid talk about her home, in which rival Spanish-mediated Mexican practices presumably took place. In addition, Bashir-Ali notes how Maria would often remain in the hallways of the school, waiting for her friends to go to class so that she would not be seen going to ESL classes. The latter space marked her as immigrant, as Mexican and uncool. In contrast, the hallway was a safe house, a space in which she could construct her African-American subjectivities in activities with her peers.

In Bashir-Ali's account of Maria's experiences, Marxian 'spirits of the past' and the 'names, slogans and costumes' and finally the 'borrowed language' do not pertain to her Mexican life experience. Rather, they seem to have a home in her physical, social and psychic surroundings in the present. As she immerses herself in that part of her environment described as 'hip-hop' and 'African-American', Maria is afforded the ambits within which she can exercise her agency and engage in identity work. In this sense, the study makes the point that one can never consider agency in isolation from social structure. However, it is rather *presentist* in that it lacks close attention to how Maria's past in Mexico, embodied in the present in the family structure, plays a role in her apparent acts of agency. In effect, it acts as a 'residual' structuring element in her life 'effectively formed in the past, but . . . still active . . . as an effective element of the present' (Williams, 1977: 122). The presentism of the study cannot be remedied without more information about Maria's past and more information about her home life and so I cannot comment further as regards these angles on Maria's experiences.

CONCLUSION

The final part of this chapter has been devoted to a modest attempt to frame Bashir-Ali's account of Maria's experiences as historically, culturally, multimodally and physically mediated and situated. In doing so, the aim has not been to position her as a free active agent who chooses to be African-American and wilfully imposes this identity on her day-to-day practices, doing so against great odds. Rather, she may be seen as someone who brings to bear on her day-to-day experiences a constellation of realities via her life project of becoming an American and gaining acceptance in her preferred peer groups, in short as someone whose agency only makes sense in terms of what it is structured by. I could obviously say more about Maria if I had access to more data relevant to her case. However, my intention here has been less about building up Bashir-Ali's study so that it is something that I can thoroughly engage with and more about presenting it as a convenient example to which I can apply my emergent thinking about agency shaped by history, culture, multimodal resources (including language) and space.

These parameters, derived as they are from my readings of scholars ranging from Bourdieu to Ortner and Archer, are by no means exhaustive. They are, however, an attempt to reverse a tendency to prime agency over structure that I see in so much (most?) work on identity in applied linguistics. This tendency is curious when one considers how the general poststructuralist approach that I cite above is so imminently social in nature. However, the tendency to marginalise structure in favour of agency exists not least because so much identity research focuses on individual case studies and the struggles and conflicts engaged in by individuals as they become American, become French, gain a voice as an English speaker or obtain cultural and social capital. The case study is no doubt an effective methodology; however, within it, there needs to be an approach to identity, subjectivities and agency which does not move structure to a secondary plane.

NOTES

1. This chapter is an expanded version of a section of Block (2009).

REFERENCES

Ahearn, L. 2001. Language and agency. *Annual Review of Anthropology* 30: 109–37.
Appadurai, A. 1990. Disjuncture and difference in the global cultural economy. In *Global Culture: Nationalism, Globalization and Modernity*, ed. M. Featherstone, 295–310. London: Sage.
Archer, M. 2000. *Being Human: The Problem of Agency*. Cambridge: Cambridge University Press.
———. 2007. *Making Our Way through the World*. Cambridge: Cambridge University Press.

Bakhtin, M. 1981. *The Dialogic Imagination: Four Essays*. Austin: University of Texas Press.

Bashir-Ali, K. 2006. Language learning and the definition of one's social, cultural, and racial identity. *TESOL Quarterly* 40(3): 628–39.

Bauman, Z. 2005. *Liquid Lives*. Cambridge: Polity.

Baumann, G. 1999. *The Multicultural Riddle: Rethinking National, Ethnic and Religious Identities*. London: Routledge.

Beck, U. and Beck-Gernsheim, E. 2002. *Individualization*. London: Sage.

Benwell, B. and Stokoe, L. 2006. *Discourse and Identity*. Edinburgh: Edinburgh University Press.

Berger, P. and Luckmann, T. 1966. *The Social Construction of Reality*. Harmondsworth: Penguin.

Block, D. 2007. *Second Language Identities*. London: Continuum.

———. 2009. Identity in applied linguistics: the need for conceptual exploration. In *Contemporary Applied Linguistics* (Vol. 1), ed. Li Wei and V. Cook, 215–32. London: Continuum.

Blommaert, J. 2005. *Discourse*. Cambridge: Cambridge University Press.

Bourdieu, P. 1977. *Outline of a Theory of Practice*. Cambridge: Cambridge University Press.

Braudel, F. 1993. *A History of Civilizations* (New edition). London: Penguin.

Bucholtz, M. and Hall, K. 2005. Identity and interaction: a sociocultural linguistic approach. *Discourse Studies* 7(4–5): 585–614.

Comaroff, J. (John) and J. (Jean) Comaroff. 1997. *Of Revelation and Revolution: The Dialectics of Modernity on a South African Frontier* (Vol. 2). Chicago: University of Chicago Press.

de Certeau, M. 1984. *The Practice of Everyday Life*. Berkeley: University of California Press.

Duranti, A. 2004. Agency in language. In *A Companion to Linguistic Anthropology*, ed. A. Duranti, 451–73. Oxford: Blackwell.

Giddens, A. 1979. *Central Problems in Social Theory: Action, Structure and Contradiction in Social Analysis*. Berkeley: University of California Press.

———. 1991. *Modernity and Self-Identity: Self and Society in the Late Modern Age*. Cambridge: Polity.

———. 2000. *Runaway Word: How Globalization Is Reshaping Our Lives*. London: Routledge.

Hall, D. 2004. *Subjectivity*. London: Routledge.

Harvey, D. 1989. *The Condition of Postmodernity*. Oxford: Blackwell.

Latour, B. 1987. *Science in Action: How to Follow Scientists & Engineers through Society*. Cambridge, MA: Harvard University Press.

Marx, K. 1972[1852]. The eighteenth Brumaire of Louis Bonaparte. In *The Marx-Engels Reader*, ed. R. C. Tucker, 432–525. New York. Norton.

Ortner, S. 1989. *High Religion: A Cultural and Political History of Sherpa Buddhism*. Princeton, NJ: Princeton University Press.

———. 2005. Subjectivity and cultural critique. *Anthropological Theory* 5(1): 31–52.

———. 2006. *Anthropology and Social Theory: Culture, Power, and the Acting Subject*. Durham, NC: Duke University Press.

Parekh, B. 2000. *Rethinking Multiculturalism: Cultural Diversity and Political Theory*. London: Palgrave.

Riley, P. 2007. *Language, Society and Identity*. London: Continuum.

Scollon, R. and Scollon, S. W. 2003. *Discourses in Place: Language in the Material World*. London: Routledge.

Shilling, C. 2004. Physical capital and studied action: a new direction for corporeal sociology. *British Journal Sociology of Education* 25(4): 473–87.

Taylor, C. 1989. *Sources of Self: The Making of the Modern Identity*. Cambridge, MA: Harvard University Press.

Vertovec, S. 2007. Super-diversity and its implications. *Ethnic and Racial Studies* 30(6): 1024–54.

Wallerstein, I. 2004. *World-Systems Analysis: An Introduction*. Durham, NC: Duke University Press.

Weedon, C. 1997. *Feminist Practice and Poststructuralist Theory* (2nd edition). Oxford: Blackwell.

Wenger, E. 1998. *Communities of Practice*. Cambridge: Cambridge University Press.

Williams, R. 1977. *Marxism and Literature* (New edition). Oxford: Oxford University Press.

Part II

Researching Identities and Identities in Research Practice

Introduction

Marilyn Martin-Jones

As in the previous part of this volume, the chapters in this part show how the close study of local practices in multilingual settings opens a window on wider social and ideological processes. The focus here is on the role of language ideologies and communicative practices in the construction of identities and in the building of different kinds of social relationships. All three chapters are underpinned by a poststucturalist view of identity: identities are seen as multiple, fluid and always 'under construction' (rather than unitary, stable and fixed over time). In keeping with a broad, social constructionist approach, identification is seen as a discursive process: that is, identities are conceived of as emerging in and through social action and interaction in different settings. At the same time, the specific processes of identification captured in each of the chapters are represented as embedded in wider relations of asymmetrical power and in transnational contexts where different discourses about identity circulate.

Each chapter focuses on the construction of identity in a different kind of multilingual space and each reveals the complex and situated nature of the ways in which people draw on the linguistic and semiotic resources available to them in negotiating identities in these spaces and in navigating dominant discourses. What the authors have in common is that they are all doing research with linguistic minority groups that are part of wider diaspora in which, as Blackledge and Creese put it, languages "carry the weight of 'culture' and distant territories".

The chapter by Eleni Mariou is based on research conducted, in northern Greece, with teenagers of Pontian Greek origin. Mariou focuses primarily on two teenagers from this wider study. These are two girls who relocated with their parents from Georgia to Greece in the 1990s, after the demise of the Soviet Union. By the time Mariou's study was carried out, they had received most of their schooling in Greece and spoke standard Greek, as well as Russian and Pontian Greek (a language variety that was originally spoken in the Pontos area of the Black Sea coast, to the northeast of present day Turkey).

Mariou gives an illuminating account of the discourses of language and identity encountered by these teenagers in the different social spaces of their lives: in institutional worlds, such as the school, and in their local lifeworlds, at home and in their immediate peer group. At home, especially among older members of the family, there was a distinct orientation to discourses about Pontian Greek heritage and about cultural traditions. The Pontian variety of Greek was seen as emblematic of a Pontian identity. These discourses evoked a place of origin—a distinctive homeland—that only existed prior to the displacement of Pontian Greeks from the Black Sea area and is now part of collective memory.

At school, there was a contrasting orientation to discourses about standard Greek, about the Greek nation and Greek history and to local ideologies of Greekness. The girls also encountered explicitly discriminatory discourses about 'Russo-Pontians'—particularly among their peers at school. These discriminatory discourses echoed wider nationalistic discourses and prejudice about 'immigrants' in Greece. Drawing on consecutive interviews with these two girls, Mariou gives us revealing insights into the ways in which they negotiated these discourses in their daily lives at home and at school, consciously avoiding use of Pontian Greek at school (for fear of being overheard), and then drawing on different language resources and blending features of standard Greek, Russian and Pontian Greek in their conversations with different interlocutors at home and with their friends. The two girls had clear views about what counts as 'being Pontian' or 'being Greek' but differed somewhat in the degree of allegiance they expressed towards their Pontian heritage.

The chapter by Adrian Blackledge and Angela Creese draws on linguistic ethnographic research carried out in complementary schools in different urban settings in the UK. The chapter provides vivid accounts of interactional processes involved in the negotiation of identities in complementary school classes, focussing in particular on Bengali schools in Birmingham and Turkish schools in London. The complementary school teachers and organisers in the study were committed to 'passing on' the heritage of their home country to the next generation. This included the national language, folk talks, cultural artefacts and specific cultural practices. Their practices and their vision for the schools were guided by "a nationalism which clung to territorial and linguistic roots", or what May and Fenton (2003) have called an "out-of-place nationalism". However, as Blackledge and Creese point out, this nationalist ideology was a potent discourse of identity and was partly shaped by the wider nationalistic discourses about English and citizenship being articulated in different areas of public life in England.

Nevertheless, as the chapter clearly shows, when linguistic and cultural resources travel across times and spaces, they take on different meanings for new generations. They are appropriated and re-evaluated. They are sometimes appropriated and recast and sometimes abandoned. Thus, community organizations like complementary schools become terrains for these processes of re-evaluation and appropriation and for the negotiation or contestation of the discourses of identity produced and reproduced by older generations within the diaspora.

Blackledge and Creese give us detailed insights into the ways in which young people who attend Bengali and Turkish classes challenge the discourses of identity that they encounter in class and how they playfully adopt differing subject positions, drawing on the wide range of communicative resources in their repertoires, sometimes going along with the activities planned by their teachers and sometimes appropriating them and turning them to their own purposes.

We also see how complementary school classes can become terrains for struggles over ideologies of language and language learning, especially where teachers represent languages as separate, bounded systems and insist on monolingual performance of language 'skills'. Classroom interaction in the classes described in this chapter involved regular 'haggling' and 'bartering' over linguistic practices, with classroom talk being intensely heteroglossic in nature.

The chapter by Frances Giampapa moves us on from research investigating the situated construction of identities, in different cultural and historical contexts, to a consideration of the relationship between researcher and researched and to the negotiation of researcher and participant identities in research in multilingual settings. Again, Giampapa is writing about a linguistic minority group with wide diasporic links: Italian Canadians in the city of Toronto. She shows that, in the course of a doctoral research project in this setting, she engaged in different self-positionings and was herself positioned in different ways by different participants in her study. These positionings related to her own history and to her past and present identities, "as a Canadian-born, Australian-raised, straight female of Italian heritage, from a working class background (with a middle class education) and with an immigrant past narrated through [her] family history".

Giampapa's narratives from the field throw into sharp focus the complex and ever-changing nature of the researcher-researched relationship and of the challenges involved in attempting to build a democratic and dialogic relationship of the kind that is called for in recent writing on critical ethnography. She also offers some thought-provoking reflections on the question of what 'being an insider' means. She says: "On the one hand, my own linguistic and cultural experience afforded me an insider identity, which at times allowed me to connect with the participants' lived experiences. On the other hand, my authenticity and legitimacy as Italian Canadian and as an insider was also questioned in various ways" (p. 102). Because of her Australian accent, she did not always 'pass' as Canadian and there were often questions about her origins.

Giampapa recollects that she often found that her 'insiderness' was being evaluated by her participants with reference to wider discourses about *italianità* that circulated in this local community, discourses that were produced and reproduced by those who exerted greatest symbolic power within local community organisations, within local government circles in Canada or among representatives of the Italian government and Italian cultural bodies. These shifting evaluations of her as a cultural and linguistic "insider" or "outsider", as not Italian enough, or as not having the right gender or sexuality, led to her being either included or excluded from certain fieldwork sites and from close engagement with particular groups. This, in turn, made it difficult for her to fully represent the voices of all those that she encountered during the course of her fieldwork in Toronto. Giampapa's chapter reminds us all of the need for reflexivity throughout the research process and for a keen awareness of the ways in which our identities and histories as researchers shape our experiences in the field and, ultimately, our research narratives. This discursive thread, relating to the need for reflexivity, is woven in and out of the remaining chapters of this volume and it is picked up and elaborated in intricate ways by other authors.

REFERENCES

May, S. and Fenton, S. 2003. Ethnicity, nation and 'race': connections and disjunctures. In *Ethnonational Identities*, ed. S. Fenton and S. May, 1–20. Basingstoke: Palgrave.

4   Pontian Greek Adolescents
The Negotiation of Identities in an Urban Context in Northern Greece

Eleni Mariou

The research presented in this chapter focuses on a group of teenagers, who relocated to Greece with their families from the former Soviet Union, principally from Georgia and Russia. They are part of a wider community of Pontian Greeks, who have their origins on the southern coastal region of the Black Sea. They speak a language variety which is called Pontian/Pontic Greek (Mackridge, 1991; Agtzidis, 1997; Anthemides, 2002).

The participants in my study were all girls. When I carried out the research (2003–4), they were between fourteen and seventeen years old. They and their parents had been born in Georgia, when it was still part of the Soviet Union. Like many other Pontian Greeks, the girls in my study arrived in Greece, with their families, in the early 1990s, after the demise of the Soviet Union. They now reside in the north of Greece, in eastern Macedonia. They speak Pontian Greek and they also speak, read and write Standard Greek, having acquired it after their arrival in Greece. And, in addition, three of them speak some Russian.

HISTORICAL BACKGROUND

The Pontian Greeks take their name from the word Pontos, i.e. sea, their place of origin. The Pontos area is situated to the northeast of present day Turkey, on the Black Sea coast. It extends 100 km, from Sinope in the west to Georgia in the east (Bruneau, 2000).

The presence of the Pontian Greeks in this area dates back to the establishment of Greek cities along this stretch of the Black Sea coast, from the eighth to the sixth century BC (ibid.). The region was briefly organised as a kingdom (Trezibond) from the second century BC. Successive wars with the Romans ensued and eventual Roman occupation. During the Byzantine Empire (sixth to fifteenth century AD), the Greek colony on this coast enjoyed a long period of consolidation and prosperity. However, the fall of the Byzantine Empire marked a significant change in the fortunes of the

Pontian Greeks (Fotiades, 2000). With the establishment of the Ottoman Empire and with the fall of Trebizond in 1461, Pontian Greeks started to flee to parts of the Caucasus, to Georgia and Russia, and, as a result, the diaspora of the Pontian Greeks came into being (Fotiades, 2000).

The most recent migration of the Pontian Greeks to Greece started after the collapse of the former Soviet Union. From 1989 until 1995, there was a major exodus of Pontian Greeks from Georgia and Russia. This population movement continued on a diminished scale until the end of the 1990s (Notaras, 2000).

AIMS AND SCOPE OF THE STUDY

The aim of the study reported here was to investigate the discourses about language and ethnic identity encountered by young Pontian Greeks in their contemporary lives in Greece. I focussed primarily on the contexts of family, peer group and school, and documented the young people's accounts of the different discourses about language and identity that they came across in these different contexts. I also documented the four girls' accounts of their use of language at home, in their local lifeworlds, with a view to determining how they drew on the different languages in their communicative repertoire in giving expression to a Pontian Greek identity. In addition, I documented their accounts of their use of language with their friends. These included some speakers of Pontian Greek and some young people who only spoke Standard Greek. Lastly, I conducted research in the institutional context of the school and I investigated the discourses about language and ethnic identity in the official discourse of the Greek educational authorities.

MINORITY GROUPS, MULTILINGUALISM AND THE DISCURSIVE CONSTRUCTION OF IDENTITIES

The study builds on poststructuralist and critical approaches to the sociolinguistics of multilingualism among linguistic minorities. Within this tradition of research (e.g. Gal, 1989; Heller, 1995, 1999, 2007; Woolard, 1985, 1998), the emphasis has been on the investigation of the ways in which language practices and values are embedded in and shaped by wider historical and cultural contexts, political economies and asymmetrical relations of power. The theoretical foundations for the adoption of critical, poststructuralist approaches lie in the work of the French social theorist Pierre Bourdieu (e.g. 1991). Bourdieu characterised language as a form of symbolic capital which could be converted into economic and social capital. He also argued that the value of a particular language variety within a linguistic market stems from its use and legitimation by dominant social groups, via institutional processes such as schooling. The outcomes of such processes of legitimation are that less powerful groups in society come to accept the dominant form of linguistic capital as inherently superior to their own linguistic resources. These arguments form the basis of his much cited theory of symbolic domination.

In developing a critical, poststructuralist approach to multilingualism, Gal (1989) and Woolard (1985) built on the basic premises put forward by Bourdieu but drew attention to one major shortcoming in his model of symbolic domination, namely the emphasis on the workings of symbolic power and the lack of a means of accounting for practices of resistance or to the emergence of alternative linguistic markets.

Turning to the long tradition of linguistic anthropology, Woolard (1998) began to explore the study of language ideology as "a promising bridge between linguistic and social theory" (1998: 27). She argued that:

> It allows us to relate the micro-culture of communicative action to political economic considerations of power and social inequality, to confront macro-social constraints on language behaviour, and to connect discourse with lived experience. (ibid.)

Heller (2007) shares this commitment to the study of language ideologies and describes the aims of research in this area as follows:

> This area of enquiry investigates the discourses in which processes of attribution of value to linguistic forms and practices are inscribed, along with the processes of construction of social difference and social inequality with which they are associated. (2007: 15)

Pavlenko and Blackledge (2004) focus specifically on the discursive construction of identities in multilingual settings and point to five characteristics of identities in such settings. I touch here on the first three of their characteristics, because they are particularly relevant to my study: firstly, the location of identities within particular discourses and ideologies of language. Pavlenko and Blackledge argue that "ideologies of language and identity guide ways in which individuals use linguistic resources to index their identities and to evaluate the use of linguistic resources by others" (2004: 14). The second is the embeddedness of identities within relations of power: Bourdieu's notion of symbolic domination is relevant here and his insistence on the process whereby subordinated groups in society come to perceive the language of dominant groups as superior to theirs. Third is the multiple and hybrid nature of identities: in multilingual settings, individuals take on different identities, shifting between them as they move across contexts. Their language practices are likely to be more mixed and hybrid in local lifeworld settings, where they are least likely to monitor their language use and when they are least aware of their use of language being evaluated.

In conceptualising the ways in which identities are discursively negoti-ated, whether it be in face-to-face interaction, in personal narratives of experience or in institutional discourses, Pavlenko and Blackledge (2004) drew on positioning theory (Davies and Harré, 1990; Harré and Van Lan-genhove, 1999). They note that Davies and Harré (1990) originally devel-oped the notion of positioning with reference to conversational interaction, but they argue for the extension of the scope of the concept "to all discur-sive practices which may position individuals in particular ways" (2004: 20). They go on to describe three different types of identities:

> *[i]mposed identities* (which are not negotiable in a particular time and place); *assumed identities* (which are accepted and not negotiated), and *negotiable identities* (which are contested by groups and individuals). (2004: 21)

In this study, I found these categories particularly useful in exploring the specific range of discourses of identity that traversed the lives of young Pontian Greeks living in northern Greece. The research was transcontex-tual in nature—taking account of different contexts such as their homes, their peer group and their schools—so as to try and capture the different discourses encountered by the young people, the ways in which they were positioned by these discourses and the ways in which they responded to these positionings.

RESEARCH APPROACH ADOPTED IN THIS STUDY

I adopted a linguistic ethnographic approach (Blommaert, 2007; Ramp-ton, 2007; Creese, 2008) combining close analysis of interview data with historical research, analysis of educational policy documents and school-based observation. I began with historical research related to the Pontian Greek diaspora. I then carried out consecutive semi-structured interviews with the four participants in the study for the duration of one year from 2003 to 2004. Eight interviews were conducted with three participants and seven with the fourth participant. Each interview was a continuation of the previous one. Certain issues came up again and again and were considered in depth with each participant. In preparing for each interview, I listened to the recording of the previous interview and took notes. During each interview, I asked for clarification of points that had come up in previous interviews and revisited with each participant the themes that were most salient in their accounts. The interviews constituted the main body of data. All of the interviews were transcribed in preparation for the data analysis.

So as to build an understanding of the educational ethos of the schools they attended and of official Greek government discourse about educational policy with regard to minority groups, I gathered a number of policy docu-ments. This involved library and web-based research.

In analysing the interview data and the policy documents gathered during the study, I focused on stretches of discourse that made explicit reference to identity, to 'Greekness', to specific cultural and linguistic practices and to the notion of ethnicity.

TWO OF THE RESEARCH PARTICIPANTS: XENA AND NORA

In this section, I focus on two of the four participants in my study and I present the main insights gleaned from the consecutive interviews with them. First, I describe their linguistic repertoires and their accounts of the ways in which they drew on the resources in their repertoires while conversing with family members. I then go on to consider their accounts of what it meant to 'be Pontian Greek'. And, after this, I focus on dominant discourses that positioned them in different ways.

Linguistic Repertoires and Language Practices at Home

Xena

Xena was born in Georgia and migrated to Greece with her family when she was six years old. Her mother tongue, until she was six, and the language spoken at home was mainly Pontian Greek. Her command of Standard Greek is now fluent and she also speaks Russian. Both her parents are of Pontian Greek origin. I began my interviews with Xena when she was still at school, at the age of sixteen.

At home, Xena drew on all three of the language varieties in her spoken repertoire. Pontian Greek was dominant at home, but the use of Standard Greek and Russian was also common. Xena mainly used Pontian Greek with her parents and grandmother. She also used Russian with her mother. With her brother and sister-in-law she used Standard Greek or Russian, as well as Pontian Greek. In sum, she switched from Pontian Greek to Russian and Standard Greek depending on the context, the identity of her interlocutors and the topic of the conversation, as we see in interview Extract 4.1.

> Extract 4.1
> *Eleni: Which language do you think is more dominant at home?*
> *Xena: Pontian Greek. But at home it's complicated. I mean if you were my relative, maybe I would start to speak to you in Pontian, then Greek and a little bit of Russian in between, so that's why I am saying to you it's a bit of a mess. (Int. 4 l. 75–78)*

Reflecting a wider ideology about speaking one language at a time being a social norm, Xena made a rather negative evaluation of the multilingual practices of her home life.

Nora

Like Xena, Nora was born in Georgia and also moved to Greece, with her family, when she was six years old. She lived with her parents and her brother. Her parents were both Pontian Greek. She spoke Pontian Greek and Russian. She was also fluent in Standard Greek. At the time when the interviews were conducted, Nora was seventeen years old.

Nora was brought up speaking Pontian Greek at home and, for her, Pontian Greek had close associations with the family environment (see Extract 4.2).

> Extract 4.2
> *Nora: I think my family was important because of the language to start with . . . the Pontian Greek we spoke at home and that I grew up with it, we were surrounded by it, the dances that I really wanted to learn, our traditions, and our relatives . . . they said that we should try and speak Pontian Greek and we should continue and shouldn't forget it. (Int. 7 l. 47–51)*

In this response, Nora made an explicit link between language and Pontian cultural traditions and, specifically, the distinctive Pontian folk dance tradition. She clearly assumed and affirmed a Pontian identity with reference to her home environment. In the same interview, she also indicated that no Russian was spoken at home.

Language, Culture and Pontian Identity

Xena

Xena talked about her Pontian Greek identity as being closely bound up with family values and beliefs. As we see in interview Extracts 4.3 and 4.4, she made frequent reference to the values passed on to her by her parents.

> Extract 4.3
> *Xena: My family played a significant role in the way I grew up, the way I live at home, my values, etc. (Int 5 l. 159–60)*

> Extract 4.4
> *Xena: My parents had this mentality, they grew up there* [in Georgia] *but they had Pontian values and beliefs, so, that influenced me and it also influenced my Pontian identity. (Int 8 l. 79–81)*

What we see here is a broad acceptance, by Xena, of a Pontian identity. This identity is a mantle that has been passed down over the generations in the diaspora. In Pavlenko and Blackledge's (2004) terms, this is an assumed identity. In Extract 4.5 below, she returned to the same theme and made an explicit link between the affirmation of a Pontian identity and the use of both Pontian Greek *and* Russian at home, with family members.

Extract 4.5
Xena: I mean, regarding the Russian and Pontian Greek language, and my Pontian origins, these are mainly due to my family, my morals and values. (Int 5 l. 165–66)

Having been at school in Greece since she was six years old, Xena had also adapted to the use of Standard Greek, to Greek perspectives on history and culture and to ways of 'being Greek', but she still saw her main cultural orientation and her ethos as being Pontian, as she noted in Extract 4.6. She also implied that she was comfortable enacting both identities.

Extract 4.6
Xena: Well the way of thinking is Greek because I grew up here but my habits and rules and ethics are Pontian. (Int. 4 l. 192–93)

In contrast, her parents clearly engaged in strict boundary marking between 'being Greek' and 'being Pontian'. In Extract 4.7 below, we have a glimpse into her parents' discourse about Pontian identity—an identity that is embedded in a history separate from that of mainland Greece and an exclusive one; for them, one cannot be Greek *and* Pontian.

Extract 4.7
Xena: Sometimes they [parents] *are not happy about the way I think and are afraid I might change. For example my mum sometimes says 'You have adopted too many Greek habits, you hang around with too many Greeks' (she laughs). (Int. 7 l. 28–31)*

We see the same exclusive definition of Pontian identity in the words of Xena's father.

Extract 4.8
Xena : Yes . . . erm . . . something happened once . . . I think they [her classmates] *mentioned about 'Russopontians'. And I said 'I feel more Greek than they do' . . . and my dad said 'You are not Greek, you are Pontian, they are two different things'. (Int 3 l. 165–67)*

Yet, when I pursued the question of ethnic identity with Xena, she expressed her sense of self in markedly different terms, stressing the inclusion and blending of different identities, as we see in Extract 4.9.

Extract 4.9
Eleni: So, if someone would ask you, what are you, in terms of your ethnic identity, what would you say?
Xena: I feel it's a mixture of everything.
Eleni: If they asked you what are you, what would you say?

> *Xena: As I said before ... I'd say altogether everything* (laughing)*, a mixture, how did we say it? Greek-Pontian-Russian? (Int 5 l. 123–29)*

A brief note is needed here about the use of 'Russian' by Xena and the other participants in this study. They used the term to refer to the Russian language (the official language of the former Soviet Union) and to Russian and Georgian culture, including food, music and so on. These cultural and linguistic elements were closely intertwined with Xena's family life and with Pontian Greek culture and language use.

Nora

A slightly different picture emerged in the case of Nora. When I asked her about the link between language, culture and identity, she indicated that 'being Pontian' was associated with sole use of Pontian Greek and with observing Pontian cultural traditions. As we see in Extract 4.10 below, she explicitly rejected the use of Russian, Georgian or Turkish as an expression of Pontian identity.

> Extract 4.10
> *Nora: I would just say I am Pontian and that we have traditions and that ... but without the language it would be weird ... erm ... when they ask where I am from and I say I am Pontian, it means I don't speak Georgian or Russian or Turkish, it's Pontian Greek at home, so, the language signifies this and I want to show I am Pontian ... so, yeah, it is important and it is one more reason why I feel Pontian. (Int. 7 l. 71–79)*

When asked about the relationship between Pontian Greek and Standard Greek, Nora implied that Pontian Greek was a language of belonging, her "mother tongue", bound up with her relationship with her family.

> Extract 4.11
> *Eleni: Is the Pontian Greek language, a separate language for you?*
> *Nora: Yes it is.*
> *Eleni: In terms of what?*
> *Nora: Well . . . since I was young I grew up with it and it is my mother tongue, that's why I say it's separate for me. It's not about the grammar or its relation to Greek, it's my mother tongue . . . the language I grew up with. (Int. 6 l. 146–52)*

Doing 'Being Greek'

I also wanted to probe Xena's and Nora's views on growing up in Greece and becoming part of contemporary Greek life. When I asked Xena if she ever felt 'Greek', she responded as follows:

Extract 4.12
Xena: Well, as for being Greek the biggest influence is the environment I live in. I grew up here, that's why . . . The Greek part of it, I mean the reason why I feel Greek is also because of the school. It's the most important reason. (Int. 5 l. 158–61)

School had clearly played a key role in her socialisation into a Greek way of life and into Greek culture and history. In Extract 4.13, we also see that she was expressing an allegiance to Greece as a nation (in opposition to 'Russia'):

Extract 4.13
Xena: I guess I now have the Greek mentality. When my parents talk to me about the former U.S.S.R. . . . . I always support or mostly support the Greek side . . . not Russia. My parents you see, they can't feel they are Greek, like me, because I lived it at school, I saw it and that is what I learnt. They don't know Greek history, so they can't understand it. (Int. 3 l. 154–59)

As with Xena, I asked Nora whether she saw herself as being 'Greek'. She indicated that she did but 'in a different way'. As we see in Extracts 4.14 and 4.15 below, she clearly leaned towards a Pontian identity despite the discourses she encountered about 'people who do not belong in Greece'.

Extract 4.14
Nora: Erm . . . well . . . I feel I am Greek but . . . in a different way. I have always heard my family and relatives say that we are the pure Greeks and that Greece is our country . . . and that the Greeks have no right to say to us that we don't belong here and that we are not Greek, because the fact that we were not born in Greece doesn't mean we are not Greek by origin. (Int 7 l. 30–34)

Extract 4.15
Nora: Well, I . . . erm . . . they are more or less the same . . . my country is Greece, there is no way that Georgia is my country . . . I feel more Pontian. (Int 7 l. 88–89)

In these extracts, we also see Nora drawing on a discourse about Pontian identity that she had encountered in her family: this is a discourse oriented to a common past and to a 'pure', idealised identity historically linked to Greece, with the sojourn in Georgia being seen as no longer relevant.

Coping with Discriminatory Discourse

Both Xena and Nora spoke of negative experiences outside the home and of their encounter with a popular, disparaging discourse about 'immigrants' and about linguistic and cultural difference. This discourse circulated within their peer group and often involved the use of labels like 'Russo-pontians' (as we saw in the interview with Xena, in Extract 4.8 above). Xena and Nora spoke of some of the strategies they used for coping when confronted with this discriminatory discourse. Xena said that she tried to avoid speaking Russian or Pontian Greek when outside the home. She also said that she mainly socialised with Pontian peers and that when they were in the company of monolingual speakers of Standard Greek, they tried to avoid being overheard speaking Pontian Greek or Russian. This strategy is described by Xena in Extracts 4.16 and 4.17 below:

> Extract 4.16
> *Xena: Erm . . . yes, sometimes . . . for example, if I am among Greeks I will be careful if I say something in Pontian or Russian and I will try and say it but not very loud because I noticed that when it happens, other Greeks look at you and it's not very nice. (Int 4 l. 94–96)*

> Extract 4.17
> *Xena: Well, my cousin is Russopontian because his mother is Russian. But I think it has now come to be a racist term. There is no basis to use this term apart from the language, which most of us speak and which is Russian, nevertheless it has negative connotations. They segregate us. (Int 6 l. 127–30)*

Nora also talked about the negative labelling of Pontian Greeks by fellow Greek students at school. She said that she found the use of the name 'Russopontian' offensive. She indicated that she had not had direct experience of discrimination but she could sense the negativity associated with such labelling, through the comments made by some of her classmates, regarding people from other countries. In Extract 4.16, she recalled classroom discussions about 'immigrants'.

> Extract 4.18
> *Nora: Well yeah, many times, when they used to say in the class that the Albanians and Russopontians came here and took our jobs, I had had enough of it . . . and when our teachers said we should study and go to university and have a proper job and then the students said 'Even if we study, the Albanians and Russopontians take our jobs'. (Int. 5 l. 42–46)*

Nora also talked about the particularly negative attitudes that her brother had encountered. He had been twelve years old when they had moved to Greece and had had to leave school, because he could not cope with the discrimination he experienced. These experiences had clearly affected Nora, and she indicated that these were the reasons why her friends were mostly Pontian. She said that it was not easy knowing she was Greek with a Pontian dimension to her identity. She hid her Pontian Greek identity at school and assumed a Greek identity, in her effort to be accepted and part of the majority.

She still felt ambivalent about the dominant culture and affirmed her Pontian roots and the dual nature of her identity. This ambivalence comes over clearly in Extract 4.19.

> Extract 4.19
> *Nora: Well I would say I am Greek in a way but first Pontian . . . I think it's like I have two countries, one is Greece and one is Pontos but sometimes I hesitate to say I am Greek or I have bitter feelings, due to past experiences.*
> *Eleni: I see. So, since you have lived in Greece for so long, is it the reason why you feel Greece is your country?*
> *Nora: Yes . . . I mean I grew up here and I know the life here, it is my country but I told you, I don't feel it a hundred per cent. (Int. 4 l. 158–64)*

Thus far, drawing on the interview data from my study, I have shown how Xena and Nora made reference to three different discourses of identity: Firstly, they evoked an enduring discourse about Pontian identity transmitted across generations in the diaspora. Xena's parents actually imposed an exclusive version of this identity, indicating that it was not possible to be Pontian *and* Greek. This rather idealised and exclusive account of their family identity contrasted sharply with the multilingual patterns of communication at home, involving the use of Pontian Greek, Standard Greek and 'Russian'. Secondly, they referred to a dominant discourse related to 'Greekness' and Greek citizenship and history in school. Taking on this identity involved acquisition of Standard Greek and the development of a capacity to use this language in legitimate ways in the institutional world of the school. Thirdly, they talked about a discriminatory discourse that they encountered in their peer group at school. This discourse reflected wider discourses about immigration in Greek society. Xena and Nora dealt with this by downplaying their Pontian identity at school and foregrounding their 'Greekness'. They also tended to form friendships with young people who had a similar background.

OFFICIAL EDUCATIONAL DISCOURSES: FURTHER CATEGORIES AND LABELS

I turn now to other identities imposed on young people like Xena and Nora within the institutional worlds of education. Here, I am drawing on my analysis of the educational policy documents gathered for my study.

The official discourse of the Greek state represents the school population as being made up of Greek students, 'repatriated Greeks' and 'foreign students' (e.g. students of Albanian, Bulgarian, Georgian, Russian or Ukrainian origin). The category of 'repatriated Greeks' includes Pontian Greeks. These are classic 'imposed identities' of the type defined by Pavlenko and Blackledge (2004). Categories such as these guide educational policy and the planning of educational provision. Official documents published by the Greek Ministry of Education and Religious Affairs on 'cross-cultural education' stipulate the following:

> A school can only be described as cross-cultural when repatriated Greek and/or foreign students account for at least 45% of the total student body. (Greek Ministry of Education and Religious Affairs, Cross-Cultural Education)

Thus, in some official governmental discourse, young people of Pontian Greek origin are defined as 'different' from the dominant majority and as qualifying for special educational provision. For example, recent legislation on cross-cultural education, states:

> The aim of cross-cultural education is to set up and run primary and secondary classes that provide education to young people with a specific educational, social or cultural identity. (Greek Ministry of Education and Religious Affairs, 1996: Law 2413/1996, Cross-Cultural Education, FEK 124, Chapter I, Article 34)

However, despite the policy rhetoric, the curriculum in 'cross-cultural' schools is often much the same as in other state schools. The main defining characteristic of such schools is that a substantial proportion of the students speak Standard Greek as a second language. A few schools have reception classes, although this provision is on the decline. A few others have 'withdrawal classes' which provide formal instruction in Standard Greek. However, this provision is made available on a piecemeal basis and it depends on demand, on staff availability and on the commitment of head teachers.

In any case, the girls in this study did not, in fact, attend a cross-cultural school. They went to a school where Standard Greek was the only legitimate language and where no account was taken of the learning needs or their cultural background and experience.

As I developed my analysis of the educational policy documents, it became clear that there was a fundamental contradiction at the heart of official discourse about linguistic and cultural difference. In addition to being characterised as having a "specific educational, social or cultural identity", the descendants of Pontian Greeks are also defined as 'homogenes', as having common ancestry with citizens of the Greek state. Usage of the term 'homogenes' is explained as follows by Papassiopi-Passia (1999):

The term 'homogenes' is used mainly to describe an individual who does not have Greek nationality but instead has Greek ethnicity. It is a foreigner who, however, is linked to the Greek nation usually through common language and religion, with common traditions, but above all with a common Greek national consciousness. (Papassiopi-Passia, 1999, 32, translated from Greek)

No definition is offered by Papassiopi-Passia for the notion of "common Greek national consciousness".

It would be interesting to see how these contradictions in policy discourses are actually played out in different schools in Greece where there are significant numbers of Pontian Greek students. Classroom-based research of a linguistic ethnographic kind is needed to shed light on some of the following kinds of questions: Which of these contradictory discourses of identity are taken up by teachers working with students of Pontian origin? How do these official discourses shape interactions between teachers and students within the daily routines of classroom life? And with what consequences?

CONCLUDING REMARKS

In this chapter, I have described some of the ways in which two young people of Pontian origin in Greece were positioned by the discourses of identity they encountered, within local lifeworlds and within the institutional space of state schools. I have also presented their accounts of the ways in which they navigated these discourses across these different contexts. Xena and Nora were 'becoming Greek' while, at the same time, retaining an affiliation to their heritage language and culture. Xena was engaging more with the dominant language and culture whereas Nora said that she did not feel "a hundred per cent" Greek. They both affirmed a Pontian identity at home and, along with other young people of Pontian descent, they drew on different resources in their communicative repertoire in displaying this identity; although, from the accounts above, it is clear that Xena felt more comfortable than Nora moving in and out of different language varieties and expressing a hybridised Pontian identity.

In the official discourses of the Greek educational system, they were categorised and positioned in contradictory terms as 'different from' but also 'the same' as the dominant majority group. The official discourse of policy documents gave due recognition to the significant presence of 'repatriated Greeks' in the school population but this discourse only had a bearing on educational practice in 'cross-cultural' schools. In the schools attended by the girls in this study, it was assumed that all students were 'Greek' and that Standard Greek was the only legitimate language of study. Moreover, the undertow of prejudice manifested in peer group discourse about

'Russopontians' made the girls wary about revealing their Pontian identities among members of their peer group who did not share their background.

The Pontian Greeks are a special case, because they speak Greek, but their language variety is a distinct one which has been developed over the centuries in settings that are geographically and politically remote from Greece. Research with minority groups such as the Pontian Greeks, who are perceived as both 'the same' and 'different' from the dominant majority group, gives us fresh insights into the ways in which identities are imposed, assumed or negotiated in context, and into the consequences of these processes of identification for young people whose families have moved across national boundaries.

In this chapter I have also tried to demonstrate the value of transcontextual research of this kind, working ethnographically across the spaces of the lives of young people of migrant origin, and conducting consecutive, semi-structured interviews. In these ways, we can build an account of the different ways in which young people such as these are positioned by discourses of identity and the ways in which they respond to this positioning. We can also throw into sharper focus the contrast between the subtle and hybrid ways in which heritage identities are assumed and recast and the narrow uniformity of the monolingual identities imposed through national educational systems.

REFERENCES

Agtzidis, V. 1997. *Euxine Sea Diaspora: The Greek Settlements in the North-eastern Regions of the Black Sea.* Thessaloniki: Kyriakides (translated from Greek).

Anthemides, A. 2002. *Hellenism in Euxine Sea Countries: Pontos-Tsar Russia-U.S.S.R-Commonwealth of Independent Nations (700 B.C.–2000 A.D.).* Thessaloniki: Malliaris (translated from Greek).

Blommaert, J. 2007. Commentaries: on scope and depth in linguistic ethnography. *Journal of Sociolinguistics* 11(5): 682–88.

Bourdieu, P. 1991. *Language and Symbolic Power.* Cambridge: Polity Press.

Bruneau, M. 2000. *The Diaspora of Pontian Hellenism.* Thessaloniki: Herodotos, 27–50.

Creese, A. 2008. Linguistic ethnography. In *Encyclopedia of Language and Education.* Vol. 10, *Research Methods in Language and Education,* ed. K. King and N. H. Hornberger, 229–41. New York: Springer.

Davies, B. and Harré, R. 1990. Positioning: the discursive production of selves. *Journal of the Theory of Social Behaviour* 20(1): 43–63.

Fotiades, K. 2000. The Greeks of the former U.S.S.R.: the genesis of the diaspora. In *The Diaspora of Pontian Hellenism,* ed. M. Bruneau, 65–92. Thessaloniki: Herodotos (translated from Greek).

Gal, S. 1989. Language and political economy. *Annual Review of Anthropology* 18: 345–67.

Greek Ministry of Education and Religious Affairs (online). Cross-Cultural Education, http://www.ypepth.gr/en_ec_page1547.htm (accessed 23 July 2008).

Harré, R. and van Langenhove, L. 1999. *Positioning Theory.* Oxford: Blackwell.

Heller, M. 1995. Language choice, social institutions and symbolic domination. *Language in Society* 24: 373–405.

———. 1999. *Linguistic Minorities and Modernity*. London: Longman

———. (ed.) 2007. *Bilingualism: A Social Approach*. Basingstoke, Hampshire: Palgrave Macmillan.

Mackridge, P. 1991. The Pontic dialect: a corrupt version of Ancient Greek? *Journal of Refugee Studies* 4(4): 335–39.

Notaras, G. 2000. The sensitisation of the Greek state to the problem of the Greeks from the former U.S.S.R. In *The Diaspora of Pontian Hellenism*, ed. M. Bruneau, 311–25. Thessaloniki: Herodotos (translated from Greek)

Papassiopi-Pasia, Z. 1999. *Law on Nationality*. Thessaloniki: Sakkoulas (translated from Greek).

Pavlenko, A. and Blackledge, A. 2004. *Negotiation of Identities in Multilingual Contexts*. Clevedon: Multilingual Matters.

Rampton, B. 2007. Neo-Hymesian linguistic ethnography in the United Kingdom. *Journal of Sociolinguistics* 11(5): 584–607.

Woolard, K. A. 1985. Language variation and cultural hegemony: towards an integration of sociolinguistic and social theory. *International Journal of the Sociology of Language* 66: 85–98.

———. 1998. Introduction: language ideology as a field of inquiry. In *Language Ideologies: Practice and Theory*, ed. B. B. Schieffelin., K. A. Woolard and P. V. Kroskrity, 3–47. New York: Oxford University Press.

5 Negotiation of Identities across Times and Spaces

Adrian Blackledge and Angela Creese

Any study of multilingualism and identities is situated in and subject to its social, cultural, political, and historical context. Investigation of multilingualism today is conducted at a time of increasing movement of people across borders, and of rapid development of accessible forms of communication which take little or no account of territory. Both of these dimensions, the global movement of people and the development and availability of digital communication, are factors which play into our understandings of multilingualism in late-modern societies. Linguistic practices move across time and space, changing as they go, taking with them old affiliations, at times shedding these affiliations and accruing new investments. In this process of movement and change linguistic practices come to constitute a terrain for competition, a point of negotiation, a market-place where some practices are valued more highly than others, and where the value of certain practices changes with each new political economy.

In this chapter we report some of the findings from a research project which investigated multilingualism in complementary schools in four English cities.[1] The research project consisted of four interlocking case studies with two researchers working in two complementary schools in each of four communities. The case studies focussed on Gujarati schools in Leicester, Turkish schools in London, Cantonese and Mandarin schools in Manchester, and Bengali schools in Birmingham. Complementary schools, also known as 'supplementary schools', 'heritage language schools', or 'community language schools', provide language teaching for young people in a non-statutory setting. One of the specific aims of the research project was to investigate how the linguistic practices of students and teachers in complementary schools are used to negotiate young people's multilingual and multicultural identities. Each case study identified two complementary schools in which to observe, record, and interview participants. The classes ran for between two and three hours, either in the evening or at the week-end. After four weeks observing in classrooms, two key participant children were identified in each school. These children were audio-recorded during the classes observed, and also for thirty minutes before coming to the class and after leaving class. We interviewed stakeholders in the schools including teachers and administrators, and the key participant children and their parents. In all we collected 192 hours of audio-recorded interactional data, wrote 168 sets of field notes, made 16 hours of video recordings, and interviewed sixty-six key stakeholders. A more detailed account of the methods used to collect documentary and home-based data are outlined in Creese et al. (2008).

Our observations in Birmingham, Leicester, London, and Manchester provide insights into the ways in which multilingualisms are emerging and changing, and raise questions about heritage, the remembered nation, and the transmission of languages which carry the weight of 'culture' and distant territories (Blackledge and Creese, 2009a). Those who take responsibility for maintaining and transmitting their languages to the next generation invest in a multilingual future, but not necessarily a version of multilingualism which is always acceptable to their students. The movement of language and languages across time and space often comes to have different meanings for the urban, urbane, young people who attend complementary school classes. These are classrooms where linguistic practices are haggled over and bartered for, in negotiations conducted in the heteroglossic language of the young multilingual. Flexible verbal repertoires enable the students to negotiate subject positions which may at times be at odds with the discourses of the complementary schools (Creese and Blackledge, 2010). In touch with global popular culture, these are young people who habitually incorporate in their linguistic portfolio features of global capital such as Bollywood film, hip-hop, rap, and bhangra music, together with the language of the latest dvd releases, and new web-based resources. This is not to say that the students we met and listened to were always in opposition to the linguistic and cultural resources on offer in their complementary schools. In fact at times they were very much involved in their learning, proud of their multilingualism, and of their heritage. What we often saw was that the students engaged in an activity planned by the teacher, accepted it to some extent, then appropriated it and used it for their own purposes. They were both in and out of their learning, accepting and rejecting, engaged and subversive, "having it both ways" (Rampton, 2006: 367). They did not fully accept a version of multilingualism which was based on long-distance or out-of-place nationalisms or heritages, or one based on the separation of languages (Blackledge and Creese, 2008, 2009a). Rather, they played with their rich linguistic assets, taking from their teachers what they needed, and using language on their own terms. Of course every interaction was different, and sometimes these negotiations resulted in teachers having things their way instead. There was almost always a sense of ambiguity, or at the very least a sense of students and teachers (and for that matter parents and friends) investing in language as heritage associated with other times and places, at the same time as remaking and reinventing it for the transnational setting in which they found themselves. Here we agree with Adam (2000: 133), that "time and space constitutes an indivisible unity where space always implicates time and vice versa". This is where our ongoing debate lies: at the interstices of nation, heritage, global movement, and new communication. In short, at the interstices of space and time.

NEGOTIATIONS IN TIME AND SPACE

The complementary schools set out to teach the heritage of the home territory through folk stories, narrative accounts, cultural artefacts, festivals, rituals and performances, offering them to the next generation as inheritance. The concept of the nation accrued particular salience in the schools. This was not, however, precisely the same phenomenon as the ideology of 'one-language-equals-one-nation'. It was not the dominant culture represented by, and constructed in, the dominant language, nor was it the simple equation of language, culture, nation, territory and state. Rather, it was nationalism at a distance (Anderson, 1998; Glick-Schiller and Fouron, 2002), an out-of-place nationalism (May and Fenton, 2003), a nationalism which clung to territorial and linguistic roots at least partly because the new environment was powerfully and determinedly nationalistic in its turn. It was a nationalism at home in another place, and perhaps even another time. But for at least some of those we spent time with and listened to, it was nonetheless a nationalism which was of central importance to their sense of themselves, and to their sense of who they wished their community of children and young people to be.

The present chapter focuses on data collected in and around the Bengali schools in Birmingham, and the Turkish schools in London. We are able to represent only a glimpse of the interactions we observed in and out of classrooms (for a fuller account see Blackledge and Creese, 2010). In the first example, a teacher in one of the Bengali schools is lecturing his young students about symbols of Bangladeshi nationhood. He has discussed the national flower, national bird, national poet, the national anthem, and the national flag. He moves on to the national fish:[2]

Example 5.1

T: jaatio maas <*national fish*> national fish. ei desh theke tumaar abbu kin-e aane naa ilish maas, ilish maas kine naa, ilish maas khaao naa? <*from this country don't your father and mother buy hilsa fish, don't they buy fish, don't you eat hilsa fish?*>

Rumana: zaanraam naa <*I don't know*>

T: tumi zaano naa? <*don't you know?*>

Rumana: maas khaai naa, aamraa maas khaai naa <*don't eat fish, we don't eat fish*>

T: [sarcastically] maas posa, naa, naa, maas motte-i khaaiyyo naa, zibon-e khaaiyyo naa. etaa tus korlei bipodh. maas khaai-lei bipodh. ekhbaar zodi maas khaiyyalaao aar ekhbaar golaa-e posa laagizaae ei golaa aar zindigi-te bhaalo hobenaa. shutorong maas khono din khaaibaanaa Abbu aane naa aar Bangladeshe kichu chaaibaanaa. Bangladeshe gesso khono din? <*fish is rotten, no, no, you should never eat fish if you touch it there may be danger, eating fish is dangerous, if you eat fish once and find it rotten in the throat then that feeling will remain with you as long as you live, therefore don't ever eat fish, your father doesn't get it and you should not ask for anything from Bangladesh have you ever been to Bangladesh?*>

Rumana: dui aasilaam <*I was two*>

T: tumi dui aasilaa ni aar er por-e aar gesso naa? ekhon tumi khoto? <*were you two then and after that have you never been? how old are you now?*>

Rumana: dosh <*ten*>

T: tokhon tumi HUA HUA [imitating an infant's cry] khorso, tumaar ammu tumaake feeder-e dudh dise, tokhon tumito maas khaao naai, theek aase aar gesso naa. jaawaar shombhobonaa khub kom, achchaa, achchaa. <*at that time you cried HUA HUA your mother fed you milk from a feeder then you didn't eat fish. all right, you haven't been since then. the possibility of going is remote, ok ok*> *(classroom video recording, Bengali school)*

Having asked the students whether they eat the national fish, the teacher appears to be surprised by Rumana's response: 'aamraa maas khaai naa' <*we don't eat fish*>. He assumes that Rumana and her family eat the traditional Bangladeshi food. In our analysis we frequently encountered examples of students using parody to subvert the official discourse of the classroom, or to clash with the discourse of their peers. Unusually here, however, the teacher uses parody and mimicry to mock his students. Billig argues that 'ridicule is a cost-effective means of social discipline' (2005:198). The mocking laughter that greets a childish error is a powerful means of discipline. The teacher adopts a parodic, double-voiced discourse (Bakhtin, 1994) to mock the student who says her family doesn't eat fish. This is neither simply the voice of the teacher nor the voice of the student, but incorporates something of each. It is also the voice of one who argues strongly that 'fish is rotten', a voice which is an exaggeration of the student's 'we don't eat fish', and a voice which clashes with the teacher's own view of the symbolic importance of the national fish. This is what Billig (2005) calls disciplinary humour, an exaggerated mocking of the child's voice as a form of punishment. The authority of the teacher is reinforced by disciplinary laughter as he defends the national symbol against the student's 'mocking transgression of their customs' (Billig, 2005: 206). The teacher's mocking discourse continues as he ironically suggests that if the student does not eat fish, she should not ask for anything from Bangladesh. The teacher's disciplinary discourse further continues as he mocks the student for not having visited Bangladesh since she was two years old. The teacher represents the student's voice as that of a baby ('at that time you cried HUA HUA'), and seems to suggest (in a curious logic) that she has been prevented from eating fish by an over-dependence on milk from a feeder cup. It is as if (for the teacher) the child has rejected Bangladeshi nationality in saying that she doesn't eat fish, and the national symbol, imposed by the teacher, becomes a site of contestation and negotiation.

The second example is from classroom observation in the other Bengali school in the Birmingham case study. T is the teacher, and Shahnaz a ten-year-old girl:

Example 5.2

T: Bangladesher teen taa national day aache, jaatio dibosh <*Bangladesh has three national days, national events*> national day not national anthem

Shahnaz: independence day

T: etaa Banglae ki bolbe shaadhinota dibosh Ekushey February shohid dibosh aage bolo Ekushey February shohid dibosh <*in Bangla it is shaadhinota dibosh 21st February is shohid dibosh first say 21st February is shohid dibosh*>

Shahnaz: ekushey February shohid dibosh

T: er pore aashlo shaadhinota dibosh <*after that comes shaadhinotaa dibosh*> independence day, independence day is not Bangla, it is English. Banglae holo <*in Bangla it is*> shaadhinota dibosh

Shahnaz: chaabbish-e March <*26th March*>

T: shaadhinota dibosh

Shahnaz: chaabbish-e March <*26th March*>

T: lastly nine months we fought against Pakistani collaborator

Shahnaz: language day

T: language day holo ekushey February. Chaabbish March independence day. Sholoi December, after nine months bijoy dibosh <*victory day*> Pakistani occupied army ke aamraa surrender korchi <*we made the occupied forces of Pakistan surrender their arms*> Al Badr against our independence war ke aamraa chutaaisi <*we chased them out*> How many national days in Bangladesh?

Shahnaz: three

T: Bangladesher jaatio dibosh koiti? <*how many national days in Bangladesh?*>

Shahnaz: teen ti <*three*>

T: Shaadhinota dibosh ebong bijoy dibosh chilo 1971. Bhasha dibosh chilo 1952. Aar bhaasha dibosh kon din chilo 52. Tokhon amraa choto <*independence day and victory day was in 1971. Language day was in 1952. Language day was 52 when we were young*> Inshaallah eta every day jodi aamraa every day discuss

kori taahole bhaalo <*by the grace of God it is good if we discuss this every day*>
(*classroom audio recording, Bengali school*)

Here the teacher instructs the students through content which refers to a narrative of collective remembering in relation to the nation. Curriculum content is strongly nationalistic, and appears to have the aim of instilling in the young language learners an understanding of key dates and events in the making of the Bangladeshi nation. The ten-year-old student seems to have some pre-existing knowledge of the historical context, and is prepared to volunteer this. For example she offers the date of Bangladeshi independence from West Pakistan, and is confidently able to do so in Bengali. The teacher moves comfortably between Bengali and English within and between sentences, and in his final statement uses the common Islamic expression 'Inshallah', derived from Arabic, and also Bengali and English. Language teaching here invents for the young students a sense of national belonging which is firmly rooted in narratives of collective memory. The teacher's stories of poignant martyrdoms and heroic victories, remembered as 'our own', serve the purpose of reproducing the national memory and imagination (Anderson, 1983).

In a third example, from observation in one of the Turkish schools, the teacher is teaching Turkish in the context of a traditional Mother's Day celebration. The participants are the teacher (T), a student (S1) who wears a digital audio-recorder, and other students (Ss). Typically, the episode begins with a dictation activity, in which he is dictating the lyrics of a traditional Turkish Mother's Day song. He plays the Mother's Day song on a boom-box:

Example 5.3

T: [switches music on] dinliyorsunuz. sizde söyleyin dans yapabilirsiniz <*you are listening. you can sing along too, you can dance*>

S1:   hadi <*let's do it*>

S2:   hey dance Turkish style. Turkish style 'düğün' <*wedding ceremony*> [laughs]

S1:   hadi halay çekelim. halay çekelim <*let's do folk dancing. . let's do folk dancing*> do you know how to halay çek? hadi halay çekelim <*do you know how to do folk dancing? let's do folk dancing.*> whoever is doing it with me? Halay çekelim.<*let's do folk dancing*> hey just come, just come, just come man. fuck you. it's gonna be joke. hey, hey [dancing] I know how to do it. AAHH MY PENIS!

S3:   [laughs uncontrollably]

T: [switches music off. wants students in two groups so that they can sing together. switches music on again]

S1:   wait . shush I'm gonna sing [coughs to clear his throat] evet <*right*>

T: söylüyoruz. <*we are singing*>
S1:   hoy Ismet, let's sing. kimsenin güleceği yok kimsenin güleceği
            yok [singing along to music] LA LA LA LA LA LA LA [exagger-
            ated, loud] yeah. [to a student] give me that ball please. please
            [T is singing, some students are singing and clapping]
T: Gökhan dışarı. <*Gokhan get out*> sen dışarı. <*you get out*>
            Hakan dışarı. . <*Hakan get out*> başkanın yanına gidiyorsunuz.
            annelerinize söyleyin beni görsün. <*you are to see the principal.*
            tell your mother to see me>
            (classroom audio recording, Turkish school)

S1 seizes an opportunity to subvert the activity, bursting with enthusiasm
when the teacher suggests that the students can dance to the traditional
music. The second student picks up on S1's intonation, and suggests that
they should dance 'Turkish style' in the way that would be typical at a Turkish wedding. The Turkish word 'halay' refers to a folk dance performed in
a circle. S2 invokes the wedding, appropriating one traditional ritual (the
wedding) in order to mock and subvert another (celebration of Mother's
Day). S1 continues in English and Turkish, inviting all to 'just come'. At
this point S1 is shouting loudly, whereas S3 is laughing uncontrollably. Our
field notes for this session read as follows: *'The music plays and the boys
rap dance, make odd faces and produce funny noises. S2 is now setting
the tone in the group of boys. They are imitating folk dance movements'*.
The students here both introduce elements of popular culture ('rap dance'),
and parody traditional folk dance. By both means hostility to the official,
traditional, authorised activity is constituted. It is an act of sameness and
difference, based in the traditional, to traditional music, but at the same
time creating something new, making change by recontextualisation. This
is not mere repetition but appropriation, the subversion of ritual by presentation of a new version of the traditional which creates a momentary
suspension of conventional hierarchies. The introduction of 'rap dance' is
comic not least because it is anachronistic, an element of the 'folk-culture'
of the people which impinges on the authorised heritage of school activity.
The mockery of the traditional dance (odd faces and funny noises) becomes
a comic parody of the official discourse. Notwithstanding this, there is a
sense in which the creation of the parody partakes of the activity which the
teacher is seeking to create. This is very different from non-participation.
It is participation, but on the terms of the students rather than the teacher.
They use the tradition, the heritage, to create their own order, to challenge
the existing hierarchy, and to claim their freedom, however ephemeral.
They populate traditional discourse with their own local social languages
and voices for their own purposes (Lin and Luk, 2005: 89). In mocking the
dance they mock the tradition, but at the same time mock themselves. This
is ambivalent laughter, at once positive and negative, creating a 'contradictory world of becoming' (Bakhtin, 1968:149). It is as if the students will

only participate in the 'heritage' they are offered if they can put their own stamp on it, taking it as their own, and usurping it. S1 dances, but ends the dance with a cry of 'AAH MY PENIS!' as coarse language becomes the centre of the unofficial world. S1's cry subverts the formality of the dance, but at the same time he laughs at himself. This is an inclusive joke, a laugh at the expense of the people but also with the people. At this point the teacher attempts to organise the students to sing the Mother's Day song. Again picking up his cue for subversive action, S1 is quick to take the floor. He clears his throat with a cough which exudes seriousness and respect. Here 'evet' is stylised, adopting the voice of a professional singer, as he prepares to sing. At first he calls on the help of another student (Ismet) to help him with the song, just as he had called on others to help him with the dance. Ismet does not join in, but S1 goes ahead, at first singing the song rather hesitantly, but apparently respectfully. After a few moments he changes tone, singing 'LA LA LA LA LA LA LA' in a comic, grotesque, exaggerated voice which serves to undermine the activity. It may be that S1 did not know the words of the song very well, and so lost confidence and reverted to the comic. Whatever the reason, there is more than one voice evident here: the voice which attempts to participate in singing the Mother's Day song, and the voice which subverts the celebration, and exudes hostility to the authorised heritage. Although some students are engaged in the activity, the teacher breaks off from this to admonish the group of boys who have treated Mother's Day as an opportunity for carnivalesque humour, and dispatches them from the classroom with a threat to involve their mothers (Blackledge and Creese, 2009b).

In each of these three examples, and in many more like them, time and space constitute an indivisible unity, where space implicates time and vice versa (Adam, 2000). In negotiations around the contemporary significance of the hilsa fish, in stories of heroic conflicts in the making of the nation, and in the performance and subversion of traditional Turkish festivals and rituals—here as elsewhere students and teachers negotiate identities across time and space.

LANGUAGE IN A TIME OF TRANSITION

What are we left with when we can see change occurring before our very eyes—when we can see the old constraints interacting dynamically with new possibilities? What does the study of multilingualism mean when linguistic practice is increasingly diverse? First, the study of language in use is never separate from the study of society. The construction of difference through the relative permeability of linguistic boundaries challenges our expectations about how sociolinguistics connects to social theory. Linguistic variability is rapidly changing, as the meanings of linguistic features change for their users. At the same time, the demand for separation of languages is often associated with a need to drop anchor and hold on to what is known and to what is owned. Second, the study of language is inevitably the study of power, as we come to understand in increasingly nuanced ways how access to linguistic resources is associated with access to economic and cultural resources. Those who control the circulation of linguistic resources also often control other forms of capital. For this reason the study of language often gives us a window into the exercise of power. Third, it is in the study of voice, and of voices, that we are able to bring into close-up the subtle and nuanced ways in which negotiations occur in language. In our study we saw many occasions in which young people, their teachers, and their parents negotiated a path through rough ideological terrain by gaining access to and making creative use of particular linguistic resources. These resources, and these negotiations, were not equally accessible to all, or accessible at all times or in all spaces, but it was in the complex, myriad voices of the students, families and teachers that we came to understand something of ideologies and practices at work. And fourth, there is a pressing need for further research into and development of pedagogy for bilingual education which is 'adaptive, able to expand and contract, as the communicative situations shift and as the terrain changes' (García, 2009: 8). In this project we saw something of the changing communicative situation, and the changing linguistic terrain.

We listened to the voices of school administrators, principals, teachers, canteen assistants, instructors, students, siblings, parents, visitors, and others who came into contact with our audio- and video-recorders, and with our research team's sharp-eyed observations. But these were not the only voices we heard. Every utterance bore the tastes and traces of other utterances across space and time. Every word we heard in the discourse of teachers, in the responses of their students, in the fragmented interactions occurring in the seams and cracks of classroom routines, in the alternative economies which young people developed in opposition to the official worlds of their lessons, in the borderlands of students travelling to and from school, and in their family homes—everywhere we saw that 'each word tastes of the context and contexts in which it has lived its socially charged life' (Bakhtin, 1981: 293). In all of these contexts language lay 'on the borderline between oneself and the other . . . it becomes one's own only when the speaker populates it with his own intention, his own accent, when he appropriates the word, adapting it to his own semantic and expressive intention' (ibid.). Frequently we heard voices which bore the traces of other voices; voices appropriated and reiterated in new contexts so that they accrued new resonances; voices creatively imbued with the colours and textures of other voices. Nation-building narratives, national symbols, and traditional rituals, all had their place, and all were negotiated anew. Not that this population of voices within voices was a straightforward process, or one which could always be easily identified. Such is the delicacy of the threads caught up when histories brush up against histories, and worlds against worlds, that even close analysis may not easily discover them. Nor is the appropriation and assimilation of the traces of other voices necessarily a conscious act, or one with specific intentions. More often, voices are populated with fragments of other voices, accents, and intonations, in a critical interanimation of language which 'discovers itself already surrounded by heteroglossia' (Bakhtin, 1981: 295). It is in just such heteroglossic talk that we are able to engage with the tensions and contradictions which co-exist at the heart of the linguistic practices we have heard, and the identity positions which they constitute.

In heteroglossic talk is a tension between an institutional ideology which holds that languages should be kept separate in the language-learning classroom, and the communicative realities of real classrooms where there is flexible use of linguistic resources to make that learning happen (Creese and Blackledge, 2010). In heteroglossic talk is the dynamic coexistence of students' positioning as both complicit in and resistant to institutionally imposed identities, and students' simultaneously serious and carnivalesque participation in classroom lessons. In heteroglossic language we understand (at least) 'two voices, two meanings, and two expressions' (Bakhtin, 1981: 324). The comic, carnivalesque language of students in classroom interaction, the parodic talk of students and teachers who mock the talk of others, the appropriation and simultaneous contestation of 'cultural heritage' artefacts such as traditional folk tales (Creese et al., 2010), wedding dances, Mother's Day celebrations, and nation-building narratives—all of these and more are discourses in which dialogue is embedded, 'a concentrated dialogue of two voices, two world views, two languages' (Bakhtin, 1981: 325). They are discourses which become sites of negotiation, holding in tension beliefs, values, and attitudes which often clash and collide, but which at the same time co-exist and correspond. This is where the creative struggle with another's discourse resides and plays out—in the internally persuasive word which is at the same time complicit and resistant. A clash with another's word may become a clash with one's own word, as the struggle goes on and is never completed. Within almost every utterance we encountered in and out of the eight complementary schools, there was an intense interaction between identities imposed institutionally, and students' own subject positioning. Captured in our transcripts, each utterance is a 'considerably more complex and dynamic organism than it appears when construed simply as a thing that articulates the intention of the person uttering it' (Bakhtin, 1981: 355). In the complementary schools in Birmingham, Leicester, London, and Manchester we saw multilingual young people, and their linguistic practices, at a particular moment in time and space, as complementary schools were emerging as economies where linguistic resources were commodities to be bartered for and bargained over in the new linguistic market-place.

MULTILINGUALISM, DISCOURSE AND ETHNOGRAPHY

Doing ethnographic research allows us to tell a story—not someone else's story, but our own story of some slice of experience (Heller, 2008: 250). In one sense our story is no more than a slice of experience: we open doors which are not often opened by outsiders, and we look in at whatever we can see and eavesdrop on whatever we can hear, and make our story out of the 'lived stuff' (Rampton, 2006: 394) of others. But at the same time what we see and hear *is* more than just a slice of experience. Adopting a theoretical and analytical perspective which combines the ethnographic with the linguistic, and which engages the dialogic thought of Bakhtin, we are able to tell a story which connects a cacophony of linguistic practice with histories and territories, with traditions and heritages, with pedagogies and ideologies, and with the changing worlds of digital communication and globalisation (Blackledge and Creese, 2010). That is, although when we open those doors we might only see and hear that which is before us, our analytic gaze takes us beyond the immediate, to other times and other spaces. Those other times and spaces include the tangible pasts of narrated events in the making of nations, exemplified by stories of martyrdoms, liberation struggles, and heroic deeds. They also include artefacts associated with the construction of the 'home' territory: traditional folk tales, festivals, food, and flags. They include histories of migration, and at times multiple migrations. And, most importantly, they include local time and space, as young people live out their lives in the complex cosmopolitan worlds of their neighbourhoods. In these cosmopolitan worlds new multilingualisms emerge, as young people use a vast array of linguistic resources which constantly change and develop, and which derive their linguistic features from many sources, including those associated with religious texts, the 'homeland' national heritage, a wide range of popular cultural forms, coarse, vernacular insults, academic English, non-standard English, and many more. These complex linguistic repertoires bear the traces of past times and present times, of lives lived locally and globally. These are the voices of young people whose 'communities'—their teachers and parents—want them to experience and to learn something of a 'culture', a 'heritage', a nation or territory, which now lies at a distance. Our story is one of linguistic resources evolving in practice as they come to accrue new values, affiliations and allegiances. It is a story of language in flexible use and up for grabs, language traded, exchanged, bartered, wrangled over, and negotiated. It is a story of language ideology and practice changing as it moves across time and space.

NOTES

1. ESRC no: RES-000–23–1180. Our research colleagues in the team are: Taşkin Baraç, Arvind Bhatt, Shahela Hamid, Li Wei, Vally Lytra, Peter Martin, Chao-Jung Wu, and Dilek Yağcioğlu-Ali.

2. Note on transcription

In keeping with the theoretical approach to linguistic practice which emerged from this work, we make no distinction between different 'languages' in the transcribed data. We use romanized transliteration for all languages, and represent each 'language' in the same way.

(.)	pause of less than a second
(2.5)	length of pause in seconds
speech	transcribed speech
<speech >	translated speech
CAPITALS	loud
( )	speech inaudible
[ ]	'stage directions'

REFERENCES

Adam, B. (2000). The temporal gaze: the challenge for social theory in the context of GM food. *British Journal of Sociology* 51: 125–42.

Anderson, B. (1983). *Imagined Communities*. London, Verso.

———. (1998). *The Spectre of Comparisons: Nationalisms, Southeast Asia, and the World*. London: Verso.

Bakhtin, M. M. 1968. *Rabelais and His World*. Translated by H. Iswolsky. Bloomington: Indiana University Press.

———. 1981. *The Dialogic Imagination: Four Essays*. Edited by M. Holquist; translated by C. Emerson and M. Holquist. Austin: University of Texas Press.

———. 1994. Problems of Dostoevsky's poetics. In *The Bakhtin Reader: Selected Writings of Bakhtin, Medvedev, Voloshinov*, ed. P. Morris, 110–13. London: Arnold.

Billig, M. 2005. *Laughter and Ridicule: Towards a Social Critique of Humour*. London: Sage.

Blackledge, A. and Creese, A. 2008. Contesting 'language' as 'heritage': Negotiation of identities in late modernity. *Applied Linguistics* 29 (4): 533–54.

———. 2009a. '*Because tumi Bangali*' : Inventing and disinventing the national in multilingual communities in UK. *Ethnicities* 9(4): 451–76.

———. 2009b. Meaning-making as dialogic process: official and carnival lives in the language classroom. *Journal of Language, Identity, and Education* 8(4): 236–53.

Blackledge, A. and Creese, A. 2010. *Multilingualism: A Critical Perspective*. London: Continuum.

Creese, A. and Blackledge, A. 2010. Translanguaging in the bilingual classroom: a pedagogy for learning and teaching. *Modern Language Journal* 94(2): 103–15.

Creese, A., Blackledge, A. and Wu, C.-J. 2010. Folk stories and social identification in multilingual classrooms linguistics and education. *Linguistics and Education* 20(4): 350–65.

Creese, A., Baraç, T., Bhatt, A., Blackledge, A., Hamid, S., Li Wei, Lytra, V., Martin, P., Wu, C.-J. and Yağcıoğlu-Ali, D. 2008. *Investigating Multilingualism in Complementary Schools in Four Communities*. Final Report. RES-000–23–1180. Birmingham: University of Birmingham.

García, O. 2009. *Bilingual Education in the 21st Century: A Global Perspective*. Oxford: Wiley-Blackwell.

Glick Schiller, N. and Fouron, G. 2002. *Georges Woke Up Laughing: Long Distance Nationalism and the Search for Home*. New York: Duke University Press.

Heller, M. 2008. Doing ethnography. In *The Blackwell Guide to Research Methods in Bilingualism and Multilingualism*, ed. Li Wei and M. Moyer, 249–62. Oxford: Wiley-Blackwell.

Lin, A. M. Y. and Luk, J. C. M. 2005. Local creativity in the face of global domination: insights of Bakhtin for teaching English for dialogic communication. In *Dialogue with Bakhtin on Second and Foreign Language Learning: New Perspectives*, ed. J. K. Hall, G. Vitanova and L. Marchenkova, 77–88. Mahwah, NJ: Lawrence Erlbaum.

May, S. and Fenton, S. 2003. Ethnicity, nation and 'race': connections and disjunctures. In *Ethnonational Identities*, ed. S. Fenton and S. May, 1–20. Basingstoke: Palgrave.

Rampton, B. 2006. *Language in Late Modernity*. Cambridge: Cambridge University Press.

6 Authenticity, Legitimacy and Power
Critical Ethnography and Identity Politics

Frances Giampapa

In the fields of sociology, geography and anthropology, critical debates have taken place with regard to the nature and effects of the relationships of power, positioning, representation and identity (e.g. racial, ethnic and gender to name a few) that are constructed between researchers and their participants in the research process (see Gilbert, 1994; Henry, 2003, 2007; Herod, 1999; Mullings, 1999; Thapar-Björkert and Henry, 2004; Sanghera and Thapar-Björkert, 2007). From a reflexive standpoint, research in these fields has explored key methodological issues that address the importance of researcher and participant identities and the ways in which participants exercise power to position the researcher and control access to their community. Furthermore, research across these fields illustrates clearly that a researcher's identity is integral to both the process and the product of the research (see Henry, 2003).

These debates have led many of us who are doing critical linguistic ethnography to cast a critical lens on the way in which the dynamics of relations of power, positioning and identity give rise to possibilities and constraints during the data collection process; and on the ways in which participants' roles as gatekeepers and cultural brokers can reposition the researcher in various ways.

This chapter offers a reflexive account on issues related to power, positioning, and identity within my doctoral research (Giampapa, 2004a, 2004b). I will explore these issues in two ways: firstly, by critically reflecting on what it means to conduct critical ethnography, and on how researchers are positioned through their methodological choices and training. Here, I will be drawing broadly from the social sciences to illuminate the debates around identity, power and positioning that inform what it means to be a critical ethnographer; and secondly, by providing an analysis of three cases from my doctoral research, I will illustrate the ways in which 'being in the field' brings forth a set of complexities that are necessary points for analysis when conducting critical ethnographic research.

In this part of the chapter, I will be referring to my research experience in the field and demonstrating how my identities and positioning across the diverse spaces of *italianità* (i.e. Italianness), in the Italian Canadian world in Toronto, were shaped and contested through a process of dialogue between myself and the participants (see Giampapa, 2004a), a process in which power, positioning and identities were fluid, multiple and shifting. Thus, what I hope to show from these methodological reflections is the need to problematise the way we, as researchers, think about our own multiple identities, and how, in turn, our participants' positioning of us as research-ers plays a role in not only gatekeeping (that is, excluding or including us in particular spaces in the field) but how this shapes what we see and how we analyse issues of identity, positioning and power.

METHODOLOGICAL POSITIONINGS: UNDERSTANDING ISSUES OF IDENTITY AND POWER

Ethnographic research has always focused on the ways in which: (1) the subjectivity of the researcher works to bridge theory and data; and (2) the researcher establishes and maintains a collaborative relationship with participants in order to develop a 'holistic' account of the emic point of view. The aim is, of course, to ensure as far as possible that the researcher has, through a number of methodological means, checked, for example, the credibility of the picture that is being produced (see also Hornberger, 2006). Within critical qualitative methodologies and ethnography, in par-ticular, there is a concern with the researcher's role in constructing and shaping the research process and in questioning 'whose' voices are truly being represented within the research.

Calling for a critical engagement with the process of research, Cameron et al. (1992) draw attention to issues of power in the research process and propose a research approach that moves beyond simply research 'on or even for' the participants but 'with' the participants through an empowerment-oriented approach. The spirit of what Cameron et al. (1992) convey is cer-tainly in keeping with the essence of what critical ethnography proposes: namely, that democratisation of the research process is key, and that issues of researcher power, biases and beliefs, representation and authority are central to the research process. When these issues arise, they constitute 'methodological rich points' (Hornberger, 2006: 221). In Hornberger's terms, these are "points of experience that make salient the differences between the ethnographer's world and the world the ethnographer sets out to describe" (ibid.: 222).

The process of research is not unproblematic and it does not always go far enough in truly achieving what Cameron et al. (1992) envisage as an empowerment-oriented approach to research. Thus, whereas critical eth-nography situates knowledge as co-constructed, produced and negotiated through the dialogic exchanges between researcher and participants, the researcher is still positioned centre stage and the issues of power in the research process are not problematised sufficiently to capture the heterogeneous nature of the sites of research and the power relations within them.

In general, the notion of power is conceptualised within critical ethnographic research as not fixed but negotiated through a reciprocal process of exchange between the researcher and the participants. According to Cameron et al. (1992), this means that we need to "take into account the subjects' research agenda, involve them in feedback and sharing of knowledge, consider representation and control in reporting of findings" (cited in Hornberger, 2006: 224).

As already noted, critical ethnography calls for a recognition of the ways in which researcher's beliefs, values, and experiences underpin the questions posed and the analytical gaze that is cast on the research. Cameron et al. (1992: 5) state:

> Researchers cannot help being socially located persons. We inevitably bring our biographies and our subjectivities to every stage of the research process and this influences the questions we ask and the ways in which we try to find answers.

As complex social beings we are located by and produce discourses of identities that shape and reconfigure the way in which we negotiate our identities and positionings with participants. As researchers, our own histories, forms of social and linguistic capital, and ways of representing ourselves, are not neutral and carry with them degrees of 'value'. Thus our own forms of capital carry a currency that has to be negotiated so as to allow us to claim the right to enter particular discourse sites.

As a researcher I am not only positioned by the discourses of the academy with regards to my identity as a researcher, and the responsibilities attached to the production of research knowledge and the process of research, but I am also a social agent with multiple identities. My identities are also historically and politically located across time and space. That is, my past and present identities are embedded within my history as a Canadian-born, Australian-raised, straight female of Italian heritage, from a working class background (with a middle class education), and with an immigrant past narrated through my family histories. Furthermore, my personal and academic life trajectories led me from Australia to Canada to pursue doctoral research. These diverse identities were played out in different forms within the field as I conducted my doctoral research in the Italian Canadian world in Toronto and had an impact on the complex relationships forged with my research participants.

As a critical ethnographer, I understand the importance of locating the researcher in the research and of taking account of the ways in which my identity narratives have to become part of the research itself.

However, in my doctoral research, negotiating my researcher identity and reconciling this with my multiple identities led to a complex set of interactions with my participants across time and space that yielded outcomes that were unexpected.

To embed, analyse and question one's subjectivity as part of the research process is not simply about questioning notions of objectivity and neutrality in the field and the ways in which a researcher may influence the data or the 'results' but rather critically understanding the ways in which researcher identities inevitably shape the relationships forged with participants across time and space and how this opens and closes the possibilities for building an account of the social and communicative practices of participants, within and across different spaces of their lives. In fact in conceptualising the 'field' itself, England (1994: 81) makes the following point:

> 'the field' is constantly changing and . . . researchers may find that they have to manoeuvre around unexpected circumstances. The result is research where the only inevitability seems to be unreliability and unpredictability. This in turn ignites the need for a broader, less rigid conception of the 'appropriate' method that allows the researcher the flexibility to be more open to the challenges of field work.

When I first embarked on my doctoral research, I believed, to some degree, that my self-positioning as a second generation Italian Canadian would afford me insider status on entering the field. Furthermore, as noted above, as a critical ethnographer conducting research that focussed on issues relating to ethnicity, language and power, I was aware of the need to critically examine my role, biases and attitudes, and the power differentials between myself and the participants.

However, my training as a researcher did not lead me to problematise the construction of my 'researcher identity', and the dominant models from which this was constructed. Henry (2007) highlights this point with regard to her researcher positionality on entering the field as a feminist researcher within a broad South Asian diaspora. She links her research training experience and the ways in which discussions with her supervisors were framed within a set of assumptions that positioned her as a "Western researcher entering a foreign field" (2007: 73), without any consideration of the complexities embedded within this researcher model and her positionality (i.e. as a female student researcher of South Asian origin). Henry recounts that whereas she had a strong understanding of issues related to power relations, positionality and privilege, it was less clear on how this might be personally experienced once in the field. My own experiences as a student researcher, as a so-called insider within the Italian Canadian community, resonate with Henry's experience. My research training did not prepare me for the issues relating to my identities that arose in the field and/or for the possible positionings from my participants. These are key issues that warrant a deeper reflection and critical understanding within the research training process.

This brings into the frame "questions of collaboration, authority and representation" (Hornberger, 2006: 223). In research training courses, it is not enough to consider only issues related to the credibility or transferability of research. It is also important to consider methodological and theoretical issues related to over-interpretation and reporting of research findings, the dialogic and collaborative nature of the researcher-participant relationship, as well as the ways in which participants' voices are represented and the limits to claims made about their lifeworlds. A greater level of critical reflexivity is needed in conceptualising and constructing fieldwork. England (1994: 82) concurs:

> Reflexivity is self-critical sympathetic introspection and the self-conscious *analytical* scrutiny of the self as researcher. . . . reflexivity is critical to the conduct of fieldwork; it induces self-discovery and can lead to insights and new hypotheses about the research questions. A more reflexive and flexible approach to fieldwork allows the researcher to be more open to any challenges to their theoretical position that fieldwork almost inevitably raises.

In my own work, critical reflection on the ways in which I was implicated in the production of discourses of Italianness turned out to be important to the way I framed and analysed my research, and made it possible for me to attend to the multiple voices that emerged within my research (i.e. those of my participants and my own). As I analysed the data gathered in my research project, I found that I needed to reflect on how my self-identification and positionings within the Italian Canadian world were shaped by my own history and experiences. As noted earlier, my multiple identities include: being Italo-Australian as well as claiming Italian Canadianness, and being multilingual (i.e. a speaker of Australian/Canadian English, 'standard' Italian and a southern Italian dialect). These identity inscriptions were read and performed not only linguistically but also through my body, and through my behaviour, talk, dress, actions, in short, through all the semiotic means by which social agents are judged and positioned across the Italian Canadian world.

Moreover, identities are not solely about where we come from but 'who we might become' and how representations of 'who we are' factor into how we represent and position ourselves. There is a dialogical relationship between both past and future in the construction of identities within the present. Complex discourses of identities are at work within the interplay of self-positioning and positioning by others across and within different spaces. As Hall and du Gay (1996: 4) state:

> Precisely because identities are constructed within, not outside, dis-
> course, we need to understand them as produced in specific historical
> and institutional sites within specific discursive formations and prac-
> tices, by specific enunciative strategies. Moreover, they emerge within
> the play of specific modalities of power, and thus are more the product
> of the marking of difference and exclusion, than they are the sign of an
> identical, naturally constituted unity—an 'identity' in its traditional
> meaning (that is, an all-inclusive sameness, seamless, without internal
> differentiation). Above all, and directly contrary to the form in which
> they are constantly invoked, identities are constructed through, not
> outside, difference.

During my fieldwork, my identities and the participants' interpretations
and positionings of me as Italian Canadian were constructed within the
micro-level exchanges that took place across the diverse research sites and
through the different stages of the research process. At the same time, my
identity claims and performances were shaped and influenced by macro-
level discourses of Italianness that were (and still are) produced and debated
within the Italian Canadian world. These wider discourses are largely produced and reproduced by social agents who have discursive control over
what counts as being Italian Canadian and over the social positionings
that are tied to different symbolic and material resources. In particular,
these agents include white, heterosexual, male, first generation Italians/
Italian Canadians (e.g. Italian Canadian politicians, media representatives, academics, local representatives of Italian Canadian institutions and
organisations, Italian government representatives). They produce dominant
discourses of *italianità* where being positioned as the "right" Italian Canadian means, for example, speaking standard Italian, investing in high culture, being Catholic, heterosexual male, and Italian Italian (i.e. a 'native'
Italian who is an educated urbanite).

As Bourdieu (1991) notes, the exchange of linguistic and cultural capital, and the position that agents hold within the market, are dependent
upon the 'legitimacy' and 'authority' of who is speaking, under what social
conditions, and the nature of what is being said. The (re)production of
these discourses of Italianness and the degree of resistance to them were
central to my research. I also took account of the ways in which I was part
of or outside of these discourses, due to either my own self positioning and/
or my participants' positioning of me. The research was carried out in the
late 1990s. It involved eighteen months of concentrated fieldwork followed
by further periods in the field as needed during which I continued to engage
with specific groups of participants.

The 're-packing' of my identities by participants varied, and also shifted
even across interactions with the same participant. Thus, there were occasions and spaces when I was positioned, at one point in time and in a particular space, as a so-called cultural/linguistic insider and then, at other times

and in other spaces, repositioned as an 'outsider'. This shows the limitation of the insider/outsider dichotomy. One can never be a 'complete' insider or outsider within a given research site, particularly in light of the role and the very nature of one's function as a researcher (see Foster, 1994).

In the following section, I will draw on narratives from the field in relation to two Italian Canadian youth participants—Salvatore and Paolo— and one Italian Canadian lesbian, gay, bisexual and transgendered (LGBT) group. These two individual participants and this particular group provide examples of the way in which my own multiple identities and "Italianness" came into question. I was positioned by them in particular ways that included and excluded me from certain discourses and spaces in the research. Issues of authority, legitimacy and power were intertwined through the way in which I was positioned by these participants and raised theoretical and methodological concerns in the data collection and analysis process.

CONTESTED IDENTITIES AND POWER: NARRATIVES FROM THE FIELD

> *We do not parachute into the field with empty heads and a few pencils or a tape-recorder in our pockets ready to record the "facts".* (England, 1994: 84)

The journey into the field began in late 1998 with entry into university-level Italian language classes and into local community contexts in Toronto. I spent over a year being a participant observer in the classes, identifying and working with the participants in my study. Through the contacts I had in the university Italian-language classrooms, and the Italian Canadian community, I was able find Italian Canadian youth participants who had varied experiences of 'Italian Canadianness', and this ultimately led to the building of a small sample of eight Italian Canadian participants who became the focus of my research. The main field journey involved triangulation of methods such as: (1) interviews (individual and focus group interviews, and special themed interviews around work, religion, sexuality, and travelling to Italy); (2) the shadowing of core participants across different spaces such as the home, university classrooms, social spaces and workplaces; (3) auto-ethnography where the core participants became the 'ethnographer' audio-recording their interactions across diverse settings; (4) questionnaires; (5) participant identity narratives and travel diaries reflecting on the 'trip to Italy' as a transnational experience; (6) newspaper documents; and (7) researcher diaries.

Over the eighteen months of fieldwork I became acutely aware of the need to situate the eight Italian Canadian youth voices within the wider macro-level discourses that were present within the Italian Canadian world, and that I also needed to find other 'voices' that are often left unheard and unrecognised within the community. With this in mind, in 1999/2000, I approached Italian Canadian youth groups and another significant group that was making its mark on the Italian Canadian community: this was FUORI, a lesbian, gay, bisexual, transgendered (LGBT) group. This group was extremely active within the Canadian and wider Italian Canadian community, as well as the queer community and had a presence at the Toronto Gay Pride event each year. It was during this event in 2001 that I approached FUORI members and made contact with their president. What then followed was a series of visits to their weekly group meetings in the Gay Village, which oftentimes were thematically organised (e.g. experiences of being Italian Canadian and gay; talks by health service and outreach workers; and other organizations such as PFLAG [Parents and Friends of Lesbians and Gays]) and I also organized a focus group interview with members. The participants in this interview were all male.

Entering queer Italian Canadian spaces, as a straight Italian Canadian female, proved to be more problematic than I had initially thought, and I debated how well I would be able to negotiate this site and understand the identities that were performed within them. I had long discussions with my supervisor on this, who was also a gay man. However, these did not unravel some of the ways in which I was positioned by FUORI members, even though I had claimed an Italian Canadian researcher identity and had explained the focus of my research. England (1994: 87) notes that it is not about being able to 'speak' for a particular community but rather it is studying "a world that is already interpreted by people who are living their lives in it". She argues that research becomes "an account of the 'between-ness' of their world" (ibid.) and that of the researcher.

As stated earlier, on the one hand, my own linguistic and cultural experiences afforded me an insider identity, which at times allowed me to connect with the participants' lived experiences. On the other hand, my authenticity and legitimacy as Italian Canadian and as an insider was also questioned in various ways. Many times I was asked: "Where are you from?" or "You don't sound Italian (Canadian)". As Visweswaran (1994: 115) notes, "the question 'where are you from?' is never an innocent one, yet not all subjects have equal difficulty answering" (cited in Henry, 2003: 233).

In the case of one of my participants, Salvatore, this was one of the first questions I was asked, and the way he positioned me as Italian Canadian was based on whether I looked and behaved Italian enough and whether I sounded Italian enough. This was linked to his self-identification and discourses of Italianness. In fact, in his words, his self-identification as Italian Canadian leaned more "towards the Italian side rather than the Canadian side" and he struggled with the possibility of losing his heritage through Anglicization, which he referred to as "being cakerized". In one interview, he put this as follows: "I have always dreaded the fact of losing my heritage. I refuse to be 'cakerized'" (Giampapa, 2004a: 214). He showed intense resistance to being Anglicized and insisted that he was "Italian Italian" (i.e. a 'native'

Italian). He talked about debunking the stereotype of what he sees as the Italian Canadian who maintains minimal links with Italy through customs and food but never ventures across the Atlantic to make the 'real' transnational link to the homeland. He also recalled being told in Italy that he acted and looked "more Italian" and didn't "give off that American, Americano thing" (Preliminary Interview). Looking and acting 'more Italian' rather than being positioned as a typical North American affirmed and legitimised Salvatore's linguistic prowess, acknowledged his behaviour and appearance as 'Italian' and strengthened his claims for social positionings within the Italian world.

Self-identifying and self-positioning in this way, Salvatore initially found it difficult to position me as Italian Canadian because I sounded more Anglicized and I didn't look Italian Canadian enough to him. That is, I didn't dress in a particularly European way or have the same linguistic and cultural experiences because of my Australian upbringing. I had to negotiate and manage this discourse of *italianità*, and claim my position as an 'authentic' and 'legitimate' Italian Canadian in order to be able to enter the various discourse sites in which he performed his identities. This included the home and his workplace where he confided in me about his failed attempts to forge relationships with other Italian Canadians in order to speak (standard) Italian.

Through a dialogic process, in which I got Salvatore thinking about different discursive constructions of *italianità*, he began to reconsider my position as Italian Canadian due to the fact that I had travelled to Italy, that I spoke standard Italian, and that, in his mind, I was engaging with Italian culture through my interest in the Italian Canadian community. For Salvatore, being Italian Canadian was strongly tied to the 'trip to Italy', the transnational experience where he could claim a "wider scale identity" (Specialized Interview) beyond his Calabrese roots. During his visits to Italy, he was acknowledged and confirmed as 'Italian Italian', due to the fact that he spoke standard Italian, as well as his regional dialect.

For Paolo, the question of my location within the discourses of *italianità* was not addressed in this way but through my positioning as an Italian Canadian female with a different regional background from his own. My gender and my non-Calabrese background denied me access into one of the key spaces in which Paolo performed his *italianità*—that is his mother's hometown 'paese' club. This space was significant for Paolo: it made it possible for him to be legitimately positioned as the type of Italian Canadian that he wanted to be. Paolo's self-identification was deeply rooted in his regional heritage as Calabrese, and for him this meant not even acknowledging that his Canadian side played a role. He had this to say about his socialisation as a Canadian:

> No. To tell you the truth I don't think so. It did maybe a negative role . . . I guess it's the way I was brought up. I am Italian. I'm just Italian. (Preliminary Interview)

Regardless of the fact that he was born in Canada, he refused to claim a subject position other than 'Italian', and this was strongly connected to speaking the Calabrese dialect, which he saw as the most important part of his linguistic repertoire. As he states: "I feel proud knowing my dialect . . . I feel the dialect is more important because of the interactions I have with the people I know" (Interview 2).

The social networks that Paolo engaged in were predominantly tied to his family and this included his mother's hometown 'paese' club. This regional club functioned as an important site for Paolo's engagement in his heritage—linguistically and culturally. However, as noted above, entering this site became impossible for me, not only because he positioned me as a regional outsider but also because of my gender. The only way to gain access to this club was either to have been born in that specific Calabrian town, or to be married to or the child of someone from that Calabrian town.

Whereas he stressed that this was an all male club, he added that women were allowed to be members. However, no woman ever came to the actual site of the club because 'it just wasn't done'. My interest in this boundary-marking was piqued, and I certainly made several attempts to try and arrange a visit because Paolo talked at length about being the youngest board member, being positioned by the older members as a young Italian Canadian who valued his heritage by engaging in and organising club events, and who spoke the Calabrian dialect. It was these forms of cultural capital that had gained him respect and access to other symbolic and material resources. However, my gender, my regional heritage and the forms of cultural and linguistic capital that I possessed positioned me in Paolo's eyes as an outsider. Thus I did not have the legitimacy or authority to enter this site.

In these two examples, I have tried to show how my insider role as Italian Canadian was constructed and reconstructed in different ways and how I was positioned in terms of my *italianità*, and in Paolo's case also in terms of my gender. I have also tried to demonstrate the power that these participants had in positioning me in ways that denied access to sites and information, even after spending a considerable amount of time in the field with them.

The final example that I will discuss illustrates the issues that arose as a result of crossing spaces of sexuality and as a result of my decision, as an Italian Canadian heterosexual female, to research what it meant to be Italian Canadian and LGBT. FUORI was created to "promote Italian or Italian Canadian culture in the gay and lesbian community . . . as well as to bridge the gap between the gay and lesbian community and the Italian community" (Focus group Interview 1). As noted earlier, I spent a considerable amount of time in the field working with FUORI and attending their meetings, and I was also invited to attend and participate in a workshop regarding what it means to be Italian Canadian and gay. It was at that meeting that one member stated that 'we need more girls [lesbian women] to come to these events'. Having spent time with this group attending specific evening talks (such as the one organized by PFLAG) and having self-identified early on in the process as an Italian Canadian researcher, I thought I had also indexed my identity as a straight Italian Canadian female. My explanations for doing my research, and in particular for wanting to work with groups that were not always 'permitted' to have a voice within the Italian Canadian community seemed to go unnoticed.

In this respect, FUORI's own agenda became intertwined with my research, and they saw me not simply as a researcher but a potential member and lesbian advocate for their group. Sometimes I felt like an imposter for not 'coming out' and directly stating that I was a straight woman. At other times, I wondered whether this really mattered as I was trying to account for their interpretation of their social world and the way they negotiated their identities across and within an Italian Canadian world that positioned them on its periphery.

In this latter case, becoming embedded within the LGBT community through FUORI, and being on their members' list created a different identity position that I had to deconstruct and problematise during the course of my fieldwork. The complexities of this positioning by these participants and the rapport that was created during the fieldwork permitted a view into the texture of their lives and the way in which this group functioned within the fabric of the Italian Canadian world. These were important insights into the lived experiences of participants who may have been framed as 'marginalised' by the Italian Canadian world but who were resisting and asserting a presence within it. But, as a researcher, I was caught up in their discourse of Italianness, despite my own attempts at self-positioning, and I needed to recognise, analyse and problematise this (see Giampapa, forthcoming).

CONCLUSION

In researching issues of identity and power, my own self-identification and positioning came under scrutiny, and the way in which I was positioned by different research participants had implications for my role as the researcher, my claims to italianità, their positioning of me within the Italian Canadian world and my access to various research sites.

Entering a research field, even one known to a researcher, is a complex process. There are always issues that arise in relation to the researcher's identity, his/her relationships in the field and the shifts and changes that take place as a result of the research process. Researcher identities and power are negotiated and managed, and power is not only exerted by the researcher. Research participants can also exercise their power to question and to provide or deny access to the very sites where identities are performed. My purpose in writing up these field narratives is to make more visible the ways in which we construct the field and the relationships within them. As critical ethnographers, we need to be keenly aware of these processes. My account also raises points for consideration with regard to current models of research training and with regard to the methodological toolkits used to negotiate and understand the social worlds that we observe. These points need further critical reflection and analysis in light of the diversity of research methodologies and tools that are now at our disposal, and, in light of the increasingly diverse, social spaces within which knowledge is now being co-constructed.

REFERENCES

Bourdieu, P. 1991. *Language and Symbolic Power*. Cambridge, MA: Harvard University Press.

Cameron, D., Frazer, E., Harvey, P., Rampton, M. B. H. and Richardson, K. 1992. *Researching Language: Issues of Power and Method*. London: Routledge.

England, K. 1994. Getting personal: reflexivity, positionality, and feminist research. *The Professional Geographer* 46(1): 80–89.

Foster, M. 1994. The power to know one thing is never the power to know all things: methodological notes on two studies of Black American teachers. In *Power and Method: Political Activism and Educational Research*, ed. A. Gitlin, 129–45. New York: Routledge.

Giampapa, F. 2004a. Italian Canadian youth and the negotiation of identities: The discourse on Italianità, language and the spaces of identity. Unpublished doctoral dissertation. Toronto: OISE/UT.

———. 2004b. The politics of identity, representation, and the discourses of self-identification: negotiating the periphery and the center. In *Negotiation of Identities in Multilingual Contexts*, ed. A. Pavlenko and A. Blackledge, 192–218. Clevedon: Multilingual Matters.

———. Forthcoming. The politics of 'being and becoming' a researcher: identity, power and negotiating the field. In F. Giampapa and S. Lamoureux, eds. (Special issue) Voices from the field: identity, language and power in multilingual research settings. *Journal of Language, Identity and Education* 10(3).

Gilbert, M. R. 1994. The politics of location: doing feminist research at "home". *The Professional Geographer* 46(1): 90–96.

Hall, S. and du Gay, P. 1996. *Questions of Cultural Identity*. London: Sage.

Henry, M. 2003. 'Where are you really from?': representation, identity and power in the fieldwork experiences of a South Asian diasporic. *Qualitative Research* 3(2): 229–42.

———. 2007. If the shoe fits: authenticity, authority and agency feminist diasporic research. *Women's Studies International Forum* 30: 70–80.

Herod, A. 1999. Reflections on interviewing foreign elites: praxis, positionality, validity, and the cult of the insider. *Geoform* 30: 313–27.

Hornberger, N. 2006. Negotiating methodological rich points in applied linguistics research: an ethnographer's view. In *Inference and Generalizability in Applied Linguistics: Multiple Perspectives*, ed. M. Chalhoub-Deville, C. Chapelle and P. Duff, 221–40. Amsterdam: John Benjamins.

Mullings, B. 1999. Insider or outsider, both or neither: some dilemmas of interviewing in a cross-cultural setting. *Geoform* 30: 337–50.

Sanghera, G. and Thapar-Björker, S. 2007. Methodological dilemmas: gatekeepers and positionality in Bradford. *Ethnic and Racial Studies* 31(3): 543–62.

Thapar-Björkert, S. and Henry, M. 2004. Reassessing the research relationship: location, position and power in fieldwork accounts. *International Journal of Social Research Methodology* 7(5): 363–81.

Visweswaran, K. 1994. *Fictions of Feminist Ethnography*. Minneapolis: University of Minnesota Press.

Part III

Taking Account of Trajectories

Multilingualism across Social Spaces

Introduction

Monica Heller

The two chapters in this part ask us to think about multilingualism not as the property of an individual, an institution or a fixed geographic space, but rather as dynamic social practices. They put movement in the centre of their reflection, understanding social categories not as given but as constructed, and the process of their construction as having a temporality and a spatiality which sociolinguistics, with its historical concentration on the here and now, has tended not only to under-theorise but also to methodologically neglect. The result is that for many of the questions we ask (about individual multilingual repertoires, about what happens to immigrant children at school or adults at work, about language education policies, and so on), we don't have the data because we haven't focussed on collecting them.

Both authors are centrally concerned with the question of what happens to immigrants to Europe, specifically to the UK, in the early twenty-first century. They ask what kinds of social positions are open to them, and what kinds they seek to negotiate. They ask what kinds of linguistic resources are available to them, and how they do (or do not) mobilise them in the course of their lives, especially for consequential activities like getting health care or a job. Put differently, they ask how language is implicated in the positioning (by self and others) of immigrants in the UK.

By asking their questions in this way they are in fact advocating a move away from the static category of "immigrant". This category, treated as a count noun, invokes assumptions about uniformity, specifically, that all "immigrants" share the label because they have something fundamental in common. From this assumption it is but a short leap to treating all "immigrants" as basically the same, both in terms of their characteristics and in terms of the stability of those characteristics. The only trajectories possible are from there to here, and once here, from other to familiar.

What brought "them" "here" is a process which tends to be neglected in the literature, although postcolonial approaches have done a great deal in the way of insisting that such processes must not be taken for granted and semiotically erased. What happens once "they" are "here" has traditionally been understood as a dichotomous choice between ghettoization and assimilation, which raises the unanswerable question of how to identify the point at which any individual passes over from one category (them) to another (us). Rather than remain locked in this conundrum, the authors suggest that we treat all categorization as a process, requiring action on the part of all participants.

Further, they suggest that analysing such action requires putting together the processes whereby bodies are transported through space with the distribution of linguistic resources, and, although they do not mention this specifically, with the distribution of the right to attribute value to linguistic and other resources, and to judge the performances of others. Seen this way, "immigrants" become the product of intensive discursive work, which takes bodies, sets them moving through space in some ways, assesses the value of their social capital (including the trajectory which brought them onto the market in question in the first place), and then constrains their mobility and their social positioning (though, with any luck, these constraints are not total and some room is left for manoeuvre).

What is at stake here, then, is grasping the complex intertwining and intersections of trajectories. The focus here is on the trajectories of individuals, who not so coincidentally share certain paths, although the authors are careful to point out that those paths are a great deal more complicated than the prevailing notion that they consist of a simple and singular movement from point A to point B. Once that initial complexity is admitted, of course, it becomes necessary to ask what constrains it; that is, what shapes does it tend to take despite its complexity, and why. It also becomes necessary to ask what further opportunities and obstacles it presents, and how people navigate them (accepting them, resisting them, trying to get around, over or under them), as well as what the consequences of their actions may be, for them and for others, and indeed for the very conditions of their mobility or lack thereof. But those trajectories clearly do not exist in a vacuum. Something explains why they even exist, and why those particular bodies, and not some others, are caught up in them.

In addition, something explains their shape. In this regard, it is important to attend to the intersecting trajectories not only of people, but of institutions. There are people who end up working in what is often referred to as "immigrant services", from state officials to social workers to lawyers to housing officers to language teachers. There are the neighbours and the babysitters and the employers (with any luck) and the teachers and the bankers and the person who runs the fruit and vegetable stand on the corner, whose lives intersect for social organisational reasons other than (or in addition to) the discursive institutionalisation of "immigration". And there are the trajectories of the institutions, their practices and their discourses. To begin with, the notion that learning something called "English" in addition to something "else" called, say, "Panjabi", is not ideologically neutral, but is, rather, the emergent product of a long history, in this case, of the

European nation-state and its colonial expansion. One can work out similar genealogies for institutions like community centres, schools, courts of law, or hospitals, just to name some of the central institutions whose trajectories, and whose sense-making, intersect with those of discursively produced "immigrants" (and "English teachers" and indeed "sociolinguists").

Sometimes these trajectories connect in such tightly-knit ways that it is almost impossible to do anything but go with the flow. Sometimes the connection is looser, and opportunities for creative and even consequential action greater. Despite the attention these chapters give to social action, or to individual agency, it remains the case that unless we follow the trajectories of the actors and their actions through, unless we ask what their consequences are, we will not have much useful to say about agency beyond identifying that action happens, that it happens more under certain conditions than others, or that it comes from some kinds of people more than others—that is, we will be able to describe its form, but not its structuring effects (if any, of course). Similarly, without attention to the genealogy of action, we cannot explain why it happens, when it happens, where it happens, who is involved or the form it takes.

Finally, I would like to draw attention to the problem of subjectivity. So far, I have focussed on the ways the chapters by Cressey and Baynham insist on putting the question of "immigration" into movement, on seeing it as a process, not a thing, and how linguistic, spatial, temporal (and, presumably, other symbolic and material) resources are mobilised in the production of the category "immigrant", in the definition of its meaning, and in the consequent constraints on what people inside and outside that category can do about their positioning with respect to it. But I think seeing things this way also raises the question of how people understand these processes from within, that is, what it means to be categorised as "immigrant", or as "ESOL teacher", in a certain place and at a certain time.

In order to understand agency, in other words, I want to argue that we need to understand subjectivity, that is, the sense it makes to construe categories in certain ways, and to embrace them, resist them, tinker with them or ignore them. How people mobilise linguistic resources of course needs to be understood as a function of what they have access to and how social categorization organises that access. But it also needs to be understood as a problem of sense-making; paths imposed, chosen or dug through a mountain of obstacles are matters of investment in ways of being in the world, whether mastered or desired or something in between.

By putting the notion of trajectory front and centre as a mode of sociolinguistic enquiry, these chapters go beyond a first-order equation of immigration with movement, and open up instead a fruitful way of asking questions about social organisation more generally. They also invite reflexion on the ways in which trajectories call for rethinking what we mean by language in relation to society in some quite fundamental ways.

7 Cultural Geography and the Retheorisation of Sociolinguistic Space

Mike Baynham

In preparing this chapter I found myself asking how I became interested in its topic. The answer lies in a series of seminars on narrative in which I was involved in the early 2000s, whose focus might loosely be called explorations in post-Labovian narrative theory. One seminar, with a focus on identity, shaped some of the contributions to the volume *Discourse and Identity* (De Fina, Schiffrin and Bamberg, 2006). Another seminar, on the topic of narrative in time and space, became half a theme issue in *Narrative Inquiry* (cf. Baynham, 2003; De Fina, 2003; Galasinska, 2003; Georgakopoulou, 2003) and shaped the book which Anna De Fina and I edited on *Narratives of Dislocation* (Baynham and De Fina, 2005). As I will discuss later, it was through an effort to retheorise Labov's orientation category, in his writing on narrative, that I became interested in cultural geography. But why narrative? This had been the topic of my doctoral research in the 1980s, a topic which I left aside during the 1990s, years spent in Sydney, when my research concentrated primarily on literacy studies. I returned to the topic when I came back to the UK in the 2000s. It was at this point that I realized the radical unanswerability of the question that had informed my doctoral fieldwork: "what made you come to England?" As I myself answered a similar question ("What made you leave Sydney and come back to England?") which was asked over and over again, often in incredulous tones on my return to England from Australia, this became an object lesson on how narratives shape and reshape reality. For each questioner, each audience, the story was told/is told in subtly different ways, sometimes as a small, allusive narrative in the sense that Bamberg and Georgakopoulou (2008) have identified, a transitory conversational moment, sometimes a larger, baggier story, more copious in detail, more revealing.

THE INTERFACES BETWEEN SOCIOLINGUISTICS AND GEOGRAPHY: A BRIEF GENEALOGY

In turning to cultural geography for retheorizations of time and space, I was aware that geography had been an influence in what we can broadly call dialectology/sociolinguistics since its origins in the later decades of the nine-teenth century. The dialect geographers, such as Gillieron (1902) and Wen-ker (cf. the discussion of his contribution in Mitzka, 1952) to name the most famous, had mapped the distribution and diffusion of dialects in geographi-cal space and indeed the interaction of dialect diffusion with geographical features: boundaries, borders, channels of communication. Dialect maps described or interpreted the distribution of dialect features, using descrip-tive theoretical artefacts such as the isogloss or isogloss bundle. Apparently concerned with the spatial distribution of dialects, the driving force of this movement was in fact temporal/historical: the reconstruction of earlier forms of the language through the evidence of the present and the specification of the laws or tendencies governing its evolution, an instance of the obsession with origins in nineteenth century scholarship. Gramsci started life as a lin-guist, studying at the University of Turin with the dialect geographer Matteo Bartoli, and writing later of this period in the following terms:

> One of the great intellectual 'regrets' of my life is the deep wound I inflicted on my dear professor at the University of Turin, Bartoli, who was convinced I was the archangel sent to destroy the neo-grammarians once and for all. (Antonio Gramsci, March 19, 1927, cited in Ive, 1999)

So, from *its foundational moments*, sociolinguistics has been spatially and temporally located, drawing on the resources and artefacts of geog-raphy, conducting empirical investigations, challenging and refining the sound laws proposed by the neo-Grammarians.

I want to move on now to *a second moment* in sociolinguistic history also deeply influenced by geography, the emergence of urban dialect geog-raphy or dialectology. I would like to locate this broadly in the emergence of the city as an object of study in the modern period, coterminous it seems with the emergence of sociology as an academic discipline. As the impact of the industrial revolution became felt throughout the nineteenth century, writers such as Dickens, Zola and Mrs Gaskell, political theorists such as Engels, activists and philanthropists, Charles Booth in London and Flor-ence Kelley in Chicago engaged with the social deprivation and deprivation of the industrialised city. Both Booth and Kelley pioneered the mapping of social disadvantage through their maps of poverty, another instance of our geographical theme, here the emergence of the map in social theory:

> The Chicago maps produced at Hull House represent an important early effort to supplement social research with maps showing the spa-tial patterns of demographic phenomena. In addition, the Hull House maps presented a model for social activists in the use of maps as per-suasive tools. (Center for Spatially Integrated Social Science, http://www.csiss.org/classics/content/35)

The urban sociology of Georg Simmel (1903), brought to North America by Robert Park in the early years of the twentieth century (cf. Park, Burgess and McKenzie, 1925), informed the development of the distinctive and influential Chicago School of Sociology, with its emphasis, on the one hand, on large-scale surveys, drawing on census and other statistical data, and on the other hand, on the close ethnographic study of neighbourhoods and social and professional groups (cf. Thomas, 1983: 389). As Ruth Cavan shows, the Chicago School systematized and turned into a methodology the maps of poverty of earlier activists:

> Ecological studies consisted of making spot maps of Chicago for the place of occurrence of specific behaviors, including alcoholism, homicides, suicides, psychoses, and poverty, and then computing rates based on census data. A visual comparison of the maps could identify the concentration of certain types of behavior in some areas. Correlations of rates by areas were not made until later. (Cavan, 1983: 415)

The reason I am developing this line of thought is that the Chicago programme looks surprisingly similar to the structure of Labov's urban dialectalogical studies, initially in New York, later in Philadelphia, which again combined large-scale survey methodology with ethnographic neighbourhood studies. We can see this in the way that Labov (2001) introduced cartographically the study of linguistic change in Philadelphia, through a succession of maps that zoom through scales, from region to city to neighbourhood to housing block.

In Figure 7.1 the Philadelphia metropolitan area is contextualised within its region.

In Figure 7.2 neighbourhoods within the city are contextualised within a map of the metropolitan area.

In Figure 7.3, family networks are contextualised within a neighbourhood map.

Midway through this cartographic contextualisation, in a section entitled scopically, "A Direct View of the Blocks", Labov pauses to introduce pen portraits of the neighbourhoods selected for the study "as seen through the eyes of the fieldworkers". He guides his reader as follows:

> It may be helpful here to provide a sketch of the physical and social layout of each block, as seen through the eyes of fieldworkers as they entered the block and made initial contacts. (Labov, 2001: 57)

Using a striking narrative technique, Labov overlays the scopic authorial stance characterised through the succession of maps, with an embodied evocation as if through the eyes of the fieldworkers entering the research site. Embedded in narrative overview is the scene as perceived by the fieldworkers, a bringing in of subjectivity. Here he evokes the moment of entry into the

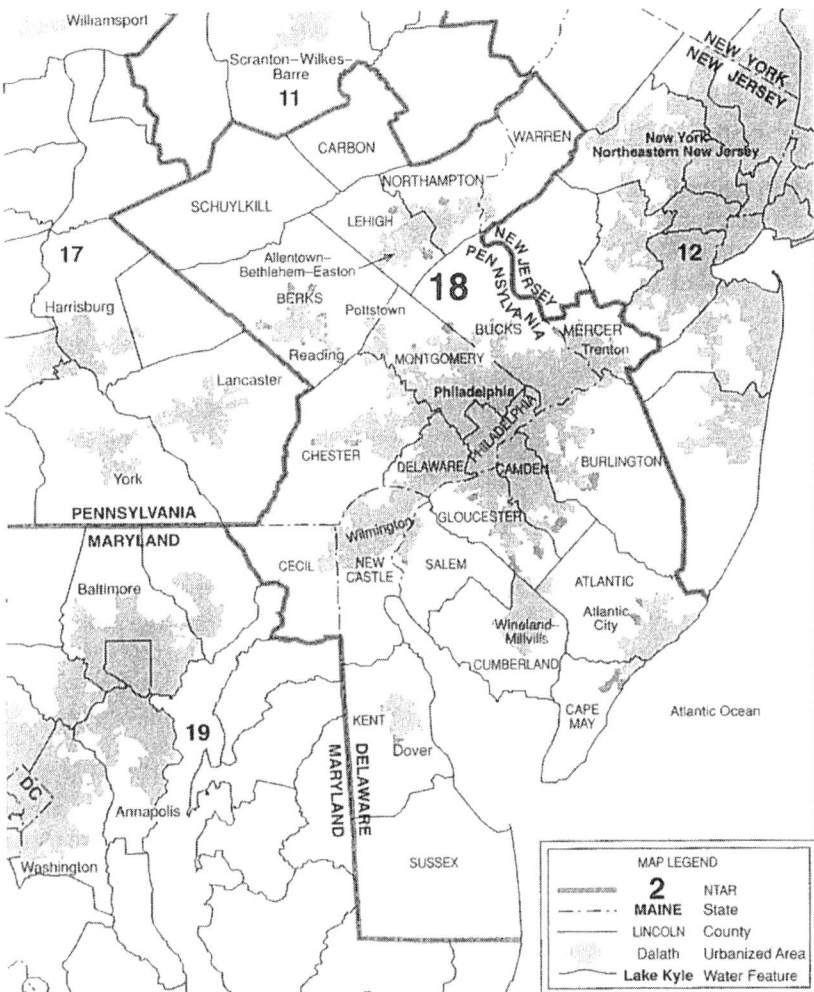

Figure 7.1   Metropolitan area contextualized within region. From Labov, W. (2001). *Principles of Linguistic Change: Social Factors.* Oxford: Blackwell, 43. Reprinted with permission.

field, a key moment in the story/trajectory of the research. Commenting on research of this kind, the postcolonial geographer Blunt (2003) writes:

> More than ever before, scholars working in other disciplines in the humanities are thinking and writing in explicitly spatial terms, most notably in terms of multiple geographies and the multiple and contested spaces of identity, which are often articulated through spatial images such as mobility, location, borderlands, exile and home. (Blunt, 2003: 75–76)

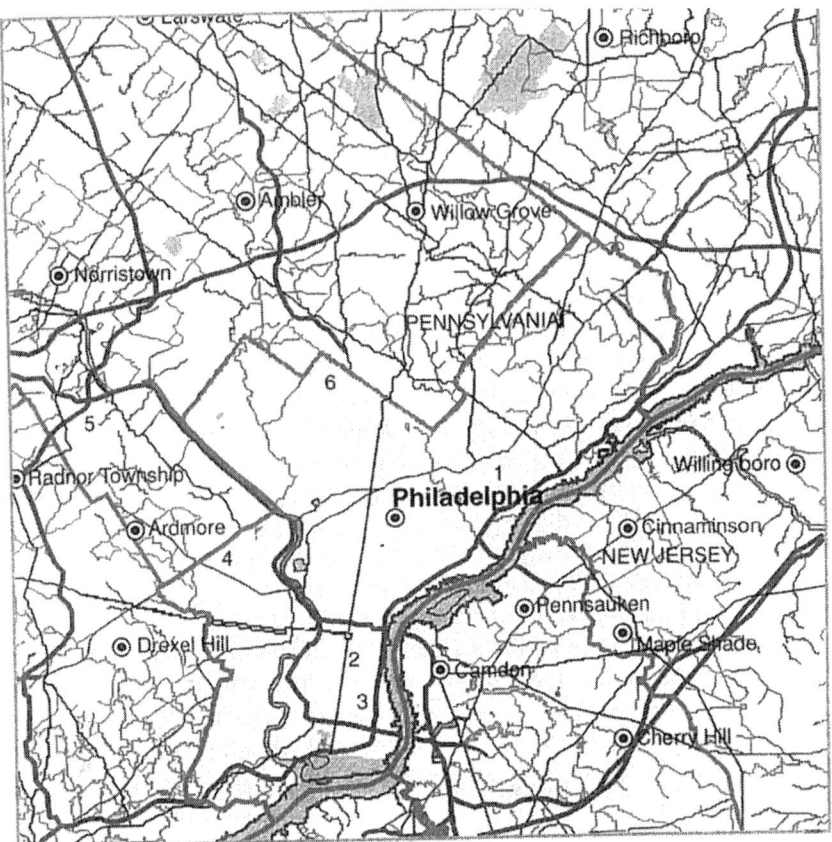

Figure 7.2   Neighbourhoods contextualised within metropolitan area. From Labov, W. (2001). *Principles of Linguistic Change: Social Factors.* Oxford: Blackwell, 45. Reprinted with permission.

It would be not altogether implausible to link the modernist sociolinguistics of urban dialectology with human geography more generally, or indeed the project of rehumanizing geography called by some "humanistic geography" (Castree, 2003):

> The attempt to re-humanize human geography took the form of close and careful studies of individual and group 'lifeworlds'. Two classic examples were David Ley's (1974) exploration of gang 'turf' rivalries in poor inner city neighbourhoods in Philadelphia and Graham Rowles' (1978) detailed analysis of a group of old people's attachment to their homeplace. (Castree, 2003: 170)

From this perspective, the at-homeness of the fieldworker in the field is another means of anchoring the research story in the humanizing lifeworld.

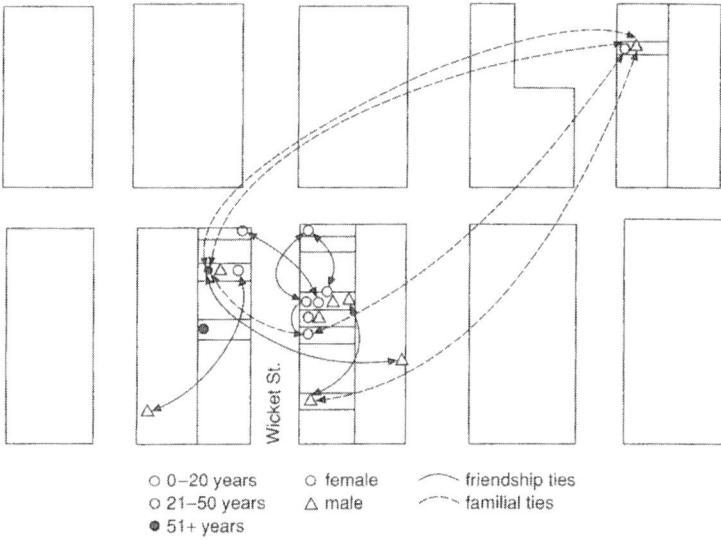

Figure 7.3   Family networks contextualised within neighbourhoods. From Labov, W. (2001). *Principles of Linguistic Change: Social Factors*. Oxford: Blackwell, 52. Reprinted with permission.

In this section, I have tried to show, in the briefest terms, how the methodology of urban dialect geography modelled rather closely in some aspects the working methods of Chicago School sociology, linking the large-scale survey with the small-scale neighbourhood ethnographic study. I have not had the time or opportunity to reconstruct a full intellectual history, just to sketch an outline. In essence, I would like to associate correlational sociolinguistics (establishing links between linguistic phenomena and social phenomena such as class, age, gender) with the modernist sociological project of theorizing the city, profoundly influenced as I have suggested by geographical concepts and rhetorics, not least those of mapping.

My *third sociolinguistic moment* takes us into the dynamics of the present, which I am going to call a performative sociolinguistics. Why performative? I'm referring here to the formative influence of interactional sociolinguistics, itself influenced by ethnomethodology and conversational analysis (CA), which brings to the fore the construction of the social world through talk, in the moment of interaction and encounter. If the focus of correlational sociolinguistics is on the establishment of links between linguistic items (sounds or words), typically taken atomistically, one by one, and social phenomena, the shift in performative sociolinguistics is to a relationship between the linguistic and the social which is dynamically enacted or performative, in the sense that Butler (1990) has made current. It involves a focus on holistic analysis of interactions, texts, events and practices. It is this performative sociolinguistics that I think resonates with the perspectives of cultural geography, as articulated for example by Blunt (2003) earlier. The narrative construction of the fieldworker's move into the field, the crossing of a threshold into someone else's space, the strange that becomes familiar, destabilizes cartographic certainties. It is this step that Labov's fieldworkers are taking willy nilly, even if recuperated into the positivist frame by means of the Observer's Paradox. So, in this third moment, sociolinguistic space becomes an environment that is inhabited, made over through identity work. It is, for example, an "ordinary" corner of Philadelphia as the fieldworkers take hold of and make it over, thus transforming it through their research activity into a consciously theorised sociolinguistic space. This point is made memorably for me by de Certeau in his juxtaposition of language and space/place:

> Thus a North African living in Paris or Roubaix (France) insinuates *into* the system imposed on him by the construction of a low-income housing development or of the French language the ways of "dwelling" (in a house or a language) peculiar to his native Kabyle. He superimposes them and by that combination creates a space in which he can find *ways of using* the constraining order of the place or of the language. (de Certeau, 1988: 30, my emphasis)

I will return to the fieldwork moment in the next section, through an examination of the use of spatial constructs in a study of space and placement practices in Adult ESOL classes, but will finish this section by mentioning the theoretical challenge in moving beyond the local face-to-face orientation implied here and in the humanistic geography described above. The theoretical challenge that I have in mind is that of how to link the face-to-face encounter with larger-scale phenomena. I am thinking here of the work of Blommaert, Collins and Slembrouck (2005) and would argue that the problem of scale is a rhetorical as well as a theoretical problem and, as we have seen in relation to the use of maps in framing the fieldwork for Labov's Philadelphia study, a problem of multimodal rhetoric at that.

EMPLOYING SPATIAL CONCEPTS IN RESEARCH ON ADULT LITERACY AND ESOL PROGRAMMES

In the second half of this chapter, I will show the theoretical challenge of linking face-to-face encounters with large-scale phenomena in a study conducted in the UK with colleagues (Simpson, Cooke and Baynham, 2008; Baynham and Simpson, 2010) and the usefulness of spatial constructs in so doing. The study was based in Adult Literacy and ESOL classes in two Colleges of Further Education, one in London (Rushton College) and one in Yorkshire (Borderlands College). In our fieldwork, we were observing the interactional routines in Adult ESOL classes and conducting interviews with college lecturers and with Adult Literacy and ESOL students. The interviews gave us particular insights into the local institutional processes related to student placement, assessment and progression. The challenge that faced us was that of linking the interactional practices of the ESOL classes, and the insights from the interviews, with the wider institutional practices and wider political processes related to the education of refugees and 'asylum seekers' in the UK. One way in which we approached this challenge was by employing meso-level spatial concepts such as 'liminality' (Turner, 1969), the appropriation of space (de Certeau, 1988), and 'vertical trajectories' (Bernstein, 1999). I turn first to the ways in which we applied the notions of liminality and the appropriation of space.

ESOL AND LITERACY PLACEMENT PRACTICES

This project started with a question: how do ESOL or bilingual students get placed or place themselves in literacy and/or ESOL classes? Whereas colleges or centres in multilingual cities or neighbourhoods might have well-developed ESOL provision, their literacy classes also show huge linguistic diversity. At around Entry Level 3 and Level 1 on the National Qualifications Framework, bilingual students might end up studying in either. What are the institutional and personal practices at play when the decision is made about whether an ESOL or a literacy route is taken at Entry 3 or Level 1?

A key underlying idea of this project is that there are two dimensions to placement: that prospective students are placed in particular types of provision and particular types of classes and that students place themselves in particular types of provision (ESOL or Literacy, under the *Skills for Life* [SfL] framework). This links with ideas in identity work and positioning theory (Baynham, 2006): people position themselves and are positioned (there is obviously also an implicit spatial metaphor in the notion of positioning). So looking at an issue which is apparently "down to earth" and practical , such as how students get placed in particular classes, very soon brings in issues of positioning and identity. How do students place themselves; how are they placed as ESOL or Literacy students? How indeed do they place themselves onto vocational track courses, rather than in SfL provision at all? These are the kind of issues that are raised when we start to look below the surface of student placement.

LIMINAL SPACE IN A COMMUNITY CENTRE

This ESOL Entry 2+ class meets two mornings a week from 9.30 to 12.30 in the Borderlands Community Centre, part of the off-site programme of Bradshaw College. There are twelve students in the group, all women, except for one young male student, a migrant worker from one of the Eastern European new EU accession states. The majority of students are asylum seekers, living in the housing estate surrounding Borderlands, from Congo, Somalia, Eritrea, Algeria, Palestine and Turkey. One student is from the local settled Pakistani community. The majority of students are recruited by word of mouth; the asylum seekers also come to Borderlands for a drop in morning. Some students have been referred to these classes from other sites, because the level is more suited to their needs and because of the crèche. Their classes are held in a large open room, the first which a visitor enters coming into the building. Its grilled windows look out onto a pedestrian precinct with a newsagent, chemist, post office and medical practice. It is also the room through which parents and children must pass to access the crèche, the toilets, and other teaching rooms. On the other side of a closed door is the lively hubbub of the crèche. Occasionally children are brought through to the toilets, and a more enterprising child might break out and run once or twice around the teaching room, before being intercepted and shepherded back into the crèche room. Through all this Sue and the students maintain focus, despite the comings and goings. The students arrive in a piecemeal way, sign the register then start in on individual work, talking quietly to their neighbours. They seem to have grouped themselves in language groupings (e.g. Somali and Arabic). Sue circulates, talking to students individually and in small groups. She has a special late note worksheet on the table nearest to the door.

Sorry I'm late

Because . . . .

It strikes me that one of the issues in this class is that of setting boundaries and creating a pedagogical frame in this very fluid and open ended space. Sue does this very effectively through framing activities, but this excuse sheet is part of the process. Sue then brings this stage of the lesson to a close by collecting the folders in and transitioning to a spelling test (all the while people are moving quietly across the room to other offices or classrooms). A father arrives with the child of one of the students; she leaves to settle him in the crèche. Sue moves into the main body of the lesson, linking it back to the lesson last week and introducing some SfL materials and realistic examples of different kinds of notes and messages. She asks the question: What are they? Why have they been used? (While this is going on Fatima arrives late and rather distressed. Sue settles her down, talking sympathetically in a low voice and I notice not insisting that she complete the late excuse worksheet.) Sue goes on to contrast the different notes and messages in terms of formality/informality of register. The next phase of activity is an SfL exercise on openings and closings in letters and messages. Sue groups the students carefully for the activity, in pairs or individually. The next activity is a story sequencing one, followed by a break. After the break, Sue introduces a role play which the students engage in with some gusto, involving a mother taking a child to the doctor. Viktor throws himself with some gusto into the part of the badly behaved boy!

REFLECTIONS ON THE OBSERVED LESSON

One of the most striking aspects of the lesson is the way that Sue and the students created a busy and focussed pedagogic space out of the "anteroom" in which the class is situated. It is impressive how they manage to maintain concentration. The whole situation evokes for me the concept of "liminality" (Latin limen = threshold). Liminality is a theoretical construct, developed by the sociologist Turner (1969) in his work on ritual to characterise circumstances of "in-between-ness", "neither one thing nor the other". The class is literally situated in an in-between space, in a kind of anteroom where everyone must be able to pass through freely. The liminality of the physical space is echoed in the "in-between-ness" of the asylum seekers' life situation, in a kind of in-between space before the decision to grant refugee status is decided. In this case the liminality can become a way of life; as Sue points out in her interview, decisions can be indefinitely prolonged over as much as five years. The class seems to be characterized by an attitude of "carry on as if", despite the fact that a student's life in this country could be abruptly terminated by a decision not to allow asylum.

UNSAFE SPACE

To think about placement brings in the question of the places where students end up. This could be a classroom in a purpose built college, or in a nineteenth century school building with its separate entrances for girls and boys (another instance of spatial segregation) adapted for the use of twenty-first century students, some of whom for a completely different set of reasons may be in women-only classes. The place where students end up may not be in a purpose built educational site at all, but may be off-site, in a community centre with many purposes, only one of which is educational. Access to particular spaces may be constrained by a range of factors, for example for parents of pre-school children, the question of whether there is crèche provision available. For a disabled person, the class they want to attend on the second floor of an old building without wheelchair access might as well be on the moon. People do not have equal access to particular places. Selma, one of the students we interviewed, shows how access to a particular place (in her case school) can be arbitrarily cut off due to bullying and harassment from male students:

> Selma is originally from Turkey and has been in the UK for over twenty
> years. She is embarrassed about her English and usually tells people she

has been here for less time. She went to school in Turkey until she was 13 and then asked to leave because she was being harassed by the secondary school boys. Her parents were unable to find another school for her and so she stayed at home helping in the house and helping her mother to raise her younger brother. (Notes from interview with Selma)

Poignantly this scenario is repeated when Selma marries and comes to England and a perceived danger again cuts Selma off from education:

During that time Selma went to English classes for the first time. However, the classes took place "down a dark street" where one of her friends was attacked, and then Selma herself was approached one evening. After this incident her husband did not permit her to go to class any more, saying he did not want Selma "to die in this country". (Notes from interview with Selma)

The sense of dangerous space is carried on in Selma's feelings about her teenage daughter whom she accompanies to school:

The class she is in now suits her because it is near her daughter's school; although her daughter is 15 Selma walks her to and from school every day. She is scared that what happened to her will happen to her daughter, as she is "very beautiful" and because London is "very dangerous". (Notes from interview with Selma)

Similar experiences of unsafe space are expressed by another student, Victoria:

Victoria, a literacy student from Zimbabwe, explained how a threatening encounter with a male student in X College deterred her from going back to the institution. Victoria said that after the incident she felt very nervous about being in the college. The attention she got from men at the college made her feel really uncomfortable. She was glad to be out of the place because she didn't want to be in a college where she feared for her safety. It was clear that X's associated problems of street gangs, knife and gun crimes had also played a critical role in Victoria's constructions of the college as a threatening and 'unsafe' space for her to be in.

APPROPRIATING SPACE

Cultural geographers suggest that people occupy and make over places, appropriating spaces through their practical activity. For example, Sue, the Borderlands ESOL teacher, was teaching her off-site class in the open plan room close to the entrance to the community centre as described above.

She and the students needed to appropriate that space. It was striking to observe how effectively Sue and the students created a learning space out of quite unpromising conditions.

MOVING ON AND UP: ABSTRACT SPACES, LEARNING PATHWAYS AND QUALIFICATIONS LADDERS

As well as the physical and social spaces where students end up, there is another more abstract dimension to the spatial practices of placement. Students are assessed and placed according to the SfL national levels (Pre-Entry to Level 2), which create, in effect, an abstract space that they move through as they progress, through achieving qualifications, towards ever higher levels. The strong spatial metaphors at work in such discourses (moving *up* a level) suggests the value of examining how progression is constructed as a spatial process:

> So the . . . the idea, the course is to move up . . . move on, into Entry 3 ESOL but to . . . to contextualise it, so that instead of doing, say, the Skills for Life materials which are about somebody . . . other . . . well, I can't think of what . . . you know, everything they learn will be about . . . the language will be around child care, but it's still at Level 3 . . . Entry 3. (Interview with Carrie)

The language of levels and of the qualifications framework constructs learning, progress and achievement in terms of what Bernstein (1999) calls "a vertical trajectory" (see Moss, 2000, for a discussion of this). Students move up and on through ever higher levels which can be aligned with other kinds of achievement and qualifications (GCSE English for example). SfL is currently evaluated through performance in moving students through this vertical trajectory, measured by performance in exams. A horizontal trajectory would map student achievement not just through the vertical movement through qualifications, but through achievements that cannot be quantified in exam passes: ability to speak with and make friends with neighbours, for example, or increasingly informed participation in children's schooling. In Rushton College, none of the students speak English outside the classroom except in service encounters such as shopping, going to the doctor's and so on. There was a general agreement that by coming to ESOL classes they could now do a lot of things they were previously unable to do. One student, Naima, expressed this as follows, when she was asked how she felt about speaking to different kinds of people:

S: Especially English person. I used to feel—nervous . . . nervous or something. They speak very fast. What if she ask me and I can't

do anything? Especially doctor [laughter] . . . I had to take someone with me.

MC: Just in case?

S: Yeah, I don't understand. Now actually I can tell my problem to
doctor, or to my son's school. (Interview with Naima)

This is an example of a horizontal trajectory: achievement and progress
that cannot be measured in terms of a vertical trajectory of qualifications.

What is interesting is how the abstract spaces of a national framework of SfL levels are similarly made over and appropriated by users as
we noticed with the physical and social spaces described above, with the
values of certain levels shifting over time. The exam itself, and the Level
2 literacy qualification, are not valued by employers, contends Raminder,
one of the literacy tutors. She attributes this to the narrow range of literacy skills it tests:

> Employers don't value the Level 2 exam because I did a little work at
> the College as well, last (. .) last year. I did a bit last year, and the year
> before last. And again they were all doing Level 1 . . . um Level 2 exams.
> [. . .] in the literacy. And again it was all multiple choice questions.
> And I got to . . . I couldn't quite understand why employers weren't
> valuing a Level 2, um, qualification. (Interview with Raminder)

A qualification can be set at a particular point on a qualifications ladder
with equivalences established between other qualifications. But if it is not
taken up and valued, if it is not "inhabited" as it were by its users, it won't
become established but remain an empty valueless shell. The qualifications
ladder creates a graded abstract space which students move through, on
and up, but like other kinds of space, if this is not appropriated and valued
it becomes meaningless.

The qualifications ladder has consequences which can again "wash
back" to influence student placement, as our research in Rushton College
makes clear:

> Classes up to Entry 3 have a parallel literacy course, called e.g. ESOL
> Entry 3 Lit. Students are placed on these courses because they have a
> "gap" between their speaking and reading/writing. The concept of the
> "gap" is a key motif in discussions around literacy and how to place
> students correctly. Jane also believes that the Cambridge exams now
> in place at Rushton in the ESOL department have forced the depart-
> ment to place students more according to their literacy rather than their
> speaking because many of them are struggling with the Cambridge
> reading and writing exams, and they are obliged to do all "modes" to
> get through a level. (Field notes)

The way the exams are structured, in particular the requirement to pass all modes, structures the placement practices, demonstrating the way that the abstract space of the qualifications ladder, shapes and influences student deployment into classes. Both spaces are intimately interconnected.

Another kind of example of this differential valuing and its consequences can be found at Rushton. It seems that for the ESOL department at Rushton the vertical trajectory of levels is not equal between ESOL and Literacy:

As we learned from our interviews, the department has clear guidelines about how people get placed at a level if they are ESOL students: an ESOL level is regarded as a level below literacy; i.e. ESOL Entry level 3 is counted as the equivalent of Entry level 2, literacy. So, some students (e.g. Ahmed, see the interview below) have done E3 ESOL already and are now doing E3 literacy. The equivalence of levels (or the lack of equivalence) is something that is locally interpreted. And, as our study revealed, both staff and students share this interpretation. There is a strong sense that ESOL is seen as a lower level, or something that you "finish" and then move on from. ESOL is associated with slower progress and with low level speaking, as shown in this extract from a conversation with Ahmed which took place in the classroom with other students present:

MC: Can you compare this class with the ESOL class?

A: Yeah. The ESOL class . . . the ESOL class is, you know, is, like, just basic English, but here is, you know, more writing, reading, writing.

MC: More writing?

A: More writing . . . writing and spellings.

MC: So when you say basic English, what do you mean?

A: Basically just, you know, speaking and they give some, you know, some . . . Grammar . . . grammatic words . . . easier. In ESOL they do missing words like . . . easy words . . . missing words, tense, past tense . . .

MC: Yeah.

A: present tense, words, which one is right and that.

MC: Right.

A: Then, basically, grammar specialist is better, I think, is ESOL class.

MC: For grammar?

A: Basically it's lower than this class I know it is hard to write letter, how to, er, mistake your letter and improve with it. And it's better this . . . this is like quality of writing, and the thing, you know, you know.

M: Yeah, I know what you mean.

A: More improving in here.

MC: Yes.

A: [So that's what I mean.]
MC: [Addressing the class as a whole] Do you all agree with him?
Ss: Yeah . . . Yeah.

So here it seems that, in terms of progression, moving from ESOL to Literacy is definitely a move on and up the progression ladder. In terms of de Certeau's (1988) notion of the appropriation of space, users shape and reshape abstract notions such as progression, through rating one type of provision more highly than another. They thus alter the "pre-fabricated" design of the SfL levels which does not, in itself, suggest that a given level in ESOL should be differently valued than "the same" level in Literacy. To try and explain why that might be I will go on to look at space in relation to centre and periphery.

LEARNING SPACES: CENTRAL AND PERIPHERAL

The notion of central and peripheral learning spaces may be useful in considering the relationship between off-site and on-site courses and also, as I have suggested above, in considering the relationship between Literacy and ESOL sub-areas of the SfL framework. Progression is constructed as movement from ESOL to Literacy or onto vocational courses. Lynne, one of the tutors, talked of one student 'who clearly was an ESOL student', who had been in the UK for a number of years and who wanted to join a literacy class ('He probably felt he was moving on from ESOL.'). Progression was also constructed as movement, either actual or desired, from off-site to main site. It seemed that the off-site *Pathways to Working with Children* course, run in a community centre on a housing estate, was of a lower level than the equivalent course run on the main site. As one member of our research team wrote: "There is very much the sense that this is a lower level 'poor relation' to the next level childcare courses and that C is very unclear of the level required for her students to be able to get onto those courses" (Field notes).

CONCLUSION

The argument of this chapter has been that spatial constructs have been crucial to the development of sociolinguistics and, informed by concepts derived from cultural geography and elsewhere, are of central use in a performative sociolinguistics. Using as an example research into space and placement in Adult ESOL classes, I have tried to show how both physical and social spaces can raise issues of access, how spaces are appropriated, made over and used and how the levels and qualifications ladders of a curriculum framework are saturated with spatial metaphors, well described by Bernstein's (1999) "vertical trajectory". I have shown how there is an obvious washback from the qualifications ladder, into the placement process, leading to students being placed in terms of literacy level rather than spoken language and have suggested that some of these processes can be explained in terms of notions of central and peripheral space. Students, teachers and curriculum managers, as well as other key players such as employers, inhabit and shape curriculum and qualifications spaces, valuing some, devaluing others and these spatial and ideological processes are influenced by shifts in the directions of policy.

REFERENCES

Bamberg, M. and Georgakopoulou, A. 2008. Small stories as a new perspective in narrative and identity analysis. In *Text and Talk* special issue: Narrative Analysis in the Shift from Texts to Practices, ed. A. De Fina and A. Georgakopoulou.

Baynham, M. 2003. Narrative in time and space: beyond 'backdrop' accounts of narrative orientation. *Narrative Inquiry* 13(2): 347–66.

———. 2006. Performing self, family and community in Moroccan narratives Of migration and settlement. In *Discourse and Identity*, ed. A. De Fina, D. Schiffrin and M. Bamberg, 376–97. Cambridge: Cambridge University Press.

Baynham, M. and De Fina, A. (eds) 2005. *Dislocations/Relocations: Narratives of Displacement*. Manchester: St Jerome.

Baynham, M. and Simpson, J. 2010. Onwards and upwards: space, placement and liminality in adult ESOL classes. *TESOL Quarterly* 44(3): 420–40.

Bernstein, B. 1999. Vertical and horizontal discourse: an essay. *British Journal of Sociology of Education* 20(2): 157–73.

Blommaert, J., Collins, J. and Slembrouck, S. 2005. Spaces of multilingualism. *Language and Communication* 25: 197–216.

Blunt, A. 2003. Geography and the humanities tradition. In *Key Concepts in Geography*, ed. S. Holloway, S. P. Rice and G. Valentine, 73–91. London: Sage.

Butler, J. 1990. *Gender Trouble: Feminism and the Subversion of Identity*. New York: Routledge.

Castree, N. 2003. Place: connections and boundaries in an interdependent world. In *Key Concepts in Geography*, ed. S. Holloway, S. P. Rice and G. Valentine, 165–185. London: Sage.

Cavan, R. S. 1983. The Chicago School of Sociology 1918–1933. *Journal of Contemporary Ethnography* 11: 407–20.

de Certeau, M. 1988. *The Practice of Everyday Life*. Berkeley: University of California Press.

De Fina, A. 2003. Crossing borders: time, space, and disorientation in narrative. *Narrative Inquiry* 13(2): 367–91.

De Fina, A., Schiffrin, D. and Bamberg, M. (eds) 2006. *Discourse and Identity*. Cambridge: Cambridge University Press.

Galasinska, A. 2003. Temporal shifts in photo-elicited narratives in a Polish border town. *Narrative Inquiry* 13(2): 393–411.

Georgakopoulou, A. 2003. Plotting the "right place" and the "right time": place and time as interactional resources in narratives. *Narrative Inquiry* 13(2): 413–32.

Gillieron, J. 1902. *Atlas Linguistique de France* (13 volumes). Paris: Champion.

Ive, P. 1999. Gramsci and the so-called 'linguistic turn' (a discussion and dissertation abstract). *International Gramsci Society Newsletter* 9 (March): 42–45, http://www.italnet.nd.edu/gramsci/igsn/articles/a09_12.shtml (accessed 5 May 2007).

Labov, W. 2001. *Principles of Linguistic Change: Social Factors.* Oxford: Blackwell.

Mitzka, W. 1952. *Handbuch zum Deutschen Sprachatlas.* Marburg: N. G. Elwert Verlag.

Moss, G. 2000. Informal literacies and pedagogic discourse. *Linguistics and Education* 11: 47–64.

Park, R. E., Burgess, E. and McKenzie, R. 1925. *The City.* Chicago: University of Chicago Press.

Simmel, G. 1903. *Die Grosstädte und das Geistesleben.* Dresden: Petermann.

Simpson, J., Cooke, M. and Baynham, M. 2008. *The Right Course: An Exploratory Study of Learner Placement Practices in Adult ESOL and Literacy.* London: NRDC.

Thomas, J. 1983. Chicago Sociology: an introduction. *Journal of Contemporary Ethnography* 1: 387–95.

Turner, V. 1969. *The Ritual Process.* London: Routledge and Kegan Paul.

8   Diaspora Youth, Ancestral Languages and English as 'Translation' in Multilingual Space

Gill Cressey

Alijaun, a ten-year-old boy from Balsall Heath in Birmingham, UK, told me with great conviction that '*pani* tastes different than water'. *Pani* is Panjabi for water. In his bilingual experience, taste is evidently not just a function of the body but also a function of the mind and of language and the culture it carries. To translate *pani* simply as water does not translate the meaning of water in different environmental and social contexts; it does not convey tasting different.

This chapter is about young people's English as 'translation' in diaspora space (Brah, 1996) in multilingual neighbourhoods in Birmingham, UK. Stuart Hall's term translation (Hall, 1992) challenges the idea of assimilation and gives space for a complex performance of migrated cultural practice and a shifting pattern of belonging. Based on ethnography with young people living in Britain and retaining transnational links with ancestral homelands, this chapter uses young people's accounts of their daily conversations to examine the place of English in their common lives. In this sense of translation, English becomes a medium of communication between people with a myriad of mother tongues. The narratives of the young people take bilingualism in English and in mother tongue to be the norm; and by this they mean being bilingual in competence, attitude and function and, in some cases, origin (Skutnabb-Kangas, 1984). Chain migration means that there are new migrants arriving from 'homelands' into the diaspora neighbourhood with limited English and 'native-speaker' fluency imported direct from 'home'. Translation in this context reverts to its other narrower meaning. This is of particular significance when the new arrival is the young person's wife or husband.

The quotations in italics come from transcribed interviews and group interviews with young people aged between fourteen and nineteen, in the Sparkbrook ward of Birmingham, UK, and accounts of local multilingual practice are derived from the findings of an ethnographic study I conducted in the same neighbourhood over a five year period from 2000 to 2005, on 'diaspora youth and ancestral homelands'. *(M)* stands for young man, *(F)* stands for young woman and alternative first names have been used to replace the young people's real names. Sparkbrook is an inner city neighbourhood of a big city; it has received successive waves of immigrants to meet Birmingham's labour needs. The young people interviewed for this study are all British born children and grandchildren of Pakistani or Kashmiri immigrants. Many Pakistani and Kashmiri immigrant workers came after the Second World War in the 1950s and 1960s. First, men came to work in foundries and factories; later their families came to join them.

> Zubair (M)
> *Dad was first generation from Mirpur (Kashmir side). He lived in a house—there were ten men, five on the night shift and five on the day. He never learned the language, never saw the need, just stuck to his own and later on took me to translate from when I was young to doctor's or the housing or wherever.*

Whereas professional translating and interpreting services use the term translate to involve text and 'interpret' to involve spoken language, common usage of the word 'translate' can mean either or both of these. Zubair's use of the idea of 'translate' is a recollection of going with his father to the doctor's or the housing department: his dad spoke in Panjabi and, to the best of his ability, he told the doctor or official what his father had just said in English. Whereas such childhood experiences could be the basis of a research study, this is not the main focus of this chapter. Rather this chapter is an exploration of cultural translation as discussed by cultural theorists such as Bhabha (1992) and Hall (1992). Stuart Hall uses the term translation to describe those group identities constructed by people who have left their homelands forever and now have lives that cut across frontiers. They retain links with their parent's places of origin and their traditions and cultural and language practices, but have no illusion of return. The narratives of the young people in my ethnographic study present an opportunity to assess the degree to which the young people could be considered translated; and their attitudes to use of the English language are an important part of their story and identity.

> Bilaal (M)
> *I'm bilingual yeh, but no you couldn't say I'm bicultural. I've got one culture (British Pakistani) but two languages. I'm better at English than Panjabi but I'm not culturally English, not at all.*

In *The Black Atlantic* Paul Gilroy suggests that the term diaspora should be "cherished for its ability to pose the relationship between ethnic sameness and differentiation: a changing same" (Gilroy, 1993: xi). Bilaal, a young diaspora man living in the UK, exemplifies this by claiming that 'British Pakistani' is one culture. He claims that he has not assimilated and become English just because of his fluency in English language, but is part of a changed diaspora which includes being multilingual and monocultural.

A diasporic perspective acknowledges the ways in which identities have been and continue to be transformed through relocation, cross-cultural exchange and interaction (Gillespie, 1995). Diaspora conjures up meta-phors of travel and of identities in a process of transition, with members of diaspora communities engaged as 'cross-cultural navigators' (Parekh, 2000); or translators translating identities and cultures across contrasting settings in time and space. Translating the definite article between English and Panjabi languages appears to be relatively straightforward compared with translating between Pakistani culture, British-Pakistani culture and other cultures in Britain including the dominant English culture influenced by US and European cultures.

> If in a given society certain groups can be identified in terms of ethnic, cultural or linguistic characteristics, these will become salient features, perceived as such by the individual and used by him for ethnic, cultural or linguistic categorization. (Hamers and Blanc, 1989: 119).

For all of these young people, their socio-cultural reality is complex and like Bilaal they categorise their own lives in terms of multiple, contingent options and combinations. Their self-categorisation does not have to mean that they harbour separatist sentiments. The young people talk a lot about mixing and interacting with diverse groups of people at work or at college or within neighbourhood settings such as sports and social events.

> Jabal (M)
> *If you don't interact then you don't learn and if you don't learn then you're going to be naïve and dumbstruck about what's going on around you. So I think it is good to interact—I don't see no reason why you can't.*

According to Avtar Brah (1996: 16),

> 'diaspora space' (as distinct from the concept of diaspora) is 'inhabited' not only by diasporic subjects but equally by those who are constructed and represented as 'indigenous'. As such, the concept of *diaspora space* foregrounds the entanglement of genealogies of dispersion with those of 'staying put'.

Jabal is clearly in favour of people, who finding themselves inhabiting the same diaspora space in an urban neighbourhood, interact in order for each person to be aware of their social setting and in order to learn and extend the range of understanding that each person has access to.

English is often used as the language in common within the neighbour-hood between multilingual residents but which English? Between young people it is often vernacular English, whereas say in the mosque or in business transactions people try with varying levels of success to speak 'standard' English. *Nadim (M)* described it like:

> *having a switch in your brain that has three settings: fully English, Panjabi or both.*

Nadim is pointing out that bilingualism is not just about competence in two distinct languages and cultures, but is about contingency and an ability to switch repeatedly and to use both together in order to express oneself as a whole bilingual or multilingual person. Nadim's three settings have a range of variations in between the settings from standard to vernacular English, from stylised Asian English to Panjabi with English vocabulary adopted within it, to Panjabi learned from grandparents from rural Panjab; and 'both'. Furthermore, as Ben Rampton (1995) has reported, young people in British inner city diaspora communities have developed a stylised Asian English. He found stylised performance of Asian English common in local adolescent discourse and described it as a subterfuge used to undermine white authority figures.

> Al Hasan (M)
> *My mates call me Honky because I just speak normal English all the time, I don't vary: like, this is who I am wherever, whenever. When they're together they speak, like, street English, mixing in their latest lyrics and phrases from hip-hop raps and fake Jamaican and bits of village slang in a mixed-up chat. But I just stick to English no matter what, even this English girl told me that's weird.*

Al Hasan is slightly mocked by his peers for not joining them in using 'mixed-up chat', the term they have chosen as his nick-name is a New York Black American vernacular derogatory term for White man. So, in being called Honky, Al Hasan is being told that his allegiances are too close to White authority figures.

I witnessed a group of young men hanging around outside a youth club building on a summer's evening. Some of them appeared to be British Pakistanis, some of them I know to be, and others appeared to be African-Caribbean or mixed race. A White police officer pulled up in a marked car and asked them what they were up to. They replied 'nothing to worry about, officer' in standard English and also switched from informally chatting with each other in Birmingham-dialect English to casually speaking in Panjabi or Patois to one another. It seemed to be a game of provoke and undermine the lone English speaking police officer. Likewise the young people have told me that they use Panjabi in school to 'leave out' the teachers.

> Babar (M)
> *I speak Patwari but I have problems with it they can tell I'm from here. My grandparents used to really make jokes out of me speaking*

my own language. The funny thing is because I've got mixed friends and I've got Sikh Panjabi friends and I've got friends from other places like Afghans so I pick up little bits and bobs from everyone . . . somehow I've made my own language.

Les Back and Anoop Nayak rounded off their book *Invisible Europeans?: Black People in the 'New Europe'* with lyrics by the Birmingham based musician 'Apache Indian' and described how:

He performs and expresses himself through snatches of Jamaican patois, Punjabi and a culturally diverse vernacular English. This language is part of a wider urban experience and symbolises the dynamic culture of Birmingham. (Back and Nayak, 1993: 143)

I imagine that Donna Haraway would love this because in 'A Cyborg Manifesto' she argues that we need to speak together 'a blasphemous heteroglossia' so that our common language doesn't always turn out to be that of the dominant (Haraway, 1991).

Homi Bhabha comments that culture as a strategy of survival is both transnational and translational. It is translational in reaction to spatial histories of displacement making the question of how culture signifies or what is signified by culture a rather complex issue that needs a social response within specific contextual locations and social systems. Translation is a process of the construction of culture and invention and reinvention of tradition (Bhabha, 1992). He uses the idea of translation to discuss the ways in which identity is negotiated and performed in the course of cultural transition. This is a related but different use of the term translation than the term used for taking text in one language and then writing a text in another language attempting to approximate in meaning as closely as possible to the first text. For one thing the majority of the language use that the young people are referring to is spoken and therefore could perhaps be thought of as interpreted rather than translated. For another there are not simply two languages involved; there are dialects, local vernacular, language appropriation and creative mixes in play too. There are also shared cultural meanings that are impossible to interpret or translate from one language and culture to another.

Nabila (F)
Our dialect is sweet. Some ways of thinking and saying things in it I just can't explain to you in any other language, when I want to think about those I have to think in our language. It's like certain music don't sound right on a piano only on a harmonium.

What is most interesting to Homi Bhabha is that which cannot be translated culturally. He draws our attention to the challenge faced in the articulation of cultural differences of dealing with what cannot be translated because it has no equivalent. The example this chapter opened with quoting Alijaun about the translation of 'water' is a good example of this. Another example is expressing the idea of 'Biraderi': extended family as understood in culturally specific terms by Pakistani people both in Pakistan and in the diaspora. There is no direct equivalent to 'biraderi' in English. Perhaps the closest would be 'clan'. In order to convey the meaning of 'biraderi' to me using English, Al Hasan resorted to reference to 'Black' cultural terminology.

Al Hasan (M)
One word I always drop into English in our language is 'biraderi'. They're called 'biraderi', like Aunty Taj is our biraderi (not direct family exactly) 'cause of being the same caste, lineage, tribe, village . . . kind of thing . . . your people. How can I explain it to you? The only equivalent here would be . . . well, there isn't really that here. You know how the Black man says 'brethren' or 'blood' or 'bro'' we say 'biraderi'.

Even when there is a direct equivalent in English, sometimes multilingual people think more naturally and fluently in a particular language of choice for particular purposes.

Tahira (F)
I was always sharper at Maths than the rest because I could think about Maths in Panjabi.

Tahira explained to me that there are certain tasks and topics that she thinks about in Panjabi even though she is a fluent English-speaker with a colloquial Birmingham accent. An example she chose was that she can do Maths in Panjabi and thinks about it using the methods taught to her at home in Panjabi, but then she finds it nearly impossible to explain her method or to defend her answer in English to the Maths teacher at school. Just like '*pani* tastes different than water', certain thoughts need to be thought in Panjabi; and Maths is easy in Panjabi but hard in English.

Hassan (M)
When I'm in Pakistan I say I'm Pakistani, in Britain I say British. It depends like who you're talking to and it depends where you are. The way I see it, patriotism and things like that I don't believe in really. The world's big with so many countries. You don't have to be patriotic to wherever you travel to or even live. You travel wherever you can learn the language, learn the culture. It's more about your self.

Hassan's contingent attitude to adapting his language and culture according to where he is, who he is with and what is happening is fairly typical of the attitude of many other British Pakistani young people I interviewed. They are resistant to being restricted by categories and labels into monocultural, mononational boxes.

Fareeda (F)
I was born in England, my parents are Pakistani and I would say I am Pakistani first although I don't always feel Pakistani probably . . . but I think it is because I am not white so I am not English as such and I maybe look more Pakistani so therefore I am Pakistani. When I speak our language I count myself in 'apne' (one of us) and I mean Pakistani. I never call myself Asian, never, never.

Identity is very topical and significant among young people. Often they will identify themselves as 'a Muslim', 'a Christian', 'a Sikh' etc. They are tagging themselves/naming themselves/marking themselves out. But what does this mean? If they identify with being a Muslim, does this mean they are knowledgeable, practising, members of religious organisations or worshipping congregations—no, not necessarily. It means that they are showing their allegiances in a social and political world that is divided and demands declarations of allegiance one way or another from us all.

Karl Mannheim published influential work on 'the problem of generations' (Mannheim, 1928) which formed the foundation of modern generation research. He contended that within each society there can be a number of differentiated generation units each developing its own style and consciousness. The idea of generation linked to theories of assimilation and of language shift leads to a notion that each generation post migration gets more assimilated and makes less reference to the culture of the 'homeland'; likewise that each generation post migration loses 'homeland language' and shifts towards adoption of the dominant language in the place of settlement, eventually leading to 'death' of 'mother tongue'. However, chain migration patterns interrupt this neat proposition. Chain migration means that not all older people arrived at the same time as each other in Britain. On the whole, Pakistani and Kashmiri men arrived years before their wives joined them in the UK, and in many cases children stayed with their mothers and arrived with them having lived apart from their fathers in the 'homeland'. Also, young people are still arriving having married British born young people. Several of the British born young people interviewed for this study are married to cousins who are 'first generation' immigrants. All of the respondents have been through or are going through the British education system. Whether they have done well in the terms of that system or not, their years of education in English medium set them apart from their parents and from newly arrived migrants. Many families span a great spectrum of schooling and educational experiences and of degrees of literacy (in English or in Urdu or both). Very few of the respondents learned English from one native-speaker parent and another language from the other native-speaker parent. Some have learned at least two spoken languages in the family from the beginning from bilingual parents; others learned a mother tongue in the family first and later learned English at school. Many learned at least two languages in their extended family from a mixture of bilingual relatives and mother tongue speaker relatives. For example, one young woman learned Patwari from conversations between her grandmother and parents in the home and English from conversations with her older brother and her parents. When she started school her English was reinforced and extended both formally and informally. She became literate in English and through supplementary education at Mosque she became semi-literate in Urdu and in Qur'anic Arabic.

There are powerful tensions confronting them concerning whether and how they will participate in community life. As young people they see many issues acutely as if for the first time as they shed childish naiveties on their transition to adulthood. As their awareness heightens to issues affecting their lives of the past and the future, they have very sharp perceptions to offer. During this period of life they are struggling to make sense of their subjectivity of their relationships with other people and key institutions. They are not passive in this process but exercise agency and choice. In their struggles for identity and coherence, there is a reflection of the struggles of all of us for a secure sense of selfhood and self-worth.

Language choices play a significant part in exploring and asserting identity, naming, cultural belonging and allegiance. Ability to code-switch is a resource for constructing a sense of self and of community. These young people are very adept at language crossing and this becomes part of their repertoire for showing where they stand. For example when Pakistan won a cricket game in June 2009 I drove through Sparkbrook, an iconic Pakistani neighbourhood in Birmingham, and there were street celebrations going on. There was a convergence of young people driving through the streets waving Pakistan flags from the windows and roofs of the cars, leaping out and setting off fireworks on the roadside and jumping back into the cars. Outside the local Pakistani restaurants there were crowds with flags and with clothing and face paint to show their support for the Pakistan cricket team. In this celebration the language in the air, the chants, the chat was colloquial Panjabi because that fitted perfectly into the occasion. The same young people could be in school or college the next day using 'standard' English to communicate with their teacher, vernacular English with Panjabi and Patois mixed in at break times with their friends and Panjabi with English thrown in at home in the evening with extended family. In the background there would be as much likelihood of a Bollywood movie in Hindi as a Hollywood movie in North American English on the television screen. Then an elder in the family may regain the remote control and summon an Urdu speaking religious commentator into the living room. This is a portrait of local diaspora multilingual practice; it is normality for the young people involved. They are sufficiently competent in more than one language to be able to code-switch between colloquial and official language practices; they have a positive attitude to using more than one language and to mixing and matching; and they choose which form of language to use to fit the function for which language is required (Skutnabb-Kangas, 1984).

Due to the diaspora practice of endogamous marriages, still frequently involving migration of one partner from the 'homeland' to Britain, translation of language and culture continues within a transnational direct link. Ongoing chain migration means that rather than being part of a diaspora that results from one episode of exodus and migration, these young people are accustomed to being part of a community of constant migrations and new arrivals from the 'homeland' to the extended family in the UK. One of the main reasons for new arrivals is still marriage between a Pakistani citizen and a British citizen; then the husband or wife arriving to join their spouse in the UK. Migration is a normal part of community life and displacement is routine for the community no matter how much it is a dramatic change for the individual.

Ishrat (F)
I think of myself as British and Pakistani not just British cos at the end of the day we're brought up in England and we're British in that way but we are brought up by and around Pakistanis and we can't you know forget that our parents are from Pakistan. My husband's from there too so it carries on.

Hassan (M)
It's good for me that I know that way of life. I want my children to have that too. If I could afford it I'd keep taking them backwards and forwards so that they can know about their culture and keep up speaking our language fully. Now they are small and their Mum speaks our language with them, they got English off TV and now nursery.

An extended family gathered for a meal that I was invited to. A young man called Ansar told me that he never speaks Panjabi, only English because *'English from round here is my language'*. His mother then entered the room and asked him a question in Panjabi and he replied in Panjabi effortlessly. I said that I thought he just said that he never spoke Panjabi and he said *'I mean when I'm out'*. His sister Memona, who is bilingual in English and Panjabi, spoke Panjabi throughout the occasion and her explanation to me for this (in English) was that she married at a young age to a man who came here to join her from Pakistan so her language at home with him and with their children is Panjabi. She said she mostly uses English in dealings with institutions such as hospitals, utility companies, benefits agencies and her son's school. Meanwhile her children were chatting to each other in English about a PSP game using a lot of gaming specific terminology.

Memona and Ansar's sister-in-law Naz arrived and greeted everyone, then started conversation with some other young women in Panjabi. Later, their brother (her husband) arrived and greeted everyone in English and proceeded to discuss football with some of the family in English responding to a football game that was on in the background with English commentary. Their children are aged one and three. Ansar started asking the three-year-old in English if he can speak English now; the child looked bemused; then he asked him in English *'D'you go nursery now?'* and the child answered in English *'Yes I go nursery and ride bikes'*. It is a Birmingham dialect habit to drop the 'to' from this sentence. The child's mother said in Panjabi that she is going to learn English from her son now. This is a typical chain diaspora (Cressey, 2006) situation where newly arrived spouses reintroduce and reinforce use of mother-tongue Panjabi and their British born wives or husbands translate and interpret as they have done since a young age for their parents or grandparents, while using English with British-born siblings, friends, nieces and nephews. As diaspora youth they are part of a 'changing same' (Gilroy, 1993); as one of the young people put it:

Hanif (M)
Identity can be flexible and like . . . it can change. For a number of years you could live somewhere and get influenced by the stuff you do, the people you hang round with but then if you move somewhere else or with other people then, even though it might have been fixed for a number of years, it can stay like that for the rest of your life but you might say it can also change.

As Hoffman has commented in the debate over language shift, "[T]here are many forms of language life before language death" (Hoffman, 1991: 239) and life in a chain diaspora is one version of that multilingual life. Stuart Hall's use of the idea of translation is a way of naming the emergence of new and changing cultural identities and cultural practices, drawing on different cultural traditions at the same time.

It may be tempting to think of identity in the age of globalization as destined to end up in one place or another: either returning to its 'roots' or disappearing through assimilation and homogenization. But this may be a false dilemma. For there is another possibility: that of 'Translation'. (Hall, 1992: 310)

Hall's term translation is a better description for what is happening culturally in the lives of these young British Pakistani and Kashmiri young people than assimilation. Assimilation suggests surrender to the hegemony of dominant cultures and suggests inclusion in a 'host' society. English as the dominant language of the UK can be thought of as displacing languages such as Panjabi through assimilation, but that view overlooks a significant array of multilingual practices. The narratives of the young people inter-viewed show that they have counter hegemonic identifications; they do not feel accepted and included in British society and they claim the right to be part of a mixed multi-racial and multi-cultural society rather than being excluded from so-called 'host' whiteness and Englishness. Tradition, including the language of their place of origin, is a resource for their counter hegemony and anti-racism; translation allows them to reinvent tradition for new times and contexts. This places them in a quandary about their rela-tionship to the English language. It is the official language for use in school, college and workplaces in England, it is the dominant language in Birming-ham and it is also an international language widely used for transnational communication and media communication. They are proficient in its use, but identification with the diaspora community and continuing bilingual-ism and local multilingual space in the neighbourhood have led them to use variations and mixes of their own as a strategy of being 'translated'.

REFERENCES

Back, L. and Nayak, A. 1993. *Invisible Europeans?: Black People in the 'New Europe'*. Birmingham: AFFOR.

Bhabha, H. 1992. Postcolonial criticism. In *Redrawing the Boundaries*, ed. S. Greenblatt and G. Gunn, 437–65. New York: Modern Language Association of America.

Brah, A. 1996. *Cartographies of Diaspora*. London: Routledge.

Cressey, G. 2006. *Diaspora Youth and Ancestral Homeland*. Leiden: Brill.

Gillespie, M. 1995. *Television, Ethnicity and Cultural Change*. London: Routledge.

Gilroy, P. 1993. *The Black Atlantic: Modernity and Double Consciousness*. Cam-bridge, MA: Harvard University Press.

Hall, S. 1992. The question of cultural identity. In *Modernity and Its Futures,* ed. Stuart Hall, David Held and Tony McGrew, 273–327. Cambridge: Polity Press.

Hamers, J. and Blanc, M. 1989. *Bilinguality and Bilingualism*. Cambridge: Cam-bridge University Press.

Haraway, D. 1991. A cyborg manifesto: science, technology, and socialist-feminism in the late twentieth century. In D. Haraway, *Simians, Cyborgs, and Women: The Reinvention of Nature*, 149–81. New York: Routledge.

Hoffman, C. 1991. *An Introduction to Bilingualism*. Harlow: Longman.

Mannheim, K. 1928. The problem of generations. In K. Mannheim, *Essays on the Sociology of Knowledge*, 276–322. London: Routledge and Kegan Paul.

Parekh, B. 2000. *Rethinking Multiculturalism: Cultural Diversity and Political Theory*. Basingstoke: Macmillan.

Rampton, B. 1995. *Crossing: Language and Ethnicity among Adolescents* (Real Language series). London & New York: Longman.

Skutnabb-Kangas, T. 1984. *Bilingualism or Not?* Clevedon: Multilingual Matters (first edition in Swedish, 1981).

Part IV

Visual and Semiotic Perspectives on Multilingualism

Introduction

Mark Sebba

In this part are four chapters which each, in different ways, develop methodologies which extend the boundaries of multilingualism research. Until fairly recently, it would have been reasonable to say that most multilingualism research was carried out within a set of sites, and using a set of methods, which were largely in keeping with the concerns and methods of sociolinguistics more generally. On the one hand, we had macro-level studies, drawing broad-brush pictures of multilingual communities, linguistic minorities in particular. On the other hand, micro-level investigations in multilingualism were typically concerned with spoken language—family conversations, perhaps, or classroom interactions or service encounters—and although by definition more than one language was usually involved, relatively few studies involved more than one *mode*, the spoken one. Over several decades, research in bilingualism and multilingualism developed and fine-tuned its methods. Yet despite a great diversity of approaches, orientations and research sites, the focus broadly remained on spoken language, face-to-face interaction, and, frequently, institutional settings.

The last decade and a half, however, has seen many new opportunities and directions for multilingualism research. Firstly, development of research in literacies and the textually mediated environment has led to many more studies which either focus specifically on practices of reading and writing, or include the study of the written mode alongside the spoken. Secondly, digital technologies (including the internet and mobile telephony) have brought a new range of digital literacies and practices which researchers have gradually embraced, both as research sites and as methodologies or tools. Thirdly, linguistics has begun, later than some disciplines and perhaps rather painfully, to engage with the *visual*—the images, signs and spatial arrangements of the world around us—and thus to enter the world of multimodal research, where the language (spoken or written) is just one of several modes in the semiotic landscape. At the same time, there has been a new awareness and understanding of the relationship between the researcher and the researched, and the development of critical approaches like Critical Discourse Analysis and Linguistic Ethnography which have both redrawn the limits of the object of study and introduced increased expectations of reflexivity on the part of the researcher.

These developments have made their impact on research in multilingualism as well as linguistics more broadly. For example, *Multilingual Literacies* (the title of a collection of papers on this topic, edited by Martin-Jones and Jones [2000]) is no longer a term which needs extensive explanation to the uninitiated. The *multilingual internet* likewise has its book (Danet and Herring, 2007). Multilingual multimodality, in the sense of texts combined with images and text-as-image, has been addressed on several fronts, for example, through a chapter on multilingual signage in *Discourses in Place* by Scollon and Scollon (2003) and by many contributions to the emerging Linguistic Landscapes paradigm, e.g. those in Gorter (2006), Shohamy and Gorter (2008), Jaworski and Thurlow (2010), as well as research on multilingual advertising by Piller (2003), Kelly-Holmes (2005) and Androutsopoulos (2007).

The four chapters in this part each extend the study of multilingualism through their engagement with types of data and new methodological approaches.

In 'Material Ethnographies of Multilingualism: Linguistic Landscapes in the Township of Khayelitsha', Christopher Stroud and Sibonile Mpendukana examine the language of advertising billboards in an urban setting characterised by both linguistic richness and severe economic disadvantage. In their study, they find that the multilingual compositions in public texts are shaped in part by the nature of consumption within the society: as they put it, 'flows of social and linguistic meaning that serve to reproduce late modern structures of consumption in the process also refigure notions of language and multilingualism'. Multilingualism, they suggest, needs to be approached as 'as a resource variously defined in different technologies and across different semiotic artifacts and spaces' whereas linguistic landscape, rather than being approached as a site of linguistic *localisation* should be studied in terms of multilingual *mobility*, where 'multiple encodings of a discourse are transfigured across signage, contexts and languages'. 'Fixed' signage, thus, is not so much a 'discourse in place' (cf. Scollon and Scollon, 2003) as a 'discourse across places,' and not a discourse of language alone, but very centrally, one of economics.

Many studies in the area of multilingualism have investigated bilingual *behaviour*, but very few have looked at the way that bilinguals, especially those from linguistic minorities, *experience* their bilingualism in their personal lives. In 'Experiences and Expressions of Multilingualism: Visual Ethnography and Discourse Analysis in Researching Multilingualism among Sámi Children', Sari Pietikäinen develops methods for doing just this, using drawings and photographs from a project with school-age children from the Sámi minority, not all of whom had strong language skills in Sámi. These *visual* methods of expression, she says, 'seemed to enable children to find their own voice and agency, regardless of language skills' and thus could serve as a source of empowerment for the children, as well as a resource for the researcher. In her conclusion, Sari Pietikäinen argues in favour of applying 'a more heteroglossic understanding of multilingualism' in terms of multimodal practices, and for a notion of 'voice'—the individual's capacity to mobilise linguistic and semiotic resources—as a way of understanding how the individual can achieve agency, identity and authority.

The final two contributions to this part are both explorations of the internet as a resource for the study of multilingualism. In 'Ethnographic Perspectives on Multilingual Computer-Mediated Discourse: Insights from Finnish Football Forums on the Web', Jannis Androutsopoulos and Samu Kytölä discuss the role of ethnography in researching computer-mediated discourse, in this case in the form of on-line football forums which include contributions in several language varieties, including learner varieties and 'mock' learner varieties of English. They propose that the sociolinguistic analysis of multilingualism online is enriched when done in combination with 'persistent observation/immersion' by the researcher, and an 'ethnography of text'. Direct contact with participants is also potentially beneficial, providing background information and a better understanding of, and rapport with, the online community. Participants' own accounts of their online behaviour, on the other hand, need to be interpreted cautiously by the researcher.

'Multilingual Nation Online? Possibilities and Constraints in the UK on the BBC Voices Website' by Bethan Davies, Tommaso Milani and Will Turner could itself be described as an 'ethnography of text', although here the focus is not on the use of multiple languages within the website, but on the website itself as an example of the thematisation of multilingualism in digital media through its portrayal of Britain as a multilingual nation. In this chapter they introduce new descriptive frameworks for analysing websites in terms of layout and navigation, which are needed to understand 'the ways in which the particular context created by the design and architecture of the website both facilitates and constrains online language debates'. In other words, both the ideological content of the website and the responses from readers or participants are partly constructed by the form of the website itself.

The four chapters in this part each point the way to new developments in the study of multilingualism: on the one hand they look to new kinds of data to be explored in the study of multilingualism—digital media, public signage, children's drawings. On the other they look to new ways of understanding bilinguals' engagement with the world and their experiences of it.

REFERENCES

Androutsopoulos, J. (2007). Bilingualism in the mass media and on the internet. In *Bilingualism: A Social Approach*, ed. M. Heller, 207–30. Palgrave Macmillan.

Danet, B. and Herring, S. C. (eds) 2007. *The Multilingual Internet: Language, Culture, and Communication Online*. Oxford: Oxford University Press.

Gorter, D. (ed.) 2006. *Linguistic Landscape: A New Approach to Multilingualism.* Bristol: Multilingual Matters.

Jaworski, A. and Thurlow, C. (ed.) 2010. *Semiotic Landscapes: Language, Image, Space.* London: Continuum.

Kelly-Holmes, H. (2005). *Advertising as Multilingual Communication.* Basingstoke: Palgrave Macmillan.

Martin-Jones, M. and Jones, K. (ed.) 2000. *Multilingual Literacies: Reading and Writing Different Worlds.* Amsterdam: John Benjamins.

Piller, I. (2003). Advertising as a site of language contact. *Annual Review of Applied Linguistics* 23: 170–83.

Scollon, R. and Scollon, S. W. 2003. *Discourses in Place: Language in the Material World.* London: Routledge.

Shohamy, E. and Gorter, D. (eds) 2008. *Linguistic Landscape: Expanding the Scenery.* London: Routledge.

9 Material Ethnographies of Multilingualism
Linguistic Landscapes in the Township of Khayelitsha

Christopher Stroud and
Sibonile Mpendukana

In a recent collection of essays on transition in contemporary South Africa, *Fine Lines from the Box: Further Thoughts about Our Country* (2007), the author Njabulo Ndebele suggests that 'what is going on in [South African] townships carries the defining characteristics of our new society' (2007: 104), and adds that "[t]he informal settlements and all the problems they present—are they not a vital context in which we can define, plan and build for ourselves?" (2007: 104). Dlamini (2009: 112) likewise points to the important role that townships have played and continue to play 'in the constitution of the public sphere, the evolution of nationhood, citizenship and identity in post-apartheid South Africa' by providing a "fertile ground for embodied agency and the possibility for emancipatory politics" (154).

At the same time, contemporary township spaces are also semiotically refigured as spaces of consumption, where emergent new subjectivities and desires, mediated in new cultures and discourses of commodification (cf. Mbembe, Dlamini and Khunou, 2004: 500), find expression in a 'politics of aspiration' (Nuttall, 2004). In this regard, South Africa is typical of late-modern societies in general, where consumption is emerging as "the primary site of identity formation . . . through the intensive marketing of life styles in niche markets" (Bucholtz, 2007: 165). As new encompassing identities of Self as consumer present with new repertoires and discourses for talking about subjectivity, taste, aspiration and choice (cf. also Machin and Van Leeuwen, 2003), so is there a reordering of the social significance of linguistic resources available to speakers. Studies of the sociolinguistics of identity, voice and agency are thus increasingly shifting to the study of style (Bucholtz, 2007).

In this chapter, we explore some of the processes whereby forms of language and concepts of multilingualism are introduced into township space, and in particular how these forms acquire social meaning through circulation in commercial signage. The questions we ask: In township contexts, does the development of new subjectivities of consumption facilitate the emergence of new forms of language and multilingualism? If so, in what ways? More specifically, how are (new) social identities semiotically represented in consumer discourses? What role do different languages play in these representations? How do linguistic items acquire social meaning and indexical value through multimodal representations of social identity?

In order to account for how linguistic resources emerge as recognisable and socially meaningful varieties, Agha (2003: 2007) has built a theory of context, identity and style around the reflexive work of identity construction that speakers regularly engage in. The essence of his theory recognises that speech practices are circulated across discursive artifacts such as narratives, printed cartoons, newspapers, magazines, and novels, and elaborated in metadiscursive commentary. Over time, these practices may become socially recognised, or *enregistered*, as indexical of particular social attributes. Agha underscores how enregisterment is best studied by analyzing large-scale semiotic events and the modes of their interconnectivity. One such large-scale semiotic event is public *signage*, a ubiquitous form of commercial representation that most clearly and consistently articulates new discourses of subjectivity. Commercial discourses in the form of adverts on public signage provide important metapragmatic representations of language in the context of multimodally mediated narratives of authenticity and commodified selves.

Methodologically, we approach these questions from the vantage point of a material *ethnography* of multilingualism, which views the study of textual and semiotic artefacts and objects as a core source of knowledge about ethnographic practices and as sites where global and local perceptions and representations of subjectivities come together. Blommaert (2008) makes a case for a (full-blown) ethnography of textual exegesis, claiming

> it seems to me that 'practices' is artificially separated from that of products. However, practices always yield products so that such products therefore contain traces of these practices and can disclose their nature, and that products yield practices. (Blommaert, 2008: 12ff)

Rowsell (2006) approaches texts from the perspective of the 'concept of tracing—tracing people, practices and places in texts', where texts represent a material realisation of systems of people, discourses, ideas and beliefs' (211) that can be used to uncover the ideologies and trajectories of practices in concrete 'spaces of production'. Pahl (2002) employs the notion of *sedimentation* to capture 'how childrens' *habitus* was inscribed into social practices and then sedimented within texts' (Pahl and Rowsell, 2006: 2). In other words, the materiality of texts comprises traces and sedimentations of identities and social practices. Approaching this ethnographically allows an understanding of how flows of semiotic artefacts in a wider social, material and political context realise fundamental features of agency and voice.

In the next section, we explore some of the semiotic processes whereby forms of language and concepts of multilingualism are introduced into Khayelitsha and acquire social meaning through discourses of consumption. In the discussion section, we will suggest that the approach we take to the circulation of representations of identity in informal township spaces carries implications both for the notion of linguistic landscape, and for our understanding of multilingualism. Ultimately, we argue that multilingual landscapes also speak to how disempowerment and empowerment is represented, circulated and reproduced.

KHAYELITSHA AS A SEMIOTIC SPACE

Types of Signage

The study is located in the Western Cape township of Khayelitsha, a community situated thirty kilometers outside of Cape Town and home to more than 1 million people. Khayelitsha exhibits all the complexities of South African townships, with a rampant poverty of shack-dwellers co-existing side by side with the ostentatious wealth of their more affluent neighbours in new up-market housing estates. Khayelitsha is a predominantly isiXhosa speaking community, although there are significant numbers of other African language speakers due to in-migration from other parts of South Africa and the continent beyond (Deumert and Mabandla, 2006). A semiotic reflex of poverty is the distribution of varieties and registers of language, and the access that different speakers have to valuable symbolic, political and economic markets through the codes they master. English, specifically, is present in forms of *peripheral normativity* resulting from the insertion of global forms into local semiotic economies of language (cf. Blommaert, 2008; Blommaert, Huysmans et al., 2005).

In Khayelitsha, language flows across chains of semiotic artefacts of different types, although signage, especially commercial signage, is the most visible and varied. We can identify two main types of commercial signage in terms of the material and socioeconomic constraints of their production, what we here call, *high* and *low* investment signage respectively.[1] High investment signage is part of long production chains involving various stakeholders and large-scale, industrial production techniques. The products and services on offer are only available through professional service providers, and are thus value-added and capital intensive. Both local government authorities and the commercial agencies that produce this signage closely monitor all stages of its production with respect to content and design, as well as placement in 'up-market' and economically up-scaled places—in what Scollon and Scollon (2003) refer to as *authorized spaces*. In Khayelitsha, such spaces comprise areas enclosed in barbed-wire, such as schools and hospital grounds, as well as main squares and busy shopping centers, taxi-stands and main squares, locations that maximise a diverse, potential readership, and that encourage a contemplative gaze—almost one of aesthetic appreciation—towards the signage.

In contradistinction to high investment signage, public displays of language in low investment signage are primarily found in transactional contexts where the form of signage is constrained by the material and spatial constraints of resource-scarce networks of production and consumption. This type of signage is usually produced by local trades-people themselves, sometimes with the assistance of a student or neighbour known for his/her artistic prowess, and fashioned from local materials easily available and affordable in the community (cardboard, zinc, or building surfaces and local paints). The signage is mainly positioned in direct relation to the outlet. In all examples, the products represented are local and traditional products and activities of everyday necessity, that is, basic food-staples and herbal remedies for medical ailments.

The two types of signage employ distinct techniques and processes of semiotic formation and organise practices of language into identifiable repertoires in different ways (cf. Stroud and Mpendukana, 2009, 2010). They predispose to different types of interaction between the reader and the text. In this chapter, we restrict our focus to how high investment signage is multimodally constructed, spatially located and circulated in the community.[2]

Genre and Identity

The notion of *genre* captures the social relations and material conditions of production and consumption that determine the semiotic representation of subjectivities of consumption. Genres organise multilingual (and multimodal) resources into complexes of functions and forms that encode communicative events recognisable by community members as conventional performances of a particular *type* of communicative act (Blommaert, 2008; Bauman and Briggs, 1992). A genre sets up a particular set of expectations as to type of topic/form of register, attitudinal stance, and interactional roles appropriate to a given speech event, and thus serves to orientate interlocutors to the production and reception of discourses. The way in which language and discourse are used in any concrete instance of a genre has been conventionalised and regularised over time, so that every unique performance of a particular speech event shares common features with other instantiations of the genre. However, Bauman and Briggs (1992: 142) note that 'generic specification . . . cannot be accomplished by the examination of texts alone, but resides rather in the interaction between the organisation of the discourse and the organisation of the event in which it is employed' (cf. French, 2000).

Genres may be made up of subgenres. In high investment signage, one subgenre of advertising organises how commercial identities, affective stances and footings associated with a product are represented. One common type of genre deploys multimodal resources to represent identities configured around a juxtaposition of elements of modernity and tradition, and of the local and the global, and that are *ascribed* (Pavlenko and Black-ledge, 2004) to particular hybrid role-figures and manifest as a *personifica-tion*. The message is that whoever possesses such a product also acquires the personal qualities and outlook on life depicted in the advert.

A typical example of a genre of personification is found in the King Korn advert seen in Figure 9.1.

This billboard juxtaposes images of the modern with the traditional, partly in how it depicts the woman as half modern, half traditional (thereby symbolising contemporary city life) and partly through the figuration of the advertised product, King Korn beer, which is a modern way of brewing Afri-can traditional beer. Here, we observe a figure of a woman with so-called 'relaxed hair' and contemporary clothing, wearing make-up and lipstick, all features of modern fashion conscious women, and suggestive of a young woman typical of a late-modern service economy. However, in addition, her face has white dots made with ocher that symbolises a traditional African/Xhosa woman and that also identifies her as a woman who customarily brews and serves local beer in the local township bars, the 'shebeens'. This signage is characterised by suggestion, innuendo and the ambiguity of the traditional and modern in how femininity is depicted, and clearly encodes a shift in the perception or ascription of femininity from the traditional older woman beer-brewster to a younger and more late-modern service provider.

The advertisement also contains an image of a traditional clay pot filled with traditional African beer and alongside it there is an image of a packet of King Korn Mtombo-Mmela home brew. The clay pot foregrounds and repeats the theme of tradition depicted in the female figure in a directional

Figure 9.1   King Korn beer advert. Photo taken by author.

reading from left to right, although the packet is clearly an item to be found on a modern super-market shelf. The layers of *Given* and *New* (cf. Kress and Van Leeuwen, 2006) in the rightmost cluster of objects juxtapose a *Given* and traditional way of brewing beer with the *New* packet of King Korn meal. Likewise, there is a suggestive *Ideal-Real* (cf. Kress and Van Leeuwen, 2006) structure in the relative positioning and perspective between the bowl of beer and the packet. The salience of the modern packet is also reflected in its *size* relative to the pot of beer, clearly underscoring how the traditional is incorporated into the modern. This way of representing the product thus also serves to lift it out of the traditional shebeen and into modern circuits of consumption. Interestingly, the isiXhosa text, *Ndim' lo*, can be roughly translated with 'It is I', a phrase that clearly underscores the link between the personality/subjectivity of the woman and the product. The King Korn brew advert is thus very explicit in creating an identity linked to the product. This, then, is a message of syncretism of the old and the new and the local and the global; social change and modernisation of traditional characters and products subtly expressed in the movement across the given and the new and the ideal and the real.

Typically, in this and other high investment signage, genres of personification present with clear reading paths through the multimodal composition, and distinct and separate principles for how the visuals and verbals are kept separated. Furthermore, different languages are presented as distinct with no hybridity or code-mixing. In the bulk of the examples we have studied in other work (e.g. Stroud and Mpendukana, 2009, 2010), language separateness is manifested and reinforced through design parameters, such as spatial placement. For example, English is typically constituted in high investment signage through the fact of its location in prominent positions of high information value and salience, occupying the *Ideal*, or top, position in a composition, whereas isiXhosa is more frequently found in the *Real*, or bottom, position.[3] English is also found more often in position *Given*, or leftmost, thereby contributing to its construal as a linguistic point of common departure, the unmarked case, whereas isiXhosa in position *New*, constructs it as socially contested—or at the very least, carrying novelty. Furthermore, English is also found in functions expressing authority, respect and formality. On the other hand, isiXhosa is clearly used in the construction of local figures/voices—voices that may thus be refracted and interpreted through the dominant and more audible voice of English as a matrix language in linguistically juxtaposed signage (cf. Stroud and Mepndukana, 2009).

Scale

Another characteristic design feature of genres of personification in high investment signage is the imaginative use of *scale*. Scale refers to the fact that linguistic forms are organised into hierarchically ordered codes and economies of value (Blommaert, Collins and Slembrouck, 2005a, 2005b). In the following advert for Cadbury's chocolate (Figure 9. 2), the semiotics of the billboard create powerful scale effects, because much in the design of this signage generates associations to distance and even *erasure* (Irvine and Gal, 2000) of the local, with few, if any, deictic pointers to the immediate context.

The wording on the billboard, '*sweet-talk waya waya*', is a hybrid construction that uses an urban African form, *waya-waya*, with the meaning 'to go on and on' and an English compound noun which together roughly translates as 'sweet-talk non-stop'/non-stop sweet talk. The phrase *waya-waya* is popularly predominantly associated with nice times, which drives home the message put across by the advertising company of drawn-out, pleasurable moments—up-scaled and apart from the immediate here-and-now. Contributing to this scale effect is the fact that the English language text is highly edited so as to conform to standard centre norms of English. Likewise, the phrase *waya-waya*—a pan-African expression common to many African languages—suggests non-localness and distance/extension, iconically signalling longing, aspiration and anticipation, covering as it does many different language groups and spaces, as well as directly referring to iterative and pleasurable times.

Although it is not as apparent in these examples, in the larger corpus of signage from which they are taken, scale is also manifested in the way in which English is presented as a linguistic system which is less permeable, that

Figure 9.2   Advert for Cadbury's chocolate. Photo taken by author.

offers more linguistic integrity, and that spans many more sentence types and functions than is the case with isiXhosa or other African languages. These latter languages frequently occur as translations or in compounds as loans. Again, there is a clear tendency towards *monolingualism* in both English and isiXhosa and *monomodalism* as either verbals or visuals.

As indicated in the sub-section 'Types of Signage', high investment signage is characteristically found in up-scaled environments, where many people gather, and where exposure to the advert is greatest. This placement also contributes to the currency and social meaning of the linguistic resources layered into the composition. One might conjecture that the forms of language that may, in a near future, gain greater currency and popularity are most likely those found in signage situated in such heterogeneous and mobile sites in which there is a physical circulation and movement of many people. We could in fact hypothesise that the characteristics of mobility and flux characterising public spaces will increasingly become projected onto forms of language found in these sites through processes such as *fractal recursivity* (Irvine and Gal, 2000), where the public nature of place is reflected in perceptions of language variants. This would be one aspect of the circulation of forms contributing to indexical meaning.

Dialogicality

A characteristic feature of much high investment signage in Khayelitsha is its aggregate 'inter-semiotic, interdiscursive, dialogicality' (Scollon and Scollon, 2003: 23) with other signage and other registers. In the following suite of signage (cf. Figures 9.2 and 9.3), we see clearly how this dialogicality comprises a central process in the circulation and establishment of the scaled multimodal resources of genres of personification.

Figure 9.3　Later version of advert for Cadbury's chocolate. Photo taken by author.

As in Figure 9.2, the presupposition in the discourse is that particular identities and personal success in social relationships may be achieved through purchase of the luxury item of chocolate. In the original advert (Figure 9.2), there is a clear link between the product, a 'sweet', and the phrase '*sweet-talk waya waya*' written in clear bold-text in the same sized fonts as the introductory PS.

This message of romance is suggestively (re)contextualised in new forms, modalities and media, thus comprising larger chains of meaning (re)construction of this particular discourse that reaches across a range of media. For example, the *Holla yo lurv* signage is in direct dialogue with the Cadbury's chocolate billboard. Firstly, there is the recontextualisation of the same product, just noted, across different representations with an expansion/elaboration/itemisation of the noun phrase 'sweet talk'. Whereas the original billboard suggested what might be meant by 'sweet-talk waya waya', this signage goes a step further by actually displaying multiple examples of such talk. These examples are linked to a second recontextualisation of the message in the format of a televised competition on *Yo TV*, which aimed to promote the product on children's television by getting contestants to come up with winning examples of 'sweet talk'. Thirdly, all the examples of 'sweet talk' displayed on the billboard are authentically composed by young people who are '*sweet-talking waya waya*' through the medium of SMS (short message service) language. In other words, the product message is recontextualised in a specific register and new technology, namely the register of short messaging, with its numerous orthographic abbreviations and truncated grammar, a choice of register that is clearly oriented towards a youthful target-market. The fourth resemiotisation implies a remodulation or reframing of the animator/principal in terms of a (transnational) imagined Black persona through the orthographic rendering of African American Vernacular English (AAVE) pronunciation *Holla Yo* and a local approximation to an unspecified transnational Black pronunciation, orthographically rendered as '*Lurv*', in *Holla Yo Lurv*.

These 'complex re-orderings of textualised meanings' (Silverstein and Urban, 1996; Blommaert, 2008) serve many metapragmatic functions (Agha, 2007): they provide a commentary on stylistic variation; they elaborate on semantic relationships and they illustrate different forms of discourse ('*sweet talk*' versus '*holla yur lurv*'); they comment on permissible code-switches and they highlight ambiguities ('waya waya'/love is forever).

The process of multiple resemiotisations of discourse (Iedema, 2003) resembles that noted by Johnstone (2009) who points to the importance of *intertextuality* in the emergence of registers, genres and varieties and their associated indexical meanings. Referring to the 'standardisation' of the American lect Pittsburghese, Johnstone notes how t-shirts carrying typically Pittsburghese words and phrasings circulate across different markets, are sold in different venues and enter into intertextual chains with other examples of Pittburghese in the media such as online lists and folk dictionaries. All these forms contribute to speakers' experience of the social meanings associated with a form.

On Participation Structures

The conditions of mobility and the contemplative gaze possible with high investment signage allows a complexity of design with multiple layers of context such as colour and spatial positioning that carry rich semantic and pragmatic meanings. Linguistically, these investments find expression in a variety of possible production formats and participation frameworks (Goffman, 1981) where the reader may be constituted through different reading positions, as audience, by-stander or ratified participant, as well as in different author positions (animator/principal /author etc.).

Viewing the Cadbury's billboard from this perspective throws up four different possible reading positions. For example, the phrase '*PS, I love you*' is indicative of a message from afar through its associations with a written register (letter, SMS, or email) which positions the reader as a 'non-proximal' interactant/recipient of distant others with whom there is some indication of an intimate relationship. However, there is also the possibility of reading this billboard from the role perspective of a by-stander/over-hearer (ratified or not), or of an audience to a podium event, creating shifts in footing and alignment with the message.

Depending on whether the billboard is read as a podium or stage event, or as a demand or offering, readers are positioned as non-present/non-proximal—engaging with distant others—or as deictically anchored first and second person.

Johnstone (2009) emphasises the important role of speakers' social and geographical mobility for processes of enregisterment. She points out that the life experiences and histories of speakers' encounters with different ways of speaking, contribute to the metapragmatic and metadiscursive processes that single out and mark particular ways of speaking as carrying out particular types of social meaning. The different participation frameworks embedded in a high investment composition mimic in some sense speakers' different life experiences and histories of encounters with different linguistic forms. Furthermore, the multiple footings, alignments and reading positions among readers reproduce a participation structure that bears more than a superficial resemblance to the loosely configured and multiplex social networks identified by Milroy and Milroy (1992) to be behind linguistic change and the uptake of novelties generally.

DISCUSSION

We have noted in the above some of the ways in which identities of consumption are figured and reproduced multimodally, and how linguistic items and forms of multilingual organisation are accorded social meanings, circulated and inserted into local communities. We have suggested that, in township contexts, the development of new subjectivities of consumption is bound up with the emergence of new forms of language and multilingualism.

The approach taken here, a material ethnography of multilingualism, presupposes and speaks to a particular understanding of core notions such as *linguistic landscape* and *multilingualism* itself. In the perspective advanced here, the notion of linguistic landscape becomes a resource for the study of the social circulations of meaning in society, and signage then becomes one form of linguistic recontextualisation in a chain/network of resemiotisations across (economically differentiated) technologies, artifacts and spaces. It suggests an approach to linguistic landscapes in terms of a sociolinguistics of multilingual *mobility* rather than linguistic *localisation*, where one would need to look at how multiple encodings of a discourse are transfigured across signage, contexts and languages. A linguistic landscape is nothing less than sedimented products of a socially and economically determined articulation of (community) multilingual resources. This is in line with contemporary work that critically addresses conceptualisations of space and the methodology of its study (cf. e.g. Shohamy and Gorter, 2009).

The approach we have taken here also carries implications for how we understand multilingualism. We have noted how a particular material ethnography encourages a specific organisation of language, manifest in textual structure, and principles of monitoring and use of textual space, particular forms of linguistic hybridity and creativity, and interactional orders and forms of resemiotisation. This suggests that we approach multilingualism as a resource variously defined in different technologies and across different semiotic artifacts and spaces.

To what extent, then, in the township context, might emerging commercial economies of identity translate into empowering registers of selfhood and agency? And, if so, to what extent? Or do new discourses of Self continue the social reproduction of disadvantage?

In all essentials, high investment signage appears to reinforce traditional and hierarchical conceptions of language and multilingualism, and recontextualise traditional and disempowering subjectivities (e.g. of femininity) in new discourses of late-modern consumption. Bourdieu's distinction between 'the taste of necessity' and the 'taste of luxury' is useful in thinking about how representations of consumption link market economic discourses with individual sensibilities and social change or reproduction (Stroud and Mpendukana, 2009). The taste of necessity refers to 'the popular aesthetic of 'the subordination of form to the function', whereas the 'taste of luxury' is 'the mode of representation, the style . . . an aesthetics that differs in the distance of their users to economic necessity and practical urgency' (Bourdieu, 1984: 23). High investment signage encapsulates the essence of the taste of luxury. In our corpus in general, this signage represents and reproduces a particular idea of language, language separation and hierarchisation, where social valuations of English as an up-scaled register of aspiration, linking transnational styles to local contexts, exist side by side with multimodal representations of isiXhosa as (marginally) embedded in frames of modernisation. At the same time, the play on social and linguistic hybridity found in some high investment signage is "strategically recontextualised" (Gal and Woolard, 2001) for consumerist purposes. In this way, potentially subversive and disruptive linguistic practices have been "domesticated" in the name of consumption, and appropriated to the taste of luxury. This is reinforced in how the advertising genre reproduces a familiar semiotics of femininity as subservient and aspiration as material and devoid of practical urgency. The Bourdieusian idea of taste as socially instilled and hierarchically ranked suggests that such semiotically mediated subjectivities of consumption in high investment signage may comprise a powerful "materialisation of relationships of power" (Styhre and Engberg, 2003: 120), that, in the end, contribute to the reproduction of the *status quo*. And, in fact, these representations are circulated across linked chains of signage, and thus throughout society, in what is reminiscent of an almost Foucauldian net of power, that predisposes to a "social envisioning" (Peters, 1997; Mazzarella, 2004) of local society, and the social, political and aesthetic values of language that may be more conserving than socially transformative.

NOTES

1. In other work, we have discussed this signage with respect to the types of space/place they are found, e.g. spaces of luxury versus necessity, or in terms of their top-down versus bottom-up characteristics of production (cf. e.g. Stroud and Mpendukana, 2009)
2. This is not to deny the importance of locally produced (commercial) signage in this context, and new studies should look at the synergies between types of signage.
3. This King Korn advert is an exception as it is a triptych and therefore not organised primarily along centre-margin principles. We chose this advert because it illustrated well how a product is linked to an identity.

REFERENCES

Agha, A. 2003. The social life of cultural value. *Language and Communication* 23: 231–73.
———. 2007. *Language and Social Relations*. Cambridge: Cambridge University Press.
Bauman, R. and Briggs, C. 1992. Genre, intertextuality, and social power. *Journal of Linguistic Anthropology* 2(2): 131–72.
Blommaert, J. 2008. *Grassroots Literacy: Writing, Identity and Voice in Central Africa*. London and New York: Routledge.

Blommaert, J., Collins, J. and Slembrouck, S. 2005a. Polycentricity and interactional regimes in 'global neighbourhoods'. *Ethnography* 65(2): 205–35.

———. 2005b. Spaces of multilingualism. *Language and Communication* 25: 197–216.

Blommaert, J., Huysmans, M., Muyllaert, N. and Dyers, C. 2005. Peripheral normativity: literacy and the production of locality in a South African township school. *Linguistics and Education* 19: 374–403.

Bourdieu, P. 1984. *Distinction: A Social Critique of the Judgement of Taste.* Cambridge, MA: Harvard University Press.

Bucholtz, M. 2007. Shop talk: branding, consumption, and gender in American middle-class youth interaction. In *Words, Worlds, and Material Girls: Language, Gender, Globalization*, ed. B. McElhinny, 371–402. New York: Mouton de Gruyter.

Deumert, A. and N. Mabandla. ms. i-Dollar eyi one! Language, communication networks and economic participation: towards an inclusive economy. Unpublished paper presented at the conference *Accelerated and Shared Growth in South Africa: Determinants, Constraints and Opportunities*, 18–20 October 2006, Johannesburg.

Dlamini, J. 2009. *Native Nostalgia.* Johannesburg: Jacana Press.

French, B. 2000. The symbolic capital of social identities: the genre of bargaining in an urban Guatemalan market. *Journal of Linguistic Anthropology* 10(2): 155–89.

Gal, S. and K. A. Woolard. (eds). 2001. *Languages and Publics: The Making of Authority.* Manchester: St. Jerome Publishing.

Goffman, E. 1981. *Forms of talk.* Philadelphia: University of Pennsylvania Press.

Iedema, R. 2003. Multimodality, resemiotization: extending the analysis of discourse as multi-semiotic practice. *Visual Communication* 2: 29–57.

Irvine, J. and Gal, S. 2000. Language ideology and linguistic differentiation. In *Regimes of Language*, ed. P. Kroskrity, 35–83. Santa Fe: SAR Press.

Johnstone, B. (2009). Pittburghese shirts: commodification and the enregisterment of an urban dialect. *American Speech* 84(2): 157–75.

Kress, G., and van Leeuwen, T. J. 2006. *Reading Images: The Grammar of Visual Design* (2nd edition). London and New York: Routledge.

Machin, D. and van Leeuwen, T. J. 2003. Global schemas and local discourses in Cosmopolitan. *Journal of Sociolinguistics* 7(4): 493–512.

Markus, H. and P. Nurius. 1986. Possible selves. *American Psychologist* 41(9): 954–69.

Mazzarella, W. (2004), 'Culture, globalization, mediation', *Annual Review of Anthropology*, 33, 345–67.

Mbeme, A, Dlamini, N. and Khunou, G. 2004. Soweto now. *Public Culture* 16(3): 499–506.

Milroy, L. and Milroy, J. 1992. Social networks and social class: toward an integrated sociolinguistic model. *Language in Society* 21: 11–27.

Ndebele, N. 2007. *Fine liner from the box: further thoughts about our country.* Johannesburg: Umuzi.

Nuttall, Sarah. 2004. Stylizing the self: the Y generation in Rosebank, Johannesburg. *Public Culture* 16: 430–52.

Pahl, Kate. 2002. Ephemera, mess and miscellaneous piles: texts and practices in families. *Journal of Early Childhood Literacy* 2(2): 145–65.

Pahl, K. and Roswell, J. (eds) *Travel Notes from the New Literacy Studies Instances of Practice.* Clevedon: Multilingual Matters Ltd.

Pavlenko, A. and Blackledge, A. (eds) 2004. *Negotiation of Identities in Multilingual Contexts.* Clevedon: Multilingual Matters.

Peters, J. D. 1997. 'Seeing bifocally: media, place, culture', in A. Gupta and J. Ferguson (eds). *Culture, Power, Place: Explorations in Critical Anthropology.* Durham: Duke Univesity Press, 75–92.

Roswell, J. 2006. Corporate crossings: tracing textual crossings. In *Travel Notes from the New Literacy Studies: Instances of Practice*, ed. K. Pahl and J. Roswell, 195–219. Clevedon: Multilingual Matters.

Scollon, R. and Scollon, S. 2003. *Discourse in Place: Language in the Material World*. London: Routledge

Shohamy, E. and Gorter, D. (eds) 2009. *Linguistic Landscape: Expanding the Scenery*. New York and London: Routledge.

Silverstein, M. and Greg, U. (eds) 1996. *Natural Histories of Discourse*. Chicago: University of Chicago Press

Stroud, C. and Mpendukana, S. 2009. Towards a material ethnography of linguistic landscape: multilingualism, mobility and space in a South African township. *Journal of Sociolinguistics* 13(3): 363–86.

———. Forthcoming. Multilingual signage: a multimodal approach to discourses of consumption in a South African township. *Social Semiotics*.

Styhre, A. and Engberg, T. 2003. Spaces of consumption: from margin to centre. *Ephemera: Critical Dialogues on Organization* 3: 115–25.

10 Experiences and Expressions of Multilingualism

Visual Ethnography and Discourse Analysis in Research with Sámi Children

Sari Pietikäinen

This chapter[1] investigates multilingualism as a complex phenomenon which pervades different social, historical and cultural processes but is also manifested in the everyday practices and experiences of multilingual individuals. Consequently, multilingualism can be examined at a macro-sociological level, where political and ideological issues are at stake: research on how language policies are designed and implemented is one example of this (see e.g. Heller, 2007; Kelly-Holmes, Moriarty and Pietikäinen, 2009; May, 2005). But multilingualism can also be investigated at the level of an individual's lifeworld, paying attention to their personal experiences of the language situation in question, and exploring how they see possibilities opened up by languages, the constraints that may exist and, finally, the choices that can be made (Burck, 2005; Pietikäinen et al., 2008; Pietikäinen, 2010). As an illustration of these interrelated processes, this chapter examines multilingualism in an indigenous language community focusing on the experiences and expressions of young Sámi children, and explores how visual ethnography and discourse analysis can be used to understand and represent the functions and values of languages and ways of using languages for them. To this end, the present chapter investigates how the youngest generation of Sámi speakers experience, express, and discuss the multilingualism present in their daily lives.

The chapter draws on my long-standing ethnographic and discourse analytical research on multilingualism in the Sámi community and particularly on work with Sámi children in the Finnish side of Sámiland. In this chapter, I focus mainly on visual and discursive data from one case study consisting of photographs taken by a group of Sámi children and the conversation that centred on these photos, but I will also make use of other ethnographic and discourse data related to these children and their community. The argument that I wish to make in this chapter is that this kind of multimodal data can help in investigating the different ways speakers express, experience, and make sense of the multilingualism present in their daily life and may help to shed light on the complex and often ideologised and politicised relationships between languages and their implications for identity and agency in an endangered, minoritised and multilingual context, such as the Sámi community.

The case study also highlights some of the conceptual and methodological work going on in rethinking multilingualism in minority language contexts (cf. Heller, 2007; Jaffe, 2007; Pietikäinen, 2010). The case study comes from a larger research project called 'Northern Multilingualism' which aims at examining discourses, practices, and experiences of linguistic diversity in the North Calotte area (for further information, see http:// www.northernmultilingualism.fi).

THE SHIFTING MULTILINGUAL ENVIRONMENT OF SÁMI CHILDREN IN THE NORTH

The multilingual environment that this chapter focusses on is that of Sámiland. This area, also known as Sápmi, Lapland and the North Calotte, stretches from the northernmost part of Norway, Sweden and Finland to north-east Russia. It has always been a multilingual place, not only because of mobility linked to traditional livelihoods centring on reindeer herding, hunting, and fishing, but also because of cultural practices such as the seasonal move between summer and winter habitats and trade (in furs, tar and dried fish). Contemporary multilingualism is related to education, media, new technology and tourism (cf. Pietikainen, 2010). In this context of the new globalised economy, and with the novel types of job opportunities and the market value of locality it brings, the value, function and experiences of multilingualism and particular languages, such as Sámi, are also being renegotiated (cf. Heller, 2003).

The 'old' and 'new' mobility and shifting values and functions of languages mean that Sápmi is a multilayered multilingual area—a constantly changing contact zone (Pratt, 1987) between nine endangered indigenous Sámi languages, other minority languages (kven and meänkieli) in the area, and majority languages, whether they be national languages (Norwegian, Swedish, Finnish, Russian) or global languages such as English and Spanish imported by tourism and technology (cf. Pietikäinen et al., 2010). For the Sámi children this multilingual environment is particular in the sense that they are perceived to be the future generation of the endangered Sámi languages, and their relation to these languages, be it easy or complex, is often under scrutiny. A historical trajectory has moved Sámi languages from being central communicative resources in indigenous communities to the margins of the twentieth century nation-states of Finland, Sweden, Russia and Norway, and in the wake of the Sámi movement, particularly since the 1970s, they have been redefined as one of the forms of cultural capital in the multilingual northern environment. This route and its milestones are very familiar from the histories of other marginalised minority languages, as their positions and value are closely related to the broader issues of constructing homogeneous nation-states as well as questions of linguistic rights, globalisation and economic and technological development (Heller, 2007; Jaffe, 2007; Kelly-Holmes, Moriarty and Pietikäinen, 2009). All these changes transcend localities, resulting in reorganisation of existing language relations and in the creation of new forms of linguistic and semiotic actions.

The endangerment of the Sámi languages started in the early twentieth century when the once-solid community Sámi languages were pushed into the margins of the nation-states, resulting in Sámi language marginalisation and language shift. Before World War II, Sámi languages were regularly learned as mother tongues and widely used as primary means of daily interaction in the community. The community was, however, never monolingual: many people knew not only different Sámi languages but also Finnish and other majority languages, depending on where they lived and how they earned their living (Lehtola, 2000: 186–87; Lindgren, 2000). Whenever necessary, majority languages were learned as additional languages. Further, Finnish was both an official language and the language of education and administration in the Finnish side of Sápmi. Knowledge of Finnish gradually became more common, and ultimately a necessity during wartime, when many Sámi people were evacuated from their traditional habitations to regions speaking only Finnish (cf. Lehtola, 1994). The post-war years since 1945 and the modernisation process that swept across the world had lasting effects on Finnish and other Nordic societies and, consequently, on the Sámi community. Industrialisation changed the ways Sámi earned their living—one example being reindeer herding—and also affected the use of languages (cf. Kulonen, Serujärvi-Kari and Pulkinnen, 2005; Lehtola, 2000). The historical and social trajectories of Sámi in the last fifty years or so have changed Sámi languages from being (strong) community languages into endangered languages known only by a few people.

Today it is estimated that among approximately 60,000 to 80,000 Sámi people, half speak one of the nine Sámi languages. The dominant language is Northern Sámi, with approximately 30,000 speakers throughout Sápmi, whereas other Sámi languages have only very few speakers in a very local language community, with as few as 250 to 400 speakers each (Aikio-Puoskari, 2005; Kulonen, Serujärvi-Kari and Pulkinnen, 2005). In practice, this means that the role of a Sámi language varies among its speakers: whereas for some the Sámi language is their mother tongue or a daily resource for communication, for others it is studied at school or encountered later in life or it may be a shrinking register used only for ritual purposes.

The indigenous languages are very important for identity issues, and are highly politicised in Sámi communities; however, both language competence and the lack of it mark people and place them within a hierarchy of

'Sáminess'. At the individual level, people have to come to terms with their own linguistic identity, which may or may not include the Sámi languages, and its implications (e.g. being Sámi without competence in the indigenous languages or being one of the few fluent speakers of Sámi or something in between). The present Sámi community can be seen as an example of truncated multilingualism (Jacquemet, 2005; Blommaert, Collins and Slembrouck, 2005) where the competences and usages of the languages are often organised around specific topics, domains or activities. Spaces, activities and people as well as their relations are, at least partly, defined and regimented by competence in Sámi or lack of it.

Furthermore, in a transnational Sámiland, where the norms and regimes of different nation-states, regions and regional and indigenous governments, communities, domains and contexts overlap, people's needs, opportunities or desires to use several languages in their everyday lives become increasingly more acute owing to economic, cultural and linguistic flows introducing different languages, new practices, other genres and language commodities. In the Sámi context, the forces that have a particularly strong impact on the language situation and the needs of Sámi people are linked, on the one hand, to political and linguistic rights, but, on the other, to global processes, such as media and tourism, the main sources of revenue nowadays. The youngest generation of potential Sámi speakers lives in a very different world from their grandparents and has very different affordances and constraints to learn and use languages, Sámi included.

The need for methodological innovation in my research with multilingual Sámi children became apparent gradually in the course of my research on Sámi media and various revitalisation projects and activities in the Finnish side of Sámiland (see Pietikäinen, 2008; Dufva and Pietikäinen, 2006). In this context, I had come into contact with several Sámi adults who had voiced their concern about the role of Sámi languages in the lives of their children, their competence in these languages and motivation, emotions and affordances related to learning and using indigenous languages. I had myself observed the children in various events in the local community and only seldom heard them use Sámi languages (usually in a festival or special occasion singing in Sámi). Another observation was that education was often mentioned as a key element in both the endangerment of Sámi languages and their revitalisation, and the children taking part in Sámi education was seen at the centre of these processes. These observations together with explicit suggestions by community members led me to examine Sámi children and their language practices and experiences.

I started to work with Northern, Inari and Skolt Sámi children in 2004, by participating in their school activities, mainly just observing language practices in classrooms, during breaks and school lunch, observing the use of language interaction among the kids and between the kids and the teachers. During these observations it became apparent that while the children used Sámi with their teacher in the classroom activities, they tended to use Finnish when interacting with each other (asking to borrow a pencil, rechecking the homework, etc.) and even more outside the formal classes (plays and games during the break happened almost solely in Finnish). The teachers confirmed this pattern and wondered about the reason. As in most of the cases they thought that the question was not so much about competence in Sámi but rather something else.

The photographing case study discussed in this chapter focussed on a group of Sámi children who were taking part in predominantly Sámi language education in the Finnish part of Sámiland. These children had a multilingual repertoire, but a particular one: officially they were classified as Northern or Inari Sámi speakers (i.e. it was their first language or mother tongue) but in practice, however, they were all fluent in Finnish; in many cases, Finnish was their strongest language whereas their skill in Sámi languages varied. In this sense they presented many of the typical characteristics of the youngest generation of Sámi language speakers. Their ages were between eight and twelve at the time the data were collected between 2004 and 2006. The photo case study I will discuss comes from a particular set of case studies focussing on Sámi children in Sámi medium education. These studies involved different types of methods and data, including on-site observation, questionnaires, written stories, drawings, and photographs, and the aim of each was to examine the multilingual experiences and expressions of these children. Whereas ethics is an important aspect in all research, working with children in a small community underlines it even more. In this research, at every step, the children's participation was voluntary; their consent and that of their parents, as well as that of the teachers and the governors of the schools were sought to conduct the research. As an application of the principles of action and ethnographic research, throughout the process, children's suggestions and ideas were invited and heard.

VISUAL ETHNOGRAPHY AND DISCOURSE ANALYSIS IN WORKING WITH MULTILINGUAL SÁMI CHILDREN

The motivation to use visual ethnography combined with discourse analysis in my research arose from three interrelated aims and needs. First, as I was interested in examining how the Sámi children experience and talk about languages around them, I looked for ways to explore their feelings and thoughts about their linguistic environment and, consequently, ways in which they could represent their experiences. This meant opting for a multimethod approach. Apart from interviewing and observing these children, as well asking them to fill in questionnaires and write stories about Sámi language, I turned to visual ethnography because, as Pink (2007: 17) argues, by paying attention to images we can develop new ways of understanding individuals, social relations, material cultures and ethnographic knowledge itself. From a discourse analytical perspective, the ways of representing are always intertextual, i.e. connected to previous ways of representing and to particular ways of seeing (Pietikäinen and Mäntynen, 2009). Consequently, visual representations, like verbal accounts, contain traces of activities related to particular languages as well as traces of the value and function attributed to them. The details in visual representation can be reflective of a larger system of values and function related to languages.

I also felt that allowing and encouraging the children to also use visual resources to represent their experiences would mean that at least some of the obstacles related to literacy skills might be overcome, as visuality would provide an alternative way of communicating, particularly for the children with limited writing skills or who otherwise preferred communication without words. This fieldwork strategy links to the view of language as a multimodal, semiotic system and to the view that 'languaging' means using all the resources that you have, visual included (cf. Pietikäinen et al., 2008; Pietikäinen, 2010). The need to develop different kinds of activities for the children to express their experiences with and to elicit knowledge about their experiences from multiple perspectives related also to the acknowledgement that all languaging happens within a particular genre and that genre structures linguistic and visual action (cf. Pietikäinen and Mäntynen, 2009). For example, a questionnaire frames the activity as question-answer pairs where the informant (the child) can only answer the questions put forward and within the space given for each question. Genre structures the action also in the sense that it presupposes prior knowledge or awareness of the genre conventions: writing a story can only be accomplished if the writer not only knows how to write but is also familiar with the genre convention related to narrative, its structure and central features. Consequently, a change in genre may allow and facilitate different kinds of action, and in the context of this study the genre innovation was related to the visual genres of drawing and photography.

Finally, many qualitative research methods, including interviews, observations, written tasks etc., easily foreground the researcher's prior knowledge and agency in the research setting and tend to impose their agenda even when conscious efforts are made to minimise this (cf. Martin-Jones and Jones, 2000). This is particularly true of a research setting with children owing to the huge power imbalance between an adult and a child. Hence approaches geared towards participatory action research were applied with the aim of granting greater space and independence to the participant's agency. Against this background, visual case studies, one focussing on drawings and one on photos, were developed, paying particular attention to the visual aspects of the Sámi children's experiences of their languages.

The ways in which the research is designed and the data collected have important implications for the analysis of the data. The analysis in this chapter starts with the recognition that photographing, just like talking or writing, is part of social action, with implications for knowledge, identity and agency (cf. Mavers, 2007). Different types of visual and written representations bear varied relations to the phenomenon under scrutiny: they represent different types of knowledge and experiences that may be understood in relation to one another. In practice, this implies an analytical process of making meaningful links between different research experiences and materials such as photographs, drawings, field diaries, interviews, local texts and practices, and previous research. The aim is thus not to form a complete record of the research but a set of different representations.

The second starting-point is the multi-functionality of each image (cf. Kress, 2010; Mavers, 2007); the same image may simultaneously be driving different meanings in different situations and consequently any analysis of images should account for their ambiguity of meaning. This diversity of meaning invested in visual images is fundamental to their analysis, and depends on who is looking. The same image may have a variety of meanings invested in it at different stages of ethnographic research and representation, as it is viewed by different eyes and audiences in diverse temporal, historical, spatial and cultural contexts (e.g. a picture in the interview, at the school exhibition, in this chapter). Therefore it is important to seek to understand the individual, local and broader cultural discourses in which photographs are made meaningful, in both fieldwork situations and academic discourses (Pink, 2007: 67–68).

Consequently, the analytical processes around the multimodal data in this chapter involve negotiation of local, ethnographic and discursive meanings and interpretation of the images made by children, drawing on various sources of meaning. The images can be interpreted in relation to the producers' (children's) account of them, in relation to the conventions of the visual culture of the Sámi and the local environment and in relation to previous research in a similar context and on similar issues and, finally, in relation to my own position and knowledge about these topics. Notably, visual images are made meaningful through the subjective gaze of the viewer, and each individual produces these visual meanings by relating the image to their existing personal experience, knowledge and wider cultural discourses (Pink, 2007: 82). The image itself represents the point at which these different meanings intersect, thus linking the contexts of research and analysis (cf. Pink, 2007: 126). To borrow discourse analytical terminology by Scollon and Scollon (2001, 2004), these images can be seen as a nexus point where different meanings collide and come together, affecting each other and making people take issue with them.

CASE STUDY OF COLLABORATIVE PHOTOGRAPHY: PICTURING SÁMI LANGUAGES

The visual case study discussed here focusses on ways in which Sámi children represent their Sámi language experience by means of photography. The idea was to focus on the visual mode so that the children could express themselves through an alternative, non-language-related, mode. As Bezemer and Kress (2008) note, different modes have different affordances, potentials and constraints as there are always gains and losses in each selected mode. After having drawn, being interviewed, having written stories and answered a questionnaire, the children in this case study were provided with yet another way of expressing their experiences and also moving away to some extent from the issues of language skills and class-room practices underlying and structuring much of the previous case studies.

To this end, a collaborative ethnographic photography case study was planned, again together with the teachers, in an attempt both to understand and make visible children's language experiences. In this case, the children became 'researcher photographers' who were invited to take pictures and were encouraged to use photography to illustrate, document and reflect upon their languages and environment (cf. Mizen, 2005; Pink, 2007). Ethnographic photography is not only about examining visual culture but, as Pink (2007: 66) argues, rather it potentially constructs continuities between the visual culture of a particular locality and that of the collaborators in the research. Thus with this case study, the aim was to create photographic representations that refer to local visual cultures and simultaneously respond to the interest of the research, i.e. examining the children's experiences of their multilingual environment.

This case study also draws from ideas developed by Savolainen (2004) in the pedagogic method that she calls 'empowering photography'. She describes how empowering photography aims at stimulating the exploration and construction of the subject's life story, family ties and their own identity. The grounding idea is equality in that inviting people to take pictures themselves about their lives and reflect upon them means that the inherent power of the photographer is replaced by interaction and dialogue, and the testimonial power of the photo is being called into question in order to emphasise the subjective experience and visualisation of it. Photographing, talking about one's own pictures and representing them to others may help one in finding a voice and agency in one's own life situation.

Based on these ideas of collaborative research, ethnographic and empowering photography (cf. Hodge and Jones, 2000; Pink, 2007; Savolainen, 2004) and linked to the aim of this research project, to examine the experiences of multilingualism of the Sámi children, a photograph project entitled 'Where Is My Sami Language?' was planned together with the teachers and children. The experiences of previous case studies involving these children were also used in planning and carrying out this particular case. In the end, thirteen children from Northern Sámi and Inari Sámi classes took part in this case study.

In practice, the project developed in four stages. (1) Orientation: we planned the topic together with the children and their teachers and formulated the task of taking pictures, with a disposable camera, of people, places, and events that the children themselves felt were important to them and related to their Sámi languages. The phrase 'where is my Sámi language?' was chosen to represent the key focus of the photography: to find out and show where and with whom the children see their indigenous languages. Even at this early stage we agreed that a practical outcome of this project was a photo exhibition of these pictures at school. This also meant that each photo was presented with the signature of the photographer, i.e. the child, and therefore in the context of the photos, the children are, by their own choice, not anonymised. (2) Photographing: an active period of three weeks for taking pictures. The children were encouraged to follow their own ideas and feelings about where, when and about whom to take pictures, as long as they followed the agreed task. The children were free to take the camera with them to school, and also back home, with them in their free time, etc. (3) Photo processing and discussion: after taking their pictures, the children returned their cameras for the pictures to be developed with the help of a professional. As with the drawing case study, we had a one-to-one discussion about the photos and each child explained to me how each photo related to their experience of the Sámi languages. While learning a lot about the places, people and events that these children had taken pictures of, I also heard stories of their late grandparents, early childhood memories and family networks and practices. Towards the end of the discussion, I asked each child to choose one picture of particular importance to them for the photo exhibition. These discussions were taped and transcribed, yielding altogether over seven hours of discussions. (4) Exhibition: with the help of adults involved with the project (the professional photographer, the teachers and myself) the children framed the one photo they selected for the exhibition, named it and, if willing, gave a brief description of the photo, choosing themselves what language they used. The children chose the place for their photos on the walls of the school designated for this purpose and hung their photos. In the end we had a photo exhibition that generated enthusiasm among the local community and school, including considerable media coverage.

The photos can be seen to reflect these children's sense of the Sámi language environment and its place in their lives. From a methodological point of view, these composite images contribute to the research process by giving the participants the opportunity to select and emphasise aspects of their linguistic and cultural environment, and are part of the final published representations of their understanding of the role and place of Sámi languages and culture (cf. Goopy and Lloyd, 2006).

In order to give an overview of these photos, an inventory of the visual aspect of Sámi languages as experienced and represented by the Sámi children was made. The elements that most often appeared in these photos (n = 308) were people (23 per cent), followed by nature (21 per cent) and animals (20 per cent). Together these three topics appeared in two-thirds (64 per cent) of all pictures. When seen closer, the recurring visualisations in these photos are family members; northern nature and sceneries; and reindeer. Linking to the photographing task—to take pictures of the most important people, places and activities linked to the Sámi language—the children mostly pictured key aspects of Sámi culture, i.e. family, nature and reindeer, an essential aspect of Sámi cultural practices and traditional livelihoods. If we look closer at each of these three types of visualisation, the typical members of the family appearing in these photos are siblings, father and grandmother, as example 10.1 below, a photo taken by a Northern Sámi-speaking girl, illustrates:

The particularly important people for these children's Sámi language seem to be their fathers and grandmothers. Among the 308 photos there was only one picture of a mother (who is not a Sámi speaker). Instead, there were many pictures of fathers (driving a car, driving a snowmobile, walking in the snow, making coffee on an open fire), suggesting that for these children Sámi is more the language of the father than the mother. The social context at least partly explaining this is linked to Sámi livelihoods and to the region where these children live: the reindeer herders stay in the area and are typically Sámi men. The photos also illustrate the transgenerational impact on these children: the grandmothers, who typically belong to the pre-language-shift generation of Sámi people with Sámi language as their first language, were remembered by the children as the ones who talked to them and taught them in Sámi from their early childhood. Some of the children chose to take pictures of various Sámi artefacts such as a scarf, a rug bag or shoes. These items were often related to a story or event concerning their grandparents: the artefacts were made, used, or given by a

Example 10.1   Family—a photo by Maria Saijets: Cáfestellan (a coffee moment).

Example 10.2   Nature, a photo by Anni-Maarit Seipijärvi: Palava puu (a burning tree).

Sámi speaking grandparent who had passed away by the time the study was carried out. The photos illustrate children's networks and the languages associated with them.

The second most frequent element figuring in the photos was nature. The most frequently photographed theme among the photos were vast scenic landscapes and particular locations (a tree, a river, a fell) all linked to the Sámi language in their experience. Example 10.2 above, taken by a ten-year-old Inari Sámi girl, Anni-Maarit Seipijärvi, illustrates these types of photos.

The photos show that for these children, nature in the northern region was the most important Sámi place. If these photos are located in the cultural and social environment of Sámi, we begin to see a possible relation of the nature topic and the most important place for these children: the traditional livelihoods and Sámi ways of living are closely linked to the seasonal cycle of nature and many of the cultural practices were—and still are—regulated by the seasons. Even today, people, particularly reindeer herding families, take into account what is called 'the reindeer year', referring to the tasks and practices related to herding the reindeers. The importance

Example 10.3   Reindeer—Jussa Seurujärvi Rätkim (reindeer round-up).

of nature for the Sámi people is also reflected in the rich Sámi vocabulary related to wildlife, weather and geographical formations—after all, the language is famous for having over a hundred words related to snow, describing its different characteristics (cf. Gaski, 1997; Aikio-Puoskari, 2005).

The third most frequent element in the children's photos was animals (a dog, swans) and most often a reindeer. The picture in example 10.3 is taken by an Inari Sámi boy at the time when he participated for the first time in the reindeer round-up.

The reindeer is embedded deep in Sámi tradition and cultural practices. It is known as 'the animal of life', as in the old days it provided all that was needed: means of transportation, food and material for clothing. Reindeer herding, the round-up in particular, is also a social event as it requires the efforts and cooperation of several families. The events are typically multilingual as the round-ups gather Sámi people from different generations and regions. However, Sámi language has a special function in relation to reindeer: many of the words related to physical appearance of reindeer and to the reindeer herding practices exist only in Sámi and therefore at least some skill in Sámi is required.

These photos suggest that the trajectories through which the Sámi language enters these children's world are linked to key aspects of Sámi culture: family, nature and reindeer.

Among the 308 photos, there were very few pictures of the school or the teachers, although other data related to these children suggest that education is one of the main domains in their lives in which they hear and use

Sámi. The absence of these pictures could be interpreted as an indication that the children themselves did not experience the formal language learning context being important for their Sámi language—rather they represented the effect of that education. There were also very few pictures of the children's friends. When asked, the children responded that usually their friends could not speak any Sámi (coming from non-Sámi families) or if they did know some Sámi, they felt it was easier and quicker to speak Finnish with them.

From a methodological point of view, this visual case study had several functions. Apart from providing a very rich and illuminating way to examine visual representations of the children's experience of Sámi language, it also had other implications. First, it contributed to the valorising of Sámi languages, at least for the period of the photograph project. Perhaps the photos, and particularly the exhibition and perception of photographing as something interesting and 'cool', enhanced the value of Sámi, at least for the moment, making it appear more attractive not only in the eyes of the participants, but in those of other students at the school as well. I was repeatedly asked by other children at the schools when I would be visiting other, Finnish speaking, classes to take pictures. Second, as a researcher, I felt that the level of engagement and enthusiasm in this case study was higher than in others carried out with the same children. As the dialogue became easier and children themselves started to introduce topics and initiate interaction, the sense of closeness also grew. In all, the photography project developed, at least in a certain respect, into a collaborative and an empowering activity, devoid at least some of the patronising tone as it was based on respect and collaboration rather than authority or norms. The project also seemed to provide the children with an opportunity to become the producers of knowledge rather than just being receivers of it in the school context.

DISCUSSION

The visual ethnographic case study discussed above illustrates the simultaneous presence of different experiences and expressions of multilingualism among the youngest speakers of Sámi languages. It represents and reflects multilingual identity, social and cultural environment and relationships by making them visible, and by doing so it offers a point of reflection and ways of representing experiences of multilingualism. The emphasis on the visual mode in the case of the photographs seemed to enable children to find their own voice and agency, regardless of their language skills. Consequently, the focus moved from the languages (and skills) towards the speakers and their voice and experiences. The concept of voice might help to map the meanings of the experience of the individuals in their ways of drawing on and using socially available and conditioned resources: languages, but also genres, discourses, styles, and visualities (Pietikäinen and Dufva, 2006).

This case study can perhaps be taken as an illustration of the potential of applying a more heteroglossic understanding of multilingualism (cf. Creese and Blackledge, 2010; Jørgensen, 2008; Pietikäinen et al., 2008; Pietikäinen, 2010). This kind of 'multi-languaging' or 'polylingual languaging' (Jørgensen, 2008) seems to encourage the speaker flexibly to make use of their unique resources. In the process, one's own voice can be found and presented, and this, in turn, seems to produce a sense of agency in the multilingual, multimodal environment. It appears that the visual ethnography used in these case studies helped the children leave behind a norm of language skills and encouraged the mobilisation of their resources in order to express their feelings. Further, when language skills or language learning were not the focus, the children were freer to use their resources and make them their own. Perhaps this approach offers one view to polycentric language revitalisation in today's multilingual Sámi context. Strong evidence of the potential embedded in this kind of activity comes from the data: when the monolingual language norm was not displayed, there were no differences in capability, performance, or authorship between Northern Sámi and Inari Sámi speakers. In this light, heteroglossic multilingualism might tentatively be understood as a range of multimodal practices, characterised by situational and individual variation, temporal change, and dynamics between languages, discourses, genres, styles and visualities.

NOTES

1. This chapter is produced in the context of a research projects *Northern Multilingualism: Discourses, Experiences and Practices of Linguistic Diversity in the North Calotte*, (http://www.northernmultilingualism.fi) and Peripheral Multilingualism (www.peripheralmultilingualism.fi) funded by the Academy of Finland. My warmest thanks go to the children, their parents and teachers for making the research reported here possible.

REFERENCES

Aikio-Puoskari, U. 2005. The education of the Sámi in the comprehensive schooling of three Nordic countries: Norway, Finland and Sweden. *Gáldu čála* (February 2005), http://www.galdu.org

Bezemer, J. and Kress, G. 2008. Writing in multimodal texts: a social semiotic account of designs for learning. *Written Communication (Special Issue on Writing and New Media)* 25(2): 166–95.

Blommaert, J., Collins, J. and Slembrouck, S. 2005. Spaces of multilingualism. *Language & Communication* 25: 197–216.

Burck, C. 2005. *Multilingual Living: Explorations of Language and Subjectivity*. Hampshire: Palgrave Macmillan.

Creese, A. and Blackledge, A. 2010. Translanguaging in the bilingual classroom: a pedagogy for learning and teaching? *The Modern Language Journal* 94: 103–15.

Dufva, H. and Pietikäinen, S. 2006. Sami languages: Between hope and endangerment. *British Studies in Applied Linguistics* 21: 47–60.

Gaski, H. (ed.) 1997. *In the Shadow of the Midnight Sun: Contemporary Sami Prose and Poetry.* Karasjohka, Norway: Davvi Girji.

Goopy, S. and Lloyd, David. 2006. Documenting the human condition in everyday culture: finding a partnership between ethnography and photo-documentary. *International Journal of the Humanities* 3(5): 33–38.

Heller, M. 2003. Globalization, the new economy, and the commodification of language and identity. *Journal of Sociolinguistics* 7(4): 473–92.

Heller, M. (ed.) 2007. *Bilingualism: A Social Approach.* Basingstoke and New York: Palgrave Macmillan.

Hodge, R. and Jones, K. 2000. Photography in collaborative research on multilingual literacy practices: images and understandings of researcher and researched. In *Multilingual Literacies*, ed. Marilyn Martin-Jones and Kathryn Jones, 299–318. Amsterdam: John Benjamins.

Jacquemet, Marco. 2005. Transidiomatic practices: language and power in the age of globalization. *Language and Communication* 25: 257–77.

Jaffe, A. 2007. Discourses of endangerment: contexts and consequences of essentializing discourses. In *Discourses of Endangerment*, ed. A. Duchene and M. Heller, 57–75. London: Continuum.

Jørgensen, J. N. 2008. Polylingual languaging around and among children and adolescents. *International Journal of Multilingualism* 5(3): 161–76.

Kelly-Holmes, H., Moriarty, M. and Pietikäinen, S. 2009. Convergence and divergence in Basque, Irish and Sámi media language policing. *Language Policy* 8(3): 227–42.

Kress, G. 2010. *Multimodality: A Social Semiotic Approach to Contemporary Communication.* London: Routledge.

Kulonen, U., Seurujärvi-Kari, I. and Pulkkinen, R. (eds) 2005. *The Saami: A Cultural Encyclopaedia.* Helsinki: SKS.

Lehtola, V. 1994. *Saamelainen evakko: rauhan kansa sodan jaloissa.* Helsinki: City saamit.

———. 2000. Kansain välit—monikulttuurisuus ja saamelaishistoria. In *Beaivvi Mánát: Saamelaisten juuret ja nykyaika*, ed. I. Seurujärvi-Kari, 185–96. Helsinki: SKS.

Lindgren, A. 2000. *Helsingin saamelaiset ja oma kieli.* Helsinki: SKS.

Martin-Jones, M. and Jones, K. 2000. (eds) *Multilingual Literacies.* Amsterdam: John Benjamins.

Mavers, D. 2007. Investigating how children make meaning in multimodal maps. *Reflecting Education* 3(1): 24–28.

May, S. 2005. Language rights: moving the debate forward. *Journal of Sociolinguistics* 9(3): 319–47.

Mizen, P. 2005. A little "light work"? Children's images of their labour. *Visual Studies* 20(2): 124–39.

Pietikäinen, S. 2008. Sámi in media: questions of language vitality and cultural hybridisation. *Journal of Multicultural Discourses* 3(1): 22–35.

———. 2010. Sámi language mobility. *International Journal of the Sociology of Language* 2010(202) : 79–101.

Pietikäinen, S., Alanen, R., Dufva, H., Kalaja, P., Leppänen, S. and Pitkänen-Huhta, A. 2008. Languaging in Ultima Thule: multilingualism in the life of a Sami boy. *International Journal of Multilingualism* 5(2): 79–99.

Pietikäinen, S. and Dufva, H. 2006. Voices in discourses: Dialogism, Critical Discourse Analysis, and ethnic identity. *Journal of Sociolinguistics.* 10(2): 205–224.

Pietikäinen, S. and Mäntynen, A. 2009. *Kurssi kohti diskurssia.* Tampere: Vastapaino.

Pietikäinen, Sari., Huss, L. Laihiala-Kankainen, S., Aikio-Puoskari, U. and Lane, P. 2010. Regulating multilingualism in the North Calotte: the case of Kven, Meänkieli and Sámi languages. *Acta Borealia*, 27(1): 1–23.

Pink, S. 2007. *Doing Visual Ethnography*. London, Thousand Oaks and New Delhi: Sage.

Pratt, M. L. 1987. Linguistic utopias. In *The Linguistics of Writing: Arguments between Language and Literature*, ed. N. Fabb, D. Attridge, A. Durant and C. MacCabe, 48–66. Manchester: Manchester University Press.

Savolainen, M. 2004. Maailman ihanin lapsi—valokuva perheessä. In *Leikin pikkujättiläinen*, ed. L. Piironen. Helsinki: WSOY.

Scollon, R. and Scollon, S. W. 2001. *Intercultural Communication: A Discourse Approach* (2nd edition). Malden, Oxford and Carlton: Blackwell.

———. 2004. *Nexus Analysis: Discourse and the Emerging Internet*. London and New York: Routledge.

11 Ethnographic Perspectives on Multilingual Computer-Mediated Discourse

Insights from Finnish Football Forums on the Web

Samu Kytölä and Jannis Androutsopoulos

Computer-mediated communication (CMC) is steadily becoming more multilingual. This development has caught the attention of researchers who have an increasing interest in adapting the traditions of research in sociolinguistics and bilingualism to new emergent socio-cultural domains, communicative contexts and technological formats (Androutsopoulos, 2007; Danet and Herring, 2007). This chapter[1] is an attempt at methodological reflection on pivotal issues in sociolinguistically and discourse-analytically oriented CMC research, and our main focus lies on the benefits that *ethnographically grounded* approaches can bring to such research. The empirical context deployed to illustrate our points here is the Finnish online football discussion forums *Futisforum* and *Futisforum2.org*, and the data we draw on is from ongoing research by Kytölä.

MULTILINGUALISM ONLINE: DISCOURSE-ANALYTIC AND ETHNOGRAPHIC APPROACHES

Research on online multilingualism so far has mainly drawn on canonical methodologies within linguistics. For instance, frameworks for bilingual spoken interaction (such as Auer, 1999) have been applied to study patterns of code-switching on the web (e.g. Hinrichs, 2006; Androutsopoulos, 2006, 2007). However, methodological reflection has recently emerged on the transferability of earlier frameworks into the forms and formats of CMC contexts (Hinrichs, 2006: 28–31; Sebba, 2008;

Androutsopoulos and Beisswenger, 2008; Kytölä, 2012). Research into 'the multilingual internet' (Danet and Herring, 2007; Leppänen and Peuronen, forthcoming) has opened up interesting avenues of investigation, including measurement of linguistic diversity online (Paolillo, 2007), English as an online *lingua franca* (Durham, 2007), language and script choice online (Warschauer, Said and Zohry, 2002; Lam and Rosario-Ramos, 2009; Lee, 2007), and code-switching within specific communities of practice (Siebenhaar, 2006; Hinrichs, 2006; Androutsopoulos, 2007; Leppänen et al., 2009).

For CMC research, a corpus-analytic or otherwise quantitative inventory can unearth overall distributions of linguistic varieties and generate very useful occurrence statistics of different types. However, corpus-analytic and quantitative approaches may overlook the pragmatics of language use in micro-level interaction and even leave it unexplained or under-contextualised. We, too, use quantitative approaches to provide overviews, inventories or backdrops of the contexts that we are researching, but the primary research approach in our respective projects has been a *qualitative*—discourse-analytic, pragmatic and interactional-sociolinguistic—one, because our common aim has been to gain insights into the rich and contextualised patterns of code choice and the sequentially unfolding code alternation in different online spaces.

The study of the multilingual internet by linguists in late 1990s to early 2000s relied on quantitative inventories and qualitative analyses of log data, with less respect to social actors' self-perceptions or the (multilingual) social action itself (Androutsopoulos, 2008). Meanwhile, largely outside linguistics, systematic online ethnographies were already being conducted with the aim of examining social actors' points of view. We build on this tradition of 'virtual' or 'online' ethnography (Thomsen, Straubhaar and Bolyard, 1998; Hine, 2000; Rutter and Smith, 2005) and link it to the sociolinguistic study of multilingual practices (Heller, 2007; Pennycook, 2007). For us, key areas of discourse-analytic-ethnographic internet research include the *emergence* of multilingual practices and communities, their *local and situated* character, the *social meanings* of multilingual language use, the *norms* governing multilingual usage in various genres, and holistic *description* of multilingual communities (see also Androutsopoulos, 2008: 3). The incorporation of an ethnographic perspective has further epistemological consequences (cf. Agar, 2006; Blommaert and Dong, 2010: 5–15): we set out to study a range of *situated, contingent uses of different language styles* by different social actors for *multiple and highly specific purposes of communication*, including identity work and social structure. Moreover, ethnography can provide a 'conceptual and methodological bridge' to other fields (Androutsopoulos, 2008: 3), while it also contributes to the 'broadening the scope of interpretation' (ibid.) and to enabling the researcher's better access to emic meanings, views and categories.

Highlighting our concern with language use, we also use the term 'computer-mediated discourse' (CMD) here.[2] Moreover, we link discourse analysis with ethnography in a combined approach, discourse-centred online ethnography (DCOE), which aims at a holistic understanding of (multilingual) processes online. Outlined in Androutsopoulos (2008), DCOE encompasses three ways of examining computer-mediated discourse practices from an ethnographic viewpoint: (1) systematic observation of online activities, (2) reconstruction of text trajectories, and (3) engagement with online social actors. In this chapter we discuss how these techniques may be used in order to gain insights into multilingual practices in a specific site of computer-mediated discourse, i.e. Finnish football communities. In particular, we focus on the first two ethnographic elements of DCOE. Like Rutter and Smith (2005), we suggest that systematic observation leads to an enhanced understanding of a computer-mediated discourse community, including its discussion topics, its regular and peripheral members and their interrelations, the emergence of sub-communities, and so on. The study of text trajectories involves tracing the history of interrelated posts and threads as well as conducting tailored searches and using forums' statistics in order to trace the history of particular language practices. Taken together, DCOE emphasises the benefit of 'being there' as computer-mediated discourse events unfold.

NATIONAL LANGUAGE AND 'VERSATILE ENGLISH' IN CMD

The type of online multilingualism investigated here is the combination of English and a dominant 'national' language (Finnish) in web environments that are clearly confined to a particular nation-state in terms of their discourse production and consumption practices.[3] Our research emphasises the considerable fluidity and variability in the uses and functions of English. Traditionally, research on the use of English in Finnish and German media discourse has focused on 'Anglicisms', i.e. words and expressions 'borrowed' from English into the respective 'recipient language'. However, researchers from discourse studies and interactional sociolinguistics have recently emphasised that English assumes a broad range of communicative functions in the discourse and linguistic repertoires of online communities in both Finland and Germany (cf. Leppänen et al., 2009; Androutsopoulos, 2007). In Finland, in particular, the importance of English has grown rapidly in various domains of life since the 1950s, first as a language of international contact and imported cultural productions, later as a desirable communicative resource in different contexts, including the internet.[4] English in Finnish CMD comes in a range of registers and styles, which partly depend on (and are indexical of) the subcultures relevant to each virtual space (e.g. fan fiction), and partly respond to specific communicative events (such as gaming). Moreover, English has currency in specific functions and positions within online discourse spaces: for example, as a base language motivated by topic or participant framework, as formulaic chunks, as slogans and routines for flagging groupness, and as personal or group emblems (usernames, signatures, slogans).

Because neither 'English' nor its uses by non-native speakers are monolithic, homogenous units, the notion of English/national language bilingualism can only be a point of entry into a highly versatile field of language use. We therefore emphasise the importance of adequate *contextualisation* for building an understanding of that language use in its historical, socio-cultural and technological context (Blommaert, 2005; contributions in Heller, 2007). Whereas much earlier scholarship on English drew upon apparently obvious, binary distinctions such as between 'native' and 'non-native', 'second' and 'foreign language', 'pure Finnish' and 'Anglicisms', we find it useful to align with constructivist approaches to language in social life and employ notions such as appropriation, entextualisation, stylisation and performance (see Pennycook, 2007; Rampton, 2006) against an ethnographic backdrop in order to tap into complex, multilingual mediascapes, such as the *Futisforums* discussed here.

THE TWO FINNISH *FUTISFORUMS*: A BRIEF OVERVIEW

Futisforum, part of the commercial website *Soccernet*, was the first Finland-based web discussion forum for football; its earliest version dates from 1996, but the current format was established in 1999. *Futisforum2.org* (henceforth *FF2.org*) was launched in 2006 independently by one activist to complement the badly managed original *Futisforum*.[5] A new space with constantly emerging new practices, *FF2.org* still carries on much of the discursive heritage from the original *Futisforum*. The *Futisforums* have developed into spaces for Finnish football enthusiasts to exchange information and opinions, form community, to negotiate and co-construct their individual and shared fan identities. The number of members is around 20,000 (*Futisforum*) and 30,000 (*FF2.org*),[6] of which approximately 15 per cent have 100 or more postings. The number of topics (discussion threads) amounts to about 40,000 (*Futisforum*) and 50,000 (*FF2.org*). Due to this sheer volume, any qualitative or ethnographic study of the forums is bound to be highly selective and based on a particular period of focussed observation.

The multilingual practices evident on the *Futisforums* must be seen within the nexus of three major socio-historical developments: the current increase of English in the macro-sociolinguistics of Finland (e.g. Leppänen and Nikula, 2007), the rapid explosion of Finns' internet usage over the last fifteen years, and the transformation of football fandom in Finland (very much driven by the *Futisforums* themselves). The forums are, from the outset, clearly targeted at Finnish speakers. This is evident in the thematic division into sub-forums that are labelled only in Finnish, the general run of topics in all sub-forums, and the predominance of Finnish in the actual discussions. However, some of Kytölä's richest data originate from settings where the use of Finnish is contested and challenged by non-Finns, Swedish speakers, or '*aficionados*' using a football-wise language less widely known among Finns. (Standard) English is also a communicative resource that has considerable currency and a wide range of uses. Whereas languages other than Finnish and English are also used, they mostly occupy specialized niches (for example, German mostly occurs in discussions on German football) and are often explicitly discouraged. Many members self-identify as Swedish-speakers, yet the actual use of Swedish remains mostly limited to topics about the Sweden or Swedish speaking Finland. Standard English is often used without meta-commentary (apologies, translations) and thus appears to be an assumedly shared code. However, frequent meta-talk in the forums about the use of English includes a good deal of criticism too. The uses of English in the forums include:

a. simple or complex lexical items (e.g. *pre-match pint*),
b. constituents in Finnish/English compounds (e.g. *jänkhäderby*, a compound that denotes a match, 'derby', between any two of the major, top-level Lapland clubs),
c. formulaic phrases (e.g. *Let's puuhast*, where *puuhast* is a mock-Anglicized abbreviation of the pejorative [in this context] Finnish verb *puuhastella*, 'to manage something in an amateurish way')
d. extended stretches of discourse (e.g. the messages in the *myll* example in this chapter).
e. the base language of some discussion threads (including the mock-Altan topics described below).

Drawing on the search facilities of web discussion forums, some of these categories lend themselves to a quantitative analysis of their frequency or to an analysis of individual usage patterns with regard to particular (clusters of) (Kytölä, 2012) participants. However, what is important is to reconstruct how these categories of English resources integrate into the distinctive discourse styles that can be observed in the forums. *Futisforum* and *FF2.org* are replete with their own 'forumisms',[7] which draw on many language varieties; also the uses of English depicted above are part of the discourse styles developed over time. Understanding them might be challenging even for native speakers of Finnish who are not familiar with these forums.[8]

RESEARCHING MULTILINGUALISM ON THE *FUTISFORUMS*

Data Gathering

The data for Kytölä's project was collected in five different phases, each one characterised by different degrees of ethnographic grounding. Taken together, the data collection spanned four years, yielding data from almost a decade. Whereas Kytölä was not able to trace the origins of some of the multilingual practices that 'were already there' upon his first visits to the forum, he has managed to document other practices during their very emergence and spread. His roles in this project thus include both that of an 'archive researcher' and that of an 'eye-witness' (cf. Rutter and Smith, 2005).

The four research phases entailed different analytical stances and methods, particularly with respect to ethnography. *Phase 1* (2004–5) initially involved getting acquainted with the community as a casual visitor, so that when conscious research began (*Phase 2*), Kytölä was already a (marginal) member in *Futisforum*. *Phase 3* (2006) involved systematic observation (with a minor degree of active participation), but in 2007 it become clear that a broader ethnographic approach was needed in order to better understand the multilingualism in the data. *Phase 4* (2008–9) involved tracing several text trajectories and unearthing connections between discourse events. The close ethnographic observation of *Phase 3* enabled Kytölä to capture the temporal structure and 'rhythm' of communicative activities in the forums. In both *Futisforum* (especially until 2007) and in *FF2.org*, several sub-forums are active all the time, and hundreds of users are contributing day and night.[9] Participating for a long time in the hectic 'rhythm' of such a community is difficult even for the devoted researcher, but doing it systematically for a focussed period enables insights that could not be gained without 'being there'. Presenting two examples from Kytölä's study, we will now illustrate that advantage of 'being there'. In line with our shared research interest outlined previously, the examples mainly involve uses of English and Finnish, standard and non-standard.

Advantages Accruing from Discourse-Centred Online Ethnography

Case 1: Mocking Turkish and Arab 'voices'

The first example illustrates how ethnographic knowledge of the unfolding of an online discourse event is beneficial to the interpretation of language use that departs from the conventional usage patterns of an online community. Key to that example is the presence on *Futisforum* of a member calling himself by a Turkish male name, Altan (changed here due to ethical considerations). Altan first appeared on *Futisforum* in early 2005, when Kytölä was already familiar with that forum (but had not planned any research into it). Altan made several friendly requests for information, expressing willingness to be included in the forum community. However, Altan's attempts were met by regular contributors with responses ranging from benevolent and helpful to malevolent and utterly racist. Many of these responses focused on Altan's distinctive English which was framed as 'bad' or 'funny'. Indeed, his English was arguably 'ungrammatical' and 'truncated', yet it was 'football-wise' entirely appropriate English (involving the use of terms such as 'transfers', 'squad', 'livescore', 'lineup', 'derby', or 'rigging'). In 2006 Altan, who had presented an interest in betting on Finnish football matches, initiated a discussion topic about an unusual match result in the Finnish League, Veikkausliiga[10] (see Example 11.1).

This short message contains several features of non-Standard English. Whereas the lack of capitalization ('i') can be relatively common in CMD (also *Futisforums*), the lack of punctuation does stand out here as more marked. Moreover, ellipticity and the subject-complement relationships here, although comprehensible, become immediately framed as non-standard (for many: 'ungrammatical') in the eyes of a person who knows Standard English well. Then, this message triggered a substantial wave of imitations: within a few weeks, dozens of 'mock-Altan' messages were posted, mostly initiating new mock-topics. Kytölä managed to document

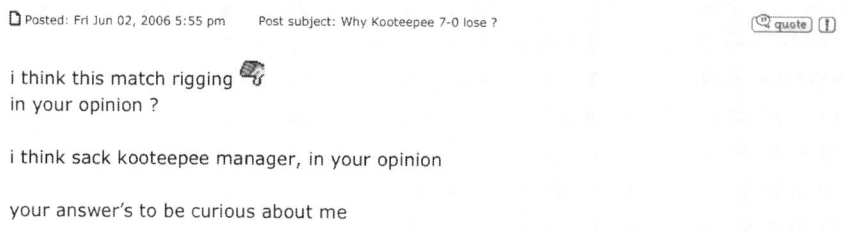

Posted: Fri Jun 02, 2006 5:55 pm   Post subject: Why Kooteepee 7-0 lose ?   quote

i think this match rigging
in your opinion ?

i think sack kooteepee manager, in your opinion

your answer's to be curious about me

Example 11.1

a.   Why Tps 5–0 lose ?
b.   Why Inter lose 5–0?
c.   Why Serbia-Montenegro 6–0 lose
d.   why san marino 0–13 lose?
e.   why Østerbr 0–7 and Sorø IF Freja 0–8 loose *(FF2.org)*
f.   Why England again penalty shoot out lose
g.   why switzerland 0 goals penalty shootout?
h.   Why Poland 1–3 lose ? *(at a Polish football forum)*
i.   Why Honka announse ouver 3000 spektators?
j.   why kalpa 2754 spektators?
k.   why russia no human rights?

Example 11.2

a total of around fifty instances, although some more disappeared from the forum. A sample of mock-Altan headings is shown below to give an idea of the variation and the non-standard features that were deployed (see Example 11.2).

The topic of the first 'mock-Altan' posts was 'a surprisingly big defeat' (a–e); later they could be about any match scores (h), attendance figures in ice-hockey (j), or even about not sport-related topics (k). *Futisforum* members also spread the 'innovation' onto the newly launched *FF2.org* (e) and non-Finnish forums (h). Similar non-standard phrases, along with other mock-Altan formulations, re-occurred with slight variations. It was clear that this formulaic recycling was deliberate and that its major function was in-group humour. If Kytölä had not been an observer in this forum for a focussed period, it would probably have been more difficult to afterwards interpret these exchanges and to capture the tenor of the contributions (i.e. the mocking) and the implicit positioning of Altan (a real or imaginary participant) within this online community. One could argue that the textual trace of the case alone still 'speaks for itself' even years after, but it would be difficult to later reconstruct, for instance, the participation framework in the 'Altan' topics (2005–6). Direct observation of discourse events such as these, accompanied by helpful field notes, puts the researcher in a good position to interpret actors' interpersonal stances or nuances of social meaning in such a complex chain of events.

However, one particular aspect of Altan's case kept puzzling Kytölä for some time: Despite the fact that Altan presented himself quite convincingly as a native speaker of Turkish and a member of Turkish football forums, many participants seemed to distrust him in that respect. Instead, there were ample references to Altan as 'fake', 'troll', 'provo[cateur]', someone else's 'side nick[name]', or a betting criminal (Finland had seen a football betting scandal the previous year). For Kytölä, however, Altan presented

Posted: Tue Mar 30, 2004 9:32 am   Post subject: feel the beet!! friiheten, bum-bum, friiiheten!!!1   quote

Ala sina suomipoika sure mina bulent voida opetta sinule huva iskuvinki jos sina tahto usi vaale naine. Sina püuta kanis naine muuta sinu kansa Türki. ☺

Example 11.3
Translation: Don't you Finnish boy regret I bulent can teach you good ways to pick up women if you want a new blond. You ask beautiful woman move with you to Türkey.

in a convincing manner as a 'real Turk', judging also from his use of features of Turkish orthography[11] and due to the authentic-looking output in non-Standard English. Altan even gave a couple of cues to his activity in a Turkish forum. Yet others' suspicions continued for a long time, implicitly and explicitly. However, the main issue here is neither Altan's offline identity nor other participants' perceptions, but rather the way in which his 'othering', by echoing his 'voice', was co-constructed by the alternation between varieties of (mock)-English and Finnish, and the pejorative discourse in relation to it.

Kytölä's reading of that aspect of the case of Altan changed several months later, when he discovered earlier cases of 'fake foreigner' *Futisforum* members. One 2004 case went by the equally Turkish name of Bulent, together with the Arabic name of Aliydah. Whereas at first sight these may have appeared to be screen names by immigrants joining the forum, a closer examination of their content and language style revealed they had been created by Finnish contributors with the purpose of articulating racist discourse on Turks, and more generally on 'the hairy arms' (*sic*; frequent emic formulation) immigrants from the Middle East, South-East Europe or even North Africa. The primary resources of that discourse were (at all levels) non-Standard 'bad' *Finnish* together with a range of non-football topics such as pizzeria ownership (a stereotypical immigrant occupation), Finnish women, Turkey, or—ironically—racism (see Example 11.3).

The use of such 'bad' Finnish in the representations of Bulent and Aliydah prompts the interpretation of them as racist fake members. In fact, Aliydah's message history revealed a sudden shift overnight from 'bad' mock-Finnish into standard written Finnish. This supports the interpretation that a fake immigrant identity was being constructed. It was also confirmed in one metalinguistic comment on Aliydah's proficiency in Finnish. This background knowledge enhanced Kytölä's understanding of the suspicions about the authenticity of the core case of Altan—several months after the real-time observations on that case. To paraphrase Blommaert (2005: 56–67), participants enter communication situations which can have a considerable amount of historical baggage.

Altan *unknowingly* carried the load of the fake-Turk, entering a space that had earlier developed into a semi-racist one where suspicions about 'Turks' were articulated. This later insight about discourse events that far preceded Kytölä's observation and data collection periods makes it somewhat easier to account for the fact that there were far more comments that were suspicious of the unfortunate Altan than responses that were helpful to him. So, this is an example on how an ethnography of digital text trajectories can inform a discourse-analytic interpretation of the data.

Case 2: 'The Myll and the Road' as jocular, in-group intertextuality

Whereas this second case differs from the first in that Kytölä did not observe it as it happened, it too illustrates the benefits of tracing text trajectories and connections. The following discourse chain occurred during Kytölä's period of participant observation (2006–7), but evaded his gaze simply because so much was going on all the time on the two *Futisforums*. The 'Myll' case at *FF2.org* caught Kytölä's eye as he was, now purposefully, searching for deliberate uses of non-Standard English, following the case of Altan. It started as is shown in Example 11.4.

This chaotic-looking thread was located under the sub-forum 'Games' (i.e. computer games, internet gaming, etc.), which Kytölä originally intended to exclude from his data collection. The participants in this thread were playing some kind of virtual ice-hockey game on another website, a joint online activity that required team cooperation and strategic planning. Most of their messages resembled casual, synchronous

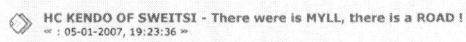

HC KENDO OF SWEITSI - There were is MYLL, there is a ROAD !
≪ : 05-01-2007, 19:23:36 ≫

There were is MYLL, there is a ROAD !

THE MYLL IDEOLOGY - NEVER FORGET !

Otsikko muutettu siitä syystä että Hoky Fyght Liigaan ei päästy ja luultavimmni sinne menee Hockey club Dynamo.

Example 11.4
Translation: Heading changed because we didn't get to Hoky Fyght Liiga and most likely Hockey club Dynamo will.

Miehekäs päätös. 👍

FAR RIGHT STRICT DISCLIPTINE AND POWERFUL LEADERSHIP BACK TO HC
SWITZERLAND JANYARY 2007 - NEVER FORGET 🏯 🏯 🏯

Example 11.5
Translation: Miehekäs päätös = a manly decision

chat (in terms of both style and the quick exchange pace of messages)
and were relatively hard to follow, even for a researcher who was familiar
with *FF2.org*. Patterns of non-Standard English were mixed throughout
the thread with colloquial 'Forumese', involving extensive use of graphic
emoticons, as is seen in Example 11.5.

Having missed the original emergence of this topic, even Kytölä could
only make sense of parts of it. Previous experience suggested that:

- 'Kendo' is an established pejorative term for the much hated ice-
  hockey among the online football community, with a reference to
  'sticks' used for 'fighting'. Accordingly, 'HC' must stand for 'Hockey
  Club'.
- 'Sweitsi' is a minimally modified spelling of *Sveitsi* 'Switzerland',
  another joke dating from the older forum, where one active member
  openly identified as a supporter of Switzerland's national team in the
  2006 World Cup.
- As for 'the myll ideology', standard Finnish *mylly* means '(wind) mill',
  whereas a specialized usage in colloquial Finnish is 'fist fight in ice-
  hockey', further shifted (at least in *Futisforum* usage) into 'any fist
  fight' or 'any fight'. Here, we see another reference to the football
  fans' conception of ice-hockey as an inferior violent game with fights.
  The spelling 'myll' appears cunningly to create an English-like lexical
  item while, at the same time, 'Finnishizing' the vowel's orthography,
  thus making the reference to *mylly* more explicit.

However, a major part of the social meaning here (cruel humour and
representation of in-group superiority) would be missed without knowledge of the intertextuality around the 'mill tattoo'. This had emerged as
a mock-topic in a sub-forum of the older *Futisforum*. Brief background
information is needed here: in 2005, the Finnish evening papers had covered a story about a Finnish celebrity's tattoo that had got an English idiom
wrong. Whereas slight variants exist, the idiom is most commonly known
in the form:

"Where there's a will, there's a way."

According to the published pictures,[12] the tattoo, however, read as follows:

"There **were** is will, there is a **road**." (our emphases)

Below is a schematic reworking[13] of the tattoo (see Picture 11.1).

In the tattoo, the word 'will' looked rather like 'mill'. Moreover, the intended cross indeed resembled a wind mill, resulting in added mockery and joking in *Futisforum* about the relationship between a wind mill and the road leading past it. Image manipulations were made with a mill and a road replacing the original cross in the tattoo. Below is our schematic version of one Futisforumist's image manipulation (see Picture 11.2).

With the help of deliberate searches for trajectories of these 'myll'-related memes, Kytölä discovered that mockery and humour related to the tattoo, the 'mill' and the 'road' continued with considerable intensity. These semiotic resources were posted in both *Futisforums*, incorporated in the already

Picture 11.1   The celebrity's tattoo.

existing 'pool of bad English', and used for joking and mocking purposes in later discussions. Deliberately 'bad' usage of 'will/mill', and the pejorative reference to a disliked sport, thus served as meaning-making resources for constructing a 'myll' discourse for solidarity and boundary marking with regard to excluded 'others' (e.g. fans of ice-hockey or fighting, 'ignorant' models, or, importantly with regard to multilingualism, users of 'bad' English). This has many similarities with the 'othering' of Turks and Arabs presented in Example 11.1.

The mocking case of Altan (2005–6) came up at the time when Kytölä was most actively engaged in participant observation of the discussion forums, experiencing the discourse as it unfolded. He was thus in an ideal

Picture 11.2   The mill and the road.

position to interpret these processes of in-group interaction and online joking. Understanding the 'Bulent-Aliydah' case was more challenging, because they had come up in an earlier period and therefore were difficult to reconstruct—these were by now 'distant' discourse events. Yet their later discovery enhanced Kytölä's understanding of the Altan case. Moreover, Kytölä had, at first, totally missed this particular source of 'bad English' as a communicative group resource, but the discovery of the cases 'HC Kendo of Sweitsi' and the related 'mill tattoo' helped him reconstruct it. This also served as a lesson that key linguistic practices can even emerge in unexpected sub-spaces, as Kytölä had—to a too great extent—ignored these 'off-topic' non-football-related discussions due to their marginal positions in the virtual spaces of *FF2.org* and *Futisforum*.

CONCLUDING COMMENTS

In conclusion, the main points of this chapter are both empirical and methodological in nature. Empirically, we find that the uses of English in these Finnish forums extend beyond conventional loanwords or borrowings and into the deliberate, highly stylized usage of non-Standard English. The English contributions to the *Futisforums* discussed above suggest that regular contributors share a co-constructed resource pool of 'bad English' from which phrases and constructions can be continuously and intertextually recycled, revised, and spread to new spaces (cf. 'entextualisation', Blommaert, 2005: 47–48) for jocular and exclusionary purposes. We demonstrated that one main function of such idiosyncratic uses of English can be to reinforce boundaries between forum regulars (who are savvy, appreciate football, know nuances of English) and various kinds of outsiders (who are ignorant, appreciate ice-hockey, use English 'wrongly').

Secondly, we suggest that systematic observation of online discourse activities and ethnography of text trajectories provide a useful hermeneutic spiral for the interpretation of online events and textual fragments which, at first sight, seem to be chaotic or inexplicable. More generally, ethnographically informed approaches to computer-mediated discourse analysis enable researchers to develop a grip on the 'rhythm' of discussion forums as a backdrop against which to interpret particular uses of language and discourse styles. Researchers are advantageously positioned to understand particular usages when they see them emerge, as they participate in the rhythm of the online forum. This is particularly useful with large and active forums such as the *Futisforums* whose all-embracing documentation is practically impossible. However, a systematic and focused observation of selected 'areas' of such forums over a period of time allows researchers to acquire some of the 'tacit knowledge' underlying the semiotic practices of key regular contributors.

Other ethnographic strategies such as tracing text trajectories and systematically contacting online actors (cf. Androutsopoulos, 2008) may be more useful when focussing on usages whose 'momentum' falls outside the necessarily limited period of systematic observation or which are located on the 'margins' of the examined virtual space(s). In addition, Androutsopoulos (2008) argues that direct contact to discourse participants can contribute to an emic understanding of language practices online, to the extent it is combined with an analysis of screen data. Yet direct inquiries about people's language use may well be misleading, because people's on-prompt reflection may turn out to be contradictory to their observed behaviour (Blommaert and Dong, 2010: 3). By contrast, combining screen data to data obtained by direct contact, such as interviews, may be particularly fruitful as it allows researchers to confront people with their own language use (or that of their community), and at the same time to check their interpretations against those by participants.

A further issue left largely outside the scope of this chapter is that of 'overhearers' or 'lurkers'. These are ubiquitous members in the overall participant framework who only read (the forums) but do not actively contribute to online content. They remain a methodological challenge for research, because they are by and large invisible, although web forum statistics may readily give information, for instance, on how many registered members have made zero postings. From the point of view of investigating multilingualism, we only get the active authors' multilingual outcomes, the visible discourse, but can only speculate on how the numerous non-writing 'lurkers' understand, like, or 'silently' react to them (cf. Rutter and Smith, 2005). A totally different (albeit arguably ethnographic) methodological combination would be needed for such an investigation.

The methodological considerations spelled out above are most directly applicable to the multi-authored, asynchronous format of web discussion forums (Kytölä, 2012). Other CMD modes may be subject to different orders of linguistic normativity, resulting in different manifestations of multilingualism, or embed a different principle for archiving old discourse. Moreover, new formats of CMD emerge frequently, often combining features from older ones. These are, therefore, likely to require different research designs and different strategies for linking discourse analysis with ethnography.

NOTES

1. We are grateful to Sirpa Leppänen and the editors of this volume for their valuable comments.

2. In early research into CMC, the emphasis was on the interactional features that were specific to the new modes of communication. Later researchers (among the very first Susan Herring) used the term Computer-Mediated Discourse (CMD), shifting the focus from the process to the product, yet acknowledging the dynamic and dialogic features in concordance with developments in discourse analysis. 'CMC' is the first—and more frequent—umbrella term calling attention to the process of interaction, whereas 'CMD' is a useful conceptual bridge to discourse-analytically oriented research (see also Herring: 2001: 612)
3. Kytölä's doctoral research investigates the use of multilingual communicative resources within Finland-based online football communities. It was undertaken at the University of Jyväskylä as part of the Research Unit for the Study of Variation, Contacts and Change in English (VARIENG), as well as the Finland Distinguished Professor (FiDiPro) project entitled *Multilingualism as a Problematic Resource*. Both projects were funded by the Academy of Finland.
4. See Leppänen and Nikula (2007) for an overview; Leppänen et al. (2009) for CMD; Kytölä (2008) for football forums.
5. The URL of *Futisforum* is http://suomifutisnet.adv1.nebula.fi/phpBB2. *Futisforum2* is at http://futisforum2.org.
6. 1 January 2011. These estimates by Kytölä attempt to exclude multiple nicknames by the same user.
7. The Finnish term used in the forums themselves is *foorumismi*; Kytölä's translation.
8. This has been testified by Kytölä in seminars and data sessions where his data have been discussed.
9. Average number of postings per day according to *FF2.org*'s statistics is 3013; average number of new topics per day is twenty-six (4 January 2011).
10. In this particular match, played on 1 June 2006, TPS (Turun Palloseura from the city of Turku) defeated FC KooTeePee (from Kotka). The final score was 7–0.
11. E.g. 'FİNNİSH', 'gençlerbirliği'.
12. The gossip magazine *7 päivää* in early July 2005.
13. We thank Ari Häkkinen, University of Jyväskylä, for editing the images.

REFERENCES

Agar, M. 2006. An ethnography by any other name. . . . *Forum: Qualitative Social Research* 7(4). http://www.qualitative-research.net/index.php/fqs/article/view/177 (accessed 19 January 2011).
Androutsopoulos, J. 2006. Multilingualism, diaspora, and the internet: codes and identities on German-based diaspora websites. *Journal of Sociolinguistics* 10(4): 520–47.
———. 2007. Language choice and code-switching in German-based diasporic web forums. In *The Multilingual Internet*, ed. B. Danet and S. Herring, 340–61. Oxford: Oxford University Press.
———. 2008. Potentials and limitations of discourse-centered online ethnography. *Language@Internet* 5 (Special Issue: *Data and Methods in Computer-Mediated Discourse Analysis*). http://www.languageatinternet.org.
Androutsopoulos, J. and Beisswenger, M. 2008. Introduction: data and methods in computer-mediated discourse analysis. *Language@Internet* 5 (Special Issue:

Data and Methods in Computer-Mediated Discourse Analysis). http://www.languageatinternet.org.

Auer, P. 1999. From codeswitching via language mixing to fused lects. Toward a dynamic typology of bilingual speech. *International Journal of Bilingualism* 3(4): 309–32.

Blommaert, J. 2005. *Discourse*. Cambridge: Cambridge University Press.

Blommaert, J. and Dong, J. 2010. *Ethnographic Fieldwork: A Beginner's Guide*. Bristol: Multilingual Matters.

Danet, B. and Herring, S. (eds) 2007. *The Multilingual Internet*. Oxford: Oxford University Press.

Durham, M. 2007. Language choice on a Swiss mailing list. In *The Multilingual Internet*, ed. B. Danet and S. Herring, 319–39. Oxford: Oxford University Press.

Heller, M. ed. 2007. *Bilingualism: a social approach*. Basingstoke, Hampshire: Palgrave Macmillan.

Herring, S. 2001. Computer-mediated discourse. In *The Handbook of Discourse Analysis*, ed. D. Schiffrin, D. Tannen and H. Hamilton, 612–34. Oxford: Blackwell.

Hine, C. 2000. *Virtual Ethnography*. London: Sage.

Hinrichs, L. 2006. *Codeswitching on the Web*. Amsterdam: John Benjamins.

Kytölä, S. 2008. Englanti huumorin ja syrjinnän välineenä suomalaisen *Futisforumin* keskusteluissa. In *Kolmas kotimainen. Lähikuvia englannin käytöstä Suomessa*, ed. S. Leppänen, T. Nikula and L. Kääntä, 236–74. Helsinki: SKS.

———. 2012. Multilingual Web Discussion Forums. Theoretical, Practical and Methodological Issues. In *Language Mixing and Code-Switching in Writing. Approaches to Mixed-Language Written Discourse*, ed. M. Sebba, S. Mahootian and C. Jonsson, 106–27. New York, NY: Routledge.

Lam, W. S. E. and Rosario-Ramos, E. 2009. Multilingual literacies in transnational digitally-mediated contexts: an exploratory study of immigrant teens in the United States. *Language and Education* 23(2): 171–90.

Lee, C. K. M. 2007. Affordances and text-making practices in on-line instant messaging. *Written Communication* 24(3): 223–49.

Leppänen, S. and Nikula, T. 2007. Diverse uses of English in Finnish society: discourse-pragmatic insights into media, educational and business contexts. *Multilingua* 26(4): 333–80.

Leppänen, S. and Peuronen, S. Forthcoming. Multilingualism on the internet. In *Handbook of Research on Multilingualism*, ed. M. Martin-Jones., A. Blackledge and A. Creese, 384–402. London: Routledge.

Leppänen, S., Pitkänen-Huhta, A., Piirainen-Marsh, A., Nikula, T. and Peuronen, S. 2009. Young people's translocal new media uses: a multiperspective analysis of language choice and heteroglossia. *Journal of Computer-Mediated Communication* 14(4): 1080–1107.

Paolillo, J. 2007. How much multilingualism? Language diversity on the Internet. In *The Multilingual Internet*, ed. B. Danet and S. Herring, 408–30. Oxford: Oxford University Press.

Pennycook, A. 2007. *Global Englishes and Transcultural Flows*. London: Routledge.

Rampton, B. 2006. *Language in Late Modernity: Interaction in an Urban School*. Cambridge: Cambridge University Press.

Rutter, J. and Smith, G. W. H. 2005. Ethnographic presence in a nebulous setting. In *Virtual Methods: Issues in Social Research on the Internet*, ed. C. Hine, 81–92. Oxford: Berg.

Sebba, M. 2008. Mixed-language texts and websites: a framework for analysis. Presentation at Sociolinguistic Symposium 17, Amsterdam, 5 April 2008.

Siebenhaar, B. 2006. Code choice and code-switching in Swiss-German internet relay chat rooms. *Journal of Sociolinguistics* 10(4): 481–506.

Thomsen, S., Straubhaar, J. and Bolyard, D. 1998. Ethnomethodology and the study of online communities: exploring the cyber streets. *Information Research* 4(1). http://informationr.net/ir/4–1/paper50.html (accessed 31 January 2011).

Warschauer, M., El Said, G. R. and Zohry, A. 2002. Language choice online: globalization and identity in Egypt. Journal of Computer-Mediated Communication 7(4). http://jcmc.indiana.edu/vol7/issue4/warschauer.html (accessed 31 January 2011).

12 Multilingual Nation Online?

Possibilities and Constraints on the BBC Voices Website

Bethan L. Davies, Tommaso M. Milani and Will Turner

In recent years, multilingualism in computer-mediated communication (CMC) has gained considerable momentum as a topic of sociolinguistic enquiry (see Danet and Herring, 2007, for an overview). Whereas research in this area has provided us with nuanced analyses of how different languages are used in CMC, what has been somewhat overlooked is that multilingualism itself can be the 'object of thematisation' in the 'new' media (however see Wodak and Wright, 2006; Ensslin, 2008; Jaffe, 2008, for notable exceptions). And this is precisely what will be brought under the spotlight in this chapter, together with a few of the theoretical and methodological challenges that online metalinguistic representations raise. For this purpose, we will take as a point of departure the BBC Voices Project website (*http://www. bbc.co.uk/voices*), a virtual discursive space which was envisaged by its creators as 'celebrating the diversity of the UK by affirming the value of regional and ethnic differences as expressed through language' (Rose and Mowbray, n.d.). More specifically, we will analyse a few excerpts taken from *Multilingual Nation*, which is a section of a broader discussion forum on the *Voices* website. These examples have been chosen because they not only offer us a snapshot of the variety—cacophony even—of ideas and beliefs about different languages that surfaced on this website, but they also allow us to show the ways in which the particular context created by the design and architecture of the website both facilitates and constrains online language debates (cf. Wodak and Wright, 2006; Wright and Street, 2007). However, before delving into an analysis of relevant extracts, we want first to offer an historical background to the Voices project, followed by a presentation of the main theoretical concepts and assumptions that inform our analysis.

THE BBC VOICES PROJECT

In 2003, a proposal was put forward within the BBC for a project on language in the UK. From its inception, this enterprise had an overt social purpose in the sense that it not only aimed 'to celebrate and explore the diverse languages, dialects and accents of the UK [. . .] at the start of the 21st century' (Rose and Mowbray, n.d.), but, in the words of Voices project director Mick Ord, it also intended to 'unite people across the UK in a shared local and national conversation' (Ord, 2005) about contemporary language use.

The project started with two main data-gathering activities: a survey of regional varieties of English carried out by specially-trained BBC broadcast journalists and an interactive website, one part of which offered an extensive asynchronous discussion forum under the heading *Your Voice*. This encompassed several sections, each of which was dedicated to a sociolinguistic topic and invited participation via an online discussion tool. *Multilingual Nation* constitutes a section within the *Your Voice* discussion forum and consists of thirty-seven separate asynchronous discussion boards, each of which is dedicated to (a) named language(s). Our main focus in this chapter will be on this section.

Voices culminated in August 2005 with a co-ordinated 'Voices Season' of programmes being broadcast across the BBC's television and radio networks. Crucially, the project was considered a conspicuous success by the members of the production team. In this regard, a market survey commissioned by the BBC in the wake of the 'Voices Season' showed that Voices items had been favourably received by audiences across the country, achieving an overall 90+ per cent approval rating among the survey's 3000 participants. In addition, 62 per cent stated that they had in turn gone on to have 'conversations about words and dialects recently' (Burgess, 2005).

LANGUAGE REPRESENTATIONS IN NEW MEDIA TEXTS: RECIPROCAL TRANSMISSION AND MEDIATISATION

Although one should always be wary of accepting statistical data at face value, the figures presented in the section above—coupled with the observation that the discussion forum on the website generated over 8500 submissions—certainly indicate that Voices contributed to initiating a 'conversation' about language(s), although this clearly transcended local and national boundaries as is shown by the many postings of internet users who defined themselves as being non-British and/or residing outside the UK. Having said that, one question remains to be answered: what kind of context did that 'conversation' take place in? Whereas the discursive space of the *Multilingual Nation* discussion boards may be seen as democratic—to the extent that anyone from any geographical location could contribute to it provided they had access to a technological device with internet connection—it would be rather ingenuous to ignore the fact that the *Voices* website is owned by a national media provider. In other words, we want to underscore here that the conversation about language took place within a context regimented by a specific 'ideological broker' (Blommaert, 1999). In this respect the notions of 'reciprocal transmission' and 'mediatisation' can help us to better explain the ideological brokerage operated by the BBC.

As has already been emphasised elsewhere (e.g. Cotter, 2010; Johnson and Ensslin, 2007), the relationship between media producers and their audiences is complex and is beyond the grasp of a linear model of information encoding, transmission and decoding. Therefore, Cotter (2010) has suggested theorising this relationship as a form of 'reciprocal transmission' of information, which she defines as 'the operation behind the interplay of texts, news practitioners, and audience (or *community of coverage*) and is what allows media to: (1) engage with the community on professional and personal levels; as well as to (2) provide content that captures facts or perspectives about social worlds in which media and community reside' (Cotter, 2010: 112, emphasis in original).

In our view, the notion of 'reciprocal transmission' is particularly apt for an appreciation of the *Voices* website, which, in the words of a member of the project team, seeks to be 'an *informed moderated* space where experience and evidence from users is *integrated* as core content for the site' (Mowbray, pers. comm., emphasis added). The terms 'informing' and 'integrating' express in this context the dynamic interplay between the BBC and its online audiences. So whereas academically-informed material is at the core of many of the linguistic articles on the website, this is not made explicitly authoritative—rather it was imagined as a way to invite contributions from the website's users. In contrast, the term 'moderating' subtly conveys the activity of the BBC in regimenting this exchange of opinions on language-related issues. The notion of 'mediatisation' can help to highlight the unavoidable ideological work inherent to this moderation process. As Johnson and Ensslin (2007: 12–13) point out, mediatisation should not be confused with the more neutral process of mediation. Whereas the latter refers 'to the general processes of information encoding, transfer and decoding' (Johnson and Ensslin, 2007: 12), the former aims to grasp the inherently ideological nature of media production, namely the fact that media workers constantly (need to) make choices about what is reported (i.e. what is deemed sufficiently 'newsworthy') and how to create appropriate synthetic relationships (Fairclough, 2001) with different audiences. Hence, it is fair to say that the 'reciprocal transmission' theorised by Cotter should not be seen as an ideologically innocent process of mediation, but as something which attends to media practitioners' ideological effects on the discursive space in which they operate.

What makes Voices so interesting in this respect is the self-conscious attempt on the part of the BBC team *not* to directly mediatise the material they were handling. Their expressed aim was to achieve an entirely 'bottom up' project that delivered 'democratic value [. . .] by providing trusted, impartial and in-depth news and information that help[s] people make sense of the world [. . .] and encourages them to engage with it' (Mowbray, pers. comm.). In part, the involvement of academic collaborators in the project was itself intended to ensure this 'impartial mediation', and thus escape the bind of mediatisation. For example, when asked what had been omitted from the website, and on what criteria, project staff were adamant that—subject to legal restrictions—there were no taboo areas as far as they were concerned. Indeed, as the website was predicated on being a channel for public views of language, a policy of *not* censoring or editorialising submitted items was actively pursued. Needless to say, invoking impartiality and claiming to know what it means to 'help people make sense of the world' are themselves ideological in character (cf. Wodak and Wright, 2006: 255). It is precisely this ideological process of mediatisation—and how it is encoded in the architecture of the *Multilingual Nation* discussion boards—that we will seek to illustrate in the next section.

MULTILINGUAL NATION

As current research on online texts has pointed out (see e.g. Lemke, 2002; Knox, 2007), the first element to consider when analysing a webpage is its relationship to the site's homepage as defined by the hyperlinks that connect the two. This allows us to understand the relative complexity of the potential 'traversals' (Lemke, 2002)—i.e. navigational pathways—followed

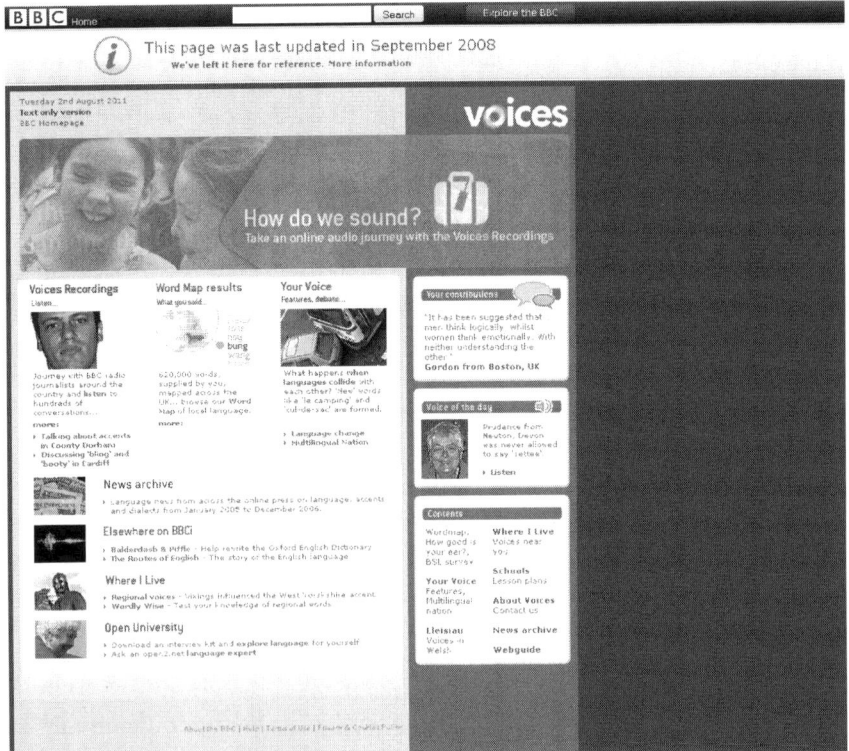

Figure 12.1　BBC Voices homepage.

by internet users to navigate to that particular webpage. Interestingly, *Multilingual Nation* features twice on the *Voices* homepage: (1) as a hyperlink in an infobite[1] (Figure 12.1) under the heading 'Your Voice' on the right-hand side of the main frame, and (2) as plain text in the 'Contents' frame in the navigation sidebar on the right-hand side of the page, again under the heading 'Your Voice'.

What is particularly relevant to observe here is the fact that only two sections of the *Your Voice* discussion forum—*Multilingual Nation* and *Language Change*—have been singled out on the homepage. Crucially, *Multilingual Nation* is not only made salient through its central position and bold type face but its access is facilitated also by the presence of a hyperlink which allows internet users to navigate to this discussion section *directly* from the homepage. Finally, *Multilingual Nation* is associated with the synthetic personalisation (Fairclough, 2001) embedded in the naming strategy of 'Your Voice'. Here, the possessive 'your' is a discursive means through which the BBC can construct a less anonymous, seemingly more personalized, relationship with each of their audiences, thus encouraging the internet users to actively interact with the website.

Introductory Page

The introductory page of the *Multilingual Nation* discussion forum is divided into three vertical sections in a margin-centre-margin formation (Kress and van Leeuwen, 2006: 198). The central part has two elements. First, there is an alphabetised list of thirty-eight language options (but arguably thirty-nine *languages*—Urdu/Hindi is presented as one option) divided into two equal columns. Beneath this, there is a flash player application where internet users can scroll through a history of language in the British Isles, showing the impact of invasion and migration. When these hyperlinks are selected, the user is taken to a dedicated webpage for that language containing the discussion board;[2] this is headed by a language article written by a linguistic 'expert'. In the left-hand margin of the introductory page, there is a navigation sidebar which offers hyperlinks within the *Voices* website and also links to the overall BBC homepage. The right-hand margin contains an image of the UK which is a collage constructed out of photographs taken by BBC broadcast journalists of participants recorded as part of the original survey. In Kress and van Leeuwen's (2006) terms, this is an example of high modality as these are naturalistic pictures used to validate the content of the site through the evidence and experience of these participants.

Within this structure, there is already evidence of ideological work. Firstly, the map of the UK serves to anchor the notion of the 'multilingual nation'. It is interesting to note that the Republic of Ireland has been erased from the picture, despite the focus on geographical rather than political boundaries signalled by the use of the term 'British Isles'. Second, although

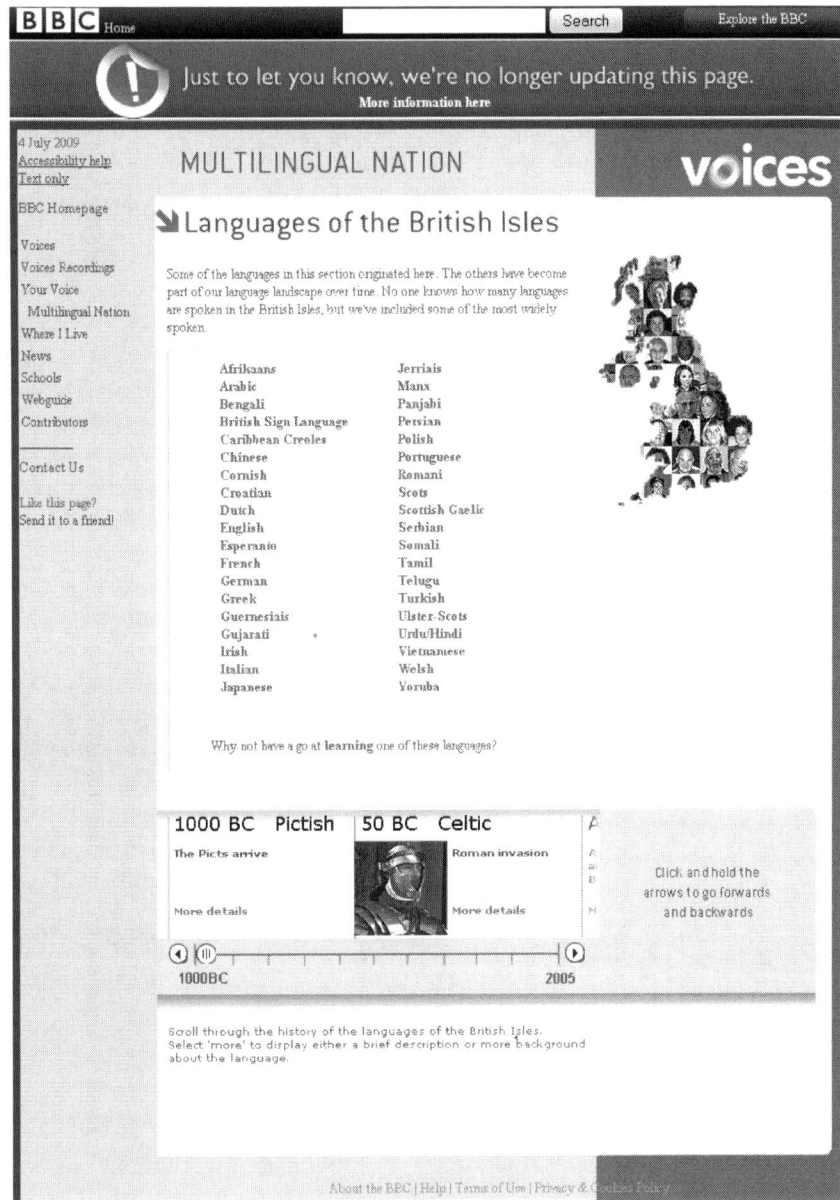

Figure 12. 2   Multilingual Nation introductory page.

there are thirty-nine languages listed, these link to only thirty-seven discussion boards. In the majority of cases, there is a one-to-one relationship
between language and discussion board, but in two cases this is arguably
not the case:

- Croatian and Serbian, which are listed separately but lead to the same discussion board
- Urdu/Hindi, which are listed together and lead to the same discussion board

From a strictly linguistic point of view, both of these pairs of languages are very closely related and arguably could be defined as dialects of one language—they are considered to be mutually comprehensible, with some differences in vocabulary (Lewis, 2009). However, each pair increases the distance between itself and its counterpart by using a different writing system:

- Croatian (Roman); Serbian (modified Cyrillic)
- Hindi (Devanagari); Urdu (Nastaliq)

Of course, whether intentional or not, the decisions to have separate listings (or not) and separate discussion boards (or not) is inescapably ideological. What is interesting is the seeming inconsistency here: both linguist-written language articles treat the languages as a pair (except when discussing writing systems), and both discuss the lack of agreement about the status of each language. Yet, a different decision has been made in these two cases: whereas Croatian and Serbian are listed separately, Urdu and Hindi are clustered together.

In this context it is interesting to note that the most heated topics of discussion in the Hindi/Urdu discussion board was the status of these language varieties, with a number of people posting comments and objecting vehemently to the grouping of the two as one language (see extracts below):

Extract 12.1
Arora from London
I agree with Vibha & Pankaj that linking these two languages is erroneous [. . .] Urdu was created using words from Hindi along with Persian and Arabic. Hindi is originated from Sanskril and uses Devnagiri Script, which I am sure Urdu does not follow. Please add Hindi as separate language with a little bit of research.[3]

Extract 12.2
Kartik Rathnam from New Delhi
Urdu does not stand any way near the great language of our country which is "HINDI". Hindi is a very ancient language derived from Sanskrit and the language evolved in INDIA. Urdu is a mixture of few languages i.e. Hindi, Persian & Arabic.

Nearly 50 per cent of the posts on this forum (11/23) rejected the concept of Hindi and Urdu being one language. Presumably, these posts would not have occurred without the ideological decision being made to group them together. Thus, the way in which the discussion boards were organised could be seen to be a defining feature in the interaction which ensued in this particular discussion board. Interestingly, only one poster on the shared Croatian/Serbian discussion board took up this topic, and it did not 'seed' (Wright and Street, 2007) the discussion in the same way.

Another issue that is worth noting regards what languages have been selected for the list on the introductory page. The inhabitants of the UK speak many more than thirty-nine languages, and therefore many have been left out from the list. The BBC gives the following representation of this ideological process on the page itself:

> The Languages of the British Isles
> *Some of the languages in this section originated here. The others have become part of our language landscape over time. No one knows how many languages are spoken in the British Isles, but we've included some of the most widely spoken.*

Thus the only *explicit* justification given for the choices made is the relative number of speakers for a particular language in the British Isles. However, when the list is inspected more closely, it is evident that this cannot be the only criterion. According to UNESCO's *Atlas of the World's Languages in Danger* (UNESCO, 2009), Guernesiais and Jerriais (and all other dialects of Channel Island French) are seriously endangered, with speakers numbering approximately 1500 and 3000, respectively. The language articles for Manx and Cornish here give estimates of their speakers as approximately 1700 and 300 respectively. It would thus seem likely that those classed as 'indigenous' languages are given preference over those that are not. Whereas we do not dispute the inclusion of these indigenous minority languages, the question is why this decision has not been made more explicit. The explanatory text could say that the list includes all those indigenous languages still judged to be spoken in the British Isles, plus the most widely spoken of those that have become part of its linguistic landscape.

In this regard, it is also unclear how the selected non-indigenous languages were judged to be 'the most widely spoken' in the UK. One obvious omission would seem to be Spanish: it is the only major Western European language to be excluded and is also a language taught in many British schools. It is also evident from the information in the flash player application at the foot of the page that Britain does have a recent history of Spanish migration:

> 1936 Spanish
> Spanish Civil War
> *Many refugees settle in the UK's major cities to escape the civil war in Spain.*

1945 Spanish
Spanish settle in London
Approximately 15,000 Spanish people settle in North Kensington, Notting Hill and Victoria to escape a fascist dictatorship and the economic crisis still looming from the Spanish Civil War.

It should be noted that out of the twenty-four extant languages named in this linguistic history of Britain, only two are not given a discussion board: Spanish and Yiddish (the reverse is also true—Yoruba and Vietnamese have no mention here, but do have discussion boards). Of course, the lack of a discussion board has practical implications for speakers of Spanish (and all other languages excluded from the list) because there is no discursive space for them to make a comment, either about the decision to leave out their language from the list or to express their feelings and beliefs about their language and multilingualism. In brief, their 'voice' is effectively silenced from this part of the *Voices* website.

But speakers of other languages, excluded from this list, do have something to say. Hebrew is one such excluded language and, in Extract 12.3 below, we see a reference to a speaker who felt aggrieved that Hebrew, her strongest language, was not represented:

Extract 12.3
Nava Freeman wrote to Voices to explain how this feels: "*When I speak Hebrew my confidence rises, because it's my mother tongue, and no one looks at me in a strange way!*"

This extract is taken from the article that introduces a general discussion board on multilingualism within another section of the *Your Voice* discussion forum. The article, written by a BBC journalist, includes several quotations taken from what internet users posted on the *Multilingual Nation* discussion boards. However, what makes Nava Freeman's contribution different is the way in which her voice has been re-entextualised in the article. Here the expression 'wrote to' marks Nava Freeman's engagement with Voices as structurally different from other internet users: it was only by *individually contacting* Voices that she could make herself heard, given that the lack of a discussion board on Hebrew disallowed her the possibility of debate about that language.

Content and Layout

The webpages which contain the discussion boards are constructed in the same margin-centre-margin structure as the introductory page. The main difference lies in the right sidebar, where internet users are offered some further links relevant to the language concerned, plus links to other parts of the *Your Voice* forum.

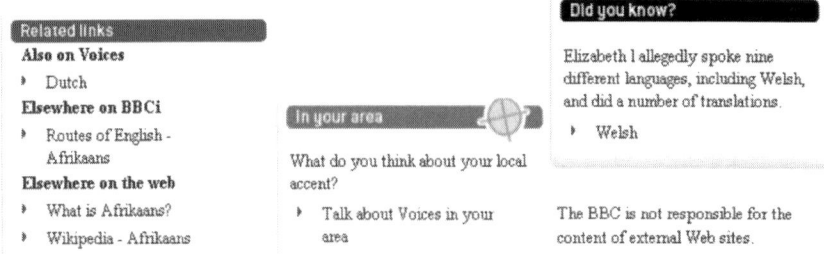

Figure 12.3   The right sidebar from the Afrikaans discussion board, shown here horizontally rather than vertically (for reasons of space).

These infobites, together with the language article preceding each discussion board, embody the 'informing' purpose of the *Voices* website. Analogous to what was observed above, the heavy usage of the deictic expressions *you* and *your* also perpetuate the establishment of a synthetic relationship with internet users. And this is repeated again in the framing of the discussion boards (see Table 12.1 below).

Content-wise, the central part of the webpages is dedicated to rich material published by the BBC which serves to 'present' the language to the internet user. This is followed by the discussion board itself. However, the material posted by the BBC is not always structured in the same way—

Table 12.1   Structural Analysis of Discursive Framing

	Format 1	*Format 2*
Heading	*Afrikaans*	*Arabic*
BBC-provided content	**Your experiences of Afrikaans** *(Series of quotations by Afrikaans speakers, collected by BBC radio journalists)* **Afrikaans in the British Isles by Viv Edwards** *(short article of approx. 250 words)*	**Page 1 of 3** - Arabic today - The history of Arabic - Names and writing system **Arabic today by Viv Edwards** *(longer article of approx. 750 words—divided over 3 pages connected via hyperlinks)*
Discussion Board heading	Your comments	
Prompt question	What is your experience of <language>?	
Hyperlink to next page of discussion board	Read more of your thoughts here	

there are two basic formats. This will be illustrated using the examples of Afrikaans and Arabic.

The key differences between the two are thus the length of the language article and whether or not there are entextualised voices from other speakers of the language. It might also be noticed that Format 1 explicitly ties the language to the British Isles in the language article heading, whereas Format 2 does not. From this, it does seem that Format 1 validates the presence of the language in the British Isles much more strongly, whereas the longer language article serves to exoticise the subject language to some extent. In particular, the entextualised quotations largely focus on speakers' *experiences* of the language. They are organized under the following subheadings:

- Who do you speak <language> with?
- About <language>
- How do you feel about speaking <language>?
- <language> today (in the UK)

Not all are used for each language, but the ordering is largely consistent. This is in contrast to the longer language articles, which are relatively depersonalised through the use of a more academic discourse which relies on the idea of fact-based truths about a language rather than invoking personal experience. Thus, from an ethnographic perspective, in Format 1 the insider's perspective is given at least as much weight as the outsider's, whereas in Format 2, the 'expert' discourse is privileged. It is interesting to note that there does not appear to be any discernable pattern in the decisions taken to use one discursive frame rather than another.

All the languages which might be considered 'indigenous' to the British Isles are discursively framed by the longer language article and have no immediate appeal to speaker's experience. In contrast, some languages which might be considered 'exotic'—such as Esperanto, Persian, Telugu— are framed by a short article and speaker quotations. In terms of what effect this had on the discussion boards, those which were discursively

Table 12.2 Categorisation of Discussion Board Languages by Discursive Framing Used.

Format 1(n=11)	Afrikaans, Dutch, Esperanto, French, German, Italian, Japanese, Persian, Polish, Tamil, Telugu
Format 2(n=26)	Arabic, Bengali, British Sign Language, Caribbean Creoles, Chinese, Cornish, Croatian/Serbian, English, Greek, Guernesiais, Gujarati, Irish, Jerriais, Manx, Panjabi, Portuguese, Romani, Scots, Scottish Gaelic, Somali, Turkish, Ulster Scots, Urdu/Hindi, Vietnamese, Welsh, Yoruba

framed according to Format 2 seemed to produce more challenges to the content presented within the framing. In particular, contributors to these discussion boards disputed 'language facts' within the expert-written language article much more frequently than those discussion boards discursively framed using Format 1. This is exemplified by the very first post on the thread on Cornish which states:

Extract 12.4
Hilary from Manchester
Native Cornish has been extinct since the 1700's. In Mousehole there is a plaque on the wall to the last recorded mother tongue speaker. The current Cornish speaking population represents a 20th century revival. Whilst I live in Manchester I was born in Cornwall. Regards Hilary

This comment was prompted by the way in which Cornish was represented in the language article where no mention was made of the controversy surrounding modern Cornish and whether it can really be considered 'Native Cornish' (as Hilary terms it). Indeed, UNESCO (2009) classes Traditional Cornish as an extinct language, in comparison to the revived versions of the language (which are not considered to be endangered, as the number of speakers is growing). This debate then gets picked up by the discussion board and it becomes the key issue, featuring in 16/24 posts.

Extract 12.5
Harry from Glasgow
Absolutely nothing against the proponents of Cornish, good luck to them, but they shouldn't deceive themselves or anyone else. The fact is that Cornish died out centuries ago, and certainly before Dolly Pentreath [. . .] it's very wrong that the article, which one would assume was reasonably objective, tries to imply that the language never quite died out—the first sentence, and phrases like "the brink of extinction" disingenuously imply a continuous tradition, which is just not true. The Cornish language revinvented in the 20th century in its various competing versions had to deal with one big problem: simply put, no-one knows how Middle Cornish was pronounced, and no-one knows the grammar of Modern Cornish. [. . .]

Harry's post (heavily edited due to space constraints) is interesting as it explicitly refers to the article itself—thus locating the source of the 'trouble'—and very precisely identifies the linguistic manoeuvres which its author uses to circumvent a discussion of the disputed status of Cornish. The first paragraph, which Harry refers to, is reproduced below:

Extract 12.6
With only a few hundred speakers today, it's hard to believe that once Cornish was the everyday language of as many as 38,000 people. However, thanks to the efforts of the revivalist movement, Cornish, while still an endangered language, continues to claw its way back from the brink of extinction.

This is very much in contrast to the approach taken by the author of the Urdu/Hindi article, who was very careful not to commit to a particular position, and referred to both varieties as 'language' within the text, before commenting explicitly on the issue:

Extract 12.7
The linguistic status of Urdu/Hindi has been the subject of fierce debate. Some argue that they be treated as the same language; others that they should be treated separately on the grounds of differences in vocabulary and word order.

Whereas it might be argued that this difference in relationship between the two discursive frames and the discussion boards they generate could be ascribed to the relative length of the expert-written article, we would argue that the effect is more to do with features of the website's architecture: the choice of discussion tool, and the relative positioning of items in the two discursive formats. The discussion tools used are asynchronous unthreaded structures, where the most recent post sits at the top of the discussion; i.e. the posts are presented in reverse chronological order. Wright and Street (2007) demonstrate, through their analysis of politically-oriented online discussion forums, that such bulletin board tools show a lower degree of discursivity than chronologically ordered and threaded tools: fewer posts act as a response to previous posts. In other words, there is less of a 'conversation'. In many respects, this is not surprising. The lack of threading makes it more difficult for a potential contributor to identify any such ongoing conversations from the outset, and if a person posting a comment does wish to signal a relationship between theirs and a previous post, they can only do so via explicit addressivity (Herring, 2001). This does occur in the *Multilingual Nation* discussion boards, albeit rarely—there is an instance of this in Extract 12.1, above. The reverse chronology also mediates against discursivity. Having located an ongoing 'conversation', the potential contributor has to infer the reverse temporal relationship between the messages (there are no time/date stamps), and also navigate backwards through the webpage(s). Crucially, where addressivity is used in *Multilingual Nation*, it rarely crosses a webpage boundary, perhaps suggesting reluctance on the part of contributors to navigate across these divisions.

Given this structure, it is perhaps unsurprising that the material published by the BBC at the top of each discussion board acts to seed debates—effectively establishing a potential topic of discussion that can form the basis for a thread. The key, then, lies in which published material is presented as being the most salient to the internet user, which is where the two formats crucially differ. This can be demonstrated using Knox's (2007) analysis of diminishing salience. He argues that webpages have a HEAD-TAIL structure, where the information that appears above the fold (visible in first screen accessed) is presented as the most important. The more scrolling that is required (and by analogy, the more navigation via hyperlinks), the less salient any item is perceived to be. Thus, the two discursive formats differ in the importance ascribed to items on the webpage—for Format 1, it is the entextualised quotations that are above the fold, whereas for Format 2, it is the language article. According to this analysis, it is then not surprising that we see more challenges to the expert-written articles in Format 2 discussion boards than in Format 1 ones. And we can also largely ignore the issue of differing article length—the requirement to use hyperlinks to access further pages diminishes its salience, and thus the internet user may never see Extract 12.7's careful attempt at neutrality (accessed via a further hyperlink), but will see the first paragraph on Cornish (made further salient by being emboldened). This is the paragraph which so irritated Harry from Glasgow (see Extracts 12.5 and 12.6).

CONCLUSIONS

Following Cotter (2010), we believe that the *BBC Voices* website can indeed be seen as a place of 'reciprocal transmission' about multilingualism, where the repeated interaction of the public with the textual formations encoded in the site's structure generated online debates in which differing views, ideas and beliefs about different languages were offered up for affirmation or contestation. Irrespective of its explicit intention to maintain neutrality and detachment, the BBC was not an impartial spectator. Whereas they may not have taken an active role in directly editing contributions, our analysis shows that the set-up of the website—and all the choices that entailed—was an act of mediatisation in itself. Interactivity was encouraged by the possibilities of engagement opened up by such semiotic strategies as synthetic personalisation and use of hyperlinks. However, the terms of that engagement were, at the same time, constrained by specific decisions taken in the structuring of the discussion forum. In all the examples discussed above, we have demonstrated the impact of website architecture on online interactions and thus that these interactions are as much a product of the context in which they are embedded as they are authored by the contributors themselves. Although as sociolinguists we might privilege the *content* of discussion boards, an analysis of the structural properties of webpages and their interactional effects is no less important.

The key methodological point here is the necessity of recognising the mediating and mediatising effect of the websites within which our primary locus of interest—people talking about language via the internet—is embedded. As Jones and Rafaeli (2000: 218, cited in Wright and Street, 2007: 854) argued:

> We must first gain an understanding of the link between technology and discourse structure [. . .] because it is technology that provides the architecture for virtual public discourse, whatever its use or associate social structure.

This chapter is an initial attempt at unpicking this relationship for the *Multilingual Nation* section of the *BBC Voices* website, and we fully recognise that we are only just beginning to understand the complexities encoded in the multiplex links between website organization, traversal patterns, discussion tool technologies, webpage content/design decisions and the way in which potential contributors actually interact with the website. And this, we would argue, is a necessary precursor to analysing the metalinguistic content of those interactions themselves. Of course, one could argue that we have privileged texts and the micro-contexts in which they were framed. Accordingly, what have been sidelined are the multiple and varied processes of media production and reception that underpin those texts. Whereas this bias might be seen as a result of our choice of a particular theoretical and methodological paradigm, we believe that the institutional limitations that constrain language-ideological research into and about the media cannot be overlooked. As Garrett and Bell cogently point out, 'It is more difficult to research production than reception (while reception is more difficult than the text itself). That difficulty is not so much theoretical as practical and interactional. Access to and acceptance by media organizations and personnel is the central problem' (1998: 19). Although we want to emphasise that the BBC Voices team has always been willing to provide us with crucial insider's information about the development of the project, the reconstruction *a posteriori* of discursive processes misses the richness of ethnographic observation.

NOTES

1. Coined following Knox's (2007) term, newsbite, which he used for similar structures in the analysis of online news websites. BBC Voices is about information (or 'infotainment') rather than news, hence the adapted terminology.
2. We use the term 'discussion forum' as an umbrella term to refer to all the online discussions contained within *Your Voice*. These are organised into sections (like *Multilingual Nation*), which each host one or more online discussions. The term 'discussion board' is used for the *Multilingual Nation* interactions.
3. These data extracts are reproduced as in the original, retaining any typographical errors. This is for two reasons. Firstly, there is high tolerance of

typographical errors within many forms of computer-mediated communication, particularly where it is perceived as being used in informal contexts, and thus to 'correct' these extracts would make it unrepresentative of the *Multilingual Nation* data. Secondly, the fact that these errors survived the BBC's moderation process shows evidence of their desire to be seen as not interfering with the 'national conversation' and thus avoiding the charge of mediatisation.

ACKNOWLEDGEMENTS

We would like to express our gratitude to the Arts and Humanities Research Council (AHRC), who are funding a three year project between 2007 and 2010 on language ideological debates on the BBC Voices website (ref. AH/E509002/1), from which this work is derived. We are also grateful to colleagues at the BBC, in particular Mandy Rose, for their support and cooperation in this project as well as for permission to reproduce screenshots from the Voices website.

REFERENCES

Blommaert, J. (ed.) 1999. *Language Ideological Debates*. Berlin: Mouton de Gruyter.

Burgess, K. 2005. *Voices Evaluation Report for BBC Nations and Regions*. London: MC & A Audience and Consumer Research.

Cotter, C. 2010. *News Talk: Investigating the Language of Journalism*. Cambridge: Cambridge University Press.

Danet, B. and Herring, S. C. 2007. *The Multilingual Internet: Language, Culture and Communication Online*. Oxford: Oxford University Press.

Ensslin, A. 2008. Thematising interwikis: Wikipedia's multilingual policy and practice. Paper presented at AILA 2008: Multilingualism: Challenges and Opportunities, Essen, 24–29 August.

Fairclough, N. 2001. *Language and Power* (2nd edition). London: Longman.

Garrett, P. and Bell, A. 1998. Media and discourse: a critical overview. In *Approaches to Media Discourse*, ed. A. Bell and P. Garrett, 1–20. Oxford: Blackwell.

Herring, S. 2001. Computer-mediated discourse. In *The Handbook of Discourse Analysis*, ed. D. Schiffrin, D. Tannen and H. E. Hamilton, 612–34. Oxford: Blackwell.

Jaffe, A. 2008. Sociolinguistic diversity in mainstream media: the construction of authenticity, legitimacy and expertise. Paper presented at AILA 2008: Multilingualism: Challenges and Opportunities, Essen, 24–29 August.

Johnson, S. and Ensslin, A. (ed.) 2007. *Language in the Media: Representations, Identities, Ideologies*. London: Continuum.

Knox, J. 2007. Visual-verbal communication on online newspaper home pages. *Visual Communication* 6(1): 19–53.

Kress, G. and van Leeuwen, T. 2006. *Reading Images: The Grammar of Visual Design* (2nd edition). London: Routledge.

Lemke, J. 2002. Travels in hypermodality. *Visual Communication* 1(3): 299–325.

Lewis, M. P. (ed.) 2009. *Ethnologue: Languages of the World* (16th edition). Dallas, TX: SIL International.

Ord, M. 2005. *Project Director's Presentation of Overview Summary—BBC Voices*. Cardiff: British Broadcasting Corporation.

Rose, A. and Mowbray, F. (n.d.) *The UK Speaks (working title)*. BBC Nations & Regions. BBC Cymru Wales.

UNESCO. 2009. *UNESCO's Atlas of the World's Languages in Danger*. http://www.unesco.org/culture/ich/index.php?pg=00139 (accessed 20 July 2009).

Wodak, R. and Wright, S. 2006. The European Union in cyberspace: multilingual democratic participation in a virtual public sphere. *Journal of Language and Politics* 5(2): 251–75.

Wright, S. and Street, J. 2007. Democracy, deliberation and design: the case of online discussion forums. *New Media and Society* 9(5): 849–69.

Part V

Interpreting Voices from the Classroom

Introduction

Charmian Kenner

A striking aspect of voices from the classroom is their rarity. In media discourse and mainstream educational discourse, we often hear what policymakers consider good practice and whether teachers are judged to be following such guidance. But we do not often hear the voices of practitioners who are attempting new ways of relating to the students in their classrooms, and less often still the voices of students themselves. This is particularly the case with regard to issues in multilingual learning, where, as Bonacina's chapter in this part points out, policies and practices are grounded in monolingual ideologies that silence or restrict the development of positive pedagogies. Bonacina's work in France highlights the 'taboo' against the use of children's first languages in many French classrooms, in a setting where multiculturalism is negatively viewed due to state policies of assimilation. However, 'monolingualising' ideologies (Heller, 1995: 374) have also been widely found in education systems around the world, even if there is a rhetorical commitment to the value of multilingualism, as shown for example by Anderson, Kenner and Gregory (2008) in an examination of the 'incoherent discourses' adopted by UK politicians and policymakers.

Meanwhile, recent research on small group interactions in classrooms characterised by multilingual diversity suggests that, where the opportunity arises, children and young people are leading the way in exploring creative uses of languages for learning. García (2009) shows how children in bilingual Spanish/English school in New York use 'translanguaging' to draw on all their linguistic resources in order to communicate most effectively and accomplish a joint task. Baetens Beardsmore (García and Baetens Beardsmore, 2009) finds a similar phenomenon in international schools in Europe, and Portante and Max (2008) analyse how children in Luxembourg classrooms negotiate meaning through the use of four languages. Such interactions take place even in situations where educational policy tries to shoehorn students into what might be termed a particular 'language box' according to the latest 'good practice'—for example, in bilingual schooling that assumes successful learning will only take place if the two languages are kept separate throughout the school day, characterised by Cummins (2010) as the 'two solitudes assumption'. Children and young people are highly alert to the pedagogies they are being asked to live by, but will often choose to subvert them to promote communication or to aid their learning.

It is therefore important that researchers find ways to investigate aspects of pedagogy that are restrictive to multilingual students, and aspects that are 'transformative' (Cummins 2001) in encouraging the development of multilingual skills and identities in the classroom. Approaches to data collection and analysis need to support and reveal the voices of students and teachers that would otherwise remain hidden. The authors in Part V demonstrate several possible pathways that can be taken:

- The researcher records and critically analyses 'what usually happens' in such a way that teachers, students and policymakers can more clearly understand the issues involved.
- The researcher provides students and teachers themselves with the opportunity to represent and reflect on pedagogies.
- Involvement in the research process enables students and teachers to construct new ideas that could lead to transformative pedagogies.

I will consider each of these in relation to the chapters in this part.

RECORDING AND ANALYSING 'WHAT USUALLY HAPPENS'

Close observation by the researcher, involving analysis from the perspective of different participants in classroom discourse, can bring to light ways in which pedagogies can be better adapted to the needs of multilingual students. This is well illustrated by the transcript from a London secondary school maths class discussed in Leung's chapter, which presents 'what happens' as Sairah, the student, tries to solve a maths problem. The teacher fails to notice that Sairah is unsure about the difference between the key concepts that are being worked on, those of 'median' and 'mode', because she perceives Sairah as a relatively fluent English speaker and takes it for granted that she will operate accordingly. Sairah, meanwhile, is baffled at certain points but is not sure how to express her lack of understanding to the teacher. The researcher, by using conversation analysis to interpret the interaction, reveals that although Sairah and her teacher are engaging positively and in many ways collaboratively, there is a significant mismatch in their respective views of the situation. In order for the student's voice to emerge, the teacher needs to be aware of the difficulties involved in gaining a sound understanding of academic concepts in a second language through classroom interaction. Leung examines current policy guidance on the learning of English as an Additional Language, revealing ways in which theoretical ideas have been misinterpreted or over-simplified, to explain why the teacher may not have recognised the problem and to suggest possible solutions.

It is not always easy to obtain such rich data on interaction from multilingual classrooms, particularly if the research focuses on students' use of languages other than the dominant one. Bonacina documents the barriers she faced when wishing to examine the multilingual interactions that might be taking place in induction classes for newly-arrived non-French speaking children in France. Access was made very difficult for her, due to the power held by the educational organisation with which she had to negotiate, representing the interests of the monolingually-oriented French state. Even when she was offered access to two induction classes, further problems arose. Although Bonacina's initial informal observations in one classroom found that children were able to use their first languages as well as French, such practices ceased to exist as soon as she explained her research focus on multilingualism. The teacher's awareness that multilingual interactions would not be officially sanctioned led to the silencing of student voices. In another classroom, multilingual practices were manufactured by the teacher in order to satisfy the researcher. Only by contacting teachers directly through an informal network was Bonacina able to access voices that challenged the power of the state. She finally found a teacher who already welcomed multilingual interactions in her classroom and was willing to participate in the research.

ENABLING STUDENTS AND TEACHERS TO REPRESENT AND REFLECT ON PEDAGOGIES

Students are continually interpreting content, pedagogies and rules of engagement in the classroom, and research approaches need to give them opportunities to represent their interpretations. In an example from previous research, peer teaching of primary school classmates by children who attended complementary schools enabled the young 'teachers' to demonstrate their understanding of pedagogies used in Chinese or Arabic class (Kenner, 2004). Role play can also be an excellent way of students displaying their knowledge; recordings of Bangladeshi British siblings playing school at home (Gregory, 1998) showed how older siblings used effective teaching strategies from primary school and complementary school to help younger children learn. In the chapter included here, Gardner and Yaacob make fruitful use of role play to investigate Malaysian children's interpretations of regulative and instructional talk in classrooms in Malaysia and the UK.

Children's interpretation of pedagogy goes beyond producing a simple copy of techniques; it involves close attention to salient features that aid or hinder learning. Gardner and Yaacob show how children acting out a role play based on their UK classroom ensure that their peer teacher holds up the book so that they can see, and reads with expression. Meanwhile, children from the Malaysian classroom raise issues such as reading an English book loudly and clearly so that the class can repeat, and reading more slowly because the English language is difficult to understand. The latter point demonstrates that children are able to critique pedagogy; when given the chance to assert themselves with a peer who is less powerful than the teacher herself, children are able to insist that approaches are tailored to respond to their needs.

Gardner and Yaacob's methodology also enables students to represent aspects of pedagogy that may not be observable by researchers. An example given in the chapter is of the 'ear bends' punishment acted out by children from the Malaysian classroom, which apparently only took place when the researcher was not present. Role play is an innovative method that demonstrates an important way of obtaining student voices and could be more widely used.

Jonsson, in her ethnographic study of bilingual schools in Sweden, also took an approach designed to augment student voice, employing several 'dialogic' research methods that offered interactive participation. These included students' drawings of their own silhouettes with the names of different languages added to show their personal significance, diaries kept on their use of languages at home as well as at school, and mp3 recordings of their interactions in formal and informal settings across an entire school day. In addition, Jonsson conducted discussion groups where students could put forward their ideas on languages and cultures, and individual interviews concerning the contents of students' language diaries. She notes that these approaches encouraged students to think about their ideas and experiences as they produced their representations. For example, the act of writing a diary became a personal reflection on language use, culture and identity. She comments that her role with the students 'became that of someone who opens a door, and allows them to enter within themselves to reflect upon their own identities'. Teachers participating in interviews as part of Jonsson's research also commented on their appreciation of this experience, because it gave them a chance to discuss issues of language development and reconsider their pedagogic practices.

CONSTRUCTING TRANSFORMATIVE PEDAGOGIES

Research in multilingual classrooms often becomes a collaborative journey between researchers, teachers and students. Jonsson gave students the opportunity to discuss not only what already took place in their classrooms, but what they would like to experience. Gardner and Yaacob show how role play can encourage students to take an active stance in expressing their ideas. In play, as Vygotsky (1978: 102) argued, children operate as though they are 'a head taller than themselves'. They behave and function at a cognitive level beyond the norm, encouraged by peers or older children. This is where they can begin to demonstrate how they would like to learn, for example through syncretising pedagogies from their different learning environments (Gregory, 1998). Students know very well what codes they are expected to live by in the classroom, but are able to explore other possibilities that may be more creative and more appropriate. In Gardner and Yaacob's work, role play generates a 'third space' that can be used by young children to switch between languages, and initiate and develop talk in order to explicitly discuss issues around learning.

For teachers, involvement in research can lead to the development of transformative pedagogies. The teacher who agreed to take part in Bonacina's study was interested in further investigating the potential of multilingual learning and became a collaborative research partner. Where research generates opportunities for students to draw on their bilingual repertoires, and teachers and students begin to investigate new ways of learning, voices from the classroom start to emerge more clearly. We then need to consider how to feed back these insights to teachers, students and policymakers so that such voices can more fully be heard.

REFERENCES

Anderson, J., Kenner, C. and Gregory, E. 2008. The National Languages Strategy in the UK: are minority languages still on the margins? In *Forging Multilingual Spaces: Integrating Perspectives on Majority and Minority Bilingual Education*, ed. C. Hélot and A. De Mejía, 183–202. Clevedon: Multilingual Matters.

Cummins, J. 2001. Empowerment through biliteracy. In *An Introductory Reader to the Writings of Jim Cummins*, ed. C. Baker and N. Hornberger, 258–84. Clevedon: Multilingual Matters.

———. 2010. Spaced out: expanding interpersonal spaces for language learning through bilingual instructional strategies. Plenary address at the conference Plurilingual and Pluricultural Education: Focus on Languages of the Wider World, SOAS, London, 20 February.

García, O. 2009. *Bilingual Education in the 21st Century: A Global Perspective*. Oxford: Wiley/Blackwell.

García, O. and Baetens Beardsmore, H. 2009. Heteroglossic bilingual education policy. In *Bilingual Education in the 21st Century: A Global Perspective*, 244–85. Oxford: Wiley/Blackwell.

Gregory, E. 1998. Siblings as mediators of literacy in linguistic minority communities. *Language and Education* 1(12): 33–55.

Heller, M. 1995. Language choice, social institutions, and symbolic domination. *Language in Society* 24: 373–405.

Kenner, C. 2004. Community school pupils re-interpret their knowledge of Chinese and Arabic for primary school peers. In *Many Pathways to Literacy*, ed. E. Gregory, S. Long and D. Volk, 105–16. London: Routledge.

Portante, D. and Max, C. 2008. Plurilingualism and plurilingual literacy among young learners in Luxembourg. In *Multilingual Europe: Diversity and Learning*, ed. C. Kenner and T. Hickey, 124–30. Stoke-on-Trent: Trentham Books.

Vygotsky, L. 1978. *Mind in Society*. Cambridge, MA: Harvard University Press.

13 English as an Additional Language Policy-Rendered Theory and Classroom Interaction

Constant Leung

Linguistic diversity in the school populations across the member states in the European Union has long been recognised by educationalists and policymakers (e.g. Baetens Beardsmore, 1993; European Commission, 2004; Tosi and Leung, 1999). In England, a country with extensive experience of inward migration in the past fifty years, the school curriculum authorities have explicitly recognised the educational needs of linguistic minority students and acknowledged the learning and use of English as an Additional Language (EAL) as an important issue. It is understood that there is a strongly articulated set of pedagogic principles and curriculum preferences underpinning the policy-sponsored EAL practice in school, and the central purpose of this discussion is to explore how far the theoretical and conceptual bases that inform policy-sponsored practice are equipped to address issues of EAL pedagogy with reference to classroom interaction. More specifically, I will examine (a) the analytic purchase of the policy-rendered theories on classroom interaction between pupils and teachers, and (b) the possible need to extend theoretical and conceptual discussions. I will examine these issues with reference to empirical data.

Conceptually there is a distinction between ideas and propositions that have been generated from research and scholarly study, and the version/s of these ideas taken up in public policy. The transplanting of ideas from one field into another tends to involve some degree of selective appropriation and rendering of the original content meaning to suit the purposes and needs of their new 'home', a process referred to by Bernstein (1996: ch. 5) as recontextualisation. Researchers and policy makers do not necessarily share the same interests, understandings and goals. In this case the transplantation involves moving ideas from research fields such as educational psychology and Second Language Acquisition into a language education policy arena. The term 'policy' is understood here to be represented by formal curriculum statements as well as official advice and guidance on practice offered to teachers.

EAL STUDENTS IN CURRICULUM INTERACTION

The state-funded school system in England has been following a mainstreaming policy since the mid-1980s. This policy encourages the integration of linguistic minority students who are in the process of developing EAL into the regular curriculum. In practice this means that linguistic minority students are put into age-appropriate classes, irrespective of their English-language proficiency. Historically the ideological foundations of this policy have been strongly shaped by the principles of equal opportunities and anti-racism. In the 1970s and early 1980s they were seen as important counter arguments against some of the segregationist provision. Withdrawal of EAL students from the mainstream curriculum to make way for specialist English-language teaching and learning was widely regarded as detrimental to the all-round quality of their education (for a fuller discussion see Commission for Racial Equality, 1986; Edwards and Redfern, 1992; Leung and Creese, 2008; Swann Report, 1985). It is a measure of policy success that EAL students, irrespective of their English-language proficiency, are routinely included in age-appropriate mainstream classes. They are expected to participate in normal and ordinary curriculum activities across all the subject areas. Additional EAL teacher or teacher assistant support is provided, although such support is subject to limited availability.

The extent to which EAL students are able to fully engage with ordinary curriculum activities is a matter of considerable official concern, as testified by the abundance of official guidance on EAL designed to set high standards of professional practice. The key question for this discussion is: is the current policy guidance built on assumptions and principles that can facilitate teacher understanding of the complexities of classroom interaction and language use with reference to EAL?

I will now turn to two episodes of an EAL student's ordinary classroom interaction with teachers. The ordinariness of these episodes can be regarded as ontologically important to this discussion because a good deal of the policy is premised on the assumption that the ordinary everyday classroom activities are the prime motor for EAL development. In other words, it is the very ordinariness of these episodes that makes them 'telling'. Perhaps it should be added here that no attempt is made to evaluate the classroom activities or the actions of the teachers and the pupil involved. It will be shown that although this particular student was apparently able to engage in interaction (and in talk) with her teachers, there were important differences in outcome. The focal pupil in the two classroom episodes was Sairah (pseudonym). She was from Iraq with a Kurdish background. She arrived in England in 2001 and lived in the north of England until 2005 when she joined a secondary school in London where the data shown here were collected. At the time of the data collection (2005 through 2006) Sairah was conversant in everyday school English. Her English (subject) assessment put her between National Curriculum Levels 3 and 4, approximately a level below the attainment norm for a year 9 pupil. The data were collected as part of an ESRC-funded project (Urban Classroom, Culture & Interaction: RES-148–25–0042) by means of a radio microphone carried by the focal pupil; the recordings were made while the pupil was engaged in ordinary non-contrived classroom activities in a number of subject areas.

The two episodes were part of a corpus of twenty hours of audio recordings. Episode 1 took place in an English lesson. At the beginning of this lesson there was some discussion on the handing-in date of some written work. Episode 2 took place about twenty minutes into a Mathematics lesson; the pupils were working in small groups or individually on exercises in topics that they had already covered.

The transcripts have been laid out in a format designed to show pupil and teacher asking questions, reasoning and reacting to each other in the exchanges. Reasoning and reacting in dialogue can be accommodated within the analytic framework provided by Eggins and Slade (1997: 198) which includes three major conversation moves of 'opening' (e.g. offer, question), 'continuing' (e.g. give reason, extend information, restate) and 'reacting' (e.g. question, contradict or reject). Reasons in the continue move would typically provide causal, explanatory or conditional information, often leading to the subsequent reaction on the part of the interlocutor/s. In the Eggins and Slade framework there are two types of reacting: 'Responses are reactions which move the exchange towards completion, while rejoinders are reactions which in some way prolong the exchange' (ibid.: 200).

In the assignment handing-in episode Sairah took initiative in a highly interactive conversation with her teacher concerning an assignment handing-in date. This lesson took place on a Wednesday. Sairah opened this exchange with a question to query the teacher's announcement that Friday was the expected handing-in date for an assignment. The teacher reacted by recounting what he had told the pupils two days previously (on Monday of that week). This led to a series of exchanges with both parties engaging in checking information (Sairah), and re-affirming a position (teacher). The frequent latching between moves suggests that both parties were quite ready with what they had to say.

In the median and mode episode the interaction between Sairah and her teacher can be seen as falling into two parts (although in real time they form a continuous stretch). In Part 1 the teacher sustained a series of six continuing moves (5, 7, 9, 11, 13 and 16) to both explicate the concept of median and to check Sairah's ability to do the calculation from a set of numbers. Sairah's replies provided answers and affirmed her understanding. From the point of view of doing Mathematics, this interaction can be seen as an instance affirming the pupil's knowledge and understanding of the concept of median.

In Part 2 the interaction appears to be a good deal more complex. At move 18 the teacher switched her attention from median to mode. Sairah did not seem to understand the concept of mode, hence her rejoinder 'Mode?' at move 19. The teacher continuing question at move 20 led to an incorrect answer by Sairah (21). The answer provided by Sairah suggests that she was still thinking in terms of median (involving the calculation of the mean of two 'middle' numbers in a set). The teacher pressed on with the same line of exposition over her next 3 moves (22,

24, 26). Sairah's rejoinder at move 27 indicates that she was still evidently working out the mean of 7 and 8 (which was not relevant to the task at hand). Her rejoinder at move 29 signals that she was still unclear about the differences between median and mode. The hitherto implicit reasoning that it is possible to have two modes in a set of numbers (move 20) was stated explicitly by the teacher in moves 26 and 30. At moves 33 and 35 Sairah appeared to take on a compliant stance in the interaction; she

Classroom Episode 13.1 Assignment Handing-in Date

Opening	Continuing	Reacting:
		respond—*italics*
		rejoinder—**bold**
1 S =wha:t (.) si:r (.) this frida:y?		
		2 T *(I've) told you that (.) asked you on monday and I'll give them back to you monday=* [answer]
		3 S =I thought you said err we can like come er and get them with you till friday like and correct them [check]
		4 T *[sorry? you can what?* [clarify]
		5 S I thought you said erm like you know normally when we come after school and er try to like improve it with yo:u?= [check]
		6 T *=yeah=* [agree]
		7 S =and then you like said that's what till friday= [check]
		8 T *=yeah [laughing] coz that's the deadline's fri[day* [counter]
		9 S [[[laughing]]
		10 T *so if you (count) wednesday Thursday and then that leaves me the friday (.) yeah ? (.) that makes s[ense* [contradict]
		11 S [er:m [acknowledge]

Key
S= Sairah
T= Teacher
(.) pause of up to 1 second
(2) pause of more than 1 second
= latching
: lengthening
[overlapping
? rise in intonation
(word) unclear words
[[ ]] noises
[ ] additional comments related to utterance

Classroom Episode 13.2   Median and Mode

Part 1

Opening	Continuing	Reacting respond – *italics* rejoinder – **Bold**
1 S: miss? 2 S: miss you know for the median when I you know compare them together I've got 7 and 7 in the middle		
		3 T: *7 and 7 in the so you've got two numbers in the middle* [engage]
		4 S: *yeah and they are the same* [affirm]
	5 T: because you've got an even number of numbers isn't it?	
		6 S: *yeah* [agree]
	7 T: so that's 1 2 3 4 5 6 7 [counting numbers on page]	
		8 S: *yeah there are 20 (.) 26* [answer]
	9 T: right so what you do is you add them up (.) the 7 and the 7 and divide them by 2	
		10 S: *oh okay* [accept]
	11 T: right? you get if it is 7 then you'll get 7 isn't it?	
		12 S: *yeah?* [engage]
	13 T: because 7 and 7 is 14 divided by (unclear)	
		14 S: *yeah (.) yeah* [affirm]
	15 S: 7 [affirm]	
	16 T: if it was different numbers if it was 7 and 8 then you would have to	17 S: *7.5* [answer]

Part 2
Opening

(*continued*)

Classroom Episode 13.2 (continued)

Opening	Continuing	Reacting respond – *italics* rejoinder – **Bold**
	18 T: what if you had if you had median (.) I'm sorry mode what then?	
		19 S: **mode?** [check]
	20 T: if you have two 7s and two 8s (2) then what would your mode be?	
		21 S: *7.5* [answer]
	22 T: no if all the rest of the numbers were appearing only once	
		23 S: **yeah** [clarify]
	24 T: and 7 and 8 was appearing twice	
		25 S: **hmmmn** [clarify]
	26 T: then you can have two modes (.) 7 and 8 because it is the most frequent number	
		27 S: **would you have 7.5?** [probe]
	28 T: no that, that (unclear) if it was the mean	
		29 S: **so if that was yeah** [clarify]
	30 T: right? if it is a mode then you can have two modes	
		31 S: (unclear) [clarify?]
	32 T: so what numbers (.) right you've got 8 more here isn't it?	
		33 S: *yeah* [engage]
	34 T: and if I gave you a set of numbers …if I gave you a set of numbers there 1 2 3 3 4 8 9 8 8 7 6 5 7 7 (.) so what's the mode there? (.) you've got 1 2 3 8s and 1 2 3 7s isn't it?	
		35 S: *yeah* [engage]
	36 T: so the mode will be 8 (7)	
		37 S: *8 and 7?* [agree]
	38 T: 8 and 7	
		39 S: *okay* [accept]
	40 T: so you have two modes (.) okay?	
		41 S: *okay yeah* [accept]

displayed alignment with her teacher by engaging—saying 'yeah'. When the teacher offered her an answer at move 36, Sairah's rejoinder signalled a continuing uncertainty as to what the numbers 7 and 8 meant. Her two subsequent responding moves (39, 41) signal compliance again and the interaction moved to a close at this point.

From the point of view of surface language features, these two episodes of interaction display many broadly similar characteristics. The live and conversational nature of the interaction manifested itself in sequential turn-taking; many of the utterances were brief and elliptical because they were premised on participant interpretation of what was said in the previous turn. This reflected the contingent and co-constructed nature of the meaning-making in interaction—participants make moment-by-moment decisions on topic introduction, maintenance and termination within broadly understood social and institutional norms and roles in context. The utterances were essentially oriented towards establishing shared understanding and task accomplishment, and most importantly for the purpose of this discussion, the register was informal and little specialist vocabulary was used. 'Median' and 'mode' in Episode 2 were the only technical terms used; they were in a sense unavoidable because they were the names of the concepts being worked upon. Yet it is quite clear that in terms of communicative outcomes, Episode 1 and Part 1 of Episode 2 are relatively happy events in that the pupil and the teacher appeared to have understood each other. The same cannot be said for Part 2 of Episode 2 in which Sairah appeared to have been trying to understand her teacher with, at best, limited success.

EAL THEORIES IN POLICY

In terms of English-language learning a 'learning by exposure and use' view appears to have been adopted. On this view, the regular English-medium curriculum (from now on 'mainstream') environment is held to be rich in communicative potential for EAL learners, and participation in subject learning activities, especially where language use by teachers is conscious of EAL needs, can drive additional language development forward. The following advice to teachers by the National Curriculum Council at the onset of the National Curriculum in the early 1990s captures the gist of this argument:

> Providing access to the curriculum for bilingual pupils means planning and implementing schemes of work which meet individual needs . . . Like all pupils, bilingual pupils should have access to a stimulating curriculum which, at the same time, helps their language development . . . Language skills may be extended in a variety of ways and some examples are given below . . .

- Work can be carried out in different language and peer groups, such as: monolingual groups to encourage the use of preferred languages [to encourage the use of minority students' first language to engage with learning tasks] . . .
- Oral and written responses at different attainment levels can be encouraged by the use of a balance of open-ended and structured tasks.
- Matrices, true/false exercises, data presentations and other display work can help to ensure that achievement is not entirely dependent on proficiency in English.
- Exercises with some repetitive element, such as science experiments, retelling stories and the use of computer software, provide a pattern which supports language development. (NCC, 1991: 1–2)

This guidance on additional language development has drawn on Krashen's (e.g. 1982, 1985) work on comprehensible input which emphasises the importance of helping language learners understand what they hear and read in their target language. The influence of Krashen's work is explicitly acknowledged in an EAL curriculum guidance document in which specific attention is drawn to his well-known conceptual distinction between language acquisition and language learning:

- The *acquired* system is a subconscious process very similar to that which children undergo when they acquire their first language. It requires meaningful interaction in the target language where the focus is on natural communication.
- The *learned* system is the result of formal instruction and is a conscious process which results in explicit knowledge about the language, for example, grammar rules. (DfES, 2006c: 12, original emphasis)

In this rendering of Krashen's work, the rhetorical articulation explicitly foregrounds the similarities between first language and additional language development. For instance, the role of comprehensible input in developing an additional language is elided to that of first language development; e.g. 'For a young child acquiring L1, understanding [comprehensible input] could be enhanced by pointing to an object; for an older pupil acquiring L2, it could be the use of diagrams or other visuals to illustrate text' (DfES, 2006c: 12). Teachers are advised that non-conscious language acquisition processes (as in first language development with infants) are more important than conscious language learning, and that, just as the case with L1 language development, EAL learners need 'regular exposure to words and structures at an early stage' through 'meaningful practice of a particular structure in the context of normal classwork' (ibid.:12). In this account there is a passing recognition of the differences between first and additional language development, but they are framed as second-order issues primarily due to two related factors: (a) time lag, i.e. additional language learners will go through what first language have done through at a later time/age; and (b) sequential language experiences, e.g. secondary school age additional language learners may already have developed the requisite knowledge in their first language, but will now need to acquire the new English-language items. On this view of language development (first or additional language), the notion of language itself is conceptualised as an undifferentiated body of linguistic knowledge and skills which, once acquired, can be put to purposeful communicative use.

Cummins' work constitutes the second source of ideas that has influenced policy. The advice on using students' first language is related to Cummins' long-held position on the potential benefits of bilingual education (e.g. Cummins, 1984, 1993, 2000). Both Krashen and Cummins stress the importance of understanding meaning in communicative context. The use of realia, visual/graphic representation and repetitive activities is quite clearly linked to the importance of enhancing contextual meaning in additional language development. Whereas Krashen treats language as an undifferentiated body of linguistic resource for communication, Cummins distinguishes between two types of language proficiency in school and curriculum contexts: Basic Interpersonal Communication Skills (BICS) and Cognitive Academic Language Proficiency (CALP) (e.g. Cummins, 1984, 1992, 2000, 2008). The former, often understood as communication for social purposes in everyday informal contexts supported by rich contextual information, is generally held to be acquired by most additional language learners in a relatively short time (about two to three years); the latter, often understood as context-reduced language for academic purposes, is known to require much more time to develop and the outcome is often much less certain.

Cummins' ideas have been configured in the current policy formation in a particular way:

> [Cummins] describes the acquisition of Basic Interpersonal Communicative Skills (BICS) as occurring within *two years* of exposure to English. Cognitive Academic Language Proficiency (CALP) to the level of their English-as-a-mother-tongue (EMT) peers, however, may take a *minimum of five years* and usually longer. Cummins's research has shown that because the pupils appear so fluent in everyday social language, teachers are unaware of the need for explicit teaching of academic language. The need for all teachers to be teachers of language in the context of their subject cannot be overstressed and nor can the advantages of such an approach for their EMT [English as mother tongue] peers. (DfES, 2006c: 14, original emphasis)

The distinction between these two types of language and their rates of development is recognised in the Ofsted framework for inspecting EAL in primary schools.

This account of Cummins' work also elides additional language development to that of first language development: that all students, irrespective of language backgrounds, would benefit from the same pedagogic considerations. Whether Cummins or Krashen would rhetorically and theoretically blur the distinction between first and additional language development in this way is a moot point. Given that both of these researchers position their work in the field of additional/second language education, this blurring of first and additional language development in curriculum and classroom contexts can be seen as a particular policy-oriented rendering. For instance, Cummins' notion of BICS is characterised as:

> *Communicative language* (conversational fluency) develops first in face-to-face, highly contextualised situations. (DfES, 2006b: 9, original emphasis)

And CALP is elaborated as comprising two components:

> *Cognitive language* is the language which develops through investigating, exploring ideas and solving problems. cognitive development accompanies the use of language for purposes such as classifying, analysing, hypothesising and generalising as well as the ability to use abstract language.

> *Academic language* is characterised by the use of the passive voice, ideas and concepts as agents, vocabulary with Greek and Latin roots, use of metaphor and personification and, most importantly, nominalisation (abstract nouns made from verbs and other parts of speech), such as *information* from *inform* and *hunger* from *hungry*. (DfES, 2006b: 9, original emphases)

The EAL and bilingual dimension is not visible in this rendering. The melding, so to speak, of aspects of Krashen's and Cummins's work in EAL curriculum policy with an assimilated L1-L2 orientation can be summarised as follows:

- EAL development within curriculum contexts is best achieved through ordinary exposure and non-conscious use that approximate to first language development processes; understanding of the meanings being communicated in context is key to this development.
- Developing 'conversational fluency' is expected to be accomplished, generally through ordinary exposure and use, within two or three years.
- Developing language proficiency for academic purposes can be a long-term process; it can be assisted or hastened up by helping learners understand the meaning of the language they are exposed to through non-linguistic semiotic means such as gestural, graphic and audio-visual information, and through appealing to learners' background knowledge.

PEDAGOGIC AND CURRICULUM UTILITY
OF RENDERED THEORIES

Krashen in Policy

Krashen's arguments on the importance of comprehensible input for additional language development, allied to his pedagogic preference for *acquisition* and not *learning*, have been used to provide theoretical and pedagogic legitimacy for mainstreaming EAL in the particular form that prevails in the English school system. As can be seen in the NCC guidance cited earlier, making the everyday activities in the ordinary English-medium curriculum understandable to EAL learners (i.e. comprehensible input) constitutes one of the, if not *the*, most important condition for EAL development. And if *learning*, particularly in terms of learning about different aspects of the English-language system, is less important than meaningful language exposure and use in everyday activities, then there is hardly any need for explicit EAL-oriented curriculum specifications for what is to be taught and *acquired*. Indeed it would be a theoretical heresy to provide conscious and explicit language learning (and teaching) opportunities. Insofar as EAL development mimics first language development, then this acquisition process will take several years. On this view, as long as teachers are making learning activities understandable, and as long as pupils are encouraged to engage in learning tasks, it is a matter of course that EAL learners will acquire English in time.

Turning to the assignment handing-in date episode it would seem that Sairah, after four years or so in England, has now acquired sufficient English language to talk to her teacher to seek clarification and to implicitly suggest that an alternative date should be set. Under the Krashenian theoretical dispensation (as rendered by policy), one would assume that in one way or another Sairah must have had the necessary meaningful exposure and use of English in the past to enable her to accomplish this in the present moment. The same can be said about Part 1 of the median and mode episode. Here Sairah was clearly able to talk and interact with her teacher. She understood what the teacher said, was able to follow the reasoning, and provided correct answers. Therefore she must have acquired the necessary language to handle this stretch of curriculum talk.

Part 2 of this episode is less straightforward. Sairah appeared to have some difficulty in following the teacher's utterances in relation to the concept of mode; these can be seen as moments of incomprehensible input. The rendered Krashenian theoretical position would suggest that Sairah did not have the necessary exposure and use to enable her to acquire the language for this particular interaction with the teacher. A Krashenian pedagogic response would be to provide more similar exposure and to make sure that such exposure is made more comprehensible, possibly by using supportive focal artefacts such as visual representations of a mode/s in a set of numbers. Over time, and with the necessary language exposure and use, Sairah would be able to handle this kind of teacher talk. This projected developmental trajectory is theoretically congruent with the rendered Krashenian perspective, and professional experience would suggest that some pupils do become more able to tackle difficult tasks through repeated experience over time. But is language exposure and use the only issue to be considered here? The two different communicative outcomes in the median and mode episode would raise doubt about this. Given that the surface features of the language use for reasoning in Part 1 and Part 2 of the median and mode episode are quite similar (e.g. counting of numbers already written down as data input, 'if . . . then' framing of propositions and 'because' constructions for principles), why did Sairah seem to have difficulty in following the teacher's questions and reasoning in Part 2? Clearly something other than language expressions or language forms is involved. I will return to this question in the final section of this discussion.

Cummins in Policy

BICS and CALP have been presented as distinct types of language. It is generally assumed that BICs is expressed through formally 'simple' language dealing with matters whose meanings are either already familiar to the people involved and/or can be gleaned from the immediate environment (e.g. teacher calling pupils' attention to start a lesson). CALP is presented as a different type of language comprising two components: cognitive language and academic language (DfES, 2006b). In this account cognitive language is understood in terms of cognitive functions: it is the 'language that develops through investigating, exploring of ideas . . . ' (loc. cit.). Academic language is defined in terms of grammatical forms (e.g. vocabulary with Greek and Latin roots . . . and nominalization' [loc. cit.]) and rhetoric features of discourse (e.g. 'use of metaphor and personification' [loc.cit.]). So, to understand an expression such as 'Industrialisation was a consequence of international trade and agrarian reform' would require CALP. On this view BICS and CALP are different types of activities accompanied by the use of different types of vocabulary and grammar.

However, the language in the two episodes of Sairah's interaction with her teachers blurs the neat division between this rendering of BICS and CALP. Is the handing-in date episode an instance of BICS or CALP? This interaction was certainly face-to-face, but was it contextualised? This interaction could only be said to be contextualised in a broad sense in that it took place in a familiar classroom and that the practice of handing in assignments would be within Sairah's experience. But the actual meanings expressed by Sairah could not have been rehearsed on previous assignment handing-in occasions because they recounted a specific sequence of events (as understood by her) on this particular occasion. And this exchange was certainly not contextualised in the sense that the meanings could be recovered from the immediate environment: Sairah and her teacher were talking about past events; very little in the immediate speech situation was related to the experience being recounted by both Sairah and the teacher. So arguably this episode is not prototypically BICS. But is it CALP? The language used by Sairah was at first glance informal. But a closer examination would suggest that it was grammatically and pragmatically apt; e.g. in move 3 'I thought you said . . . ', the use of the past tense signals appropriate politeness, and in move 5 ' . . . normally when you come after school . . . to improve . . . ', the recounting of an established practice points to complex background reasoning to support her position. Rightly or wrongly, Sairah was trying to establish the arguments for a particular case (an alternative handing-in date) by inferring from a general understanding (the normal practice of going to see the teacher after school to improve her work which would require more time); this is sophisticated reasoning expressed in pragmatically appropriate language—the stuff of academic discourse. But Sairah and her teacher were not dealing with a piece of curriculum content and exploring complex concepts such as 'industrialisation' or 'mode'. They were just trying to sort out a handing-in date for a piece of written work. So how far should this exchange be regarded as an instance of CALP?

Similar blurring of the distinction between BICS and CALP can be seen in the median and mode episode. This exchange between Sairah and her teacher was face-to-face. The language expressions, or wordings, used by the teacher and Sairah were very much interactional and here-and-now. For instance, the use of the deictic 'you' by the teacher when acknowledging Sairah's questions and when leading her through reasoning, e.g. move 3 '7 and 7 in the so you've got two numbers in the middle' and move 9 ' . . . what you do is . . . ', suggests the immediacy of this context-bound exchange. The meanings expressed in the interaction were also embedded in the focal artefacts in the immediate environment, e.g. moves 7 and 8 when both Sairah and the teacher counted the numbers written on a page. In terms of register the teacher's utterances were relatively non-technical, and much of her exposition was framed in a contingent dialogue designed to lead Sairah to the correct answers (e.g. moves 18 through 40). In the continuing moves in Part 2 of this episode (e.g. 18, 20, 22, 24, 26, 28 and 30) the teacher asked questions, repeated information and evaluated answers on a reactive and contingent basis. The formal 'if . . . then' conditional reasoning structure was used, but this seemed to be already familiar to Sairah as evidenced by the exchanges in earlier moves (16 and 17) when Sairah was able to give a correct answer. So, the language features of this episode would suggest that this is an instance of BICS, but the content meanings are very much part of the mathematics curriculum. And the apparent difficulty Sairah seemed to have in grasping the meaning of mode would suggest that she was not familiar with this concept. Furthermore, the availability of the focal artefacts (e.g. a set of numbers on a page) did not seem to help her much. So this was a cognitively demanding task encoded in here-and-now language, or more provocatively, was this a case of CALP expressed in BICS?

UNDERSTANDING LANGUAGE IN CLASSROOM INTERACTION

The discussion above suggests that there are considerable complexities in the central theoretical tenets underpinning the key policy-sponsored pedagogic principles. I will attempt to comment on two related issues in this final section: context for achieving understanding and classroom language, and highlighting relevant issues for further conceptual and theoretical deliberations for policy purposes.

Context for Achieving Understanding

Achieving understanding is self-evidently important for classroom communication (indeed any communication). Helping EAL pupils to understand what is being said is clearly an important pedagogic consideration. Making classroom communication understandable through increasing the amount of contextual meaning available in the teaching-learning context is, however, not entirely a teacher-controlled process. Cummins (2008:75) suggests that there are two components in the concept of context: 'what we bring to a task' which includes prior knowledge and interests in the task at hand, and 'the range of supports that may be incorporated in the task itself' which may include visuals and realia. From the point of view of a teacher the idea of using realia and visual representation in teaching to help make meaning more explicit may seem a relatively straightforward and familiar idea. After all illustrative pictures and diagrams can be found readily in textbooks. And the increasing use of digital interactive display technology in the classroom would suggest that the immediate teaching context can be made abundantly rich in multiple forms of meaning representation.

The value of providing this kind of contextual meaning, however, depends on the capacity of the pupils to make use of it. This capacity would be in part dependent on previous experience, present interests and tasks at hand (for a further discussion see Leung, 1996; Cowie et al., 2008: Section 3). Furthermore, it is extremely difficult to know how much contextual information is being used actively by pupils, whether we are talking about the contextual information that resides in pupils' background experience or in the immediate learning environment. Roberts (1996: 24) notes that '[c]ontextual information is frequently potential rather than explicit . . . it does not appear as readily available to participants and/or is not necessarily relevant and therefore attended to at any one time'. So context is in a fundamental sense created by participants in interaction on a moment-by-moment basis.

Given the complex, contingent, fluid and participant-constructed nature of context, it would be unsafe to assume that teachers can control the context understood and experienced by pupils, let alone their ability to increase contextual support for particular pupils at will. Pedagogically it would seem that a way forward would be to pay close attention to interactive classroom talk, for it is through attending to talk in an informed way that teachers can begin to grasp what and how pupils are making sense of the meaning in ongoing interaction. The literature on achieving understanding would clearly be a useful reference point for further pedagogic development (e.g. Bremer et al., 1996). The recent conceptual and empirical work on teacher-pupil interaction in relation to classroom-based formative assessment may also serve as a useful starting point for further development (e.g. Black and William, 1998, 2006, 2009; Leung 2004, 2005, 2007; Poehner and Lantolf, 2005).

Classroom Language

Conceptually there is little doubt that language can be used to express informal, non-technical social meanings, just as it can be used to express complex and technical meanings. In other words, language can serve different functions.

But are BICS and CALP different types of language? It is suggested that BICS is 'face-to-face' and 'highly contextualised' (DfES, 2006b: 9) and CALP is characterised by 'the use of passive voice . . . vocabulary with Greek and Latin roots . . . nominalisation . . . ' (loc. cit.). This formulation presents BICS and CALP as distinct forms of language. There is no doubt that complex and technical forms of language are used to express curriculum concepts, for example:

> The median of a set of numbers is the value of the middle number when they are arranged in ascending order. (National Strategy: 258)

> The mode indicates the item or class that occurs most often. (National Strategy: 257 http://nationalstrategies.standards.dcsf.gov.uk/downloads/pdf/ma_sf_exmp_257_259_261_036608.pdf)

Such formal definitions are generally found in textbooks and reference materials, and they constitute part of the curriculum content and language to be learned. But in the classroom a good deal of what counts as teaching and learning is interactionally realised. Professional experience, exemplified by the two episodes of classroom interaction discussed earlier, would suggest that teachers and pupils generally engage one another using forms of language that would be appropriate for the speech situation and the task at hand. Complex ideas are not always expressed in complex and formal language. As Martin-Jones and Romaine (1986: 29) observe in a discussion on a related topic: 'The relationship between language and thought processes is by no means as straightforward . . . Language skills cannot be neatly compartmentalised . . . '. This would seem to be in line with Cummins' (2008: 74) clarification on this point: 'BICS/CALP made no claim to be anything more than a conceptual distinction'.

It is often stated that BICS is relatively easy to acquire within a relatively short time, whereas CALP takes a much longer time. BICS is easier to acquire, it is implicitly suggested, because of its here-and-nowness, its face-to-faceness, and its non-technical forms. The median and mode episode would suggest that informal interactional language can be both easy and difficult, depending on participants' ability to understand the meaning being worked upon. Whereas it is reasonable to say that the routinised language associated with certain familiar and repetitive activities such as buying food in a school canteen is likely to be relatively easy to understand and to learn, it doesn't follow that using routinised language would make meaning easy to grasp. The language used to talk about 'mode' was not very different from that used for 'median', yet Sairah appeared to struggle with the concept of 'mode'. The difference may be accounted for by her capacity to apperceive the content meaning, and to bring all that she might know to bear on the communication. Seen in this light, the teaching of EAL is more than just teaching different forms of language (e.g. formal and informal), it is also about communicating content meaning (e.g. mode). In a fundamental sense this is the crux of the matter for EAL pedagogy—to achieve understanding of content meaning in classroom communication and express it in an academic register. This content-language integrated view would recast the role of contextual support. The invocation of pupils' background knowledge and the use of realia to assist understanding, for instance, are now pedagogic means to help pupils understand curriculum meaning. The language used to achieve this may take different forms for different purposes, e.g. interactional, informal language for contingent talk to explain or clarify meaning, or more formal language for textbook reading and assignment writing. (For further discussion see Gibbons, 2003; Halliday, 1999; Leung and Mohan, 2004; Mohan and Slater, 2004.)

Overall, the distinction between BICS and CALP is best understood as conceptual domains of language proficiency (i.e. not as types of language). Cummins (2008) clarifies that context and cognitive demand are not fixed quantities—they should be understood dynamically in terms of individuals' experiences and tasks. The analysis presented here suggests that complex and cognitively challenging meanings can be expressed through both here-and-now informal language and complex formal language. BICS and CALP are not labels for different types of language represented by different type of lexical and syntactic realisations. Nor are they labels for different kinds of cognitive complexity. For an absolute beginner in English-language learning, getting food in a canteen can be very difficult. But when the requisite language (food names, making a request, and so on) is appropriated, both the language and the transaction would become relatively straightforward. Furthermore, language use in social interaction can take many registers— the language used to talk to one's friends is likely to be quite different from that used when talking to the head teacher, even on social occasions. Likewise a piece of curriculum learning can comprise different forms of language, depending on the activities at hand (e.g. teacher and pupil talking to each other in one-to-one consultation, teacher reading from a book to class), the participants involved (e.g. teacher doing teacher-fronted talk, invited outside speaker addressing a pupil audience in a school assembly) and the intended learning outcome (e.g. written account, spoken report to class). In terms of learning curriculum content, informal here-and-now language is not necessarily easier to understand. For EAL pupils these are all potentially important areas of language use to be acquired, as they may not have the requisite knowledge from previous experience and prior learning at any one stage of their English-language development.

In this chapter I have tried to show that the curriculum guidance and professional advice offered to teachers are based on interpretations of theories and concepts that have (a) reified selective concepts of additional language development drawn from fields such as educational psychology, psycholinguistics and Second Language Acquisition and turned them into a thing-like language typology, and (b) overly simplified the dynamic relationship between language registers in interaction, achieving understanding in context, and curriculum meaning. Further development in EAL pedagogy will require an expanded understanding of language in use, taking into account the complex form and function relationship in language use, and the participant-constructed nature of achieving understanding in classroom interaction.

REFERENCES

Baetens Beardsmore, H. (ed.) 1993. *European Models of Bilingual Education.* Clevedon: Multilingual Matters.

Bernstein, B. 1996. *Pedagogy, Symbolic Control and Identity.* London: Taylor and Francis.

Black, P. and Wiliam, D. 1998. Assessment and classroom learning. *Assessment in Education* 5(1): 7–73.

———. 2006. Assessment for learning in the classroom. In *Assessment and Learning,* ed. J. Gardner, 9–25. London: Sage.

———. 2009. Developing the theory of a formative assessment. *Educational Assessment, Evaluation and Accountability* 21: 5–31.

Bremer, K., Roberts, C., Vasseur, M., Simonot, M. and Broeder, P. (eds) 1996. *Achieving Understanding: Discourse in Intercultural Encounters.* London: Longman.

Commission for Racial Equality. 1986. *Teaching English as a Second Language.* London: CRE.

Cowie, B., Moreland, J., Jones, A. and Otrel-Cass, K. 2008. *The Classroom InSite Project: Understanding Classroom Interactions to Enhance Teaching and*

Learning in Science and Technology—Teaching and Learning Research Initiative Final Report. Hamilton: The University of Waikato/Te Whare Wānanga o Waikato.

Cummins, J. 1984. *Bilingualism and Special Education: Issues in Assessment and Pedagogy*. Clevedon: Multilingual Matters.

———. 1992. Language proficiency, bilingualism, and academic achievement. In *The Multicultural Classroom: Readings for Content-Area Teachers*, ed. P. A. Richard-Amato and M. A. Snow, 16–26. New York: Longman.

———. 1993. Bilingualism and second language learning. In *Annual Review of Applied Linguistics* (Vol. 13), ed. W. Grabe, 51–70. Cambridge: Cambridge University Press.

———. 2000. *Language, Power and Pedagogy: Bilingual Children in the Crossfire*. Clevedon: Multilingual Matters

———. 2008. BICS and CALP: empirical and theoretical status of the distinction. In *Encyclopedia of Language and Education* (Vol. 2), ed. B. V. Street and N. H. Hornberger, 71–83. New York: Springer.

Department for Education and Skills. 2006a. *Primary National Strategy—Excellence and Enjoyment: Learning and Teaching for Bilingual Children in the Primary Years: Introductory Guide: Supporting School Improvement*. London: DfES Publications.

———. 2006b. *Primary National Strategy—Excellence and Enjoyment: Learning and Teaching for Bilingual Children in the Primary Years: Unit 1 Planning and Assessment for Language and Learning*. London: DfES Publications.

———. 2006c. *Secondary National Strategy: Pupils learning English as an additional language*. London: DfES.

Edwards, V. and Redfern, A. 1992. *The World in a Classroom: Language in Education in Britain and Canada*. Clevedon: Multilingual Matters

Eggins, S. and Slade, D. 1997. *Analysing Casual Conversation*. London: Cassell.

European Commission. 2004. *Integrating Immigrant Children into Schools in Europe*. Brussels: Eurydice.

Gibbons, P. 2003. Mediating language learning: teacher interactions with ESL students in a content-based classroom. *TESOL Quarterly* 37(2): 247–73.

Halliday, M. A. K. 1999. The notion of "context" in language education. In *Text and Context in Functional Linguistics*, ed. M. Ghedessy, 1–24. Amsterdam: John Benjamins.

Krashen, S. 1982. *Principles and Practice in Second Language Acquisition*. Oxford: Pergamon.

———. 1985. *The Input Hypothesis*. New York: Longman

Leung, C. 1996. Context, content and language. In *Curriculum Related Assessment, Cummins and Bilingual Children*, ed. T. Cline and N. Frederickson, 26–40. Clevedon: Multilingual Matters.

———. 2004. Developing formative teacher assessment: knowledge, practice and change. *Language Assessment Quarterly* 1(1): 19–41.

———. 2005. Classroom teacher assessment of second language development: construct as practice. In *Handbook of Research in Second Language Learning and Teaching*, ed. E. Hinkel, 869–88. Mahwah, NJ: Lawrence Erlbaum.

———. 2007. Dynamic assessment—assessment as teaching? *Language Assessment Quarterly* 4(3): 257–78.

Leung, C. and Creese, A. 2008. Professional issues in working with ethno-linguistic difference: inclusive policy in practice. In *Planning Change, Changing Plans*, ed. D. E. Murray, 155–73. Ann Arbor: University of Michigan Press.

Leung, C. and Mohan, B. 2004. Teacher formative assessment and talk in classroom contexts—assessment as discourse and assessment of discourse. *Language Testing* 20(3): 335–59.

Martin-Jones, M. and Romaine, S. 1986. Semilingualism: a half-baked theory of communicative competence. *Applied Linguistics* 7(1): 26–38.

Mohan, B. and Slater, T. 2004. The evaluation of causal discourse and language as a resource for meaning. In *Language, Education, and Discourse: Functional Approaches*, ed. J. A. Foley, 255–69. New York: Continuum.

National Curriculum Council. 1991. *Circular Number 11: Linguistic Diversity and the National Curriculum*. York: NCC.

Poehner, M. E. and Lantolf, J. 2005. Dynamic assessment in the language classroom. *Language Teaching Research* 9(3): 233–65.

Roberts, C. 1996. A social perspective on understanding: some issues of theory and method. In *Achieving Understanding: Discourse in Intercultural Encounters*, ed. K. Bremer, C. Roberts, M. Simonot and P. Broeder, 9–36. London: Longman.

Swann Report. 1985. *Education for All*. London: HMSO.

Tosi, A. and Leung, C. (eds) 1999. *Rethinking Language Education*. London: CILT.

14 Young Learner Perspectives through Researcher-Initiated Role Play

Aizan Yaacob and Sheena Gardner

Conducting research with young multilingual participants is challenging, particularly for those who want to access learner perspectives. Question-naires analysed quantitatively provide insights into learner experiences worded by researchers, as in the investigation of primary pupils' percep-tions towards the teaching of Science through English in Malaysia (Yassin et al., 2009). More qualitative data from interviews with pupils, class-room observation, and document collection provide a richer description of the learning experience, as in the seven country comparative and lon-gitudinal European study of primary English Language Teaching (Szpo-towicz, Mihaljevic Djigunovic and Enever, 2009) or the holistic Primary English Curriculum Innovation impact study in Beijing (Wang, Sun and Ma, 2008). These 'grown up' methods are adapted for young learners using non-verbal signs such as smiley faces or visual prompts. Written or spoken protocols are used to elicit affective and evaluative responses to questions such as 'Which activity do you like best? or 'Why did you like it?' (e.g. Shak and Gardner, 2008), but responses tend to be short, and so these techniques offer limited access to detailed or nuanced young learner perspectives on learning and teaching. One reason for this is that most learners, whether children or adults, do not have the vocabulary needed to discuss specific aspects of the lessons they experience in detail. A sec-ond reason is that learners may not be used to reflecting on their experi-ences or may be uncertain of what exactly researchers are looking for. As Pinter (2011: 212) points out,

> When a research project is conducted at school, children may think that the research task is a test, and as such it may count towards their formal assessment. This may make them reluctant to speak up or be critical in any way. Class routines, such as teachers nominating those who are allowed to speak, may also interfere with the researchers' intentions when inviting children to contribute ideas freely to a discus-sion. Children know that most tasks and questions at school have a right or wrong answer and they have this same expectation when they participate in research.

In sociodramatic play, however, children naturally move away from paper and pencil tasks and expectations of a correct answer. They can, nevertheless, draw on funds of knowledge about language, values, beliefs, approaches to classroom management and the value of education (Riojas-Cortez, 2001).

Yaacob's study of literacy practices in year 1 classrooms in Malaysia (Yaacob, 2006) involved classroom observation, interviewing teachers and children, gathering documents and researcher-initiated role play. This technique was developed because in the first data collection phase in Malaysia it was difficult to access young learner perspectives effectively using interviews. In this chapter we illustrate how data collection through researcher-initiated role play can shed light on young learner perspectives on classroom based teaching and learning in multilingual contexts.

PLAY IN RESEARCH ON SCHOOL LEARNING

Play comes naturally to children, and valuable insights about children's development are gained from observing such play in school settings. Of particular interest to us is sociodramatic role play, where children assume roles and act out parts based on events they have experienced as part of the process of making sense of their worlds. Such role play occurs naturally, so children are used to taking charge, assigning and playing roles, in words and action, with props, and using a mixture of experience and imagination to develop a story collaboratively.

Research also suggests such play is beneficial for children's development, and this, in turn, has led to research into ways of optimising such benefits through influencing play. Studies, such as Kitson (1994) and Lyle (2002), have suggested that adult intervention in play can lead to greater engagement, and that certain settings, and provision of certain kinds of props, can lead to play with more talk than others where acting is more prominent. More discussion and negotiation of roles will be evident if there are more than two people playing. Whereas these studies have tended to be in monolingual contexts, they have proved useful for us in our development of the practical details of researcher-initiated role play including the nature of adult intervention, the setting, group size and composition, props and prompts.

Researchers such as Lytra (2007) and Maybin (2006) have shown how children naturally imitate teachers and school talk, and in particular how they play with these voices. Maybin distinguishes more formal dialogue where 'students repeat what teachers say and teachers repeat and appropriate the voices of textbooks' (2006: 168) from informal talk where children 'slip rapidly between different interpretive frames, transforming work on a maths problem into play, . . . switching attention from informal chat onto a school task, . . . , or holding a number of frames simultaneously for strategic purposes'. (Maybin, 2006: 169) Although she is describing secondary school children, this notion of holding several frames in play is also important in our context, where, as we shall see, the children switch from acting out to negotiating the nature of the role play.

The main inspiration for researcher-initiated role play came not from research on playing with teacher roles and voices in school, but from the research by Gregory and her colleagues which has shown how siblings spontaneously play school at home (Gregory, 2001; Williams, 2004). In these studies, we see spontaneous play at home where older children are the 'teachers' in role plays of the literacy hour and are able to reproduce and adapt many of the teaching strategies used in schools.

THE STUDY AND RESEARCHER-INITIATED ROLE PLAY PROTOCOL

Although there is considerable evidence that children naturally play school, it was not clear whether it would be possible to persuade children to play school for our research purposes. Both personal communication from those who had tried to do this and advice on testing young learners suggested it might not work: Leena Robertson (personal communication, 2004) reported little success with multilingual young learners in the UK ('it all just broke down in giggles'), whereas Carpenter, Fujii and Kataoka (1995, cited in McKay, 2006: 85) found that asking two children to role play was 'extremely problematic' and vividly describe some of the issues in getting young children to talk.

Aware that it might not work, we developed the researcher-initiated role play technique as one among many for collecting data on the literacy practices of Malaysian children. We piloted it with Malaysian children attending school in England. The second data collection phase in Malaysia took place over three months in four primary schools in two districts of Kedah province in northern Malaysia (Yaacob, 2006). It involved observation, interviews and document collection from children and teachers of year 1 classes with thirty-five to thirty-six children aged six and seven. Children at this age usually have different teachers for Malay, English, Jawi, Science, Maths and other subjects. The focus was on literacy practices in the twenty-six English Hour lessons observed. The English Hour is similar in structure and purpose to the Literacy Hour in England (Gardner and Yaacob, 2009). To understand the pedagogic context better, observations were also conducted in other reading lessons (in Malay and in the Jawi script), and in other subjects taught in English (Maths and Science). Bahasa Malaysia (BM), or the Malay language, is today most frequently written in the Roman alphabet, but the Malaysian government is keen to revive Malay in the Jawi script (Mashkuri et al., 2001) which is an enhanced Arabic alphabet with vowels used for Malay. Children also learn about the Quran, so being able to read this script helps with Islamic studies and with preparation for Arabic which they may learn later.

In each of the four Malaysian primary schools (A, B, C, D) two groups of four children were interviewed and performed role plays in English, with three also performing role plays in Malay. The role plays lasted fifteen to twenty minutes, with some groups performing more than one lesson. Seven groups were video-recorded (the eighth group were shy and refused permission). The role plays were transcribed, with talk in Malay translated into English. For the purposes of this chapter one transcribed role play from the pilot study is included. This involved Malaysian children aged three to eight in England, UK (UK-RG0). The data set includes role plays of seven year 1 English classes in Malaysia (ME) and three Malay classes (BM) with the same children, aged six to seven, as in Table 14.1.

In each role play reading materials were available for props, and the following prompt was given by the researcher to initiate the role play. The prompt was given in English with the UK group, whereas in Malaysia, both Malay and English were used: the prompt was first given in English, then explained in Malay. The term 'role play' was used in both contexts.

Table 14.1   Role Play Contexts

Code	School & Group	Composition	Children T= child playing the teacher	Target Reading Language
UK-RG0	X-0	3 girls, 1 boy	Leah (T) Sya, Nana, Wan	English
BMUA-RG1	A-1	4 girls	Sofea (T) Ani, Qis, Farra	Malay
MEUA-RG1	A-1	4 girls	Farra (T) Sofea, Ani, Qis	English
MEUA-RG2	A-2	4 girls	Farhana (T) NF, AIN, IN, NY	English
MEUB-RG3	B-3	4 girls	Nicky (T) Wani, AA, Fay	English
MEUB-RG4	B-4	4 boys	Mokhsin (T) Awie, Sham, Helmy	English
BMRC-RG5	C-5	4 girls	NB, FAR, AS, NS	English
BMRC-RG5	C-5	4 girls	NB, FAR, AS, NS	Malay
MERC-RG6	C-6	4 boys	AF, ZN, MK, II	English
MERD-RG7	D-7	2 girls, 2 boys	AAA, MA, ZI, FH	English
BMRD-RG7	D-7	2 girls, 2 boys	AAA, MA, ZI, FH	Malay

Let's pretend that some nursery children are coming to your class to see what it is like to be in year 1. They don't know how to read so you have to teach them. One of you will pretend to be the teacher. Role play what happens in your English/ Malay/ Jawi classroom.

The introduction of an audience of younger children rather than the adult researchers was intended to provide an easier rationale, although the children also knew that the research was interested in what happens in their regular classrooms. The role plays in schools in Malaysia took place in a quiet room so that they could be performed and recorded away from distractions. The role plays in the UK were recorded outside of school in the children's homes. The role plays relate to primary classes in Malaysia and to primary classes in the UK, to early literacy in Malay in Malay-medium classes (BM), to early literacy in English in bilingual Malay and English classes (ME), and to early literacy in English in English-medium classes (UK). We now present and analyse data extracts from the role plays and we make comparisons across the three contexts of starting class and learning to read.

COMPARISONS ACROSS CONTEXTS

Starting Class in England and in Malaysia

The children's role plays tended to begin with the morning rituals for starting class. These two extracts show clearly the differences between starting class in Malaysia and in England. Please see the end notes for transcription conventions.

Extract 14.1   Starting class in Malaysia (MEUA-RG1).
(Everyone is standing up waiting anxiously to start the role play)
01   Sofea   **Hey duduklah dulu** < hey sit down first!>
02   (Farra who is playing the teacher enters the classroom and greets the students.
03   (The students stand up and greet her)
04   Farra   Good morning, class
05   All   Good morning, teacher   (slow, loud, in unison)
06   Farra   Sit down
07   All   Thank you, teacher   (slow, loud, in unison)
08   (Qis flips the pages of the English textbook)
09   Qis   **Cikgu ambik buku mana cikgu?** <teacher which book to take, teacher?>

The dialogue in lines 4–7 with its distinctive intonation patterns will be familiar to many readers as a typical way of marking the beginning of a lesson. Whereas this may resemble a parody (Maybin, 2006: 160–61) in some contexts, it was very similar to the typical opening dialogue observed in 'real' classes, and came across as a genuine imitation of classroom talk. This highlights the importance of observing and then later being able to replay the role plays and notice how the talk interacts with gaze, gesture and movement around the class, particularly by the teacher, in order to interpret the significance of what is being conveyed by the role plays.

> Extract 14.2   Starting class in England (UK-RG0).
> (Teacher Leah is sitting on a sofa waiting for the other children to come in. Children are giggling and playing joyfully at the hallway, waiting for the class to begin.)
>   3 Leah   Ring Ring (pause) Ring Ring (pause) Ring Ring (pause) Ring Ring
>   (Children enter room and greet her)
>   (Teacher smiles back and indicates where they should sit)
>   6 Sya   Hello   (Sya enters classroom smiling)
>   (Children sit in semi circle on carpet in front of Teacher)
>   7 Sya   Sit down. sit down. sit down   (telling Nana and Wan to sit down)
>   9 Leah   Put the books away (she waits till all are ready) . . .
>   14 Leah   What's your name?   (taking register)
>   15 Sya   Nantilah dulu tak payahlah lagi. Tak payah ask the name.
>   <wait a second not yet. no need to ask the name>

There is considerably less agreement to the beginning of this lesson as the group includes children from different classes in the same school, and partly for this reason there is more talk about what they should be doing. It is also clear that one of the 'learners' (Sya) is taking a leading role in organising the play.

Nevertheless, a comparison of these two short extracts highlights the main differences between starting the English Hour in Malaysia and starting the Literacy Hour in England. In Malaysia the teacher enters the class, the children rise and there is a ritual choral greeting before they turn to the appropriate page in the textbook. In England the teacher who has been sitting waiting for the children rings a bell which is a sign for the children to come into class from the playground. There are individual greetings and register is called before the lesson starts.

The differences between observing role play and observing actual lessons also begin to emerge. One difference is that non-verbal sounds and actions are verbalised. For example, teacher Leah says 'ring ring' as she rings an imaginary bell. Such verbalisations serve to highlight cues that children attend to. A second difference is that expected behaviours are verbalised in ways that are unlikely in real classrooms. For example in line 1, Extract 14.1, Sofia says 'hey, sit down first', and in line 15, Sya says 'wait a second not yet, no need to ask the name'. In these turns the students slip out of their acting roles into directing roles, and out of English into Malay. In fact, the code-switching here is a classic contextualisation cue (Gumperz, 1982) that marks the shift between on-stage and off-stage talk (see also Goffman, 1974; Arthur, 2001).

Despite these differences between school and role play, we do get a strong sense not only that the children are keen to represent what goes on in their reading lessons with accuracy, but also that they are capable of providing detailed information about the literacy events and how they should be enacted in talk in class.

Learning to Read in English and in Malay

The next three extracts show the kinds of literacy events the children select to play in their role plays in three contexts: learning to read in Malay, in English in Malaysia, and in English in England.

To learn to read in Malay the class select their textbooks from the props available and take it in turns to read sentence by sentence around the class. The students read, whereas the teacher listens and corrects any errors. This is followed by choral reading after the teacher, as words are built up, syllable by syllable:

Extract 14.3   Learning to read in Malay (BMRC-RG5).

T	pa
SS	pa
T	da
SS	da
T	**pada**
SS	**pada**
T	se
SS	se
T	ko
SS	ko
T	lah
SS	lah
T	**sekolah** <school>
SS	**sekolah** <school>

In their interviews, the adult teachers commented that reading in Malay and in Jawi was easy because you could teach it as a building process from syllable to word to sentence to text, with a focus on good pronunciation and diction. In contrast, they found they could not do this with all English words and so had to use whole words and sentences. In fact flashcards were used to teach reading in Jawi and in English, but not in Malay, perhaps because the shape of words in the Jawi script is, like the shape of English words in Roman script, a distinctive characteristic. The principle that reading in English should focus on whole words was reinforced by the absence of breaking down words into syllables in the role plays of English lessons in Malaysia, which like the Malay lessons stick to the textbooks. The normal method of teaching reading in the role plays was repetition of sentences from the textbook.

Extract 14.4   Learning to read in English in Malaysia (MEUB-RG4).
10. (Mokhsin, the teacher stands up and starts reading aloud and the other students follow)
11. Mokhsin   E IS FOR EAR
12. All   E IS FOR EAR (Awie shows a signal to Sham to stop reading and not to go over board this time and wait for the teacher)
13. Mokhsin   E IS FOR EAR
14. All   E IS FOR EAR
15. Mokhsin   ELLY ELEPHANT
16. All   ELLY ELEPHANT
17. Mokhsin   HAS TWO BIG EARS
18. All   HAS TWO BIG EARS (They all laugh)
19. Mokhsin   N IS FOR NOSE

The children demonstrated in their role play the variations that could be used in this type of activity, with the teacher leading, individual students leading, with breaks in sentences, then whole sentences, with questions and answers and so on.

Extract 14.5   Learning to read in English in Malaysia (MEUA-RG1).
38. All   WHERE ARE YOU FROM?
39. Farra   I'M FROM SABAH
40. All   I'M FROM SABAH
41. Farra   WHERE DO YOU LIVE AMIR?
42. All   WHERE DO YOU LIVE AMIR?
43. Farra   I LIVE IN TAMAN PERDANA
44. All   I LIVE IN TAMAN PERDANA
45. Farra   I LIVE IN TAMAN PERDANA TOO
46. All   I LIVE IN TAMAN PERDANA TOO
47. Farra   HAVE SOME CAKES
48. All   HAVE SOME CAKES
49. Farra   THANK YOU SWEE LING
50. All   THANK YOU SWEE LING
51. Farra   YOU ARE WELCOME
52. All   YOU ARE WELCOME

In addition to different units of reading (syllable vs phrase or clause), when we compare the reading lessons in Malay and in English, we notice that reading in the mother tongue involves mainly sitting and reading aloud. In contrast, the reading activity in English engages the whole body in ways that attend more to the meaning of what is being read. This is important, as English is being learned as a foreign language in this context.

As the students and teacher became more involved in their roles, they embellished the texts with enthusiasm and non-verbal communication, in the form of gestures and actions:

Extract 14.6   Learning to read in English in Malaysia (MEUB-RG4).
20. All   N IS FOR NOSE (Awie touches his nose)
21. Mokhsin   ELLY ELEPHANT
22. All   ELLY ELEPHANT
23. Mokhsin   HAS A LONG NOSE
24. All   HAS A LONG NOSE (Awie touches his nose again and laughs)
25. Mokhsin   T IS FOR TAIL
26. All   T IS FOR TAIL
27. Mokhsin   ELLY ELEPHANT
28. All   EELY ELEPHANT
29. Mokhsin   HAS A TINY TAIL
30. All   HAS A TINY TAIL

In Extract 14.6 there are giggles of recognition (line 24) when the boys realise they are doing the actions they have been taught to accompany the words and reinforce the meanings. Such physical reinforcement of meaning is seen across schools and groups, as in Extract 14.7 below:

Extract 14.7   Learning to read in English in Malaysia (MEUA-RG1).
71. Farra   I CAN TOUCH LEAF
72. All   I CAN TOUCH LEAF (The students move as if touching a leaf)
73. Farra   I CAN SEE A BIRD
74. All   I CAN SEE A BIRD
75. Sofea   A bird!!
76. Farra   I CAN SMELL CHICKEN
77. All   I CAN SMELL CHICKEN
78. Farra   Ok. Thirty three. I MUST WASH MY HANDS
79. All   I MUST WASH MY HANDS (students act as if washing their hands)
80. Farra   I MUST BRUSH MY TEETH
81. All   I MUST BRUSH MY TEETH (students brush their teeth)
82. Farra   I MUST COMB MY HAIR
83. All   I MUST COMB MY HAIR (Students comb their hair)

This shows how physical and verbal routines that are familiar from reading lessons can be elicited through role play. Reading routines in England are quite different, as illustrated in Extract 14.8:

Extract 14.8   Learning to read in England (UK-RGO)

17. Leah   Today we are going to read a story about Faraway Friends
18. Nana   Look you need to show it like that (pointing to the title and showing Leah how to hold the book facing the children)
19. Sya   Cakaplah with expression <say it with expression> Today we're going to read about Faraway Friends
20. Nana   I can't see
21. Sya   Show lah. Leah kena show Teacher selalu show < show you have to show teacher always shows> (demonstrates holding the book higher)
        (Leah starts reading the story slowly and softly)
23. Sya   Read with expression (showing her how to read with expression)

Rather than using textbooks or flashcards, teachers in the UK tend to read stories with the class, although they may also read poems or information texts. The stories are accompanied by pictures and the teachers generally read with expression. Both these aspects of classroom practice help convey the meaning of the words in print.

By comparing all the role plays, we can see patterns emerging for each setting. Reading English in Malaysia includes multiple variations on individual and choral reading aloud. Action is important both to accompany singing rhymes, as demonstrated by one group's rendition of 'one to three four five, once I caught a fish alive', and when incorporated into spoken or chanted choral repetition activities. Thus learning to read is an active, participatory process that bears many similarities to group singing. Through repetition of syllables, phrases, and clauses, the sounds and the rhythms become familiar to learners and are associated with the printed words in the textbooks.

In contrast, learning to read in England is a more reflective, physically passive process. Children are encouraged to notice features in the pictures and try to figure out the relationship between the spoken words and printed words through their meaning. There is no physical participation by learners, and no repetition of words or phrases. Of course there is much more to teaching reading in England and in Malaysia, but an examination of the children's role plays offers us insights into the young learner perspective on what is essentially going on—not just what is said, but the whole setting and staging of the activity. It encourages us to focus on what the children present—features that we might not notice or consider worthy of further enquiry.

YOUNG LEARNER PERSPECTIVES THROUGH ROLE PLAY

Playing school is not the same as doing school. In some ways it is less than school in that, without teacher input, the activities are unlikely to represent the full range of what happens in class. But, in some ways, it is more than school because it opens a window on learner perspectives. It does this not only in what children choose to act out, but also in the way they do this. "In the very manner in which they reproduce a voice and its generic and social connotations, . . . , speakers . . . are in a sense answering it, and saying something about themselves in the process" (Maybin, 2008: 82).

As we have seen through our comparison of role plays from different contexts, the role play technique offers insights into young learner perspectives in several ways: First, it provides a window on what learners see, and do not see, of what happens in class. For instance, in role plays in England, the teacher is imagined sitting relaxing in the classroom while the children are outside playing before class starts. This is something that could be checked with the children, or through observation, but it is probably not a scenario many British primary teachers would recognise as the norm!

Secondly, role play provides evidence of features of lessons that young learners deem significant. For instance, the 'ring ring' of the bell; the reading 'with expression'; the choral repetition in unison. These are features of the lessons that the children recognise as important for the smooth flow of the lesson.

Thirdly, role play brings out features that young learners may barely be conscious of but have nevertheless internalised. For example, the actions accompanying the choral drilling appeared almost self-consciously. Such insights provide evidence of how these lessons are experienced. Related to this, although not illustrated here,[1] are examples where learners ask the teacher to 'slow down' or complain that the reading task is 'too difficult'. Such comments point to areas where learners have difficulties reading in ways that might not be obvious in real classes if such comments are not made. Other comments show learners enjoying the activity, or keen to participate ('I want to read').

Role play works best with classroom routines that are regular, formal and involve predictable dialogue. The children particularly in the UK class were not able to demonstrate the full range of activity that takes place in the Literacy Hour. In this way it provides evidence of the level at which they understand and can reproduce routines. As Woods, Boyle and Hubbard (1999) point out, even children with very limited English can take part in role play of activities such as taking the register which are regular and provide strong language models (146).

Role play also elicits explicit talk about norms, particularly when something is not quite right, as in Sofea's utterance 'hey sit down first' in Extract 14.1 when the children realise they should be sitting in class before the teacher comes in, so that they can stand up when she enters. Such stage directions may be taken up straight away, or they may be negotiated; either way they make explicit to the group and to the researcher what children feel should be taking place.

Role play allows us to get up close to the action. The essential elements of the reading lesson are crystallised in the role play, and are preserved for further analysis through the use of video recording. The recording can be watched repeatedly, focussing on details of language(s), gesture, action and teaching routines that the children present.

Finally role play can be used as a prompt for discussion. It is possible to play a video recording back to the children, who love watching themselves perform, and to ask them to explain what is going on. This adds a further layer of data.

An Appropriate Technique for Gaining Insights into Young Learner Perspectives

Role play is particularly appropriate for use with young learners for several reasons. First, it is around age six to eight that sociodramatic role play comes most naturally (e.g. Gardner and Yaacob, 2008).

Secondly, this is an age-appropriate research strategy because it does not expect participants to respond analytically or reflexively, but rather expects them to respond kinesthetically and through familiar talk. As Shaaban (2000) points out, it is an appropriate demand for young learners of English. In a similar vein, Lefever (2006: 28–29) identifies the following characteristics of five- to eight-year-old learners of English as:

> keen and enthusiastic, curious and inquisitive, outspoken, imaginative and creative, active and like to move around, interested in exploration, learn by doing/hands-on experience, holistic, natural learners searching for meaningful messages. . . . In addition, younger learners are usually less anxious and less inhibited than older learners.

It is important then to remember that children at this age love to play, and therefore they may well make things up, or embellish certain events. Evidence from other sources is also needed.

RESEARCHER-INITIATED ROLE PLAY AS PART OF THE MOSAIC

Role play is not a complete stand alone research technique. It works well in combination with other techniques. For instance, it can raise questions to be followed up in observation or interviews. In this respect, it could be easily incorporated into the Mosaic approach to researching young learners. Clark (2001) describes this approach as follows:

> The Mosaic approach is a multi-method framework, which combines the traditional methodology of observation and interviewing with the introduction of participatory tools including the use of cameras, tours and mapping. Other tools such as drawing and role-play can also be

added. Each tool forms one piece of the Mosaic. In Stage two these pieces are brought together with parents and practitioners comments to form the basis of dialogue, reflection and interpretation. The Mosaic, which is made, is a form of documentation, co-constructed by the children and adults. (Clark, 2001: 334)

Explicit in this approach is the view that young children are the experts in their own lives, and that one of the roles of adults is to 'support . . . young children to communicate their perspectives by providing a rich array of different resources and environments' (Clark and Moss, 2005: 7). The proponents of the approach argue that role play 'can be an important tool for young children to express their feelings. This can be another way for listening to young children which can involve their whole bodies and all their senses' (Clark, 2005: 496). To the Mosaic approach of Clark and Moss (2005) we would add researcher-initiated role play and researcher-initiated drawing (Pietikäinen, Chapter 10, this volume). As we have seen, these research strategies can reveal young learners' perspectives on their educational experience, but the insights gained also need to be brought together with interview and observation data as the basis of dialogue, reflection and interpretation.

NOTE

1. Examples of this are in a draft paper available from the authors.

ACKNOWLEDGEMENTS

An earlier version of this chapter was presented at the launch of the MOSAIC Centre for Research on Multilingualism at the School of Education, University of Birmingham in April 2008.

We are indebted to Marilyn Martin-Jones for her detailed constructive suggestions on the original version of this chapter.

TRANSCRIPTION CONVENTIONS

Bold—Bahasa Malaysia
Normal—English
<*italic*>—English translation
underline—author emphasis
(laughs) -non-verbal behaviour
(pause)—pause for a few seconds
CAPITAL LETTERS—reading from the text

XXX—unclear conversation
[   ] overlapping speech
I = Interviewer
T = Teacher
Ss = Students

REFERENCES

Arthur, J. 2001. Codeswitching and collusion: classroom interaction in Botswana primary schools. In *Voices of Authority: Education and Linguistic Difference,* ed. M. Heller and M. Martin-Jones, 57–75. Westport, CT: Ablex.

Clark, A. 2001. How to listen to very young children: the Mosaic approach. *Child Care in Practice* 7(4): 333–41.

———. 2005. Listening to and involving young children: a review of research and practice. *Early Child Development and Care* 175(6): 489–505.

Clark, A. and Moss, P. 2005. *Spaces to Play: More Listening to Young Children Using the Mosaic Approach.* London: National Children's Bureau.

Gardner, S. and Yaacob, A. 2008. Role play and dialogue in early childhood education. In *Discourse and Education* (Vol. 3), ed. M. Martin-Jones and A.-M. de Mejía, 291–303. Of *Encyclopedia of Language and Education* (2nd edition), ed. N. Hornberger. New York: Springer.

———. 2009. CD-ROM multimodal affordances: classroom interaction perspectives in the Malaysian English Literacy Hour. *Language and Education* 23(5): 409–24.

Gregory, E. 2001. Sisters and brothers as language and literacy teachers: synergy between siblings playing and working together. *Journal of Early Childhood Literacy* 1: 301–22.

Goffman, E. 1974. *Frame Analysis.* Boston: Northeastern University Press.

Gumperz, J. J. 1982. *Discourse Strategies.* Cambridge: Cambridge University Press.

Kitson, N. 1994. 'Please Miss Alexander: will you be the robber?' Fantasy play: a case for adult intervention. In *The Excellence of Play*, ed. J. Moyles, 88–98. Buckingham: Open University Press.

Lefever, S. 2006. English for very young learners. *Málfríður* 22(2): 27–31.

Lyle, S. 2002. Talking to learn: the voices of children, aged 9–11, engaged in role play. *Language and Education* 16(4): 303–17.

Lytra, V. 2007. *Play Frames and Social Identities.* Amsterdam: John Benjamins.

Mashkuri Y., Zainab, A. N., Mahmud, R. and Edzan, N. N. 2001. Digitisation of an endangered written language: the case of Jawi script. Paper presented at the International Symposium on Languages in Cyberspace, Organized by the Korean National Commission for UNESCO, Seoul, Korea, 26–27 September.

Maybin, J. 2006. *Children's Voices: Talk, Knowledge and Identity.* Basingstoke: Palgrave Macmillan.

———. 2008. Revoicing across learning spaces. In *Discourse and Education* (Vol. 3), ed. M. Martin-Jones and A-M. de Mejía, 81–92. Of *Encyclopedia of Language and Education* (2nd edition), ed. N. Hornberger. New York: Springer.

McKay, P. 2006. *Assessing Young Language Learners.* Cambridge: Cambridge University Press.

Pinter, A. 2011. *Children Learning Second Languages.* Basingstoke: Palgrave Macmillan.

Riojas-Cortez, M. 2001. Preschoolers' funds of knowledge displayed through sociodramatic play episodes in a bilingual classroom. *Early Childhood Education Journal* 29(1): 35–40.

Shaaban, K. 2000. Assessment of young learners' achievement in ESL classes in the Lebanon. *Language, Culture and Curriculum* 13(3): 306–17.

Shak, J. and Gardner, S. 2008. Young learner perspectives on four focus on form tasks. *Language Teaching Research* 12(3): 387–408.

Szpotowicz, M., Mihaljevic Djigunovic, J. and Enever, J. 2009. Early language learning in Europe (ELLiE): a multinational longitudinal study. In *Young Learner English Policy and Implementation: International Perspectives*, ed. J. Enever, J. Moon and U. Raman, 141–49. Garnet: IATEFL/Reading.

Wang, Q., Sun, L. and Ma, X. 2009. An impact study of a TEYL innovation project in Beijing, China. In *Young Learner English Policy and Implementation: International Perspectives*, ed. J. Enever, J. Moon and U. Raman, 223–31. Garnet: IATEFL/Reading.

Williams, A. 2004. Right, get your book bags! Siblings playing school in multi-ethnic London. In *Many Pathways to Literacy: Early Learning with Siblings, Grandparents, Peers and Communities*, ed. E. Gregory, S. Long and D. Volk, 52–65. London: Routledge Falmer.

Woods, P., Boyle, M. and Hubbard, N. 1999. *Multicultural Children in the Early Years: Creative Teaching, Meaningful Learning.* Clevedon: Multilingual Matters.

Yaacob, A. 2006. *Malaysian Literacy Practices in English: 'Big Books', CD-ROM and the Year 1 English Hour.* Unpublished doctoral dissertation. Coventry: University of Warwick.

Yassin, S. M., Marsh, D., Tek, O. F. and Ying, L. Y. 2009. Learners' perceptions towards the teaching of science through English in Malaysia: a quantitative analysis. *International CLIL Research Journal* 1(2): 54–69.

15 Doing Ethnography in Multilingual Schools

Shifting Research Positioning in Response to Dialogic Methods

Carla Jonsson

The aim of this chapter is to discuss how the dialogic ethnographic research methods used in a two year research project about intercultural pedagogy and language learning influenced shifts in my role as an ethnographic researcher in three schools.[1] Ethnography in education can be employed in three different ways according to Green and Bloome (1997: 183): by "doing ethnography", by "adopting an ethnographic perspective", and by "using ethnographic tools". Doing ethnography means "the framing, conceptualizing, conducting, interpreting, writing, and reporting associated with a broad, in-depth, and long-term study of a social or cultural group, meeting the criteria for doing ethnography as framed within a discipline or field" (Green and Bloome, 1997: 183). It is such an approach of 'doing ethnography' that this study takes.

In what follows, the ethnographic methods employed in the study and the three schools in which the data was gathered will be briefly described. Thereafter, my shifting roles as a researcher in response to dialogic methods will be discussed. The chapter offers insights into the multifaceted roles of an ethnographic researcher.

THE RESEARCH SITE: THREE SCHOOLS

The three schools that are part of the study share the characteristics that they are independent schools situated in the greater Stockholm area, i.e. in Stockholm and nearby cities. The schools portray themselves as international schools which aim to foster bilingualism. These characteristics led me to select these particular schools for the study. Another important factor when selecting the schools was 'accessibility'. By this I mean access to as many spaces as possible (classrooms, meetings etc.). Before initiating the project I had established contacts with the three schools, which made it possible for me to enter the field without any restrictions and to gain access to the schools. The data collection began in the fall term of 2006 and was completed during the fall term 2008.

Besides the Swedish language, which is mandatory in Swedish schools, School A focusses on the teaching of Spanish. School B and School C focus on the English language. Further information about each school will be given below together with a discussion of my roles in each of the schools.

When I entered the field (i.e. the three schools) I presented my study to teachers and students (and, in the case of School A, also to parents) by saying that my aim was to study strategies used by students and teachers in the schools and that I was interested in anything that had to do with languages and cultures.

ETHNOGRAPHIC METHODS EMPLOYED

The study builds on ethnographic research methods that aim at producing qualitative data in which the voices of the participants can be heard. The methods offer the participants the possibility to participate interactively, thus enabling the research to become dialogic. An advantage of dialogic methods is that they offer "a means of shifting the positioning of researcher and researched" (Jones, Martin-Jones and Bhatt, 2000: 326). The participants in the study were active in that they contributed not only with material, but also with their reflections and analyses. The participants can be seen as agents who could influence the data that that was collected, for instance by choosing to share certain experiences.

The following methods of data collection were used in the study:

- classroom observations—teachers (in School A and School B)
- classroom observations—students (in School A and School B)
- interviews—teachers
- interviews—school board
- drawings and interviews—students (in School A)
- questionnaires—parents (in School A)
- questionnaires—students (in School B and School C)
- group discussions—students (in School B and School C)
- language diaries and diary interviews—students (in School B and School C)
- mp3 recordings during a school day (in School A and School B)
- informal conversations with teachers and students (before/after lessons, during breaks, lunch etc.)
- participation at school meetings (in School A and School B)
- collection of artefacts (e.g. material produced by students and teachers, brochures)
- collection of documents (e.g. official school documents)
- audio-video recordings
- photography

Ethnographic research is highly extractive (Heath and Street, 2008: 60–61). During my visits, I collected language data by audio-video record-ing of classroom interaction, interviews, group discussions etc., by taking photos of student-produced material, classroom interaction etc. and by col-lecting documents and artefacts. During my fieldwork I came to realize that data is not merely 'collected' but also 'given'. Participants in the study are free to choose what they wish to share. Once the purpose of my visits became clear to the students, some of them shared literacy events with me by for instance showing me artefacts or by telling me about something they had experienced, thus giving me data for the study. The methods I used involved not only the extraction of dialogic data, but the dialogue with participants itself produced further data.

ROLES AS A RESEARCHER

In the three schools my role as a researcher was quite different. Here I explore these differences, concentrating specifically on how the dialogic methods enabled these differences to evolve. Before entering the field I had given careful thought to my role as a researcher. I had planned that I would be a participant researcher (the researcher as participant, participant obser-vation). This decision was based on my role in my previous research project (Jonsson, 2005). Before embarking on the field trips for my previous study, I had seen myself as someone who would travel to the US to 'collect' data. Then, during my field trips, I realized that there were many different layers to my role as a researcher. For instance, during one occasion when I was audio-taping a play for my study I was, together with everyone else in the audience, invited by the actors to join them for a dance on the stage! The example serves to illustrate that I was invited (and expected) to partici-pate as any other member of the audience (i.e. in-group). Such invitations occurred regularly during my fieldwork. However, "only rarely can we shed features of ourselves to be a 'real' participant" (Heath and Street, 2008: 31) in the sense that although we might feel that we are/could be members of the in-group, our role as researchers always gives us another position. "Eth-nography forces us to think consciously about ways to enter into the life of the individual, group, or institutional life of the 'other.'" (ibid.: 31).

Having reflected more on my role as a researcher during my present study, I saw myself as a researcher who would participate by sitting some-where in the classroom. I realized that my mere presence would somehow affect the people and the activities in the classroom. Before entering the field, however, I did not realise exactly what being a participant researcher would mean in the different schools. It turned out that in one school at times I became the teacher's aide, in another I was sometimes seen as a representative of the school and in yet another school at times I became the person to whom one confesses. My role as a researcher in the three schools is as different as the schools themselves, yet there are some similarities. Below I will discuss and analyse the particular aspects of my shifting roles as a researcher in the different schools. Before that some general tendencies will be discussed.

On the whole, one can say that my role as a researcher was that of the participant researcher. I participated in the daily activities of the school (School A and School B). Later, towards the end of my fieldwork I gave the students tasks and invited them to participate in different activities which somewhat altered my role. I went from being more 'passive', in the sense that I was observing, filming and taking notes of the lessons planned and carried out by the teachers, to being to more 'active', offering the students tasks such as filling out questionnaires, writing language diaries, drawing etc. I deliberately chose to more actively participate with these tasks during the end of my fieldwork with the aim of not altering the situation earlier. Once the students had answered the questionnaires, they openly started reflecting more on their linguistic and cultural experiences. Below I discuss my role as a researcher at the three schools among students and teachers.

MY ROLE AS A RESEARCHER AT SCHOOL A

This school offers education from pre-school class to third grade. Pre-school class is non-compulsory and it is offered for children who are about six years old. Compulsory school starts with the first grade and the children in first to third grade are typically seven to nine years old. However, because school start in Sweden is flexible, starting when the child is six, seven or eight years old, the ages may vary (The Swedish National Agency for Education, 2010).

When School A started they only offered pre-school class and first grade. Since then, the school has been adding one grade per school year with the aim to continue adding one grade per year to the school until they reach the ninth grade. Bilingualism is a key word in the school's language policy. The school profiles itself as a Swedish school that, in addition to Swedish, offers lessons in Spanish. The students have lessons in Spanish approximately three times per week.

In the beginning of my fieldwork at School A, I chose to visit as many classes as possible in order to get a broad picture of the education offered at the school. I then changed the focus from 'width' to 'depth' and more intensively started visiting two classes. The students in my study who attend this school were in the second and third grade when the fieldwork was completed. I have followed these students since they were in pre-school class and the first grade respectively. Fieldwork was conducted at this school over five school terms.

Due to the young age of the students in School A, my role as a researcher at the school often became that of a teacher's aide. When the teachers were delivering their lessons from the front of class, I would sit down in the back of the class and take notes. However, when the teachers walked around in the classroom, the students expected me to do the same. If I sat in the back taking field notes, they would interrupt me and ask me to come and help them with whatever task they were doing. In other words, even when attempting to be non-dialogic, I was positioned by the students as someone with whom there should be dialogue. Rather than resisting this role, I would assist with the task and thus my position changed.

One day, after about a year of fieldwork at the school, one of the teachers asked her class what it was that I was doing in their school. Several students raised their hands and the teacher started allotting turns. One student said that "she looks at what we do", another student said she is "a substitute teacher", a third student said "she helps us when we have problems" and yet another student said "she studies here . . . she is looking for a job" (Classroom observation, 2007, School A; my translations). The teacher reminded the class that, just as one of the students had said, I was there looking at something. She asked the class what it was in particular that I was looking for. One student replied "how we learn Spanish and Swedish at the same time" and another student said "how we behave" (Classroom observation, 2007, School A; my translations). It is interesting to note that despite the fact that I had been at the school for quite some time and that I, at different occasions, had introduced the purpose of my visits to students and to parents, the students had so many different ideas as to what it was that I was really doing there. In their eyes I was someone who observed them (their learning strategies and even their behaviour), someone who helped them and also someone who was looking for a job.

At the same school I also had the role of a friend. The students would hug me when they saw me, ask me to sit next to them during the lesson or during lunch, ask me to come and look at a worm they had found during the break etc. I felt very welcomed by the students, and when I walked into the classrooms, students would regularly say something like, "Yeah! Carla is here today!" (my translation). Because I visited two classes at the school, the students would, when they saw me in the corridor, ask me whether I was going to visit their class that particular day. If I was not, they would ask me to visit their class soon. During lunch breaks the students would ask me to sit next to them. Sometimes, if I already was sitting next to someone, some other student could make me promise to sit next to them another day.

Towards the end of my fieldwork at School A, I more 'actively' started to collect data. Besides collecting data through classroom observations, I engaged the students in different activities that dealt with their bilingualism/multilingualism, I recorded the language of individual students with mp3 players during entire school days and I interviewed the students individually.

Among the teachers my role was, apart from the occasional role of a teacher's aide, almost the role of a colleague; for instance, I was invited to take part in teachers' further training courses (e.g. in-service training), I was included on the phone list of teachers, I had my own box for incoming post, and I was invited to parties. I was also at different occasions invited to present and talk about my research at parent-teacher meetings, which were held in the evenings a couple of times per term. The atmosphere was friendly and hospitable and I felt welcomed as one in the team. However, despite being welcomed into the in-group of teachers and principals at the school I was well aware that my role as an ethnographic researcher did not allow me to be an insider. This was accentuated on rare occasions when for instance someone would make a joke of some sort and then look at me and jokingly say something like 'do not include this in your study'. In other words, despite being welcomed into the group I was still 'the Other'. Nevertheless, by being an ethnographer, I was privy to informal and routine conversations among the teachers in ways that I would not have been had I simply appeared to observe class and interview them more formally.

I do not feel that the familiarity at the school compromised me in my role as a researcher or that my membership in the group was conditioned, e.g., that the school had certain expectations on my research. The principals and the teachers who participated in the project emphasised that they saw my study as a possibility for their school to develop. During the interviews some teachers mentioned that they appreciated the interviews because my questions gave them the possibility to reflect on their teaching practices. Teachers and principals enabled me to get access to material for my study (by offering me their time, their thoughts on education, access to their classrooms etc). Some teachers also helped me inform parents who had yet not heard about my project, and to collect 'forms of parental consent' for the students who were under age. The only times during my fieldwork when I felt that my role as a researcher risked becoming compromised was when I was asked by one of the principals to teach an in-service training course on bilingualism for the teachers at the school and when the Parents' association invited me to speak to the parents about the 'best' ways to work with bilingualism in school. I firmly declined these offers, stating that I could not combine my role as a researcher at the school with that of an 'expert' on bilingualism who offers instructions of 'how to' work with bilingualism. In both cases, my reasons for declining were accepted and understood. In all the schools, I have offered to return and report on the study once it has been concluded.

MY ROLE AS A RESEARCHER AT SCHOOL B

School B is a Swedish high school that offers education from first to third grade, which roughly corresponds to grade 10, 11 and 12 in the American high school system. The students in Swedish high schools (also called upper secondary schools) are between sixteen and twenty years old.

English and Swedish are used in School B. The school profiles itself as an international school that offers English. About 80 per cent of the subjects are studied in English (Teacher 2, 2007), with subjects such as Swedish and the first year of Civics taught in Swedish.

In the beginning of my fieldwork at School B, I chose to visit as many classes as possible in order to get a broad picture of the education offered at the school, then changed the focus from 'width' to 'depth' and more intensively started visiting one class. The students in my study were in the third grade of high school when the fieldwork was completed. I followed these students from their second grade of high school. Fieldwork was conducted at this school over three terms.

At School B, my role was significantly different from that at School A. This was mainly due to the fact that the students were older and that I entered the school team in a different manner. At School B, I primarily worked with two teachers who gave me access to their classrooms on a weekly basis and who each term gave me access to schedules, term plans, syllabi, student lists etc. I also gained access and visited lessons by other teachers, but these visits were only a complement to the other visits and did not occur on a regular basis. As with the elementary teachers, the two main teachers said that they found it rewarding to take part in the study because my visits to their classrooms and my interviews made them reflect on their own practices. Both teachers felt the need to discuss questions regarding language development and they said that my visits created a forum for this.

Because the students were high school, and there are rarely teaching aides in Swedish high schools, students there did not see me as a teacher's aide. Instead, I got the feeling that they saw me as some kind of representative of the school. For instance, when I first introduced my project I was asked by students whether the principal would see the data, whether I would report any swearing in the classroom and whether the study could affect their grades. It was as if some students at first saw me as a potential spy, as someone who would report their behaviour to the school board. Thus, I felt the need to emphasise that the teachers and the school board would not get access to the data that I collected, but that they, once the study was concluded, would find out about the results. Once the students and I got to know each other, the atmosphere became more relaxed. The students took a great interest in the study and participated in both curricular and extra-curricular activities. However, for quite some time I felt that I was regarded as a representative of the school. Many students seemed to treat me as a teacher. For instance, they most often spoke to me in English, which is the 'working language' of the school. In my data there are examples of students who are speaking Swedish or mixing Swedish and English with their friends and then change into English when addressing the teacher or me.

One day when I arrived at the school I found out that one of the main teachers in the study was on sick leave. The other main teacher had received instructions to give to the students of the absent teacher and, on his behalf, she suggested that I could do my classroom observations even though the teacher of the class was absent. She unlocked the classroom and gave the students instructions on what to do. The task was to continue writing on a text that they were later to hand in. During this lesson, some students asked me to clarify the instructions; others asked me to check the spelling, grammar etc. in their texts. At the end of the lesson the students handed in their texts to me; I erased the text on the board and closed the windows in the classroom (Classroom observation, 2007, School B). This can be seen as yet a further example of my role as a representative of the school, in this case as a substitute teacher.

As time passed, my role changed somewhat. Many students still saw me as a representative of the school and the teachers, because they saw me coming to classes with the teachers, having lunch with the teachers etc. However, to some students I became some sort of friend. During the summer after my first term at the school, at different occasions, I ran into students in the city of Stockholm, i.e. outside the school environment, and I received hugs and we chatted for a while. Before entering the field, I had hoped to create a friendly atmosphere where the participants would feel comfortable. I had not 'planned' to become friends with the participants, nor did I see it as an aim of the study. In an attempt to not make the students feel like I desperately wanted/needed to become friends with them I had, for instance, chosen not to 'hang out' with the high school students during their breaks. The younger children in the study, on the other hand, expected me to join them during their breaks. Sometimes I would talk to the high school students (both in School B and School C) during their breaks but this was not a planned method of my study and, more importantly, it was always on the initiative of the students. Perhaps it was the fact that I took an interest in the lives of the students together with the fact that the methods used to collect data were dialogic and often perceived as quite personal, that led to the development of our friendship. The students in School B and in School C shared their personal histories and experiences with me. They laughed and cried with me and they gave me so much of themselves. For the results of the study, I do not see any negative aspects of the friendship that developed naturally between me and the participants; neither do I feel compromised by it. The friendly atmosphere led to an open environment in which I believe that the students felt comfortable to share their experiences. As a result, I perceive that the friendly relations in the study were advantageous and led to richer and more dialogic data. At the end of my data collection in the schools (in School B and School C) I asked the students to stay in touch. Some participants have stayed in touch via email and others have become my friends on the social network website Facebook. I have promised to send updates on my research, e.g. publication of articles, to those participants who said that they were interested in reading the results of the study.

When the time came for me to more actively collect data by asking the students to write language diaries, take part in group discussions etc., I felt that my role as a representative of the school was long gone. Through my regular visits to the school the students had gotten to know me better and they had learned more about the aim of my research project. I experienced that the last part of my data collection at the school brought the students and me closer because the ethnographic research methods employed were dialogic in nature and offered a forum to come together and discuss personal matters such as, for instance, their experiences of how their different languages were valued in the school system, their thoughts about different cultures and their identity construction. In particular, the activity of writing language diaries proved to be a personal experience for the students through which the students trusted me with sensitive data about their languages, identities and cultures. The students at the two high schools, School B and School C, could choose to write language diaries during one to two weeks. In the diaries the students documented their literacy events, e.g. books they read and movies they saw in different languages (for a thorough description of participant diaries see Jones, Martin-Jones and Bhatt, 2000). The diaries are multivoiced in that they make reference to other people than the participant and to different types of texts (e.g. novels, movies). After the students had finished writing their diaries I met them for a diary interview where we talked about their diary, the process of writing it and about languages and cultures in general. The activity of writing a diary was dialogic in different ways. First, the process of writing in itself can be seen as an 'internal dialogue' that takes place in the participant's brain. Moreover, because the students were aware that I was going to read their diaries and use it for research, the activity of writing a diary became dialogic in a wider sense. Not only did the diaries open up and support the dialogue between the students and me, they also enable anyone who reads this research to hear the voices of the students. Thus, the dialogue continues. Finally, the diary interviews offered a dialogic forum.

The students at the two high schools, School B and School C, could also choose to participate in group discussions. The groups consisted of about four students who during approximately thirty to sixty minutes discussed questions about languages and cultures (see Musk, 2006, for a detailed discussion about group discussions). The group discussions were audio-video recorded. After concluding the data collection and after having analysed the collected material from the group discussions, I feel that the study would have benefitted by a group discussion 'interview' (similar to the diary interviews). In such an interview, I would have been able to meet with the group after taking part of the group discussion recordings to talk about their experiences of the group discussion. This would have made the activity more dialogic. As it was now, the activity was dialogic in the sense that the students together discussed questions about languages and cultures and in the sense that they knew that I would later take part of the recordings of the discussions. However, meeting the student again after the group discussion would have offered yet another dialogic forum.

MY ROLE AS A RESEARCHER AT SCHOOL C

School C is a Swedish high school that, like School B, offers education from first to third grade, for sixteen- to twenty-year-olds. English and Swedish are used in this school. The school, which is a boarding school, profiles itself as a school where students can come from abroad to learn Swedish. However, nearly all subjects are taught in English.

School C is only partially involved in the study. The primary reason was that I had worked one term at this school previously and therefore did not wish to do, for instance, classroom observations in the classes that my former colleagues taught.

Ever since I worked at the school (during the fall term of the students' first year in high school) I felt that I wanted to revisit the school and include the students in my research. When I came back to the school, it turned out that the class I originally had taught had been divided into two classes. Both these classes had new students, besides the ones I had taught. One class was about to have their finals, and due to time constraints only one of my former students in this group was able to participate in the study. Luckily, the other class was able to meet with me on several occasions. From this class some of my former students, as well as new students, participated in the study. The students in my study who attended this school were in the third grade of high school when the fieldwork was completed. Fieldwork was conducted at this school during the final weeks of spring term.

My role as a researcher in School C was different from that at the other schools, primarily due to the fact that I had previously worked at the school as a teacher. Being aware of the difficulties of doing research in a familiar setting, I decided not to do classroom observations at this school. According to Heath and Street (2008: 58), "[f]ormer teachers-turned-ethnographers" "will find it easier to grow familiar with a 'strange' site than to maintain a value-neutral stance within the 'familiar' classroom". Besides excluding classroom observations, I do not feel that my previous role as a teacher at the school had any negative effect on my data collection. On the contrary, it was my status as a former teacher that allowed me to get access to this boarding school where, to my knowledge, no previous research has been done. When I returned to the school to conduct my fieldwork, I was welcomed back to the school by students, principals, teachers and staff. Teachers in the study talked to me as a member of the in-group. For instance, during the interviews they presupposed that I knew certain things about the school's organisation, teaching practices etc. and they did not feel the need to explain everything to me. This was an advantage in a fairly 'closed' school, not used to giving access to 'outsiders'. My role as a member of the in-group also gave me access to more informal conversations (e.g. in the teachers' lounge) than at the other two schools. Some of my former colleagues freely expressed their opinions and views about the students' multilingualism. This gave me access to different registers which at times resulted in somewhat contradictory data. For instance, one teacher who spoke in an unreserved manner during our informal chats seemed to censor herself somewhat during our recorded interview. I felt that there was a difference in tone when the recorder was on and off. My role as a former colleague thus allowed me to see these two positions more clearly than at the other schools.

Some of the students in the study knew me from before because they had had me as their teacher for a term. Other students joined the study without having been my students before. I felt that I quickly became friends with several students, both with those who previously had been my student and with those who I did not know before. A special bond was established between me and the students who participated in the activity of writing a language diary. It was as if the activity of writing and sharing their diaries made us come closer. After having discussed the diaries with the students I realized that the activity of writing a diary had been quite a personal experience for some of them because the activity had made them reflect on questions that have to do with their language use, their cultures and, ultimately, their identities. During several diary interviews I felt that to some students I became the person to whom one confesses. For instance, a week before her graduation, one of the students told me that she had not shared her thoughts on some of these subjects with anyone else at the school before, except for her closest friends. After our conversation she said that she felt relieved. Throughout her entire schooling, she had not felt that she had had a regular forum to talk with any of her teachers about her language use, her cultures and her identities (Diary interview). Several students said that the diary writing had made them reflect on things that they had not thought about before. My role to these students became that of someone who opens a door which allows them to enter within themselves to reflect upon their own identities.

As mentioned above for School B, the group discussions also offered certain dialogic possibilities. After the group discussions I met the students briefly to collect my recording equipment. During these brief encounters, the students shared some of their thoughts on the activity they had just taken part in. After one such group discussion, in which five students had taken part, the students—some of whom, prior to the group discussion, had seemed to take a shallow interest in the study and some of whom had seemed almost reluctant towards participating in the group discussion—stayed for fifteen to twenty minutes and asked me questions about research in general. Their sudden interest came as quite a positive surprise to me and I gladly responded to their queries. For instance, they asked me what the difference was between a 'PhD' and a 'PhD student', whether I would be able to become a Professor, what an 'Assistant Professor' is, if the salaries were higher at university than at high school, how long it had taken me to write my PhD dissertation, how my PhD dissertation was examined, what the party after my defence was like, and whether I had received a

PhD hat. They used terms such as Assistant Professor, PhD student, PhD and wanted to understand their significance (Group discussion, 2008). Their questions showed that they took an interest in research. All of a sudden, my role as a researcher had shifted again—I was regarded as a representative of research.

CONCLUSION

My role as an ethnographic researcher evolved throughout the duration of my project. In all schools my role was first that of an observer, of someone interested in the students' schooling. Throughout the course of my study, I moved from observer to interactant in dialogues with students and teachers in the three schools. Some of these shifts were planned. For instance, when I went from being more 'passive' in the sense that I participated in activities initiated by the teachers (e.g. classroom observations) to being more 'active' in the sense that I invited the participants to engage in activities that were specifically designed for this study (e.g. diary writing and group discussions). Other shifts developed as a consequence of the ethnographic methods that were used. At the three schools different facets of my role as a researcher were highlighted. In School A through student-initiated dialogue my role became that of the teacher's aide and a friend of the students. In School B I was regarded as a representative of the school and, at first, as someone who potentially could report the students' behaviour to the school board. Later, when the students got to know me better and when they learned more about the purpose of my research, I felt that some participants saw me as some sort of friend. The last part of my data collection at the school brought the students and me closer because the ethnographic research methods employed (e.g. group discussions and language diaries) were dialogic in nature and offered a forum to come together and discuss personal matters. In School C the use of ethnographic methods, in particular the activity of writing diaries, resulted in me becoming the person to whom it was possible to confess things that had not been said during one's entire schooling. In the three schools, the use of dialogic methods opened up possibilities for the students to share their experiences with each other and with me. In sum, I feel that the dialogic nature of the ethnographic methods enabled me and the students to get close. This, in turn, made it possible for the students to trust me with sensitive data about their languages, identities and cultures.

Among the teachers, my role was that of an observer, a teacher's aide, a former colleague. Furthermore, the fact that I was present in their classrooms and that I asked questions about their classroom practices offered the teachers a space of reflection, a space where it was possible for them to address questions and to discuss practices that they otherwise did not have a regular forum to discuss.

The different aspects of my role in the three schools clearly illustrate the complexity of the role of an ethnographic researcher. In fact, it might not even be possible to detect all the intricate layers in the role of a researcher. For instance, it is difficult to know how my presence affects students who are part of the study. In one of the schools, the mother of a young girl who participated in the study told me that her daughter had told her that she wanted to become a researcher when she grows up. The mother, well aware that her daughter's interest would change many times in the course of time, ascribed this sudden interest to my presence at the school. It would be of interest to understand what it means for the students that a researcher takes an interest in their lives and their realities. Furthermore, it would be interesting to see what empowering functions ethnographic research can have and how the different facets of the researcher role affect the material that is collected.

NOTES

1. The post doc research project described in this chapter is entitled *Intercultural Pedagogy and Intercultural Learning in Language Education*. It is funded by the Swedish Research Council (ref. 724–2006–2610).

REFERENCES

Green, J. and Bloome, D. 1997. Ethnography and ethnographers of and in education: a situated perspective. In *Handbook of Research on Teaching Literacy through the Communicative and Visual Arts*, ed. J. Flood, S. B. Heath and D. Lapp, 181–202. New York: Macmillan.

Heath, S. and Street, B. V. (with Molly Mills). 2008. *On Ethnography: Approaches to Language and Literacy Research* (an NCRLL volume). New York: Teachers College Press.

Jones, K., Martin-Jones, M. and Bhatt, B. 2000. Constructing a critical, dialogic approach to research on multilingual literacies: participant diaries and diary interviews. In *Multilingual Literacies: Reading and Writing Different Worlds*, ed. M. Martin-Jones and K. Jones, 319–51. Amsterdam and Philadelphia: John Benjamins.

Jonsson, C. 2005. *Code-Switching in Chicano Theater: Power, Identity and Style in Three Plays by Cherríe Moraga*. PhD Dissertation. Umeå, Sweden: Umeå University.

Musk, N. 2006. *Performing Bilingualism in Wales with the Spotlight on Welsh: A Study of Language Policy and the Language Practices of Young People in Bilingual Education*. PhD Dissertation. Studies in Language and Culture No. 8. Linköping, Sweden: Linköping University.

The Swedish National Agency for Education. 2010. Compulsory school. http://www.skolverket.se/sb/d/2653 (accessed 23 February 2010).

16 Ideologies and Issues of Access in Multilingual School Ethnography

A French Example

Florence Bonacina

The issue of access, also aptly referred to as the "problem of access" (Delany, 1960; Prewitt, 1984), is a well-known aspect of ethnographic enquiries in both institutional and non-institutional settings. It is tackled in most textbooks devoted to ethnography (e.g. Silverman, 2000; Hammersley and Atkinson, 2007; Gobo, 2008) and has been addressed in studies conducted in fields as various as health care units (Bruni, 2006), refugee communities (Miller, 2004), courtrooms (Blank, 1987), and—of interest in this chapter—schools (e.g. Beynon, 1983; Burgess, 1991; Klaas, 2006; Troman, 1996; Wanat, 2008).

Missing, however, is an account of the issue of access in the specific case of *multilingual* school ethnography, by which I mean studies that focus on multilingualism in schools and that rely on ethnographic enquiry. Despite the vast array of ethnographic research conducted in multilingual schools, to date no account has been given of the process of gaining access to multilingual educational settings. Creese, Bhatt and Martin's (2009) reflection on team research in the process of access in linguistically and culturally diverse schools represents an exception in a field where the issue of access remains otherwise unaccounted for. Admittedly, in multilingual school ethnography the process of access is similar to the process of access to schools where multilingualism is not salient, insofar as the ethnographer has to deal, in both cases, with a highly institutionalised setting. Nevertheless, the process of access in multilingual school ethnography is distinctive insofar as multilingualism is a phenomenon that is still often disregarded or negatively perceived by those in charge of granting access. Such a mismatch, or "conflict of interest" (Hammersley and Atkinson, 2007: 52), between the researcher's object of enquiry and the researched's perceptions of such enquiry is, thus, most likely to impede the process of access. Therefore, this contribution aims to offer a personal account of my own attempts to gain access to multilingual practices in France's induction classrooms for newly-arrived migrant children; access that has been complicated primarily by monolingual ideologies held in the French educational system.

Across the different accounts of the issue of access in ethnographic research, there is a clear consensus that access is a negotiating process and that successful access negotiations depend on the relationship between the researcher and the researched (gatekeepers and/or participants). For instance, Wanat reports gaining access to different educational sites by developing "empathetic relationships" with gatekeepers (2008: 200). Similarly, Beynon reports "weaving" his way into a school by finding common interests, or "bridges", with the researched (1983: 40). A relationship of trust between the researcher and the researched is perceived as the key to be granted access to a research site (e.g. Woods, 1986; Heller, 2008). In turn, this chapter adopts the stance that access negotiations are "a relational process" (Feldman, Bell and Berger, 2003: vii) where identities are negotiated between the researcher and the researched. With a view to address the issue of access in multilingual school ethnography, this chapter focusses on the research relationship, and more specifically on *identity negotiations*, at play in the process of access. In this regard, access negotiations are reflected upon in light of Harrington's (2003) social psychological framework of access grounded in the symbolic interactionist tradition, and, more precisely, in the social identity (Tajfel and Turner, 1979; Hogg and Abrams, 1990) and self-presentation theories (Goffman, 1959). Harrington explains how these theories can be used to explain access negotiations:

> Social identity focuses on the categorization process and objectives of participants in identity negotiations, while the self-presentation literature calls attention to the call-and-response mechanisms through which identities are negotiated. In other words, social identity theory addresses the 'why' of identity negotiation, while self-presentation theory looks at the 'how' of these interactions. (2003: 604)

In this chapter, I will thus examine the 'how' and 'why' of the ethnographer's identity negotiations with gatekeepers and induction teachers in the process of access, looking in turn at the way in which the ethnographer presented herself and the way in which the researched interpreted the ethnographer's identity claims and research topic. Furthermore, I will show the way in which the 'how' and 'why' of access negotiations in multilingual school ethnography are embedded in macro-contextual ideologies—and in this study, in monolingual ideologies.

The structure of this contribution follows the "route of access" (Hammersley and Atkinson, 2007) I experienced in my fieldwork while conducting PhD research in induction classrooms for newly-arrived migrant children in France. To begin with, I briefly present the background of the study, specifying the context of France's induction classrooms, the aim and methods of the research project and my preconceptions of the field based on the research literature. I then relate the 'how' and 'why' of identity negotiations in the process of access, first with gatekeepers, and second with induction teachers. I then report an alternative route of access, which led me to discover induction teachers who hold positive ideologies towards multilingualism, and which ultimately enabled me to access multilingual classroom practices. Lastly, I discuss how the research relationship at hand in these access negotiations was rooted in—and hindered by—ideological considerations.

BACKGROUND OF THE STUDY

To integrate newly-arrived migrant children in its educational system, France operates a withdrawal (or pull-out) policy. According to this policy, newly-arrived migrant children are withdrawn from mainstream classrooms upon arrival and taught French as an additional language in induction classrooms for twelve months (see de Miras, 2002, and Goï, 2005, for detailed accounts of France's induction classrooms). Induction classrooms differ from mainstream classrooms insofar as they gather in one single class children aged between six and eleven who are all learners of French as an additional language. Although no statistics are available on the languages spoken by inducted children, a recent survey conducted in the educational district of Paris shows that, in the school year 2006–7, ninety-four nationalities were represented across sixty-three induction classrooms, with the majority of children coming from China, Algeria, Portugal, Korea, Romania and the Chechen Republic (CASNAV, 2007). Thus, induction classrooms are multilingual educational contexts. Consequently, this linguistic heterogeneity raises language policy issues such as: what language(s) should be used as a medium of instruction and what place should be given to children's first languages. However, such language policy issues are not addressed in policy documents regulating induction classrooms (MEN, 2002). Therefore, the question arises as to whether induction classrooms follow the French monolingual language policy in place in mainstream education (Code de l'Education, Article L 121–3, I, 2009).

My PhD project addressed this question and aimed to uncover the "practiced language policy" (Bonacina, 2011) of induction classrooms. I planned to investigate language-in-education policy at the micro level of one induction classroom in a French primary school; conducting interviews, participant observations and audio recordings of classroom interactions. However, given France's long-standing history of monolingual ideology in its educational system, as well as in its society at large (for an extensive discussion of France's monolingual policy see for instance Ager, 1999), I had anticipated negative attitudes on the part of educational representatives and practitioners towards my research focus on multilingualism. Previous studies conducted in France's induction classrooms report that newcomers' multilingualism is perceived negatively (Varro, 1990; Abdallah-Pretceille, 1992; Auger, 2008a, 2008b). Varro's (1990) interviews with Parisian induction teachers show that the notion of 'bilingualism' is used only to refer to the linguistic repertoire of children speaking elite languages, such as French and German, whereas migrant children's bilingualism is perceived as a "non-lingualism". Negative attitudes are also found in interviews conducted with mainstream teachers, where migrant learners are said to speak a "hybrid language" that is neither French nor their home language (Mazurkiewicz and Varro, 2001: 45). Similarly, and more recently, Auger (2008a) reports that newly-arrived migrant children's bi/multilingualism is perceived as a handicap rather than an asset to the extent that children speaking a postcolonial language do not consider themselves as being bilingual (2008b: 201). Based on these previous reports of negative ideologies held in the French educational system towards newcomers' bi/multilingualism, the question arose as to how I would obtain permission to enter schools and to access multilingual classroom practices if those same practices were to be denied or negatively perceived by gatekeepers and teachers.

ACCESS NEGOTIATIONS WITH GATEKEEPERS

During preliminary observations in a French primary school, I learned that inspectors grant permission to enter schools provided that prior informal consent has been given by both the head teacher and teachers. However, informal consent can only be gained if either the head teacher or teachers have a guarantee of the researcher's trustworthiness. Unfortunately, I did not have informal contacts in schools that had an induction classroom. Therefore, in order to be directed to primary schools that run an induction programme and to be introduced to the school staff on an informal basis, I contacted the academic centre named CASNAV (*Centre Académique pour la Scolarisation des Nouveaux Arrivants et des enfants du Voyage*) which provides teacher training and teaching material for induction teachers. Although the CASNAV is attached to the French Ministry of Education, its representatives do not evaluate induction teachers' performance and it is, consequently, a more neutral body to be introduced by than inspectors. In this sense, the CASNAV represents an "intermediate gatekeeper" (Wanat, 2008: 199) in the hierarchy of the French educational system, insofar as it occupies formal authority positions but has also informal relationships with induction teachers. Establishing a positive research relationship with CASNAV representatives was thus crucial because they would be able to facilitate access to induction classrooms by acting as "intermediaries" and "guarantors" (Gobo, 2008: 121).

Presentation of the Researcher-Self

In access negotiations with CASNAV representatives, I tried to build positive relationships that would eventually allow me to access induction classrooms. My aim was to foreground within my "portfolio of identities" certain social categories that were identifiable, salient and shared by gate-keepers (Harrington, 2003: 607–9). I thus highlighted three aspects of my identity, that of being French, that of having been a teacher, and that of being a researcher. I emphasised the fact that I had previously graduated as a teacher of French as a foreign language in France, and gave evidence of my status as a researcher. In my initial letter to the CASNAV, I provided official proof of my student status at the University of Edinburgh, a reference letter from my supervisor and head of department, as well as evidence of funding from the Economic and Social Research Council in the United Kingdom. The "psychological objectives" (Harrington, 2003: 610)—or the 'why'—underlying my self-categorisation as a teacher were to draw similarity between my concerns and those of CASNAV representatives for learners of French as an additional language, and to create common ground in addition to the mere fact that I was French. Those underlying my self-categorisation as a researcher were to reassure my interlocutors about the academic value of my investigation.

I also had to decide in what terms I was going to present my research interest in multilingualism. Based on the research literature aforementioned, I was aware of potential negative attitudes held in the French educational system towards newly-arrived migrant children's multilingualism. I was thus concerned that disclosing my research focus would jeopardise access to induction classrooms. During my initial meetings with CASNAV representatives, I observed that my attempts to address the issue of multilingualism were avoided or not taken further by my interlocutors. I concluded that my research focus was tapping into a 'taboo area' that was best avoided in order to maintain positive relationships in access negotiations. Consequently, I decided to expose my research topic in broad terms, saying that I intended to investigate "classroom interactions in induction classrooms—teacher-led interactions as well as peer-led interactions". Using the generic term 'classroom interactions', rather than the more specific term '*multilingual* classroom interactions', raised the ethical issue as to whether I had given enough information for CASNAV representatives to give me a fully informed consent to my access query, as required by codes of research practices in France (Baude, 2006) and the United-Kingdom (BAAL, 2006). Although ethically debatable, defining a research topic in generic terms is a strategy that appears in previous accounts of access. Scholars report for instance that informed consent from the start of the research is "neither possible nor desirable" (Hammersley and Atkinson, 2007: 57) and that, during access negotiations, they used "neutral topics" (Beynon, 1983: 39), "toned down" the language of their research proposal (Klaas, 2006), or were "truthful, but vague and imprecise" (Taylor and Bogdan, 1998: 33). In fact, for the researcher to be able to disclose the specificity of a research topic to gatekeepers, both the researcher and gatekeepers would need to share a set of theoretical and political orientations; which is unlikely to be the case and thus an unrealistic criterion to meet. Therefore, rather than it being a matter of being 'vague and imprecise', the issue is more that being specific might not offer greater clarity if gatekeepers do not participate in the same discursive and theoretical universe as the researcher.

Gatekeepers' Interpretation of the Researcher-Self

My identity claims of being French, a researcher and a colleague were all challenged by gatekeepers. Firstly, CASNAV representatives did not acknowledge my 'French-ness' and seemed to categorise me as an 'outsider' due to my affiliation to a British university. One of my interlocutors argued that, insofar as multiculturalism and multilingualism are not dealt with in the same way in the British and French educational systems, I could not study France's educational programmes for newly-arrived children with a "British mindset". He then stressed that, in France, integration is mediated by the French language and that, consequently, in induction classrooms, French ought to be the sole language of instruction and the sole language of classroom interaction. Secondly, CASNAV representatives questioned my actual intentions as a researcher and the real motives behind the fact that a British institution would sponsor a research project in France. Gatekeepers seemed to be concerned that I would report and subsequently criticise their models of educational provision for newly-arrived migrant children to my British funding body. Along with Burgess (1991), I thus wondered to what extent my sponsor had influenced research access because it seemed that rather than identifying me as a researcher, gatekeepers identified me as an evaluator. Thirdly, CASNAV representatives did not recognise me as one of their colleagues, a teacher, on the basis that my training as a teacher of French as a foreign language was irrelevant to the purview of teaching French as a language of instruction.

This first account illustrates the bilateral process of self-presentation (see mainly Goffman, 1959) at hand in access negotiations, whereby the ethnographer's identity claims must be recognised and approved by gatekeepers in order to be granted access. As Harrington points out, participants, and in my case gatekeepers, have 'power' because they are not "passive recipients of a researcher's impression management strategies, but are active in accepting, rejecting, or modifying the researcher's identity claims" (2003: 617). Most importantly, gatekeepers' interpretations of my identity claims were embedded in political considerations and macro-contextual ideologies. Predominantly, gatekeepers seemed to have interpreted the local discursive process of our access negotiations in the wider dialectic of France's and Britain's societal models of integration. It looked as if my dual identity of being French but working in the UK had been interpreted as a double alliance that cast doubts over my research intentions. Finally, gatekeepers interpreted my research topic and my self-categorisation as one of their colleagues against the background of their monolingual ideologies of language teaching and learning. As suspected in initial meetings, these CASNAV representatives held negative attitudes towards the use of children's first language(s) in induction classrooms. In summary, access negotiations with gatekeepers were an interactional space where all participants negotiated both the identity of the other and their own identity. However, by repositioning me as an outsider, gatekeepers were not refusing to grant access. They redefined their identity, and what it is to be part of the French state educational system—namely, to adhere to certain ideologies on integration, and language teaching and learning. That is, they asserted definitional control over all definitions of identity and co-membership, including over how I fitted in. Subsequently, they granted me access to two induction classrooms.

Access Negotiations with Induction Teachers

The CASNAV introduced me to two induction teachers in two different primary schools. Induction teachers accepted informally to be observed for a short while before deciding to contribute to a longer ethnographic study. On the strength of this informal consent, and of the support from the CASNAV, I obtained official permission from the respective inspectors to carry out two weeks of participant observations in each induction classroom and to audio-record classroom interactions. Although I was granted entry to these induction classrooms, I had yet to gain access to their potential multilingual practices because teachers might monitor their behaviour so as to present themselves as following monolingual norms. In this regard, induction teachers are gatekeepers of their classroom insofar as it is up to them to display their classroom practices. The interpersonal aspect of access negotiations with induction teachers can also be discussed in terms of self-presentation and social identity.

Presentation of the Research Topic

In both induction classrooms, I presented myself in the same way as with the CASNAV, that is, as being French, a teacher and a researcher. However, I adopted two different strategies regarding the presentation of my research topic. In the first induction classroom, I presented my research topic in broad terms, saying that I wanted to observe how teacher and pupils interact in an induction classroom. During the two week observations, classroom interactions were conducted in French as well as in children's first languages. At the end of these preliminary observations, I expressed to the induction teacher my interest in conducting a longer study in her classroom to observe more closely her use of French alongside newly-arrived migrant children's first languages. Following our agreement, I returned to her classroom a few months later. However, despite a two month observation period, I noted a conspicuous lack of any use of children's first languages to the extent that interactions were strictly monolingual in French. I thus concluded that, although I had secured entry to this induction classroom for a few months, the induction teacher prevented me from accessing multilingual practices.

Based on this first episode, I decided to adopt a different strategy with the second induction classroom and stated from the start my interest in "the way activities are conducted in the midst of the eight languages available in this classroom". During the two weeks of preliminary observations, the induction teacher did a 'demonstration class' and talked me through the different classroom activities where she would ask children to rely on their first languages. Regularly, she suspended interactions and explained why a switch to another language occurred. In brief, her awareness of the exact focus of my project had affected the naturalness of classroom talk and invalidated data collection processes. In the end, the induction teacher stated she had shown me everything she could and refused to participate in a longer period of investigation.

To sum up, access negotiations with gatekeepers gave me entry to two induction classrooms, but access negotiations with induction teachers did not give me access to multilingual classroom practices. Along with a distinction between *access* and *cooperation* (Wanat, 2008), these two episodes call for a distinction between *access* and *entry* (Harrington, 2003; Hammersley and Atkinson, 2007), whereby access is not only a matter of gaining entry into a community or institution but also a matter of being in a situation where data collection is effective.

Induction Teachers' Negative Attitudes towards the Research Topic

One way of making sense of these two access negotiations with induction teachers is to posit that induction teachers held negative attitudes towards the use of newcomers' first languages in classroom interactions and therefore perceived my research topic negatively. Indeed, once the first induction teacher heard about the actual focus of the project, she stopped allowing children to switch to their respective first language(s). In this regard, it is likely that this induction teacher realised her own teaching practices when being observed by the ethnographer and decided to readjust her practices in line with her monolingual ideology of language teaching and learning. This interpretation is all the more plausible because, during informal conversations, this induction teacher exposed a monolingual understanding of language teaching and learning. In this way, it is also possible to make sense of access negotiations with the second induction teacher. She may have held negative attitudes towards the use of newly-arrived children's first language(s) but, nevertheless, staged multilingual practices in order to please the ethnographer. Her refusal to contribute to a long-term ethnographic study may reflect the fact that during unstaged classroom practices, interactions would tend to be monolingual.

Induction Teachers' Perception of the Researcher as an Evaluator

A second way of making sense of those two access negotiations is by positing that both induction teachers categorised the ethnographer not just as a teacher and a researcher, but first and foremost, as an evaluator closely associated with the CASNAV. Although the CASNAV does not formally assess teachers' performances, it provides teacher training and support for induction teachers. Its ideologies about language teaching and learning represent therefore a model of good practice that induction teachers aspire to follow. In this sense, the first induction teacher's switch from multilingual to monolingual teaching practices can be interpreted as a fear of being evaluated as not conforming to the CASNAV's ideologies. Likewise, it is likely that the second induction teacher refused to collaborate in a long-term ethnographic study because she was reluctant to display unstaged classroom practices in front of the ethnographer-evaluator.

Perceiving the ethnographer as an evaluator is not an unusual phenomenon and has been reported in previous school ethnographies (see for instance Woods, 1986). Nevertheless, the interesting point here is that induction teachers' reactions towards an 'ethnographer-evaluator' confirm the more or less covert monolingual norms and ideologies held in the CASNAV. Furthermore, they indicate that relying on gatekeepers to introduce me to induction teachers situated access negotiations within monolingual ideologies of language teaching and learning held in the French educational system and prevented me from accessing "de facto" multilingual language policies.

AN ALTERNATIVE ROUTE OF ACCESS

Following these unsuccessful access negotiations with induction teachers, I decided to adopt an alternative route of access, and to approach induction teachers without the mediation of gatekeepers. CASNAV representatives introduced me to a CASNAV from a different educational district, where representatives let me contact induction teachers directly, via an internal electronic mailing list. Mails sent via this list were read only by induction teachers and communication was therefore beyond the influence of CASNAV representatives. I thus adopted a "bottom-up" approach to access (Silverman, 2000) by sending a call for participation to all induction teachers of this new educational district. In this way, I was able to introduce myself as someone with internal access to the educational system while dissociating myself from gatekeepers.

In the call for participation sent to induction teachers, I stated clearly the focus of my research project in the hope that teachers who held negative views regarding the use of children's first languages would naturally opt out from the study. This call for participation triggered multiple and various replies, and most importantly, some enthusiastic replies from a few induction teachers who held an ideology of language teaching and learning different from that of gatekeepers'. The following excerpt from an audio-recorded interview with one of these induction teachers is a good example:

> I'm not the kind of person who is going to tell one of my pupils: 'right, my dear, you are in France and it's to learn French. And you know, the Senegal . . . ' ((Gesture that indicates indifference)). They know that me, I am the institution, but that, at the same time, I don't endorse that

stuff about 'we're here to learn French, and that's the only thing that matters and all the rest it's a private issue'. Me, I say: 'we're here to learn French but you are Senegalese, and this, it interests me a lot'. (T2 interview 12, 350, my translation)

This positive ideology about newcomers' multiculturalism and multi-lingualism enabled induction teachers to perceive the focus of my research positively, that is, as enhancing their work and standpoints on teaching. In the end, I secured entry to an induction classroom taught by one of these induction teachers and accessed classroom interactions where more than seven languages were used.

DISCUSSION

In the following section, I would like to discuss how access negotiations reported in this chapter were influenced—and hindered by—ideologies held in the French educational system and in French society at large. Taking into account the macro-context of access negotiations is not new, and has in fact been done by several scholars conducting ethnographic research in educational settings. In his ethnography of schooling, Gilborn (1994) for instance acknowledges the influence of wider educational reforms in his access to schools. Similarly, Troman (1996) discusses the role of macro-societal values in his unsuccessful attempts to access English primary schools to conduct ethnographic research. Likewise, Klaas (2006) addresses the impact of ideologies in his access negotiations to carry out race ethnographic research in White schools in South Africa. In this section, I will focus on two ideologies that have influenced my access negotiations with gatekeepers and induction teachers: France's and Britain's ideologies of integration, and monolingual versus multilingual ideologies of language teaching and learning.

France's and Britain's Ideologies of Integration

As I have shown, my identity claim of being an insider to the French community based on my French nationality was challenged by gatekeepers who seemed to perceive me as an 'outsider', a 'foreigner', studying France's educational programmes for newly-arrived migrant children from the perspective of Britain's ideology of integration. This indicates that local discursive identity negotiations taking place during the process of access were embedded in France's and Britain's conflicting ideologies of integration. To meet space constraints, these ideologies can only be briefly summarised. Great Britain operates a multicultural model of integration whereby migrant communities are recognised as such and co-live in British society. On the contrary, France operates what might be called a 'monocultural' model of integration, whereby migrants are integrated and assimilated to the French nation, which is seen and portrayed since the Revolution as a monolingual and monocultural entity. Based on the Republican principle of 'Equality for All', migrant communities are not recognised as such—the French state remaining "indifferent to differences" (Forquin, 2000: 156). In this regard, learning French is seen as a key tenet for a successful integration and is therefore the principal aim of induction classrooms, often at the expense of children's first languages. Due to this ideological context, CASNAV representatives appear to have interpreted my focus on issues of language-in-education policy in multilingual contexts as being a focus on multilingual language practices per se; practices that they precisely discourage in favour of the sole use of French in the classroom.

Monolingual versus Multilingual Ideologies of Language Teaching and Learning

During the course of access negotiations with gatekeepers and induction teachers, I have also shown that monolingual ideologies of language teaching and learning have influenced the way in which I presented myself and my research topic, and the way in which this presentation has been interpreted by my interlocutors. According to this ideology, one's first language must be left behind in order to be able to acquire a second language. Castellotti (2001) notes that this monolingual ideology of language teaching and learning resulted in pupils' first language(s) being considered as a "real 'taboo'" (2001: 10) as they are thought to prevent second language acquisition. We recall that this 'taboo' on newcomers' multilingualism has indeed been perceived during initial meetings with CASNAV representatives and has influenced my decision to present my research topic in broad terms. In turn, the two induction teachers I first observed oriented to a monolingual ideology of language teaching and learning.

However, a bottom-up approach to access revealed that some induction teachers hold a multilingual ideology of language teaching and learning. This ideology underlies the work of a strand of French researchers who consider learners' multilingual repertoire as being strategic for language teaching and learning and as needing to be developed into a multilingual and multicultural competence (see for instance Coste, Moore and Zarate, 1997; Moore, 2008). In the specific context of induction classrooms, Auger's recent DVD designed for induction teachers (2008a) shows examples of teaching sequences grounded in children's first languages. The fact that some induction teachers endorse this multilingual ideology has not been reported in previous studies—and shows the extent to which the process of access is in itself a process of data collection (Beynon, 1983: 42; Whyte, 1984: 34; Harrington, 2003: 599).

CONCLUDING REMARKS

I have shown in this chapter the influence of ideologies in the 'how' and 'why' of identity negotiations involved in the process of access in multilingual school ethnography. During access negotiations, I tried to foreground aspects of my identity and of my research topic that would draw common ground with my interlocutors and facilitate my presence within the educational institution. However, my identity claims (of being French, of being a researcher and of being a teacher) have all been challenged by gatekeepers on the basis of wider ideologies held in the French educational system and in French society at large. In turn, the way I presented my research topic to gatekeepers was also shaped by my perception of the surrounding monolingual policy. In a similar way, I have reported how access negotiations with induction teachers have been embedded in ideologies of language teaching and learning. Access negotiations mediated by gatekeepers were especially hindered by institutional monolingual ideologies, as induction teachers most likely perceived me as an 'evaluator' closely associated with gatekeepers. However, a bottom-up approach to access negotiations revealed that some induction teachers hold multilingual ideologies, which gave me access to 'de facto' multilingual language policies in induction classrooms.

It goes without saying that this "trajectory of access" (Bruni, 2006) does not stop where this chapter finishes, and includes further negotiations to access, for instance, inducted children's language practices in small groups. Equally, this personal account of access negotiations does not claim to be prescriptive by any means. It is rather a call to consider the specificity of access negotiations in multilingual school ethnography—namely the way in which micro negotiations are intertwined with macro ideologies towards multilingualism in education and in society at large. This account shows that access strategies should therefore be part of ethnographic accounts as they are the first *loci* where ideologies are enacted, and represent, therefore, a first window onto the institution's ideologies. Thus, whereas access strategies are understood as being "designed and adjusted according to the characteristics of the organization or group observed, its type (company or institution), its size (large, medium, small or very small), and the aims of the research" (Gobo, 2008: 120), I have illustrated the fact that, in multilingual school ethnography, access strategies are also "designed and adjusted" according to the gradual manifestation of the institution's ideologies.

ACKNOWLEDGEMENTS

I gratefully acknowledge the support of the Economic and Social Research Council of Great Britain for this PhD research project. I am also thankful to Marilyn Martin-Jones, Sheena Gardner, Alexandra Jaffe, Charmian Kenner and Joseph Gafaranga for their useful comments on an earlier version of this chapter. Any shortcomings are mine.

REFERENCES

Abdallah-Pretceille, M. 1992. *Quelle Ecole Pour Quelle Intégration*. Paris: Hachette Education.

Ager, D. E. 1999. *Identity, Insecurity and Image: France and Language*. Clevedon: Multilingual Matters.

Auger, N. 2008a. 'Comparons nos langues': Un outil d'"empowerment' pour ne pas oublier son plurilinguisme. In *Conscience du Plurilinguisme: Pratiques, Représentations et Interventions*, ed. M. Candelier, G. Ioannitou, D. Omer and M. T. Vasseur, 185–99. Rennes: Presses Universitaires de Rennes,

———. 2008b. Pourquoi tenir compte des représentations des langues et des cultures? In *Immigration, Ecole et Didactique du Français*, ed. J. L. Chiss, 187–230. Paris : Didier.

BAAL. 2006. *Recommendations on Good Practice in Applied Linguistics* (2nd edition). The British Association of Applied Linguistics.

Baude, O. 2006. *Corpus Oraux: Guide des Bonnes Pratiques*. Paris: CNRS.

Beynon, J. 1983. Ways-in and staying-in: fieldwork as problem solving. In *The Ethnography of Schooling: Methodological Issues*, ed. M. Hammersley, 39–53. Chester: Bemrose Press.

Blank, P. D. 1987. The 'process' of field research in the courtroom: a descriptive analysis. *Law and Human Behavior* 11(4): 337–58.

Bonacina, F. 2011. A Conversation Analytic approach to practiced language policies: the example of an induction classroom for newly-arrived immigrant children in France. Unpublished Doctoral dissertation. The University of Edinburgh, Edinburgh, UK.

Bruni, A. 2006. Access as trajectory: entering the field in organizational ethnography. *M@n@gement* 9(3): 129–44.

Burgess, R. G. 1991. Sponsors, gatekeepers, members, and friends: access in educational settings. In *Experiencing Fieldwork: An Inside View of Qualitative Research*, ed. W. B. Shaffir and R. A. Stebbins, 43–52. Newbury Park, CA: Sage.

CASNAV (Centre Académique pour la Scolarisation des Nouveaux Arrivants et des enfants du Voyage). 2007. *Les Elèves Nouvellement Arrivés dans l'Académie de Paris: Enquête Statistique Premier Degré*. http://casnav.scola.ac-paris.fr/page.php?espace=service&doc=stats (accessed 22 March 2009).

Castellotti, V. 2001. Pour une perspective plurilingue sur l'apprentissage et l'enseignement des langues. In *D'une Langue à d'Autres: Pratiques et Représentations*, ed. V. Castellotti, 9–38. Rouen: Publications de l'Université de Rouen.

Code de l'Education. 2009. http://www.legifrance.gouv.fr/WAspad/UnCode?&commun=CEDUCA&code=EDUCATL.rcv (accessed 23 March 2009).

Coste, D., Moore, D. and Zarate, G. 1997. *Compétence Plurilingue et Pluriculturelle*. Strasbourg : Conseil de l'Europe.

Creese, A., Bhatt, A. and Martin, P. 2009. Multilingual researcher identities: Interpreting linguistically and culturally diverse classrooms. In *Linguistically and Culturally Diverse Classrooms: New Dilemmas for Teachers*, ed. J. Miller, M. Gearon and A. Kostogriz, 217–35. Clevedon: Multilingual Matters.

de Miras, M. P. 2002. *La Classe d'Initiation au Français pour Enfants Non Francophones*. Paris: L'Harmattan.

Delany, W. 1960. Some field notes on the problem of access in organisational research. *Administrative Science Quarterly* 5: 448–57.

Feldman, M. S., Bell, J. and Berger, M. T. 2003. *Gaining Access: A Practical and Theoretical Guide for Qualitative Researchers*. Oxford: Altamira Press.

Forquin, J. C. 2000. L'école et la question du multiculturalisme: Approches française, américaines et britanniques. In *L'Ecole, l'Etat des Savoirs*, ed. A. van Zanten, 151–60. Paris: La Découverte.

Gilborn, D. 1994. The micro-politics of macro reform. *British Journal of Sociology of Education* 15: 147–64.

Gobo, G. 2008. *Doing Ethnography*. London: Sage.

Goffman, E. 1959. *The Presentation of Self in Everyday Life*. Garden City, NY: Doubleday.

Goï, C. 2005. *Des Elèves Venus d'Ailleurs*. Tours: SCEREN CRDP.

Hammersley, M. and Atkinson, P. 2007. *Ethnography: Principles in Practice* 3rd edition). London: Routledge.

Harrington, B. 2003. The social psychology of access in ethnographic research. *Journal of Contemporary Ethnography* 32(5): 592–625.

Heller, M. 2008. Doing ethnography. In *The Blackwell Guide to Research Methods in Bilingualism and Multilingualism*, ed. L. Wei and M. G. Moyer, 249–62. Oxford: Blackwell.

Hogg, M. and Abrams, M. 1990. Social motivation, self-esteem and social identity. In *Social Identity Theory: Constructive and Critical Advances*, ed. M. Hogg and D. Abrams, 28–47. New York: Harvester Wheatsheaf.

Klaas, J. 2006. The complexities of conducting ethnographic race research. *Ethnography and Education* 1(3): 365–78.

Mazurkiewicz, M. C. and Varro, G. 2001. L'accueil des enfants allophones à l'école française. Un exemple parisien. *Education et Sociétés Plurilingues* 11: 38–51.

MEN (Ministere de l'Education Nationale). 2002. Scolarisation des nouveaux arrivants et des enfants du voyage. In *Bulletin Officiel Numéro Spécial 10*. Paris: CNDP.

Miller, K. E. 2004. Beyond the frontstage: trust, access, and the relational context in research with refugee communities. *American Journal of Community Psychology* 33(3/4): 217–27.

Moore, D. 2008. *Plurilinguisme et École*. Paris: Didier.

Prewitt, K. 1984. Field access: a growing problem. *Science* 223(4640): 1019.

Silverman, D. 2000. *Doing Qualitative Research: A Practical Handbook*. London: Sage.

Tajfel, H. and Turner, J. 1979. An integrative theory of intergroup conflict. In *The Social Psychology of Intergroup Relations*, ed. S. Worchel and W. Austin, 33–47. Monterey, CA: Brooks-Cole.

Taylor, S. J. and Bogdan, R. 1998. *Introduction to Qualitative Research Methods* (3rd edition). New York: Wiley.

Troman, G. 1996. No entry signs: educational change and some problems encountered in negotiating entry to educational settings. *British Educational Research Journal* 22(1): 71–88.

Varro, G. 1990. Les représentations autour du bilinguisme des primo-arrivants. *Ville-Ecole-Integration* 83: 30–46.

Wanat, C. L. 2008. Getting past the gatekeepers: differences between access and cooperation in public school research. *Field Methods* 20(2): 191–208.

Whyte, W. F. 1984. *Learning from the Field: A Guide from Experience*. London: Sage.

Woods, P. 1986. *Inside Schools: Ethnography in Educational Research*. London: Routledge.

Part VI

Building Researcher-Researched Relationships

Introduction

Angela Creese

The five previous parts in this book make connections, develop themes and explicate contexts in researching multilingualism. This final part serves in some ways as a 'PS', a final post script to remind us to dwell on the 'how' of conducting multilingual research and on the centrality of the researcher in researching multilingualism.

The four chapters here prompt us to dwell on the *processes* of conducting multilingual research: the shaping of perspectives and the way these are represented; the exploration and production of researcher-researched knowledge; the journeys that researchers and researched make together; the voices which are heard and not heard in our final research accounts. Because each chapter in this part describes an ethnographic approach to data collection and analysis, the reflexivity of the researcher in relationship to the researched is central and the four research accounts reflect on the stance, strategy and shifts the researchers take as they position themselves in the research process.

Approaches in the ethnographic tradition emphasise the plurality of realities experienced by the people being researched and the meanings they assign to objects as well as their notions of what's important and interesting (Hymes, 1968, 1980; Shaffir and Stebbins, 1991). As Hornberger records, '[I]t is not enough to enter the community simply by residing in it; rather, I enter it by establishing social relationships with its members' (1992: 160). In the researchers' accounts which follow we see the centrality of these relationships in the data collection and data analysis processes.

The chapter by Feliciano Chimbutane shows how local rationalities are shaped in the ethnographic interview process. Chimbutane's research reports on a new language policy in two rural areas in Mozambique which use local languages alongside Portuguese to educate young people. In his chapter, Chimbutane considers the different and varied roles and relationships he formed with the teachers during the research process and how these shaped the interview narratives.

Extracts from three of the twelve teacher interviews conducted in this study of language education in Mozambique are examined to show how participants strategically exploit relationships to highlight points crucial to them. The detailed and extended interview extracts provide evidence of shifts in the teachers' stance as topics arise. Because of experiences shared by both researcher and participants over a long research and policy implementation process, Chimbutane shows how shortcuts are made in explication and explanation. He describes meaning-making processes in his ethnographic journey which draw upon understandings reached through having covered common ground. In this ethnographic study, the researcher's close and detailed knowledge of the research site is apparent in the contextual analysis brought to the interview data.

The chapter by Deirdre Martin makes the case for adopting a critical ethnographic approach to research on language disabilities in multilingual settings. This field has, hitherto, been dominated by social science research which has been largely positivist in orientation. Martin shows how adopting an interpretive approach, narrowing the research lens and paying close attention to communicative practices and to the co-construction of meaning in interaction can provide new insights into the diverse and nuanced ways in which disability is managed within multilingual families. She also gives a detailed account of the advantages that accrue from combining close analyses of interaction with ethnography in such contexts. And, given the ways in which powerful institutional discourses construct and represent disability, she emphasises the need to adopt a critical research perspective and to show how local family-based practices are shaped by these discourses, with family members either taking up or challenging these discourses. Throughout this chapter, there is an emphasis on the centrality of the researcher-researched relationship in the knowledge-building process.

The chapter by Gabriele Budach also builds on the notion of experience in her research on a two-way immersion programme in a state primary school in Frankfurt Germany. Budach investigated a bilingual team-teaching pedagogy which involved practitioners from different linguistic and socio-cultural backgrounds.

She argues for expanding the scope of ethnomethodological enquiry by seeking to understand the social processes that lie beyond the moment of the interview itself. In this chapter, she focuses on the affordances of the retrospective interview which presents the interviewee not only with a space for reflection but also with enhanced possibilities to inform educational theory, policy and learning. For Budach, the retrospective interview embedded in collaborative ethnography revealed interactive episodes which built new opportunities for contributing to 'a living educational theory.' Using data from one retrospective interview, Budach argues that educational research can be viewed as collaboration between teachers and researchers in conversation in which practice is reflected on and knowledge constructed in ways to contribute to theory.

The chapter by Jaffe describes collaborative practice and shows how researcher and practitioners create 'a nexus of shared practice' which is productive in appreciating multiple perspectives, reducing hierarchies and developing shared goals. Jaffe's research context is Corsican bilingual schools. She offers a detailed vignette of the preparation of a public presentation, in 2006. She was working closely with two teachers, Pascale and Marylene, in preparing for the talk. Jaffe describes how this involved building an understanding of each other's different professional discourses and habituses. Differences in teacher and researcher professional roles and responsibilities led to energies differently employed. It also involved developing an understanding of the complexities of the processes of promotion and validation associated with efforts at language revitalisation. Thus Jaffe describes how the preparation for the talk led to new understandings not necessarily gained in other ethnographic data sets including new emic perspectives on pedagogy and development.

The four chapters in this part show us the necessity of increasing the number of voices brought into the frame. We are provided with rich accounts of the voices, experiences, knowledges and noticings of researchers working in collaborative ethnographies in diverse settings. The research accounts here make explicit the knowledge building that goes on in ethnography and show the reader how the researcher moves between the emic and the etic to look for bigger theoretical and methodological contributions to multilingual practice in different settings.

REFERENCES

Hornberger, N. 1992. Presenting a holistic and an emic view: the literacy in two languages project. *Anthropology & Education Quarterly* 23: 160–65.

Hymes, D. 1968. The ethnography of speaking. In *Readings in the Sociology of Language*, ed. J. Fishman, 99–138. The Hague: Mouton de Gruyter.

———. 1980. Language in education: forward to fundamentals. *Language in Education: Ethnolinguistic Essays.* Center for Applied Linguistics.

Shaffir, W. B and Stebbins, R. A. (eds) 1991. *Experiencing Fieldwork.* Newbury Park, CA: Sage.

17 The Advantages of Research in Familiar Locales, Viewed from the Perspectives of Researcher and Researched

Reflections on Ethnographic Fieldwork in Mozambique

Feliciano Chimbutane

In traditional ethnography the mission of ethnographers is to write accounts based on their intense participation in some initially unfamiliar social world (Emerson, Fretz, and Shaw, 1995). It is assumed that there is a potential bias in researching familiar sites or phenomena and that, in such cases, researchers may 'trade unreflectingly on what they already 'know'" (Edwards and Furlong, 1985: 22). However, this view has been challenged in postmodern ethnography (Marcus, 1995, 1997) and ethnographically-oriented approaches to discourse (Rampton, 2007) which underscore the advantages of researching familiar sites. For example, Marcus (1998) suggests that researching a familiar locale helps to achieve the depth that conventional anthropology always hoped for from long stays in the field. Drawing on his experience as a researcher and thesis supervisor, Marcus (1998) argues that this is mainly due to the fact that researchers investigating a familiar locale can use their control of language as well as their life experiences as assets to achieve such depth. However, Marcus warns that in order to make good use of such resources the researcher needs to be reflexive.

In this chapter I take this postmodern view and I offer reflections on my own fieldwork experience in Mozambique (Chimbutane, 2009; 2011). I also consider the familiarity issue from the vantage point of the research subjects (the researched) as well as from my own vantage point as researcher. Although it has long been recognised that the researched may intentionally play a role in shaping the information they share with a researcher, the tendency is to appraise this role in a negative way, associating it with biases such as the 'social desirability response bias' or with the respondents' wish to present themselves in a favourable light (Robson, 2002: 310).

Here, I take the position that the researched can use their knowledge of the researcher to express their views in a focussed and incisive way, as conversations unfold (e.g. with changes in addressees and topics). They can, for example, use shortcuts and react to the researcher's perspectives, including those not even made explicit in a particular encounter. I also show how researcher and researched position themselves, how they view each other, depending on the topics addressed, and how they populate their accounts with other social actors (e.g. with reference to past conversations). Shifts in speaker stance on the topics addressed and acquaintance with the social actors involved enable the researched to be strategically explicit or implicit in their views and achieve different positionings.

CONTEXT

Changes in Language Education in Mozambique

Mozambique is a multilingual country. There are over twenty languages and it is estimated that 87.9 per cent of the population (of about 20 million citizens) speak an African language as a first language. Portuguese, the official language, is spoken by 50.4 per cent of the population, of which only 10.7 per cent speak it as a first language (INE, 2009).

Up to 2003, Portuguese held a prestigious position as the only official language of formal education at all levels, from primary to tertiary education. It was only in 2003 that local languages officially started to play a role at primary school level, with the introduction of a pilot bilingual education programme as part of a wider curriculum reform. The bilingual programme is now running in selected rural schools throughout the country. Pedagogical and cultural reasons have been given for this innovative programme.

An early-exit transitional model of bilingual education has been devised, so that pupils can learn how to read and write in a Mozambican language first and subsequently in Portuguese. In the first three years of schooling, apart from being taught as a subject, a Mozambican language is used as a medium of instruction. Pupils then start using Portuguese as a medium at grade 4. In the first three years, Portuguese is taught as a subject. The objective in the first two years is to develop listening and speaking skills in Portuguese. Pupils start reading and writing in Portuguese at grade 3. Mozambican languages are taught as subjects up to the end of primary school. The schools running this pilot bilingual programme also continue to run the mainstream, Portuguese-only programme.

From the evidence gathered so far, it can be said that there is a positive atmosphere in the country for the use of African languages in formal education. It is seen as an innovation which provides a way of stimulating children's learning and of lending official recognition to the languages.

The Schools and Their Communities

My study (Chimbutane, 2009; 2011) was undertaken in two rural schools located in Gaza Province, one of the eleven provinces of Mozambique. The schools are in two different villages which are referred to here as Gwambeni and Bikwani.[1] Bikwani is in a Changana speaking area, whereas Gwambeni is in a Chope speaking area, but has considerable Changana influence.

Although there are some differences between the two communities and schools, in general they display similar characteristics. Both communities rely chiefly on subsistence agriculture, outward labour migration, and informal trading. Both schools are in need, in terms of infrastructure and school materials.

My Involvement with the Research Sites and the Participants

My involvement with the research sites and the researched started in 2003, when I was invited by the National Institute for the Development of Education (INDE) to design and coordinate a three year project aiming at researching the processes involved in the implementation of the bilingual programme. As a research strategy, the project team and I decided to undertake ethnographic work in a small sample of schools, including those in Gwambeni and Bikwani. My role in the project included observation of classes, interaction with key participants (teachers, pupils, parents, education authorities and NGOs), training of teachers in language-teaching methodologies, the use of standardised orthographies and the structure of local languages as well as reporting to INDE. The main objective of these activities was to provide an account that could inform policy, planning and implementation of the bilingual programme in the country.

I was also involved with the bilingual teachers in Gwambeni and Bikwani, and others across the country, as a facilitator in teacher education programmes. Thus, since 2003, I have been working in the field of bilingual education in Mozambique as a teacher trainer, researcher and adviser, either linked to government or non-government educational institutions or to the academy.

METHODOLOGY

In this chapter, I analyse data from interviews with three of the twelve teachers interviewed in the schools in Gwambeni and Bikwani. These three teachers are referred to as Mr Gwambe, Ms Cacilda, and Ms Flora. I chose these three interviewees because their discourse illustrates particularly well how teachers presented themselves and viewed me, both during the conversations and in our relations in the field. Mr Gwambe was teaching in Gwambeni and, when I did my fieldwork there, he had already been teaching for twenty-nine years (four years in the bilingual programme). Ms Cacilda and Ms Flora were in Bikwani. Ms Cacilda had been teaching for thirty-one years (three in the bilingual programme) and Ms Flora had been teaching for seven years (two in the bilingual programme).

The interviews took place during the second month of my three month long fieldwork. The interviews were open-ended. I decided to begin by presenting the interviewees with key topics of a general nature which I found relevant for the purpose of my research and then inviting them to talk freely about those topics, with a minimum of intervention on my part. My role during the conversations was mainly to ask for clarifications and elaborations and pursue new themes introduced by the interviewees. The topics addressed included the teachers' evaluation of the current implementation phase of bilingual education, their views about the value of bilingual education, their comments on parents' views about the programme and the impact of the programme on the life of the local communities.

Although I gave the teachers the choice to speak in Portuguese or their first language, all but Ms Cacilda preferred to speak in Portuguese, only switching from time to time into their local languages. Ms Cacilda was the only one who spoke extensively in Changana, her first language. She only used Portuguese on one occasion.

NEGOTIATING IDENTITIES DURING THE INTERVIEWS

Teachers Learning from Participation in the Bilingual Programme

The teachers in the bilingual programme had all been educated and trained in a Portuguese-only mainstream programme. Because of this, only very few had managed to gain reading and writing skills in local African languages before taking on the role of bilingual teachers. The few who could write in these languages had been using non-standardised orthographies. In this context, one of the values that the teachers ascribed to bilingual education in their interviews was the personal opportunity that they have been given to learn how to read and write in their own mother tongues. In Extract 17.1 below, Mr Gwambe traces his trajectory towards the acquisition of Chope standardised orthography and also expresses his recognition of the researcher's role in that learning process:

This extract evokes a trainer-trainee relationship, particularly through the terms of address: the researcher (the interviewer) is addressed as 'doutor Chimbutane'[2] and the researched (the interviewee) is addressed as Mr Gwambe. Mr Gwambe's account is chronological: it describes different developmental stages in his acquisition of reading and writing skills in Chope, referring first to his doubts when he had contact with the standardised orthographies for the first time (lines 7–12); then to the fact that, at the time of interview, he was a proficient user (lines 13–18), although he still recognised that he had difficulties in dealing with 'less common words' (lines 21–24). In lines 4–5, Mr Gwambe highlights the role of the researcher in his and his fellows' achievement '*penso eu que o doutor Chimbutane tanto nos valeu*'/'I think doctor Chimbutane was very helpful'.

Extract 17.1   Mr Gwambe's (Mr G) narrative about his learning of Chope standardised orthography (19/09/2007, 0:33:15–0:34:03)

1	F:	E como é que se sentiu na ortografia	F:	And how did you feel in using
2		na sua língua?		the orthography of your language?
3	Mr. G:	((riso))	Mr. G:	((laughter))
4		Ortografia, penso eu que o doutor		Orthography, I think doctor
5		Chimbutane tanto nos valeu.		Chimbutane was very helpful.
6	F:	((riso))	F:	((laughter))
7	Mr. G:	Saí com um pouco de dúvida	Mr. G:	I went away a bit doubtful
8		quando pela primeira vez		when for the first time
9		em 2001 ou 2002...		in 2001 or 2002...
10		quando estivemos em Chibututuine		when we were in Chibututuine
11		com o doutor X...		with doctor X...
12		saí dali ZERO mesmo!		I went away completely BLANK!
13		Mas ((riso irónico))		But ((ironic laughter))
14		eu agora leio e escrevo.		I can now read and write.
15		Já CONHEÇO exactamente o		I already KNOW the alphabet
16		alfabeto EU...		exactly...
17		de Cicopi, conheço,		of Chope, I know
18		não há problemas!		no problems!
19	F:	Imm	F:	Umm
20	Mr. G:	Escrevo até correctamente.	Mr. G:	I even write correctly.
21		É... é claro, existem algumas...		Of... of course, there are some...
22		expressões, não é... que talvez as		expressions, you know... may be the
23		palavras não são tão usuais		words that are not very common
24		na língua aqui...		in the language here...

'Us' and 'Them': Local Teachers' Challenges and Distant Programme Planners

When Mr Gwambe was addressing a different topic, I found myself positioned in a rather different way: not as someone who was associated with his personal achievements but as someone associated with the education authorities running the bilingual programme. Extract 17.2 below shows how some teachers are playing a role in adjusting the bilingual programme to the local circumstances and recognising the demands it places on learners. The matter at hand here is that, at grade 4, the transitional phase, the pupils are still not ready to cope with the demands posed by the use of Portuguese as the language of instruction. Because of this issue, there are already calls for a review of the model of bilingual education currently in place in the country. In this extract, my links with the education authorities only seem to be implied, not articulated explicitly.

In his account, the interviewee evokes a dialogue between 'nós'/'us' (lines 9, 20, 46), defined as the actors/teachers in the field, and 'them', defined as 'visitors' (line 41) and/or 'those who are long way away' (line 7) from the field. This rather vaguely defined group implies education planners, pedagogic supervisors, education advisers, etc. As the researcher from Maputo, I was clearly seen as part of this second group. The participants in the local programme are represented as those who much better understand what is going on in the classroom, whereas the others (the 'visitors') 'are unable to see what is going on', because they are assumed to be 'a long way away' from the scene.

In fact, during our conversation I did feel part of the category 'visitors' or 'those who are a long way away'. However, in my multiple roles as a classroom observer, teacher trainer and evaluator of the programme, I have repeatedly discussed the issue of transition both at Mr Gwambe's school and elsewhere. Moreover, far from being original, the idea he advanced to tackle the problem has in fact been circulating in bilingual education circles in the country for some time. The reason why the decision on the review of the model is still awaited is that it is felt that there are numerous factors hampering the performance of the pupils in Portuguese, including the lack of materials and poor teacher training, and not only the design of the programme itself.

Irrespective of whether Mr Gwambe's message was intentionally or unintentionally conveyed, taking into account the roles that I have been playing in the implementation of the bilingual programme in Mozambique and the effects that my current research may have on policy and practice, I felt that he was telling me (and all 'those who are a long way away') to listen to what the practitioners are saying and act or, at least, try to get others with authority to do so.

(continued)

Extract 17.2   Mr Gwambe commenting on the transition phase (19/09/2007, 0:02:05–0:03:58)

#	Mr. G:	Mr. G:
1	Então dizia que	Well I was saying that
2	esta inquietação que eu tenho com a	this concern I have regarding the
3	turma	class
4	é que a fase da transição	is that the transition phase
5	há um PROBLEMA que existe	there's a PROBLEM that exists ((he
6	((levanta o tom de voz))	raises the tone of his voice))
7	Só para quem de longe está	Only for a person who is a long way
8	não consegue ver isto	away is not able to see this
9	mas nós que estamos dentro,	but for those of us who are inside,
10	já conseguimos descobrir que	we are already able to find out that
11	aquela fase em que a criança NÃO	that phase in which children DON'T
12	ESCREVE	WRITE
13	na primeira e na segunda ((alude ao	at grade one and two ((he alludes to
14	que acontece na disciplina de	what happens in the Portuguese
15	Português))	subject))
16	apenas só... quer dizer,	they are only... I mean,
17	eles só CONVERSAM, só só há	they TALK, there is only dialogue in
18	diálogo em português...	Portuguese...
19	A SITUAÇÃO NÃO ESTÁ BOA!	THE SITUATION ISN'T GOOD!
20	Porque para nós falarmos assim é que	Because for us to talk like that it is
21	quando se chega já na terceira,	because when they arrive at grade
22	que é a fase da transição,	three, which is the phase for
23	é preciso conhecer o alfabeto	transition, it is necessary to know
24	e ao mesmo tempo a criança	the alphabet and at the same time
25	ESTÁ OBRIGADA JÁ A	children ARE ALREADY
26	ESCRECER E LER AO MESMO	REQUIRED TO READ AND
27	TEMPO! ((levanta o tom de voz,	WRITE AT THE SAME TIME! ((he
28	como que a sublinhar o carácter	raises the tone of his voice, as if he

Line	Original (Portuguese)	Translation (English)
29		were highlighting the illogical nature
30	ilógico da situação))	of the situation))
31	Então, há esta guerra aqui.	Therefore, there is this war here.
32	Se ali... na quarta... chega a ler um	If there... at grade four... a pupil
33	aluno, é um ESFORÇO muito enorme	manages to read, that is a huge
34	que está a acontecer ali.	EFFORT that is happening there.
35	Mas é claro lêem	But of course they read
36	mas... mas sem segurança!	but... without confidence!
37	(...)	(...)
38	Portanto, nós já falámos muito sobre	Therefore, we have spoken a lot
39	esta fase aqui.	about this phase here.
40	Já fizemos menção mesmo a algumas	We have even mentioned this to
41	visitas que já tivemos aqui	some of the visitors during the visits
42	e puderam compreender connosco	which we have received here
43	concordaram que a fase da transição	and they could understand with us
44	não está boa!	they agreed that the transition phase
45	Então nós tentamos propor alguma	isn't good!
46	ideia que na segunda classe	So we tried to propose the idea that
47	se houvesse uma possibilidade DE...	at grade two if there were a
48	ou é no terceiro trimestre	possibility FOR ...
49	em que a criança podia começar	perhaps at the third term
50	mesmo com a escrita de algumas	for children to start even with the
51	letras e... e algumas leituras aí	writing of some letters and... and
52	talvez pudesse entrar já na quarta	some reading there maybe they
53	classe com um conhecimento um	could reach grade four with some
54	pouco sólido.	knowledge in some way solid.
55	E concordaram connosco.	They agreed with us.

Teachers as 'Critics' and 'Agents' of the State Education System

The lack of materials is one of the major problems of education in Mozambique, affecting not only the newly introduced bilingual programme but also the Portuguese monolingual programme, despite the fact that Portuguese is a well-resourced language and has been used in education for generations in Mozambique and elsewhere. However, the situation in the bilingual programme is worse because teachers and pupils are not even getting the limited supply of textbooks that their counterparts in the monolingual programme get. Although there have been promises of improvement in materials production since the introduction of the bilingual programme in 2003, the state is still failing to deliver. Extract 17.3 illustrates how teachers are dealing with this issue.

As with all my interviewees, before closing the conversation, I opened a space for Ms Cacilda to raise issues not discussed up to that point, ones that she felt important to raise or simply add to what we had discussed. Noting that she had something to say but was reluctant to speak out (lines 3–4), I encouraged her to open herself up '*im . . . tlhatlha lesvi svinga xifuveni*'/'yeah . . . release whatever you have at the bottom of your heart'. Continuing to encourage her to speak, I stressed that it was important for 'us' to know what she feels, without promising to fix it (lines 6–7). My use of first person plural here was ambiguous: it could have been interpreted as a polite way of saying 'me', the researcher (in Changana), or it could have been interpreted as 'us', the decision-makers. She might have taken the latter meaning, as this is in part how she and other participants occasionally viewed me (cf. Extract 17.2). However, my intended meaning was the former one—I wanted to foreground my researcher position as a listener and co-constructor of knowledge (with her and the other teachers) but without the powers to change (at least not directly) the status quo.

Ms Cacilda started by putting herself on the side of the pupils: she attributed the poor performance of her pupils to the lack of materials and regretted the fact that she had been blaming the pupils themselves for that (lines 12–24); she then took a teacher stance and stated that 'she' and the others were working under poor conditions (lines 25–28); she concluded, saying '*loku lona bilingue lila kufamba alihumensi materiyali*'/'if the bilingual [programme] wants to move on, it has to provide materials' (lines 43–45).

She and other teachers saw the state education system as failing to provide them with the necessary resources for their normal daily teaching and learning activities. For them, the lack of materials made their work harder and hindered pupils' learning. They were both agents and critics of the system.

Extracts 17.2 and 3 show moments when the interviewees implicitly positioned me, the researcher, as their messenger or as someone who could speak on their behalf to those responsible for the implementation of the programme. This positioning is made more apparent in the following extract. In addition to the issue of lack of materials already discussed above, Ms Flora brought up another issue faced by both of the schools in the study: the poor quality of the classrooms. As in the case of Ms Cacilda in Extract 17.3 above, Ms Flora implicitly invited me to act.

(*continued*)

Extract 17.3 Ms Cacilda commenting on the lack of resources and its impact on pupils' learning (18/09/2007, 0:18:47-0:20:22)

#	Original	Translation
1	Ms C: Eeh!... asvaku sviyengetela anina	Ms C: Well!... there is nothing I can add
2	svona ((diz com ar submisso))	((she says in a submissive way))
3	F: Im, TLHATLHA lesvinga xifuveni!	F: Well... RELEASE whatever you
4		have at the bottom of your heart!
5	Ms C: ((riso))	Ms C: ((laughter))
6	F: Ahili hitasvilunghisa	F: We are not saying that we will fix it
7	kambe svalaveka ku hisvitiva.	but it is necessary for us to know it.
8	Ms C: Lexi nixilavaka muito muito!...	Ms C: What I want the most!...
9	((ainda a sorrir))	((still laughing))
10	Hikusa kusukela vaalunu anili navona	Because since I have been... I have
11	ninganavu lavaya...	been with those pupils there...
12	nako hambi vo nivasolaka, novasola	in fact though I have been blaming
13	kambe NASVIKARHATA lesvaku	them but THE REALITY IS THAT
14	avaalunu VAFUNDHA	IT IS DIFFICULT for pupils to
15	hikusvitwa ka mina,	LEARN by hearing it from me,
16	navasvivona ko ka xileti!	just seeing it on the blackboard!
17	É por isso svitekaka nkama wakuleha	That is why it takes a long time
18	hikuva uvabzeletela...	because you tell them...
19	vasvitwa...	they understand...
20	ugama se uyasvitsala...	then you write it...
21	uvaobrigara lesvaku avasviteketeli!	you require that they should copy it!
22	Às vezes vasviteka svona	Sometimes they copy it well
23	às vezes vasviteka MAL	other times they copy it WRONGLY

Extract 17.3 (continued)

Line		
24	ugama uku avasvitivi!	and in the end you want them to
25	Se lani hi lani nikuvonaka svaku...	know! So here is where I see that...
26	MINA, kumbe nivan'wanyani hitirha	I, and maybe others as well we are
27	*mal*!	working under bad conditions!
28	Hitirha *mal*	We're working under bad conditions
29	(...)	(...)
30	Se mina la aniku vona... ingava kuva	So my view is that they... we should
31	kaku hikuma *materiyali*.	have materials.
32	Hitalwa navona navani *materiyali*.	We will struggle with them
33	Hikuva akulwa navona svosvi	while they have materials.
34	hilwaka navona	Because struggling with them as we
35	holwa navona uvavangela guwa	are [currently] struggling
36	*maxji* nhambi we nawutlhela	making a clamour for them
37	usvivona svaku vanani *razão*.	but even you yourself you end up
38	Avasvivoni mbangu.	seeing that they are not to blame.
		They don't see it anywhere.
39	(...)	(...)
40	Se la nakuvona svaku ku ni...	So I find that here there is... a lot of
41	akukarhateka kakukulu lanu.	suffering here.
42	Hisvaku loko lona *bilingue* lila	So if the bilingual programme wants
43	kufamba,	to move on,
44	alihumensi *materiyali*!	it has to provide materials!
45		

Extract 17.4 Ms Flora (Ms F) commenting on the lack of materials and classrooms (21/09/2007, 0:22:27–0:23:00)

1	F:	Não sei se tens mais algum aspecto	F:	I don't know whether you have any
2		que achas que podias acrescentar		other aspect you think you should
3		quer da reacção dos alunos na turma...		add, either in terms of pupils'
4		da tua experiência como professora...		reaction in the classroom...
5		ou... da reacção da comunidade em		your experience as a teacher... or...
6		relação ao ensino bilingue.		the reaction of the community in
7				relation to bilingual education.
8	Ms F:	Eeh, só um pedido que tenho	Ms F:	Umm, I've only got one request
9		((diz a rir))		((laughing))
10	F:	Imhim	F:	Ok
11	Ms F:	De salas de aulas...	Ms F:	With regard to classrooms...
12	F:	Ok	F:	Ok
13	Ms F:	Im, temos problemas mesmo...	Ms F:	Yes, we've really got problems...
14		e o material		and the materials
15		O LIVRO!		THE TEXTBOOK!
16	F:	Imhim, então consideras	F:	Ok, so you think that
17		que esses aspectos têm de certa forma		those aspects in some way have
18		influenciado o rendimento dos teus		influenced your pupils'
19		alunos...		achievement...
20	Ms F:	Não. O LIVRO, SIM!	Ms F:	No. THE TEXTBOOK, YES!
21	F:	Im	F:	Ok
22	Ms F:	Mesmo salas de aulas...	Ms F:	Even classrooms...
23		os encarregados às vezes têm falado		the parents some times say
24		"kasi vo valungu va n'wina lava		"these bosses of yours these...
25		avamiyakeli asvilaun sva kujondzela		why don't they built classrooms for
26		ka svo sva kukombekisa ku		you to show that they like you?"
27		vamirhandza?"		We said "no! we are happy with
28		Hiku "eh! svosvi binganasvu i		what we have so far
29		svinyingi		for the time being lets keep using
30		abipfeneni bitirbisa svosvi		these they will build for us as the
31		vatabiyakela bikutfamba ka minkama"		time goes on"
32	F:	Então, é sinal de que estão cansados	F:	So, that is an indication that they are
33		de andar a construir...		tired of building...
34	Ms F:	Estão! ((rindo))	Ms F:	They are! ((laughing))

Before I closed the conversation, I invited Ms Flora to add whatever she felt important to tell me. She replied saying that she only had a request: '*só um pedido que tenho*'/'I've only got a request' (line 8). This opening implied that she viewed me as someone to whom she could direct the particular request she had (lines 11–15) and therefore someone with the power to meet her request or at least do something so that the request could be met by someone else. She appeared to be identifying me with the institution that had the power to supply their needs (books and class-rooms) and appeared to perceive me as someone whom she could use as a channel of communication.

In order to lend weight to her case for improved classrooms, she reported in Changana part of a dialogue that local teachers had had with parents around this issue (lines 22–31). Through her account she conveyed the mes-sage that the parents were tired of construction work and of maintaining the classrooms and therefore they were calling upon the state authorities to assume their responsibilities (lines 24–27).

When reporting this dialogue, Ms Flora used direct quotation, switch-ing from Portuguese, the language we were using throughout the interview, into Changana, the language that the teachers use in their communication with the parents. This was a way of lending weight and authenticity to what she was reporting, suggesting therefore that the request was not hers alone (or that of teachers alone) but also of the community served by the school, as directly quoted. Her code-switching served not only to bring in the voices of the parties directly or indirectly involved (parents, teachers and education authorities) but also to portray the stances taken by par-ents and teachers. Reported speech, particularly in direct quotation, can be viewed as a 'substantiating procedure' (Freebody, 2003: 154–55), in this case used by the interviewee to support her claim for classrooms. The use of reported speech as a way of presenting the self and others has also been reported by Maybin (2006) in her study of children's discourse.

As in the previous extracts, the discourse in Extract 18.4 set up dif-ferent subject positions for Ms Flora, as the bilingual education teacher, and for me, as the researcher. As the researcher, I began by using the sec-ond person singular form of the verbs ('*não sei se* **tens** . . . '/'I wonder whether **you have** . . . '), which indexed a close working relationship and/or one of solidarity. The pronoun '*tu*'/'you' was used here, as in all informal interactions in Portuguese. However, in formulating her request, and then backing it up with the 'voices' of members of the community, Ms Flora positioned me as a representative of the Mozambican education authorities. Ms Flora's discourse also drew in references to a range of key social actors: '*encarregados*'/'parents/caretakers' and '*valungu*'/'bosses'.

Ms Flora also revealed the tensions between the different identities (imposed and assumed) that she and other teachers had to take on: as agents of and spokespersons for the education system, on the one hand, and as critics of the system, on the other hand. The teachers are viewed by the local community as representatives of the education authorities, and are called upon to resolve day-to-day problems in local classrooms. The teachers feel that they all have the same problems: as they are forced to work in poor conditions, their role as representatives of education authorities leads them to protect their 'employers' by not showing collusion with people in the local community but mobilising it instead, telling them to be patient and assuring that the government will sooner or later solve the problem. On the other hand, finding themselves without the capacity to build the necessary classrooms, teachers demand that the education authorities should do so and strengthen their case by using the voices of the community. At this moment, in this interview, I was positioned as a representative of the education authorities or at least as a valid channel for taking the message up.

DIVERSE POSITIONINGS: RESEARCHER AS TEACHER TRAINER, POLICYMAKER, AND 'CIRCUMSTANTIAL ACTIVIST'

I departed from the premise that investigating a familiar site does not necessarily lead to biased data and analysis but can be viewed as an opportunity for the researcher to achieve the depth of insight that traditional ethnography hoped to achieve through long stays in the field (Marcus, 1998). I also indicated that close scrutiny of interview data provides insights into ways in which the researched in such situations skilfully shape their discourse based on what they know of researchers, including their orientation and interests.

I noted that authors who underscore the advantages of researching a familiar site present such advantages only from the vantage point of the researcher. I tried to go beyond this by focussing on the perspective of the researched, taking into account my own fieldwork experience. My aim was to establish how and to what extent our past acquaintance shaped the nature of my conversations with the teachers in my study. I tried to find out how this familiarity was enacted and manifested itself discursively.

The analysis presented here resonates with the view expressed in Marcus (1998). In fact, my detailed knowledge of policy and practice of bilingual education in Mozambique and my familiarity with the research sites, including the participants and their languages, helped me to understand discursive nuances and interpret contextualisation cues. Moreover, the participants did not always fully articulate their views and positionings; they were implicit in their discourse. In order to make sense of their contributions, I had to go beyond the then and there of the conversation and connect the points they were making to the wider context, and this included recalling experiences we had shared in the past.

As I have shown, the teachers and I presented ourselves to each other and saw each other in different ways depending on the topic being discussed during the interviews or evoked from previous encounters (not necessarily ones involving me). The stances of the teachers also shifted depending on who they were addressing. This included addressees evoked through narratives. I have argued that these interviews provided revealing insights: (1) into the ways in which the teachers in the study were managing different identities—identities that had been imposed or assumed; and (2) into the stances adopted by the teachers on the issues arising from their involvement in the bilingual programme. The teachers assumed different identities: as bilingual teachers, as members of the local communities, as trainees and as the subjects of my research; and they saw me as a representative of the state education authorities, as a teacher trainer or as their messenger or advocate. Their familiarity with me as the researcher enabled them to strategically present their views and positionings in an explicit or implicit manner depending on their evaluation of the significance of each discursive context.

Three categories of addressees were foregrounded in the teachers' discourse: the state or its representatives, the local communities, and me as interviewer/researcher. When addressing the state or state representatives, the teachers presented themselves as critics of the state system for not providing them with the necessary resources for their daily work, and urged it to act. The teachers used the voice of parents/local communities as a strategy to add weight and authenticate their demands. To achieve this they used reported speech, including direct quotation, as a way to make vivid themes and stances taken by them and by the parents during the reported encounters. In this sense, reported speech appeared as an authenticating strategy (Hanks, 1987). In contrast, when presenting themselves as addressing the local communities (e.g. in short narrative sequences), the teachers presented themselves as spokespersons for the education authorities.

As the researcher, I was addressed by the teachers as a planner, teacher trainer and representative of the education authorities. When evaluating the programme, teachers associated the merits and also the demerits of the bilingual programme with me, and when it came to the need for corrective actions I was viewed as part of the solution or as an ideal messenger to channel their calls to the appropriate decision makers.

Caught in crossfire, I found myself swinging between different roles, some of them actually performed in a near past: as a representative of the education authorities, as a researcher and as a 'circumstantial activist' (Marcus, 1995). I acknowledged my involvement with the education authorities, although I seldom articulated this during the interviews. However, as a researcher, I assumed that my prime mission was to produce knowledge and not to change things, although I hoped that my findings would have an impact. At the same time, I also felt that I should not overlook the calls from the teachers. I also found these legitimate, and therefore felt committed to doing something for them. In fact, in my different roles, I have also been criticising crucial flaws in the current bilingual programme and suggesting changes in the ways in which it is being implemented, including in the teacher-training component. Therefore, some of the concerns raised by teachers and local communities are also my own concerns. This seems to be an example of a situation in which a researcher acts or is called to act as a 'circumstantial activist'. As Marcus (1995: 113) has put it:

> not the activism claimed in relation to affiliation with a particular social movement outside academia or the domain of research, nor is it the academic claim to an imagined vanguard role for a particular style of writing or scholarship with reference to a posited ongoing politics in society or culture at a specific historic moment. [. . .] It is a playing out in practice of the feminist slogan of the political as personal, but in this case it is the political as synonymous with the professional persona and, with the latter, what used to be discussed in a clinical way as the methodological.

I do recognise that utterances are by nature multivoiced, dialogic and fragmented (Maybin, 2006) and therefore I am not naively trying to argue that we should take for granted that when the researched are familiar with particular researchers and their interests they necessarily convey original, coherent, and intentional messages. Indeed, as Freebody (2003) suggests, interview accounts may be coherent and relevant within the specific context of the interview, but not necessarily 'true'. I therefore subscribe to the position that the researchers should not take such messages for granted; instead they ought to be reflexive when interpreting them.

CONCLUSION

The conclusion emerging from this analysis is that not only can researchers take advantage of knowing the site and the participants they are researching but also the researched. Those being researched can, in a skilful and positive way, exploit the knowledge they have of the researchers, including their interests and perspectives, to shape their discourse. The outcome is more focussed, incisive, and contextually appropriate responses. Therefore, I hope that this chapter can, in some way, serve as a contribution towards the representation of interviewees 'as artful, reasoned and sophisticated cultural practitioners' (Freebody, 2003: 169).

NOTES

1. For ethical reasons, the names of schools, their locations, communities served, and participants are fictional.
2. In the Portuguese tradition and also in contexts with Portuguese influence, like Mozambique, the title 'doutor' applies to all those who hold a university degree (except for those from engineering fields, who are called engineers).

REFERENCES

Chimbutane, F. 2009. The purpose and value of bilingual education: A critical, linguistic ethnographic study of the rural primary schools in Mozambique. Unpublished PhD Dissertation, School of Education, University of Birmingham, UK.
———. 2011. *Rethinking Bilingual Education in Postcolonial Contexts*. Bristol: Multilingual Matters.
Edwards, A. D. and Furlong, V. J. 1985. Reflections on the language of teaching. In *Field Methods in the Study of Education*, ed. R. G. Burgess, 21–36. London: Falmer Press.
Emerson, R. M., Fretz, R. I. and Shaw, L. L. 1995. *Writing Ethnographic Fieldnotes*. Chicago: University of Chicago Press.
Freebody, P. 2003. *Qualitative Research in Education: Interaction and Practice*. London: Sage.
Hanks, W. F. 1987. Discourse genres in a theory of practice. *American Ethnologist* 14(4): 668–92.
Instituto Nacional de Estatística (INE). 2009. *Dados do recenseamento geral da população de 2007*. Online document, http://www.ine.gov.mz.
Marcus, G. E. 1995. Ethnography in/of the world system: the emergence of multi-sited ethnography. *Annual Review of Anthropology* 24: 95–117.
———. 1998. Sticking with ethnography through thick and thin. In *Ethnography through Thick and Thin*, ed. G. E. Marcus, 231–53. Princeton, NJ: Princeton University Press.
Maybin, J. 2006. *Children's Voices: Talk, Knowledge, and Identity*. Basingstoke, Hampshire: Palgrave Macmillan.
Rampton, B. 2007. Neo-Hymesian linguistic ethnography in the United Kingdom. *Journal of Sociolinguistics* 11(5): 584–607.
Robson, C. 2002. *Real World Research* (2nd edition). Oxford: Blackwell.

TRANSCRIPTION CONVENTIONS

.	stopping fall in tone, with some sense of completion
,	a slightly rising tone giving a sense of continuation
. . .	pause
(. . .)	indicates that parts of the original text have been omitted
?	raising intonation
!	emphasis (marked prominence through pitch or increase in volume)
' '	indicates the beginning and end of a direct quotation (reported speech)
((text))	contextual information
Italics	marks an utterance in a different language or the use of borrowed or nativised words
UPPER CASE	indicates louder speech than the surrounding talk

18 A Critical Linguistic Ethnographic Approach to Language Disabilities in Multilingual Families

Deirdre Martin

INTRODUCTION

This chapter examines the challenges, opportunities and implications of critical linguistic ethnographic research relating to language disability in multilingual families. The chapter discusses what linguistic ethnographic research would look like for multilingual families with children who have biologically-based difficulties learning to talk and communicate. The first section deals with traditional approaches to researching contexts with language disability and then points to the need for ethnographic research. Some key ideas of critical linguistic ethnography (LE) are presented and I outline the advantages of adopting a critical perspective for the field of multilingual language disability. Subsequent sections discuss the challenges, at different stages of the research process, for researching the language and communicative socialisation of children with language disabilities in multilingual settings. The chapter concludes with the implications of critical linguistic ethnographic research for understanding and explaining communication practices in contexts of multilingual language disability.

Children learn language in their own unique way and children with language difficulties are no different. Some children are identified, in comparison with typically developing peers, as having delay or difficulty in developing language as their primary developmental need. The term 'language disabilities' (or difficulties, disorders, pathology) refers to a spectrum of speech, language and communication needs (SLCN). It is generally accepted that multilingualism does not cause speech, language or communication difficulties and disabilities. Indeed, children with language-learning difficulties can develop multilingually (Paradis et al., 2003).

Research into language disabilities has developed within different disciplinary traditions: medicine/biological, psycholinguistics, and linguistics. In linguistics, a structural approach, in which the focus is on language as a system, dominates the field and the research methodologies are largely positivistic in orientation. Moreover, the current research base for multilingual language disability is limited (Diniz, 1999; Steinstra, 2002). In her substantial review of research studies in the field of disability, multilingualism and ethnicities, Steinstra (2002) pointed out that most research has been provider-led, orientated by a model of impact and benefit of provision to clients. With its focus on procedures and mechanisms of institutional support, this research orientation tends to overlook wider social issues and processes. As Nazroo (1998: 1) explains:

> Ethnic inequalities are important because they might point to a wider understanding of mechanisms producing inequalities in health. However, a concern with mechanisms in health inequalities research can lead to a focus on technical interventions along causal pathways, with the roots of health inequalities, wider social inequalities, being ignored.

There are therefore opportunities for research to reconceptualise the relationship between language disability and multilingualism in ways other than through this focus on impact and benefit. Sociological research orientates to client perspectives and to the perspectives of young multilinguals and their families; for example in studies of deafness (Ahmad, Atkin and Jones, 2002) and severe disability (Hatton et al., 2002).

However, there have been relatively few ethnographic and interpretative studies of language disabilities. Some studies with adults with acquired language disability following brain damage have been conducted in the US in the related traditions of linguistic anthropology and interactional sociolinguistics (e.g. C. Goodwin, 1995; M. Goodwin and Goodwin, 2001; Kovarsky, Duchan and Maxwell, 1999). Within these traditions, language socialisation is defined as "the process of integrating code knowledge with socio-cultural knowledge" (Ochs and Schieffelin, 2001: 289). Ochs (2002) has observed there is a dearth of linguistic anthropological research with children who have disabilities such as autism. This is surprising given the robust tradition of research on language and literacy socialization that has been developed by linguistic anthropologists in the US (e.g. Heath, 1983; Ochs and Schieffelin, 2001).

Within the more recent tradition of research in linguistic ethnography, in the UK, research related to language disability has also been slow to develop. In the meantime, there has been a critical turn in both traditions— in linguistic anthropological research in North America and in linguistic ethnography in the UK and further afield. The opening up of a critical dimension to language research of an ethnographic nature (e.g. Heller, 2008) offers a number of advantages for those of us who are concerned with researching the interface between language disabilities and multilingualism. First, it allows us to question dominant theories and fundamental notions about language disability and multilingualism and to document the ways in which these theories and notion are taken up and applied. Second, a critical perspective goes beyond an account of language use in immediate interactional contexts. It interrogates the ways in which different societal arrangements for managing disability shape the lives and communicative practices of children with language disability and their multilingual families, either enriching or impoverishing them. Third, research into multilingual communicative practices in contexts of language disability can provide new perspectives on "the roots of health inequalities [and] wider social inequalities" that Nazroo wrote about, in the quotation above. And, fourth, critical linguistic ethnography has the potential to represent the perspective of children with communicative disabilities in multilingual communities.

DEVELOPING CRITICAL ETHNOGRAPHIC APPROACHES

The following sections examine what research with language disabilities in multilingual families might look like from a critical linguistic ethnographic perspective. Each section considers a particular stage in the research process.

Deconstructing Discourses about Norms

Currently, spoken language by children whose communication is a cause for concern is compared normatively, either against a developmental 'average' known as Age-Stage norms or against other functional norms. Normative developmental information for English is based on research studies with young monolingual English-speaking children (e.g. Brown, 1973). Such normative comparisons are based on a rigid, monolingual view of language development and an essentialist view of language disability.

We do not know enough about multilingual language development to be able to claim when it is 'abnormal'. There is now ample evidence that most developmental language tests in this field are in English and have cultural, linguistic and tester biases as well as developmental norms that do not readily apply to multilingual development (e.g. Valdes and Figueroa, 1994; see also Martin, 2009, for a summary). Critical linguistic ethnography has the potential to unpack and challenge these institutional discourses, to demonstrate the consequences of such discourses for particular groups and individuals and, through close collaborative research with multilinguals in different settings, to create a knowledge base that affords an alternative understanding and explanation of communicative practices in contexts of multilingual language disability.

Multilingual Research Teams

Traditional research practice involving a 'lone researcher' is still commonplace (e.g. in doctoral research) yet, in multilingual settings, there are real challenges for the researcher. In particular, it is difficult for monolingual researchers who do not share the languages and cultures of their participants to achieve the level and quality of engagement that they wish with their research participants. For a range of reasons, there are still too few researchers who are members of linguistic minority communities and who are interested in researching language disabilities.

Multilingual researcher pairs or teams can precipitate a change in research practice and can, at the same time, achieve greater rigour in the research process (Creese, Bhatt et al., 2008). Different perspectives are brought into the interpretation and analysis of the participants' realities, generating more nuanced and layered understandings. Multilingual researchers already act, on a regular basis, as mediators and 'resources' for research teams and research projects. Multilingual research projects can also benefit from the creation of a multilingual advisory board and/or panel that includes multilingual members with language disabilities. Such bodies can advise the research team and can monitor and interrogate the progress of the project. Advisory bodies with representation from the researched community are a requirement in most funded research in the UK and elsewhere.

However, investigating multilingualism with members of local communities who are not researchers can raise ethical issues, along with issues related to the power asymmetries associated with differences in professional knowledge, gender and age within a research team (Martin, Stuart-Smith and Dhesi, 1998).

Gaining Access

Multilingual researchers in project teams are likely to play a key role in gaining access to potential research participants in local community contexts. They are also likely to bring knowledge of specific cultural and historical beliefs about language socialisation to inform the design of the research and to support the data collection. Researchers making contact with people with disability in multilingual settings are, of course, required to work with the principles and codes for ethical behavior for academic and professional bodies and for the ethical governance of services. These principles and codes are designed to protect families and individuals. Researchers must also obtain informed consent from participants. Some multilingual families may need interpretation/translation support at this stage, and children and adults who have substantial language disabilities may require additional support. Furthermore, research with vulnerable individuals, such as those with communication disabilities, can give rise to complex ethical situations where ethnographers may face decisions about responsible management of data.

Recruiting participants with language delay or disability in multilingual families poses specific challenges. Researchers usually gain access through family members and carers rather than negotiating directly with participants who have language disabilities. Language disability is sometimes referred to as a 'hidden' disability because families may not be aware of it or recognise it (Warner, 1999). For example, a UK survey by the National Autistic Society (2007) reported on the difficulties of identifying bilingual families within minority ethnic groups in which there are children with autism.

Researchers also access families with young children with disabilities through provider agencies as well as non-governmental organisations, such as registered charities that work with families who have children with language disabilities. On the whole, bodies like the National Autistic Society, *Afasic*[1] and *ICAN*[2] in the UK are supportive access routes. Chamba and Ahmad (2000) used a national UK database of families with members who had severe disabilities to undertake research with families in minority ethnic groups who had children with disabilities.

However, some researchers have difficulty locating a range of different kinds of multilingual families including children with disabilities. It is usually easier to make contact with families from established minority groups. Social networking strategies, such as gaining access to the family through a friend-of-a-friend, are sometimes employed (Milroy, 1980). Co-workers recruited to service providers also work with researchers to assist in gaining access to families (Martin, 2005). Harris (2003), for example, gained access to participants with disabilities who were refugees and asylum seekers, through a friend who was a member of the community. However, researchers who are members of linguistic minority communities and who use their social networks to make contact with families may find that networking raises other ethical issues, such as confidentiality (Martin, Stuart-Smith and Dhesi, 1998).

There are also issues relating to working with minority groups other than established, long-settled groups. In health, education and social welfare policy discourses, these are families who are described as 'hard to reach' or 'non-compliant'. Although recognising that there are less visible and more marginalised groups, critical linguistic ethnography interrogates these descriptors, seeking more nuanced analyses of families' engagement (of lack of engagement) with service providers.

Building the Researcher-Researched Relationship

Trusting relationships between researchers and participants emerge gradually, over time, through the creation and exploration of shared and negotiated understandings. However, there are four crucial elements in the building of researcher-researched relationships and the development of trust: the first element is the language resources of the research team. In culturally and linguistically diverse research sites, the development of trusting relationships often involves team work with interpreters and/or bilingual researchers. It is more difficult to develop a constructive and trusting relationship when these resources are limited or absent.

Secondly, researchers with a level of professional competency for working with families where there is language disability and for communication with individuals with language disability are more likely to be able to develop a trusting relationship with multilingual families from the early stages of a project. Researchers interviewing children with language disability may encounter complex challenges in the course of communicating: these can include challenges such as the child's intelligibility or engagement. Code-switching may also need to be managed sensitively to maintain trust.

Thirdly, in contexts of disability, researchers need to be prepared to manage the expectations of different families. Some may gain a high degree of confidence and trust, but need to be able to sustain the quality of that relationship, to manage expectations and dependency and to bring the relationship to an appropriate close when the research project ends. Other researchers may receive a mixed welcome from families with disabled children: on the one hand, researchers may be welcomed as bringers of benefits, such as knowledge about the needs and demands of the children and about ways of accessing support, whereas at the same time the presence of the researcher is a reminder of the children's disability and needs. Practitioner-researchers who are working as ethnographers in contexts of disability may choose to intervene and advise in response to parental questions, judging that it is entirely ethical to respond with informed advice to parents' questions about managing the family member's communication disability and language socialisation.

Fourthly, dilemmas may arise from observing parenting or family practices that researchers believe may be harmful to the child, such as 'infantalising' a child with disability, for example, carrying or feeding the child when the child *is* able to walk or feed her/himself. Researchers can address this dilemma through discussion of their observations with key family participants (see the discussion of research methods that make this possible, in the next section). Nevertheless, researchers' "reach" into family communicative practices is always controlled by the participants. Participants may prefer not to disclose knowledge or avoid issues raised by researchers that they see as having negative consequences for them.

Research Methods

At present, linguistic ethnographic practice primarily involves three field-work methods: participant observation with field notes, interviews and recording of naturally-occurring interactions. These three sources of ethnographic material become data through transcription of interactional and interview data and through amplification of field notes from initial jottings, as soon as possible after participant observation. Bringing together the three forms of data and triangulation of data sources, in this way, provides a fuller account of any moment of interaction.

Participant Observation

Participant observation is the hallmark of data collection in ethnography. In linguistic ethnography, communicative practices provide the main focus. In research focussing on local lifeworlds, the precise ways for the researcher to go about participant observation are shaped largely by the participants. In research on language disability, the researcher is focussed on systematic study of the situated practices of multilingual communication with and around the person with language disability. Hymes' (1972) mnemonic, SPEAKING, is still a useful tool for studying interrelated categories of interaction: Setting, Participant, End (purpose), Act (sequence), Key (tone) Instrumentalities (modality), Norm (rules of interaction) and Genre. Researchers who are unfamiliar with the language and cultural practices of a multilingual family are faced with a substantial task of participant observation, akin to aspects of linguistic anthropology work. The interpretative challenges are best addressed by working in a multilingual research team and/or by revisiting audio- or video-recorded data with the participants (see below for a fuller discussion of this method).

Field Notes

Field notes document actual observations of interactions and the contexts within which the interactions happen. They may start as quick jottings and drawings of the context on a notepad during the observation period and they can then be rewritten more fully and reflectively afterwards. When informed consent is given, field notes can also include photographs of the home and specific rooms where the interactions occur and photographs of any artefacts that are involved. Moreover, field notes can be used to inform future observations and interviews. They are an essential element in the interpretative process. In multilingual team ethnography, field notes can be shared and discussed by the team to generate further levels of analysis and interpretation (Creese, Ghatt et al., 2008).

Interviews with Multilingual Parents or Carers

Interviews with multilingual parents or carers make it possible to explore their feelings, attitudes and decisions relating to maintaining multilingual communication with a child who has a language disability, particularly in the light of advice from professionals who advocate monolingual practices. In a recent study of multilingual families, Kremer-Sadlik (2005) addressed issues of multilingualism and language choice for language-delay children with high functioning autism (HFA) (Kremer-Sadlik, 2005). She reported some of her findings as follows:

> Giving up the family's language is a great price to pay. One mother told me that she stopped going to church with her children because her son was unable to understand the Armenian priest's sermons. But most families disclosed that they only stopped using the mother tongue when addressing the affected child. Dinnertime observations revealed that the HFA child did not take part in family conversations, parents

did not address the autistic child often, and parents rarely used English. (Kremer-Sadlik, 2005: 1232)

A critical perspective can reveal the impact of professional discourses about multilingualism on the families involved. Kremer-Sadlik's research indicates that parents shape their multilingual communicative practices with their autistic children in line with powerful directive discourses from non-present (monolingual English) professional institutions.

There is a place in this type of research for interviews with parents and carers that are based on prepared questionnaires, in order to explore the case history of the particular family member with a language disability. However, these kinds of interviews may position the two parties in ways that constrain the outcome. For example, interviewers may feel positioned in ways that may prevent them from exploring with participants more nuanced, context-sensitive aspects of language use. Interviewees may also give responses that reflect how they are positioned by the interviewer and reports of language use may be shaped by their perceptions of the interviewer and of the interviewers' views about language. Furthermore, unless it is adapted, this interview method may exclude the actual participants with language disability.

In contrast, ethnographic interviews with participants are more like focussed, iterative conversations that revisit, each time, issues that recur with a view to drilling deeper for further meanings and interpretations. Although it is more likely that interviews will be with family members than with participants with communication difficulties, there are specialized methods that have been developed for interviewing participants with severe language disabilities and that involve the use of alternative and augmented forms of communication. Examples include computerized speech generating devices (SGDs) and lower tech resources, such as 'Talking Mats' (University of Stirling). However, applications are still relatively limited: in a recent study with participants who had severe communication disabilities, it seems that most participants reported that they did not use their SGDs in situations in which they needed them (Valiquette, Sutton and Ska, 2010: 303). 'Talking Mats' can be adapted for communication across languages with trained users although, as yet, there is no research reported with users from multilingual contexts.

Audio and Video Recordings

A common site for recording interaction between family members in disability studies is family meal times, as in Kremer-Salik's (2005) study. The development of small mobile digital video cameras, with built-in audio recorders, now allows family members to record their own interactions at home, in the homes of extended family members, in shops or in places of worship. Video data is particularly valuable for research with children with language and communication disabilities. First, visual data relating to these children's interactions with others is essential for interpreting and analysing the communicative practices involved in the co-construction of meaning. Video data not only captures the physical context; it also captures the fleeting, subtle and often unusual repertoire of verbal and non-verbal contextualization cues as well as the indexicality of interactions between these children and their interlocutors. Second, the data provides a fuller picture than was previously feasible. An advantage of the video camera is that it can go with participants to places and discursive spaces where researchers may not be permitted, such as religious ceremonies, family celebrations, bedtime routines. Whereas the scenarios are selected by the participants, reflecting their understanding of the importance and relevance of specific sociolinguistic practices, researchers can also be explicit about what their research needs are and discuss the selection of scenarios with the participants beforehand.

Third, audio- and video-recorded data can be revisited. Digital audio-video cameras facilitate the downloading of material to the computer and open up a range of possibilities for viewing and listening to recorded material. For instance, in discussion of the recorded material with the researcher, key participants in the interaction can contribute further layers of description and interpretation. The process of layering data and interpretations in this way has been compared to lamination (Maybin, 2006). Maybin's use of this term reflects the research approach first proposed by Gumperz (1982), namely that of taking the audio-recorded data back to participants and asking for their reactions. It is described by Maybin as the process when the ethnographic lens is "strengthened, further laminated, as it were, (as when layers of glass are melded together to make a stronger pane)" (Maybin, 2006: 12). Maybin was referring here to interviews she conducted with the young participants (eleven- and twelve-year-olds) in her study. The interviews centred on themes and topics that had cropped up in her audio recordings of their talk in the interstices between school activities. She notes that these interviews (with friendship pairs) provided "another point of reference from which to interpret the other data I had collected" (Maybin, 2006: 13).

In interviews such as these, participants revisit topics and themes captured in transcripts or recordings of particular communicative events in discussion with researchers and these conversations provide further material for data analysis. Audio-video material can be revisited several times, depending on the conditions for the research and the overall time frame. Similar research practices adopted by other researchers are referred to as "retrospective interviewing" (Rampton, 1995: 23) and amount simply to iterative cycles of data collection. Such iterative cycles of data collection are particularly apt for research on language disability among children in multilingual contexts: participants such as parents, other family members, siblings and/or the child with disability can be invited to recount their experiences of particular events, and to address aspects perceived to be problematic or contested. In research conducted by multilingual teams, additional advantages accrue from incorporating the perspectives of different members of the team, logged in their field notes and research journals (Creese, Bhatt et al., 2008).

Transcription, Interpretation and Analysis of Data

Transcription of the audio-recorded data for language disability research presents specific challenges. Approaches to transcription that draw on the conversational analysis tradition may use narrow transcription conventions with reference to details of non-verbal communication (gestures, eye gaze direction). The speech of some children with language disabilities may border on unintelligibility and transcripts may capture episodes of breakdown and repair. A considerable amount of attention needs to be given to phonetic and prosodic detail. Transcription needs to capture both verbal and non-verbal contextualisation cues, and other modalities of interaction, in orthographic form. Other contextual data, from observations, field notes and other layers of 'laminated' data gathering, also needs to be incorporated into transcripts wherever possible.

In multilingual contexts, transcription of spoken data can involve capturing stretches of monolingual talk in different languages. However, it is more common to be faced with the challenge of transcribing speech exchanges which involve code-switching or code-alternation (Auer, 1998) or language crossing (Rampton, 1995). In research in multilingual settings focussing on children with language disabilities, close attention is needed to the particularities of the communicative practices that arise in the conversations between the children and their interlocutors and to the recurring use of specific kinds of contextualisation cues, such as code-switching and/ or particular uses of prosody or pitch. Kremer-Sadlik's (2005) study provides evidence, based on observations, that multilingual families modify their multilingual interactions in contexts of communication disability. So, some detailed interactional evidence is now needed to gain further insights into the ways in which communicative practices are modified and into the consequences that this has. Conversational analysis is an appropriate analytic tool; however, in more critically oriented studies, analysis needs to be extended to take account of the shaping influences of institutional discourses on families' multilingual communicative practices.

As noted above, iterative cycles of data collection contribute to the interpretative layering of field notes, observations, recordings and interviews. This is a particularly effective approach to the collection of rich ethnographic and textual material for researchers who are 'outsiders' and who do not share the communicative, social, cultural or historical practices of participants in multilingual families that have children with communication disabilities. This approach can be used to steer researchers to deeper exploration of multilingual and multimodal communicative practices and to track those practices across contexts. Iterative cycles of data collection and analysis also increase the reliability of the analysis, providing checks and balances for researcher bias. Layering of data in this way makes the research more valid and trustworthy, as it interprets and represents participants' perspectives on their lived communicative experiences.

Some ethnographers argue that attending to the extraordinary-in-the-ordinary promotes our understanding of the "tacitly known scripts and schemas that organise ordinary activities" (Ybema et al., 2009: 2). However, simple immersion in the mundane and *sub*mundane of the details of everyday language socialisation may not lead to a full appreciation of the social processes that constitute them. Some orienting theory is also necessary as we begin to interpret and analyse conversational routines.

*Re*presenting Participant Perspectives in Writing Up

This section deals with the writing up of research of a critical ethnographic nature in the field of language disabilities. A central question is that of giving voice to the participants and representing their emic perspectives. This task is a particularly difficult one when the participants are children. Ochs identifies the 'colossal challenge' for linguistic anthropologists and ethnographers aiming to give an account of situated, social and cultural phenomena as if it were through the eyes of children as well as those who attend to them (Ochs, 2002: 100). Researchers not only present evidence gathered with research participants in their lifeworlds; they also *re*present this evidence through a particular interpretative lens.

The difficulties involved in gathering interactional data with participants with communicative disabilities in multilingual contexts have been highlighted in this chapter. These difficulties can easily lead to reliance on data gathered only with carers or other interlocutors so that the voices of the actual participants with disabilities are silenced. Moreover, generalisations about processes of cultural and linguistic socialisation are still commonplace and the variation in communicative practices among adults and children with language disabilities may be simplified and underemphasised (Ochs, 2002; Garrett and Baquedano-Lopez, 2002). Thus, disability can be represented in reductive, essentialist ways.

Those who adopt critical linguistic ethnographic approaches are well positioned to discern and explain the ways in which asymmetries of power are played out in the lives of participants with disabilities and to offer pointers as to how to mediate and broker these social and institutional processes. A study with Hispanic parents of deaf children in the US (Allen, 2002) illustrates how participants can be empowered to challenge the unfairness of local educational provision through the research process and demand more equitable, multilingual support for their deaf children's needs. And, as I have indicated above, a critical perspective can also be a means of unpacking the discourses which generate negative representations of disability and which often conflate multilingualism, additional language learning and language disabilities.

The use of the term '*re*presentation', in accounts of ethnographic research, is motivated by a desire to signal reflexivity in the research process. The narratives of linguistic and cultural socialization are written and rewritten. There are also contradictions and dilemmas in how participants are represented and in how language is orthographically represented. In addition, there are questions about whose voices are foregrounded, and whose perspective(s) are privileged in the final draft of a research text. Co-authoring in multilingual research teams (Creese, Baraç et al., 2008) provides some checks and balances in this regard. We are now beginning to develop research practices that are better suited to meeting the challenges of representing children and their communication partners in contexts of multilingual language disability.

CONCLUDING REMARKS

As I have shown in this chapter, research on language socialisation among children with language disabilities in multilingual contexts presents new and 'colossal challenges' for ethnographers. The chapter has examined some of the ways of responding to these challenges, considering in particular how ethnographers need to negotiate issues related to perspective-taking and representation. The chapter has also explored the complexity of language socialisation research with children in multilingual families who have a language disability and has emphasised that research with linguistic minority families raises specific issues related to power asymmetries.

I have stressed that there are issues that are particular to research in this area and that these need to be taken into account at each stage in the research process. Ethical considerations are paramount and particularly in the processes of gaining access to particular families where there are children with disabilities, especially in marginalised communities. The development of trusting relationships between researchers and participants across hierarchies of power takes time and commitment. This process needs to be informed by professional competencies and preparedness to meet parental expectations, particularly in the case of practitioner-researchers who are working at the interface of research and practice. Representation of the perspectives of participants, parents and children is a key challenge and researchers need to show considerable reflexivity in analysing their data and in writing up the research. Working within multilingual research teams adds additional value provided that the relationships within the team are equitable. Identifying inequities in service provision is an important process so that the value and benefits of the research are evident to the participants' and to the wider community.

Finally, critical linguistic ethnography offers a way to *re*present the child's perspective, the 'voice' of children living with language disability in multilingual contexts; a voice that is usually unheard.

NOTES

1. *Afasic* is the UK organisation for children and young people with communication impairments and their families.
2. *ICAN* is a charity in the UK whose aim is to help children communicate.

REFERENCES

Ahmad, W., Atkin, K. and Jones, L. 2002. Being deaf and being other things: young Asian people negotiating identities. *Social Science and Medicine* 55(10):1757–69.

Allen, B. 2002. ASL-English bilingual classroom: the families' perspectives. *Bilingual Research Journal* 26(1), 149–68.

Auer, P. (ed.) 1998. *Codeswitching in Conversation*. London: Routledge.

Brown, R. 1973. *A First Language: The Early Stages*. Cambridge, MA: Harvard University Press.

Chamba, R. and Ahmad, W. 2000. Language, communication and information: the needs of parents caring for a severely disabled child. In *Ethnicity, Disability and Chronic Illness*, ed. W. I. U. Ahmad, 85–102. Buckingham: Open University Press

Creese, A., Baraç, T., Bhatt, A., Blackledge, A., Hamid, S., Li Wei, Lytra, V., Martin, P., Yagcıoglu-Ali, D. and Wu, C. J. 2008. Investigating multilingualism in complementary schools in four communities. *Naldic Quarterly* 5(1): 20–23.

Creese, A., Bhatt, A., Bhojani, N. and Martin, P. 2008. Fieldnotes in team ethnography: researching complementary schools. *Qualitative Research* 8(2): 223–42.

Diniz, F. A. 1999. Race and special educational needs in the 1990s. *British Journal of Special Education* 26(4): 213_217.

Garrett, P. and Baquedano-Lopez, P. 2002. Language socialization: reproduction and continuity, transformation and change. *Annual Review of Anthropology* 31: 339–61.

Goodwin, C. 1995. Co-constructing meaning in conversations with an aphasic man. *Research on Language and Social Interaction* 28(3): 233–60.

Goodwin, M. and Goodwin, C. 2001. Emotion within situated activity. In *Linguistic Anthropology: A Reader*, ed. A. Durant, 239–61. Oxford; Blackwell.

Gumperz, J. J. 1982. *Language and Social Identity*. Cambridge: Cambridge University Press.

Harris, J. 2003. 'All doors are closed to us': a social model analysis of the experiences of disabled refugees and asylum seekers in Britain. *Disability and Society* 18(4): 395–410.

Hatton, C., Akram, Y., Robertson, J., Shah, R. and Emerson, E. 2002. *Supporting South Asian Families with a Child with Severe Intellectual Disabilities*. A report to the Department of Health, Institute of Health Research, Lancaster University, Lancaster.

Heath, S. B. 1983. *Ways with Words*. Cambridge: Cambridge University Press.

Heller, M. 2008. Doing ethnography. In *The Blackwell Guide to Research Methods in Bilingualism and Multilingualism*, ed. Li Wei and M. Moyer, 249–62. Oxford: Blackwell.

Hymes, D. 1972. Models of interaction of language and social life. In *Directions in Sociolinguistics: The Ethnography of Communication*, ed. J. J. Gumperz and D. Hymes, 35–71. New York: Holt, Rinehart and Winston.

Kovarsky, D., Duchan, J. and Maxwell, M. (eds) 1999. *Constructing (In)Competence: Disabling Evaluations in Clinical and Social Interaction*. Mahwah, NJ: Lawrence Erlbaum.

Kremer-Sadlik, T. 2005. To be or not to be bilingual: autistic children from multilingual families. In *ISB4: Proceedings of the 4th International Symposium on Bilingualism*, ed. J. Cohen, K. T. McAlister, K. Rolstad and J. MacSwan, 1225–34. Somerville, MA: Cascadilla Press.

Martin, D. 2005. Communities of practice and learning communities: do bilingual co-workers learn in community? In *Beyond Communities of Practice: Language, Power and Social Context*, ed. D. Barton and K. Tusting, 139–57. Cambridge: Cambridge University Press.

———. 2009. *Language Disabilities in Cultural and Linguistic Diversity*. Clevedon: Multilingual Matters.

Martin, D., Stuart-Smith, J. and Dhesi, K. K. 1998. Insiders and outsiders: translating in a bilingual research project. In *Language at Work*, ed. S. Hunston, 109–22. Clevedon: Multilingual Matters/BAAL.

Maybin, J. 2006. *Children's Voices: Talk, Knowledge and Identity*. Basingstoke, Hampshire: Palgrave Macmillan.

Milroy, L. 1980. *Language and Social Networks*. Oxford: Blackwell.

National Autistic Society. 2007. *Missing Out? Autism, Education and Ethnicity: The Reality for Families Today*. London: National Autistic Society, http://www.autism.org.uk.

Nazroo, J. Y. 1998. Genetic, cultural or socio-economic vulnerability? Explaining ethnic inequalities in health. *Sociology of Health and Illness* 20(5): 710–30.

Ochs, E. (2002. Becoming a speaker of culture. In *Language Acquisition and Language Socialization*, ed. C. Kramsch, 99–120. London: Continuum.

Ochs, E. and Schieffelin, B. 2001. Language acquisition and socialization: three developmental stories. In *Linguistic Anthropology: A Reader*, ed. A. Duranti, 226–301. Oxford: Blackwell.

Paradis, J., Crago, M., Genesee, F. and Rice, M. 2003. Bilingual children with specific language impairment: how do they compare with their monolingual peers? *Journal of Speech, Language and Hearing Research* 46: 1–15.

Rampton, B. 1995. *Crossing: Language and Ethnicity among Adolescents*. London: Longman.

Steinstra, D. 2002. The intersection of disability and race/ethnicity/official language/religion. Prepared for the 'Intersections of Diversity' seminar, Canadian Centre on Disability Studies, University of Winnipeg. Talking Mats Research and Development Centre, Scion House, University of Stirling, Stirling FK9 4NF.

Valdes, G. and Figueroa, R. 1994. *Bilingualism and Testing: A Special Case of Bias*. Stamford, CT: Ablex.

Valiquette, C., Sutton, A. and Ska, B. 2010. A graphic symbol tool for the evaluation of communication, satisfaction and priorities of individuals with intellectual disability who use a speech generating device. *Child Language Teaching and Therapy* 26(3): 303–19.

Warner, R. 1999. The views of Bangladeshi parents on the special school attended by their young children with severe learning difficulties. *British Journal of Special Education* 26(6): 218–23.

Ybema, S., Yanow, D., Wels, H. and Kamsteeg, K. (eds) 2009. *Organizational Ethnography: Studying the Complexities of Everyday Life*. London: Sage.

19 "Part of the Puzzle"

The Retrospective Interview as Reflexive Practice in Collaborative Ethnographic Research

Gabriele Budach

THE INTERVIEW IN THE SOCIAL SCIENCES

Interviewing in the social sciences has a long tradition, going back to research by sociologists such as Thomas and Znaniecki (1918–20), but it is of equal importance in social science research today. As much as 90 per cent of contemporary research (Briggs, 1986) relies on interviews as a method of data collection. This trend is paralleled by a growing interest in research methodology. There are an increasing number of publications on the conduct of empirical research in the social sciences, which include guidance regarding good practice in interviewing (e.g. Corbin and Strauss, 2008; Flick, 2009; Hollway and Jefferson, 2000; Johnson and Christensen, 2007; Kvale, 2007; C. Marshall and Rossman, 2006; Silverman, 2009).

Across the range of publications the interview appears as part of an essential tool kit for conducting empirical research. Yet, its place and value within a theory of knowledge building varies considerably. An early definition by Hyman et al. (1975) describes interviews as forms of communication that "vary from highly structured, standardized, quantitatively oriented survey interviews, to semi-formal guided conversations and free flowing informational exchanges" (Hyman et al., 1975: 112). What is laid out here as a range of variants, points, in fact, to different ontological and epistemological paradigms in social sciences. The first as part of positivism operates with highly structured, standardised formats and understands interviewing as a strategy to retrieve specific information from research participants to inform pre-established theoretical frameworks. The interview itself is therefore seen as "a potential base for bias, error, misunderstanding or misdirection, a persistent set of problems to be controlled" (Gorden, 1987: 112).

The second paradigm, referred to as interpretivism, is interested in "free flowing informational exchange" and communicational procedure that reduces the predictability of answers and understands the interview as a site in which new knowledge is actively constructed. Individual "respondents are not so much [viewed as] repositories of knowledge—treasuries of information awaiting excavation, so to speak—[but] as constructors of knowledge in collaboration with interviewers" (Holstein and Gubrium, 2002: 113). This new knowledge can be understood within the boundaries of the interview situation—a perspective that has been adopted by ethnomethodological enquiry (Garfinkel, 1967: 112; Cicourel, 1964, 1974)—or it can be interpreted beyond the actual situation of the interview and in relation to realities and social processes that are connected to the individuals' life experience and talked about in the interview.

The latter view is the one adopted by ethnographic research which relies on various sources of data—including interviews—that are triangulated in order to construct meaning across time and space. Ethnography is the broad approach within which this volume and my own research are anchored. By expanding the scope of ethnomethodological enquiry I argue that the interview has great value for understanding social processes that lie beyond the moment of the interview itself. Participants in the context of my research are educational practitioners who are seen as experienced members of specific professional communities. As individuals they are socially and historically situated and involved in educational processes where they adopt specific roles. Therefore, I wish to argue that conducting *retrospective interviews* with members of those communities create a space for reflection on joint practice which is not only useful as a method for building understanding about new realities (outside of the interview situation) and about social change as viewed from the perspective of the school, but also a valid means to inform educational theory concerned with pedagogy and learning.

CONTEXT OF MY RESEARCH AND HOW IT CONNECTS TO OTHER STRANDS OF RESEARCH

My research was based in a two-way immersion programme in a state primary school in Frankfurt, Germany. In this programme two languages, Italian and German, were taught across the curriculum to children from monolingual German and bilingual German-Italian or other mixed multilingual background (further details about the research are provided later in this chapter). One central feature of the classroom pedagogy was team-teaching which involved practitioners from different linguistic and sociocultural backgrounds (Italian-German). Aiming at building a bilingual and bicultural curriculum they engaged in a dialogue between different (national) pedagogical cultures. They thereby crossed national and institutional boundaries bringing about institutional and pedagogical change within the German school system. Creating new forms of practice on the grounds of daily educational routines, practitioners took on a key role in constructing new knowledge in multilingual education and transformative pedagogy (Millard, 2006).

I want to argue here that conducting *retrospective interviews* with those social actors served as an appropriate means to crystallise this new knowledge featuring practitioners in a leading role in the knowledge-building process. This goal resonates with previous and ongoing research in the fields of life histories and action research. Life history research uses interviews as its key methodological tool, whereas action research emphasises the role of practitioners as agents of social change and legitimate contributors to the construction of academic knowledge. Research in both fields sheds light on institutional practice and change considering different viewpoints and the role of individual agency. Life history research in the 1970s and '80s investigated links between the trajectories of individuals and the history of schooling (Smith and Keith, 1971) and studied institutional practices in relation to changes in the teaching profession which were interpreted from the viewpoint of practitioners (Lortie, 1975). The conditions of teaching and teachers themselves ceased to be viewed as interchangeable and time-less, and life histories were an "attempt to locate the immediate experiences they document within the wider context of historical background" (Good-son, 1981: 71). More recently, life history interviews have been used as a methodological tool to explore the trajectory of teachers in schools in the UK (Goodson, 1983, 1990; Goodson and Sikes, 2001), including the tra-jectories of teachers from minority ethnic groups (Pole, 1999, 2001). Other studies within the ethnographic tradition have employed a mixed meth-ods approach—including classroom observation and recordings as well as in-depth interviews with teachers—looking at language and power in the classroom mediated through language choice and code-switching around the negotiation of curricular and non-curricular knowledge (Martin-Jones and Saxena, 1996, 2003).

The study on which this chapter draws investigated bilingual team-teaching as a particular pedagogical feature and therefore relates to studies in the fields of English as a second or additional language and multilingual classroom pedagogy. Existing work on bilingual team-teaching (Arkoudis, 2003; Bourne, 1997; Bourne and McPake, 1991; Crandall, 1993; Creese, 2005; Davison, 2006; Hurst and Davison, 2005; Mohan, Leung and Davi-son, 2001) has been describing and modelling this still relatively rare edu-cational practice, but points consistently to power asymmetries between language and subject teachers and the uneven status of the languages involved. The majority language tends to inhabit higher authority and cur-ricular status, whereas minority languages are marginalised as temporary learning tools only valid in accommodating the transition of non-native speakers of English into the (monolingual English) mainstream education. In two-way immersion (or dual language education) this principle is main-tained by keeping both languages separate in monolingually taught units (Hadi-Tabassum, 2006) which excludes the possibility of bilingual team-teaching in one classroom.

This study aimed at discussing new models of good practice in team-teaching under conditions where two teachers are co-teaching in one class-room using both languages and delivering a bicultural curriculum which represents complementary parts of the teachers' individual experience. Practices of this kind are still understudied. I want to argue that *retrospective interviews* with practitioners who are involved in this type of team-teaching practice are an indispensable methodological tool and contribute in an important way to our understanding of the process of bilingual/bicultural curriculum building. Generally, I agree with Elliott (1990) that "knowledge [which is] generated within specific disciplines must not become dissociated from people's [teachers'] attempts to resolve the complex problems which emerge in the circumstances of their lives" (Elliott, 1990: 12). In very concrete terms, the curriculum development taking place in the German/Italian bilingual programme evolved around the practice of individuals whose previous experiences and new learning fed into ongoing and further curricular planning and bilingual teaching practice. The retrospective interviews revealed crucial interactive episodes in that process. They helped to elucidate the rationale and changing positions of the practitioners who brought different bodies of knowledge to their professional collaboration. Due to her transnational trajectory, the experience of the Italian teacher, in particular, was dislocated (Baynham and De Fina, 2005) and relocated in a new institutional, cultural and pedagogical context.

In this chapter, I want to argue that teachers who are involved in cross-language, cross-subject team-teaching create new types of educational practice and become agents of a "living educational theory" (Whitehead and McNiff, 2006; MacLure, 1996; J. Marshall, 2004; McNiff and Whitehead, 2002). They are no longer seen as "shadowy figures on the educational landscape mainly known, or unknown through large scale surveys" (Ball and Goodson, 1985: 6). As Becker (2002) has put it, they can become a mobilising force "when an area of study has grown stagnant, has pursued the investigation of a few variables with ever-increasing precision but has received dwindling increments of knowledge from the pursuit. When this occurs, investigation might well proceed by gathering personal documents which suggest new variables, new questions, and new processes, using the rich though unsystematic data to provide a needed reorientation of the field" (Becker, 2002: 83). Exploring the viewpoints of practitioners provides us with valuable "insights into the new moves to restructure and reform schooling, into new policy concerns and directives" (Goodson, 1992: 11). At the same time, they provide "testimonies [which] expose the shallowness of the managerial, prescriptive view of schooling" (Goodson, 1992: 13). The latter view has come to dominate educational research in times of evaluation-driven and performance indicator-based neo-liberal educational policy.

As this study demonstrates, there is real benefit to be accrued from close collaboration of educational practitioners and academic researchers. Therefore it seems appropriate to revitalise the idea of "conversational research communities" (Elliott, 1990) whose "excellence consists in the qualities they foster in their members, such as intellectual creativity, the courage to say new and interesting things to audiences who want the familiar certainties confirmed, a tolerance of intellectual deviance and methodological pluralism" (Elliott, 1990: 3). In such a forum the retrospective interview should have a central place.

THE RETROSPECTIVE INTERVIEW AS A CONTRIBUTION TO "LIVING EDUCATIONAL THEORY"

The empirical part of this chapter is built around three axes of analysis: The first situates the retrospective interview within the adopted approach of collaborative ethnography and as one particular moment in the longitudinal research process. The second axis investigates it as one specific moment of intercultural transnational dialogue within a conversational research community revolving around practices of cross-linguistic cross-subject team-teaching and bilingual bicultural curriculum development. Thirdly, the retrospective interview is located as a specific moment of educational practice in history and at the crossroads of individual life trajectories and the institutional world of a German mainstream school through which current relations of domination are being articulated.

This chapter focuses on one retrospective interview that was conducted as part of a four year ethnographic study of bilingual literacy teaching and learning in the two-way (German/Italian) immersion programme in Frankfurt. The study was carried out between 2003 and 2006 encompassing one cycle of primary schooling in the German system. From the beginning, the research process developed as a joint endeavour of teachers and academic researchers: I spent one school day per week with the same bilingual class over a period of four years. Throughout the entire research process, joint reflection on bilingual learning and current teaching practice formed an essential part of our enquiry. It took various conversational forms, including informal talk after and in between lessons, during pauses in the school yard and during lunch breaks. It also included more planned episodes of extensive, in-depth reflection, such as discussions over dinner at my home or the teachers' home. These longer discussions were recorded and analysed. They included the interview presented here.[1]

These ongoing activities of collaborative investigation and reflection also took a visible shape in specific public events. For the European Day of Languages in 2004 the German teacher and I designed posters which presented the approach to bilingual literacy learning adopted in the programme, including photographs and texts written by me, the teachers and the children. The posters were exhibited in the school corridor. Another event, an exhibition in the city's town hall in 2006, celebrated the foundation of the German-Italian parents association which was instrumental in establishing the bilingual school project. We contributed posters to that event which presented bilingual science and maths teaching.

Our collaborative research activities culminated in a joint presentation (involving me and the Italian and the German teachers) at an international conference at Frankfurt University in 2006. The presentation discussed sources, practices and experiences of intercultural maths teaching around the use of the *abaco*: a model for representing large numbers and calculating with them. This presentation highlighted the different culturally-situated view points of the teachers and the children as well as the development of new practices of intercultural maths teaching. These reflections were framed with reference to multimodality and to the challenges of cross-language and cross-subject team-teaching in a bilingual programme in the German school system (see also Budach, Dreher and Spanù, 2008).

In sum, we understand educational research as collaboration between teachers and researchers and a research conversation in which practice is reflected on and knowledge constructed in ways to contribute to theory. Therefore, the interview which will be discussed here can be seen as contribution "to an overall research enterprise [which is not] considered in isolation or [seen as] producing definitive results of its own" (Becker, 2002: 86). It is rather understood as situated within an ongoing process of engagement with reflexive teaching practice at one particular moment in time. On a time scale, the moment of the interview is located towards the end of year 3. As the Italian teacher joined the project only at the beginning of year 2, the reflection undertaken here spans over a period of two years of joint practice of team-teaching and regular conversations with me as the researcher.

ONE MOMENT IN AN INTERCULTURAL, TRANSNATIONAL DIALOGUE

Team-teaching within this bilingual programme took up six hours per week. Teaching activities were prepared and conducted by both teachers jointly. They included language and curricular content in Italian and German and an equal share of both curricular cultures. Both teachers were bilingual Italian and German speaking, but from different sociolinguistic and professional institutional backgrounds. Patrizia, whose first language was Italian, had been socialised through schooling in Italy and trained as a primary school teacher in Sardinia where she worked for several years and became a member of the Italian teaching community. Ulrike, whose first language was German, had been socialised through schooling in Germany and trained as a primary school teacher there. She has been working within a German institution for more than fifteen years incorporating the institutional culture and specific professional norms.

For both women team-teaching was a new experience through which they were encountering and needed to negotiate difference on a daily basis. Difference resided mainly in divergent teaching methods, learning materials and culturally-specific approaches to curricular planning.

Comparing maths teaching in grade 3 in a German and Italian context revealed several differences. They related to: (1) curricular progression: in Italy summing up numbers by writing them down in columns is already introduced in grade 1; (2) different strategies of calculating: there is variation in the methods of adding numbers and writing down the amount carried over from a previous sum; and (3) different tools are used to represent maths knowledge—take, for example, the *abaco* which is more consistently used in Italy.

These cultural differences were being discovered by the teachers as they engaged in primary maths teaching and they were being negotiated by the teachers through team-teaching. The process of intercultural dialogue can be described in three steps: (1) discovering difference; (2) explaining differing mathematical rationales and procedures to each other; (3) transforming learning about difference into new teaching methods that are adapted to the local circumstances of maths learning in grade 3. In following this process, the teachers were becoming sensitised to the plurality of approaches. Through their own learning they developed confidence in building plurality into the curriculum and this helped to improve the conditions for children's learning. Both teachers affirm this. The following extracts show how this dialogue was recounted by the teachers during the retrospective interview.

Example 19.1   P: Patrizia (Italian teacher), U: Ulrike (German teacher).

P: io ho avuto difficoltà essendo la prima volta insegnare matematica nella scuola tedesca. ho avuto difficoltà per capire com'è il ragionamento dei bambini oppure come gli insegnanti tedeschi insegnano la matematica [. . .] quindi io ho imparato quando abbiamo parlato tra di noi abbiamo fatto proprio gli esempi direttamente su carte come contiamo noi in italiano e come contano loro in tedesco in Germania no?

U: esatto abbiamo proprio insegnato [lachen] il mio metodo a lei e il suo metodo a me

P: prima di tutto

U: ecco

P: I had difficulty since it was it the first time for me of teaching maths in a German school. I had difficulty understanding the [mathematical] reasoning of the children and how Germans teach math [. . .] So I learned while we were talking between the two of us, really doing examples on paper explaining how we calculate [us] in Italian and how they count [them] in Germany, right?

U: exactly we really taught each other [laughing] my method to her and her method to me

P: at first

U: that's it

In the first example, Patrizia, the Italian teacher constructs herself as a novice in a new environment of schooling. However, this experience was not a process of unidirectional adaptation, it soon became mutual learning in which both teachers, the Italian and the German teacher, engaged in explaining differences observed to each other, discussing and doing exercises jointly on paper. In this way, both teachers constructed a model of "adult learning" that forms the basis of new teaching practices in their bilingual classroom (Becker, 2002).

This activity has the potential to serve as a model for negotiating cultural difference and informing intercultural pedagogy. In this bilingual programme, the intercultural dialogue was brought about by transnational migration and the internationalisation of education. It provides an example of how more plurality can be included in classroom pedagogies in ways which would not only enhance the learning of children with multiple sociolinguistic backgrounds, but also monolingual children who are often erroneously conceived as a homogenous group of learners with undifferentiated needs.

After having worked out the intercultural differences for themselves, Patrizia and Ulrike decided to teach both methods to the children. They thereby drew on their own experience of adult learning transforming the different approaches into a model that they considered suitable for the children's learning. This was a difficult decision to make in the first place, as both teachers were concerned about confusing the children by presenting them with different ways of calculating instead of just one. However, as the following example shows, their concern proved to be unfounded as the children were able to follow and understand two different approaches, just like their teachers, and, in the end, they were able to choose the approach which was more suitable for themselves.

Example 19.2

U: non era tanto difficile era meno difficile di quello che pensavo sinceramente pensavo che avessero più difficoltà invece forse avendo due persone una italiana e una persona tedesca che una spiegava così e l'altra spiegava così non si sono confusi veramente posso dire che non si sono confusi . . . mh certamente all'inizio abbiamo esercitato

P: si ci voleva molti esercizi e pazienza

U: si e poi abbiamo fatto il metodo italiano per un po' di tempo poi dovevano fare il metodo tedesco per prima capire tutte e due e poi potevano scegliere però una volta capito non c'erano problemi

U: it was not so difficult it was actually less difficult than I expected I thought they would have had more difficulty. Maybe having the two of us, an Italian and a German person, one explaining like this and the other like that, meant that they didn't get confused.

I really can say that they didn't get confused . . . mh in the beginning we did exercises, of course.

P: yes it needed lots of exercises and patience

U: yes and then we did the Italian method for some time and then they had to do the German one until they had understood both. Then they could choose, but once they had understood there was no problem

As Ulrike states in this example, the children might have been helped by the fact that they could rely on one expert per language who embodied one specific way of approaching a maths task and by the fact that both approaches were introduced as equally valuable and legitimate to the children.[2] Still, the opening to include diversity can be considered as an innovative pedagogic choice and the outcome of a productive intercultural encounter. This is in line with the idea that innovation is enhanced in situations in which "we experience ourselves as living contradictions when our values are denied in our practice" (Whitehead and McNiff, 2006: 26).

Learning from their own experience, these two teachers were daring to cross national monolithic traditions of subject teaching by amplifying the content and methods of their teaching. They were able to revise their own adult beliefs and actively engage in observing children's learning from a new perspective. They committed themselves to constantly revise and improve their teaching practice and the children's conditions for learning.

This process was embedded in a research conversation which contributed to knowledge exchange. The following example illustrates how both teachers received and applied advice from another academic who commented on our joint presentation at an international conference. Whereas the Italian and German methods were presented by the teachers consecutively, the academic suggested introducing both at the same time in order to enable children to compare and reflect on the differences between both approaches.

Example 19.3

U: mi ricordo benissimo perché la [name of professor] al convegno che dopo nella discussione a detto ma perché non presentate tutte e due metodi

P: infatti mi ricordo [. . .] non l'avevamo fatto contemporaneamente proprio perché la nostra paura era di confonderli [i bambini]

U: infatti si è si è verificato quello che a detto lei non era un problema per i bambini ci facciamo più problemi noi

P: hai ragione

U: I recall perfectly well when [name of professor] at the conference asked us why we didn't present both methods simultaneously

P: yes I remember that [. . .] no we had not done this just because we were afraid of confusing them [the children]

U: but, in fact, what she said turned out to be true it wasn't a prob-
          lem for the children it is actually us who are making it one
P: you are right

As we saw in Example 19.3, both teachers decided to introduce both methods (almost) simultaneously, and thereby demonstrated a higher level of confidence in the children's autonomy as learners. They also challenged (their own) settled beliefs which tended to be grounded in monolithic and monolingual national school systems with distinct cultural traditions. Over the two years of close collaboration, the two teachers had become more confident about engaging in innovation. This growth in confidence and reflective practice has been described by Davison (2006) as part and parcel of the development of partnership within team teaching:

> Initially struggling to adapt to routines and reluctant to change, teach-
> ers become gradually more concerned about their impact on pupils,
> then ready to respond to feedback on teaching. This model of devel-
> opment, moving from *self-concerns* to *task management* to *learner
> impact* and *teaching innovation* has been confirmed by many other
> studies as a typical development pattern for novice teacher growth.
> (Davison, 2006: 459)

As indicated above, one of the innovations introduced into the German curriculum in this bilingual programme was the *abaco*, a model to repre-sent large numbers spatially, which is common in Italian maths teaching. The teachers reflected on this innovation as follows in the retrospective interview.

Example 19.4
P: cioè e proprio un metodo molto antico molto vecchio dai Greci
          mi è sembrato una cosa originale proporlo anche nelle nostra
          classe proprio perché facendo matematica insieme sento un lav-
          oro molto indicato anche per i nostri bambini
P: [. . .] invece con l'abaco [. . .] riesci con due con due pezzi di
          pasta riesci a portare anche le migliaia i numeri grandi [risa]
U: perché in genere per questa operazione in genere non c'è materi-
          ale non c'è materiale adatto
P: infatti
U: e l'abaco invece è adatto anche per i numeri più grandi

P: it's a really old method from the Greeks, I thought this would be
          an original method to use in our class well since we were doing
          maths together I thought this would be appropriate for our chil-
          dren to work with

P: [. . .] with the abaco [. . .] you are able to represent two thou-
        sands, big numbers, with just two pieces of pasta [laughter]
U: because in general there is no appropriate material (offered by the
        German curriculum)
P: indeed
U: but the abaco is appropriate for representing bigger numbers

Innovative teaching of the kind documented above impacted on the chil-dren's learning in two ways: firstly, it diversified the means of access to knowledge by introducing a multimodal dimension (Kress et al., 2001). Through numbers and the numeric code *and* through a model, it opened up different avenues for cognitive learning and facilitated access to the cur-riculum for children with different needs; secondly, the use of the *abaco* in bilingual math teaching opened up discussion about culture and identity. The children with an Italian background identified the *abaco* as part of "their Italian culture" and started reflecting on mathematical methods as culturally based. However, it is interesting to note that, having been intro-duced to both approaches to maths tasks, some children adopted a method that was not in line with their preferred ethnic affiliation. This suggests that the appropriate method for learning relates to individual learning styles rather than to an essentialist notion of cultural belonging.

THE RETROSPECTIVE INTERVIEW AS MOMENT IN INSTITUTIONAL HISTORY

Team-teaching as it is described here generates new teaching practices and curricular change. However, as this two-way immersion project was embedded in the German context this innovative practice was also submit-ted to the constraints of the dominant institutional culture in which the German language and German curriculum, generally, have more authority and higher prestige.

Whereas both languages, Italian and German, have equal status as a medium of instruction within the bilingual project, the wider discursive order which places German as dominant can neither be denied nor neutra-lised. Even the immediate concrete work of team-teaching, such as plan-ning classroom activities and selecting teaching material, showed traces of that unequal weight and misbalance between both institutional cultures.

Example 19.5
P: abbiamo guardato prima il libro tedesco che cosa ci presente il
        libro tedesco ma non volendo solo presentare una cosa tedesca
        abbiamo guardato insieme i libri italiani di seconda e di terza in
        questo caso anche se la classe era di terza e abbiamo visto tutti

i diversi esercizi che c'erano in italiano nei libri italiani e lì abbiamo soprattutto con il consiglio della maestra tedesca secondo te questo va bene va bene per i bambini tedeschi

P: we first took the German book and were looking at what was presented there. But as we didn't just want to present German content we also had a look at Italian text books and exercises in Italian from grade 2 and 3. From there we decided especially following the advice of the German teacher what according to you would be appropriate for the German children

The words of Patrizia, the Italian teacher, shown in Example 19.5 above, shed light on the status of bilingual education and its relationship to mainstream schooling. Team-teaching in the bilingual project can be compared to activities as part of the *curriculum as practice* (Reid, 1992) which starts from the assumption that both languages, Italian and German, are equal in status. However, another level of *curriculum as institution* which refers to established institutional curricular norms enforces the authority and superior status of German, because, in addition to the bilingual curriculum, the German curriculum also has to be followed.

The quotation above evokes both discursive orders, but alludes to the superiority of German. This also shows in the way Patrizia addresses Ulrike, her German colleague. On the one hand, she creates closeness and emphasises an equal partnership in team collaboration when she uses the first person plural pronoun and states "we wanted to present both contents". On the other hand, she admits the superiority of the German curriculum when she refers to her German colleague in much more formal terms and using the third person stressing her professional status as the "maestra tedesca" whose advice needs to be followed. Furthermore, she highlights the fact that German textbooks are consulted first, and that the needs of the German children are considered with priority.

CONCLUSION

Methodological choices in research should be guided by the kinds of research questions that we want to ask. In this chapter I argue that current educational research can benefit greatly from innovative practice that is being developed by practitioners in daily teaching activity. The documentation of those practices necessitates the active contribution of educational practitioners and close collaboration between practitioners and researchers. In this context, the retrospective interview can be understood as a site where this collaboration is enacted and where new knowledge is being formulated. By looking at cross-language, cross-subject team-teaching which is carried out by social actors with different linguistic and cultural backgrounds, this case study highlights the potential of collaborative ethnographic research and its capacity to reflect on new realities of schooling in times of late modernity. These times are, of course, characterised by increasing transnational migration and the internationalisation of education. In this context, the retrospective interview helps to understand how diversity is not only a social reality which creates challenges, but it shows how diversity can be used as a pedagogical resource to address the learning and identity needs of children with different backgrounds, opening up various routes for accessing content and identifying with what is learned in more than one way.

NOTES

1. In addition, interviews (of a retrospective and/or task-based nature) were also conducted with children, parents and community/school representatives. These ethnographic research interviews were complemented by extended classroom observation and recordings of classroom interaction.
2. It was noticeable that calculation methods that were chosen by the children did not in all cases correspond to their socio-cultural background. This shows that methods are historically formed, conventionalised cultural products which have been identified as national, but which are neither essentially specific to a certain culture nor the most suitable learning tools for all members of a "national community of learners".

REFERENCES

Arkoudis, S. 2003. Teaching English as a second language in science classes: incommensurate epistemologies. *Language and Education* 17(3): 161–73.

Ball, S. and Goodson, I. 1985. *Teachers' Lives and Careers*. London: Routledge Falmer.

Baynham, M. and De Fina, A. (eds) 2005. *Dislocations/Relocations: Narratives of Displacement*. Manchester: St Jerome.

Becker, H. S. 2002. The life history and the scientific mosaic. In *Qualitative Research Methods*, ed. D. Weinberg, 79–87. Malden, MA: Blackwell.

Bourne, J. 1997. The continuing revolution: teaching as learning in the mainstream multilingual classroom. In *English as an Additional Language*, ed. C. Leung and C. Cable, 77–88. York: NALDIC.

Bourne, J. and McPake, J 1991. *Partnership Teaching: Co-operative Teaching Strategies for English Language Support in Multilingual Classrooms*. London: HMSO.

Briggs, C. 1986. *Learning How to Ask: A Sociolinguistic Appraisal of the Role of the Interviewer in Social Science Research*. Cambridge: Cambridge University Press.

Budach, G., Dreher, U. and Spanù, P. 2008. Se non è chiaro prendete l'abaco. Curriculumsentwicklung im Schnittpunkt von Zweisprachigkeit, Team-Teaching und Multimodalität. In *Écoles Plurilingues—Multilingual Schools: Konzepte, Institutionen und Akteure*, ed. G. Budach, J. Erfurt and M. Kunkel (Hrsg), 291–316. Frankfurt: Peter Lang.

Cicourel, A. V. 1964. *Method and Measurement in Sociology*. New York: Free Press.

———. 1974. *Theory and Method in a Study of Argentine Fertility*. New York: Free Press.

Corbin, J. M. and Strauss, A. 2008. *Basics of Qualitative Research: Techniques and Procedures for Developing Grounded Theory.* Los Angeles: Sage.

Crandall, J. 1993. Current directions in curriculum development for culturally and linguistically diverse children. In *Policy and Practice in the Education of Culturally and Linguistically Diverse Students: View from Language Educators,* ed. G. R. Tucker, 13–25. Alexandria, VA: TESOL.

Creese, A. 2005. *Teacher Collaboration and Talk in Multilingual Classrooms.* Clevedon: Multilingual Matters.

Davison, C. 2006. Collaboration between ESL and content teachers: how do we know when we are doing it right? *International Journal of Bilingual Education and Bilingualism* 9(4): 454–75.

Elliot, J. 1990. Educational research in crisis: performance indicators and the decline of excellence. *British Educational Research Journal* 16(1): 3–18.

Flick, U. 2009. *An Introduction to Qualitative Research.* London: Sage.

Garfinkel, H. 1967. *Studies in Ethnomethodology.* Englewood Cliffs, NJ: Prentice-Hall.

Goodson, I. 1981. Becoming an academic subject. *British Journal of Sociology of Education* 2(2): 163–80.

———. 1983. The use of life history in the study of schooling. *Interchange* 11(4): 62–76.

———. ed. 1990. *Studying Teachers' Lives.* London: Routledge.

———. 1992. *Studying Teachers' Lives: An Emergent Field of Inquiry.* London: Routledge

Goodson, I. and Sikes, P. 2001. *Life History Research in Educational Settings.* Buckingham: Open University Press.

Gorden, R. L. 1987. *Interviewing: Strategy, Techniques, and Tactics.* Homewood, IL: Dorsey

Hadi-Tabassum, S. 2006. *Language, Space and Power: A Critical Look at Bilingual Education.* Clevedon: Multilingual Matters.

Hollway, W. and Jefferson, T. 2000. *Doing Qualitative Research Differently: Free Association, Narrative and the Interview Method.* London: Sage.

Holstein, J. A. and Gubrium, J. F. 2002. Active interviewing. In *Qualitative Research Methods,* ed. D. Weinberg, 112–26. Malden, MA: Blackwell.

Hurst, D. and Davison, C. 2005. Collaboration on the curriculum: focus on secondary ESL. In *Case Studies in TESOL: Teacher Education for Language and Content Integration,* ed. J. Crandall and D. Kaufman, 41–66. Alexandria, VA: TESOL.

Hyman, H. H., Cobb, W. J. Feldman, J. J., Hart, C. W. and Stember, C. H. 1975. *Interviewing in Social Research.* Chicago: University of Chicago Press.

Johnson, B. and Christensen, L. B. 2007. *Educational Research: Quantitative, Qualitative, and Mixed Approaches.* London: Sage.

Kress, G., Charalampos, T., Ogborn, J. and Jewitt, C. 2001. *Multimodal Teaching and Learning: The Rhetorics of the Science Classroom.* London: Continuum.

Kvale, S. 2007. *Doing Interviews.* London: Sage.

Lortie, D. C. 1975. *School Teacher: A Sociological Study.* Chicago: University of Chicago Press.

MacLure, M. 1996. Narratives of becoming an action researcher. *British Journal of Educational Research* 22(3): 273–86.

Marshall, C. and Rossman, G. 2006. *Designing Qualitative Research.* London: Sage.

Marshall, J. 2004. Living systemic thinking: exploring quality in first-person action research. *Action Research* 2(3): 309–29.

Martin-Jones, M. and Saxena, M. 1996. Turn-taking, power asymmetries, and the positioning of bilingual participants in classroom discourse. *Linguistics and Education* 8: 105–23.

———. 2003. Bilingual resources and "funds of knowledge" for teaching and learning in multi-ethnic classrooms. In *Multilingual Classroom Ecologies*, ed. A. Creese and P. Martin, 107–22. Clevedon: Multilingual Matters.

McNiff, J and Whitehead, J. 2002. *Action Research: Principles and Practice* (2nd edition). London: Routledge.

Millard, E. 2006. Transformative pedagogy: teachers creating a literacy of fusion. In *Travel Notes from the New Literacy Studies*, ed. K. Pahl and J. Rowsell, 234–53. Clevedon: Multilingual Matters.

Mohan, B., Leung, C. and Davison, C. (eds) 2001. *English as a Second Language in the Mainstream: Teaching, Learning and Identity*. London: Pearson Education.

Pole, C. 1999. Black teachers giving voice: choosing and experiencing education. *Teacher Development* 3(3): 313–28.

———. 2001. Black teachers: curriculum and career. *The Curriculum Journal* 12(3): 347–64.

Reid, W. A. 1992. *The Pursuit of Curriculum: Schooling and the Public Interest*. Norwood, NJ: Ablex.

Silverman, D. 2009. *Doing Qualitative Research*. London: Sage.

Smith, L. M. and Keith, P. M. 1971. *The Social Psychological Aspects of School Building Design*. Report No. CRP-S-223. St. Louis, MO: Washington University, Graduate Institute of Education. (ERIC Document Reproduction Service No. ED 010 672)

Thomas, W. I. and Znaniecki, F. 1918–20. *The Polish Peasant in Europe and America: Monograph of an Immigrant Group*. Chicago: University of Chicago Press.

Whitehead, J. and McNiff, J. 2006. *Action Research: Living Theory*. London: Sage.

20 Collaborative Practice, Linguistic Anthropological Enquiry and Mediation between Researcher and Practitioner Discourses

Alexandra Jaffe

This chapter explores what it means to take a critical ethnographic approach to language, culture and identity within an applied anthropology framework, and considers the unique purchase on an applied agenda offered by linguistic anthropological perspectives and tools. At the foundation of this kind of applied linguistic anthropology is collaboration between researcher and practitioners; collaboration which implies the development of some shared (rather than researcher-imposed) goals and methods, the reduction of hierarchies between researcher and researched, an appreciation for multiple types of expertise, and, potentially, some form of joint authorship. In this chapter, I reflect on the complexities and potentials of this process through the lens of my own collaborative experiences with Corsican bilingual teachers and other language activists. Drawing on linguistic anthropological perspectives on talk as joint action, I argue that what is at issue in these forms of collaboration is creating a nexus of practice (see Scollon, 2001) and discourse that mediates, in some productive way, differences between researchers' and practitioners' respective professional Discourses or habituses. This is no easy task, but I will argue that this process: (a) helps to create the conditions in which local actors will use linguistic anthropological perspectives/data, and (b) is itself a form of ethnographic enquiry that has rich implications for building linguistic anthropological knowledge.

The impetus for this chapter comes out of the expanding role and recognition of applied and engaged public anthropology. This recognition has grown within the discipline (see for example commentaries by two past Presidents of the American Anthropological Association: Goodman, 2008; Peacock, 2007). Conceiving of fieldwork in collaborative terms is an integral part of this kind of work, for several reasons. As Lassiter points out, collaboration between ethnographers and those they study grows out of a dialogic view of culture, communication and knowledge production. It includes the recognition of the ways in which both ethnographers and their interlocutors "exist within and partake of a larger economy of representations in varied and complicated ways" (2005: 93), a perspective anchored in the critical anthropology pioneered by such works as *Writing Culture* (Clifford and Marcus, 1986). Collaboration, in contrast with the more affectively oriented notion of building "rapport" in order to advance the ethnographer's interests, "entails joint production, but with overlapping as well as differing purposes, negotiation, contestation and uncertain outcomes" (Marcus, 2001: 521). As a consequence, Lassiter writes that:

> collaborative ethnography is ultimately about power and, I would add, control—about who has the right to represent whom and for what purposes and whose discourse will be privileged in the ethnographic text. Americanists, feminists, and postmodernists (as well as applied and public anthropologists) have long dealt with this issue in various ways. (2005: 102)

Over the last decades, a great deal of linguistic anthropological work on indigenous, minority and 'endangered' languages has engaged with these issues of power and representation, both in research design and in the production of ethnographic texts. In 1988, Brandt characterised the field of linguistic anthropological research on languages in Native American communities as having already "changed from the solo fieldworker model . . . to the collaborative model of jointly constructed work with native speakers on goals defined by the community, tribe, school or program" (1988: 322). These close collaborations have often been partnerships in which traditional hierarchies between ethnographers and subjects are heavily mitigated, both because of ideological commitments and because of growth in community members' own professional training as linguists, educators or anthropologists (see Leap, 1988). These ideological commitments include the legitimation of local or indigenous epistemologies within a human rights framework (see McCarty et al., 2005) and in numerous cases have led to collaboration in the form of co-authorship. In some of these jointly produced texts, the outside anthropologist's voice can be subordinated to the voice and agenda of the inside partner. For example, in the introduction to their article on language-planning efforts involving five traditional Athabascan languages, Dementi-Leonard and Gilmore write that "[w]e have chosen to organize and report our findings in ways that are consistent with that knowledge base and its epistemology . . . [and] to rely more heavily on local experts, their knowledge, interpretations, and meanings, and less on scholarly outsiders' analyses and categorisations" (1999: 38).

The ethnographic research in Corsican bilingual schools that I conducted in 2000 led to the kind of researcher-practitioner collaboration that I view as the foundation of applied linguistic anthropology. This experience helped to clarify for me the importance of linguistic anthropology for the study of research collaborations in applied anthropological work. First of all, collaboration and cooperation are discursive practices and accomplishments, and thus studying—and attending—to these processes in the interaction between researcher and community partners is absolutely crucial. As Gottlieb argues in a 1995 piece about the "difference collaboration makes in the very practice of ethnography," it is important to attend to the details of variations between different types and practices of collaborative work (1995: 23), and a detailed, linguistic, interactional focus can do just that. The examples I will be using centre around the joint production of texts, where linguistic anthropology is uniquely positioned to address questions such as: (1) how particular practices of text creation reflect and constitute social relations and hierarchies, (2) how professional (and all cultural) practice is embedded in specific literacy practices and Discourses and (3) the political and ideological dimensions of the writing process and the final products alike. Secondly, the goal of applied linguistic anthropological research—the production of new forms of knowledge of interest to all participants—also has to be understood as a discursive process. This shifts the focus from an applied linguistic anthropology that takes language "X" as its object, to one that fully engages with the discursive foundations of the process of inquiry and exchange between ethnographers and the people whose lives they study. This includes an attention to the epistemological foundations of the various Discourses that collaboration brings into contact, as well as how legitimacy, identity, knowledge and equality emerge through interaction and "little-d" discourse. Ultimately, this leads us away from viewing the targets of applied research and collaboration as static, emic goals. Thus in contrast to a perspective that frames applied anthropology as responding in a relatively straightforward way to what community members want to know, I argue for a view of collaboration in applied anthropology as having the potential to shift what the people we work with think they want to know as well as what we think we understand.

Let me turn, then, to some ethnographic specifics about the workshop/conference that I organised in 2006 in collaboration with a bilingual teachers' association and, in particular, with two Corsican teachers, Marylene Menozzi and Pascale Pergola, whose classes I had observed five years earlier. I begin with a discussion of my original research in 2000 to lay two important pieces of groundwork for the 2006 event. First, there is the question of my understandings of the gaps between my professional discourse and theirs. Second, I address the kinds of relationships we built up over time that eventually led to the 2006 conference.

DISCOURSE AND DISCOURSE: EPISTEMOLOGICAL AND SOCIAL FRAMES

The first gap between my Discourse and the teachers' has to do with the direction of communication and learning. As an ethnographer, I was primarily concerned with understanding their D/discourses. I had a lot to learn—from the specific phrases and formulas that teachers trained in France use to talk about parts of the curriculum, to how they described and thought about children's developmental stages, to how they described various pedagogical goals and practices. And then there was the Discourse—or habitus—of teaching in France, teaching in Corsica, and teaching bilingually. This included their shared histories of school, linguistic and cultural experience, their formal training to become teachers, and underlying ideological premises about language, identity, learning that permeated all these experiences. The teachers, on the other hand, were not on a focussed mission to learn similar things about me; they were there to get on with their work. The point to be made here is that these differences in our professional roles and responsibilities and thus in the focus of our energies led us to have different forms of engagement with one another, and this had implications for the nature of our collaboration.

My focus on learning about their lives and practices, however, was accompanied by an effort to take advantage of every opportunity for give and take with them, and through this, to make it possible for them to learn about my perspectives and developing analyses. This included a commitment on my part to participate, in my own capacity as an ethnographer, linguist and anthropologist, in events and activities that were meaningful to them. These included several different kinds of public venues related to bilingualism and bilingual education. In these forums, I usually held more than one role: that is, I was both 'their' American anthropologist and someone who was called upon to speak by academics in the University and the Corsican academy. By the time I took part in these kinds of events, I had come to understand their mixed feelings about academics and academic knowledge. On the one hand, they thought that there was a research void on bilingual education on Corsica that needed to be filled and had a deep respect for higher education and research. At the same time, they cast a critical eye on the producers and products of that research, and disparaged researchers who did not invest sufficiently in understanding the realities of practice, or who did not make the connection, in their writing, between theory and that practice. These sentiments—expressed in a variety of informal contexts and responses to others' work—were (intentionally or unintentionally) powerful forms of socialisation for me. They reinforced my existing sensitivity to how I managed my academic stance when I represented my disciplinary knowledge and my developing understandings of bilingual education on Corsica.

These issues are hardly new ones, but I raise them to draw attention to a more general point, which is that there is an ethnographic process that needs to take place before we can make informed decisions about how to present ourselves and our work—and these presentations shape the kinds of collaborations that our partners can imagine. Additionally, we can view the work of stance "management" itself as a collaborative gesture. That is, I think that my efforts to negotiate the delicate social terrain of speaking authoritatively but not presumptuously about these teachers' practices, in forums where they were present, was a first step towards a more significant collaboration. In some of these public occasions, I did so in Corsican, a language I speak much less fluently than French, thus laying myself open to linguistic scrutiny. These efforts displayed to Pascale and Marylene my willingness to assume responsibility for my own talk and action within the social and discursive fields that mattered to them.

The second discursive gap that I encountered in my initial fieldwork had to do with how the Corsican teachers' training led them to conceptualise the disciplines that would most productively bridge the micro-level of everyday classroom practice and something more generalisable. By attending a month-long continuing education course with Pascale and Marylene near the beginning of my fieldwork, I learned that the sociolinguistic approaches offered by several of the University presenters did not meet their expectations. They felt they already knew a lot about the macro-level sociolinguistic framework, but that there was no "meso" level between this information and the micro-level demands of doing school every day. They identified psycholinguistics as the missing mediating discipline. This led me to do some work to make a case for linguistic anthropology as a possible alternative. For example, near the end of the course, I gave a presentation to the whole group on ethnographic perspectives on language and education, emphasising the way that everyday practice (including specific linguistic routines) is both shaped by and constitutive of wider social, political and ideological issues and processes. I do not think, however, that I really understood how their sentiments were related to models of the articulation of individual development and social process, a point to which I will return later.

Over the course of the year I spent doing fieldwork in their school and other bilingual schools, I took every possible opportunity to exchange ideas with Pascale and Marylene, to reveal my own perspectives and analytical processes, and to involve them as partners in a dialogue about their practice. I sought their feedback on my developing analyses as I transcribed and began to write about and present the data I had collected at various conferences. After I left, I sent them everything I wrote in French, and also translated into French some (but not all) other texts I had originally written in English.

Despite this relationship of mutual respect, support and reciprocity, I would not characterise my initial fieldwork and its immediate aftermath as being applied linguistic anthropology. This is because neither I nor the teachers involved carved out the space or created the conditions in which either of us could work through, in a focussed way, how the data that I had gathered and the frameworks I used to analyse it might be taken up to inform policy or practice on the ground in Corsican bilingual education. That is, even when we met to go over data, that review was really for my benefit, with them acting as consultants for ends defined within my own agenda. The texts that I shared with them were largely transcripts/videos and finished articles. Even when the latter were written in French, they were written for academic audiences only and it was up to Marylene and Pascale to extract relevance for their own practice or thinking.

THE DEVELOPMENT OF A SHARED PROJECT: CONFERENCE PREPARATION

My work became applied, and my relationship became a real collaboration with Marylene and Pascale four years after the initial fieldwork, in 2004, when the three of us began to work together on an international conference/workshop on bilingual education in minority language contexts. The initiative began with me, and seed money that I got from my institution to travel and establish contact with researcher-practitioner teams in Canada, New Zealand, Wales, Ireland and the Val d'Aosta. I organised these visits

Table 20.1   The Eleven Workshop Themes, as Presented in French and English

1. Gestion de l'erreur et de la norme.
   Managing « error » and the norm.
2. Gestion de la variation linguistique dans la langue minoritaire
   Management of linguistic variation in the minority language
3. Alternance/mélange des codes
   Code-switching
4. Littéracie-lecture-écriture: gestion dans les deux langues
   Biliteracy management
5. Théâtre/création dans la langue minoritaire comme outil pédagogique
   Drama and creative activity in the minority language as a pedagogical tool
6. Enseignement bilingue—citoyenneté
   Bilingual education and citizenship
7. Compétences métalinguistiques: repérage, développement
   Metalinguistic competence: identification and development
8. Enseignement bilingue et citoyenneté/valeurs d'ouverture/interculturalité
   Bilingual education and citizenship/intercultural values and identity
9. Intégration des enfants/cultures de l'immigration
   Integration of immigrant children/immigrant cultures
10. Ecole-famille-société: Liens, défis
    School-society-family: links and challenges
11. Enseignement bilingue et pratique coopérative
    Bilingual education and cooperative practice

in order to flesh out my knowledge of the literature with mini site visits and discussions, and identify key issues that were both theoretically compelling and viewed by teachers as central to their practice. Thus from the outset, I made an effort to respond to what I had come to see as an unresolved issue about where the researcher-practitioner nexus was for linguistic anthropological work in contexts of this sort.

The comparative framework and the particular case studies from around the world became the basis for discussion with Pascale, Marylene and other Corsican colleagues working on language and education. On the basis of these discussions, I developed an outline of possible workshop themes and questions, which was then circulated in the bilingual teachers' association *A Scioglilingua* in which Pascale and Marylene were key players. We used that feedback to generate a list of eleven workshop themes (see Table 20.1), which were the basis for an application for funding that we made in the name of the association to the Corsican Territorial Collectivity.

In addition to working closely and intensely together on all the details of the conference organisation—a significant form of fellowship in and of itself—these two teachers and I collaborated on two presentations we made jointly during the course of the conference. We also worked with other members of the association and colleagues at the University of Corsica doing research on bilingual education to write press releases, arrange for newspaper interviews and take part in other forms of media publicity (TV and radio). Below, I focus on just one of the presentations I developed jointly with Marylene, to explore the discourses that we brought into contact and dialogue, in our PowerPoint and in our oral presentation.

COOPERATING ON COOPERATION: JOINT AUTHORSHIP ON THE FREINET METHOD IN THE CLASSROOM

By the time Marylene Menozzi and I began work on our presentation, we had already established a keen shared interest in the topic of co-operative practice. In my original fieldwork, I had drawn up a document describing my perceptions of the goals of the cooperative pedagogies she and Pascale used, and the three of us had discussed this document at some length. Thus we were both operating with a relatively good, mutual understanding of both her teaching philosophy and the metadiscourse she used to describe it. We also shared the experience of a year's worth of examples of practice that she had enacted and I had observed and video- recorded. I did not have the entire corpus at my fingertips when we started to prepare, but I came with several videos of weekly cooperative meetings, two of which were fully transcribed. Marylene also brought data to the table: a raft of documents that she and her students had created over the last several years of teaching. We began to go through this data with the goal of selecting telling examples from the videos, transcripts and written texts to show to our anticipated audience of international researchers and practitioners and other Corsican teachers and researchers who would be attending the conference.

Going through the video and transcript data this time was quite different to what it had been in the past, when it had more or less been a "playback" event, designed to help me understand better or check my interpretations. This time, we were both actively looking for representative elements in the data, which forced us to articulate to each other both the specific elements we found interesting in a particular segment as well as how they related to Marylene's patterns of practice and to the pedagogical framework that guided her overall approach. So we were both engaged in selecting data and relating it to principles, theories, frames of analysis with the shared goal of explaining the teacher's practice to an outside audience, a point to which I will return.

At the same time, we were creating two texts: a set of PowerPoint slides and a handout for our presentation. In doing so, we were faced with very concrete decisions about how to coordinate our two discourses. The result turned out to be a somewhat hybrid document, with the following structure (names in parentheses indicate who did the talking in each particular segment during the conference):

1. Introduction/framework: socialisation to cooperative practice; the link between those practices, ideologies of citizenship, language and the sociolinguistic context (Jaffe)
2. Pedagogical philosophy of the Freinet Cooperative Movement (Jaffe/ Menozzi)
3. Project-based pedagogy (Menozzi)
4. Original documents developed in Menozzi's classes (Menozzi)
5. Transcripts plus videos of classroom practice (Jaffe's transcripts— discussion by both Jaffe and Menozzi)
6. Summary: Connections between philosophy of cooperation and models of society, identity and language learning (Jaffe)

All of the slides were bilingual (French/English) or trilingual (French/ English/Corsican); I supplied the English and consistently put it second in the texts. The presentation itself was multilingual. Marylene spoke in French and voiced Corsican data in Corsican; I spoke in French and English, providing English oral translations for anything that Marylene said that was not written in English on the slides, and providing English or French translations for any of my own comments that were not presented bilingually in those same slides.

If we look at the structure of the presentation, we can see that it opens and closes with a linguistic anthropological discourse or framework, which does give the discipline—and me—a privileged status in this particular event, which, although it incorporated and validated practitioner voices, was in fact structured from within the academy, my world. I think it is important that this took place *after* I had participated in other venues with Marylene and Pascale where the practitioner voice and educational discourse was dominant, and where my disciplinary perspective had been accepted but not central. That is, collaboration, reciprocity and power sharing can take place in a variety of forms over time.

If the academic discourse is structurally privileged, we can also find a significant integration of this discourse with Marylene's own developmental and pedagogical one in the text we put together. Traces of this integration can be found in the opening and closing slides, as well as within the body of the presentation, where we find two pedagogical discourses (the Freinet movement and project-based pedagogy) serving as key frameworks for the presentation and analysis of classroom texts (Marylene's data) and video/transcript data.

If we look at the opening slide that I used to give an overview of the presentation, the linguistic anthropological voice is dominant, but it is mitigated by some of my translation choices. For example, in the first bullet, we find the discourse of language socialisation. This represents my voice. Marylene would have used a term like "apprentissage" ("learning"). The second bullet evokes norms, values, rights and responsibilities; this is also my discourse. Marylene might have described these topics with a cover term like "savoir être"—knowing how to "be" in society, in which the components of the social contract would have been taken for granted. The third bullet uses a

1. Introduction/framework (Jaffe)

L'apprentissage de la coopération Learning Cooperation
** Comment les enfants d'une école sont socialisés aux pratiques coopératives dans des réunions de coopérative dans une école bilingue corse
- How children in a bilingual school are socialized into cooperative practice in cooperative meetings
* Les normes et les valeurs qui sont véhiculées dans la pratique coopérative: droits et responsabilités sociaux et communicatifs
- Social and communicative norms and values transmitted in cooperative practice: rights and responsibilities
* La relation entre ces pratiques et le contexte social et politique dans le cadre du remplacement linguistique (corse->français) et aussi de l'élaboration de la langue ainsi minorée
- The relationship between these practices and the political and social context of language shift and revitalization
* L'articulation de la pratique coopérative et polynomie: appartenance à une communauté de pratique qui n'est pas uniquement linguistique mais communicatif et social.
- The relationship between cooperative practice and polynomy: belonging to a community of practice that is not solely linguistic, but communicative and social.

Slide 20.1

French paraphrase to translate my term "language shift" but it also uses the term "élaboration" to describe the language revitalisation process. This term was widely used by sociolinguists in the Corsican context, and was part of the Corsican-specific professional discourse of bilingual education with which Marylene and other Corsican teachers were very familiar. The same can be said of the term "polynomy," a concept of linguistic unity based on acts of mutual recognition/legitimation within a community of practice pioneered by the Corsican sociolinguist Jean-Baptiste Marcellesi, and widely used in the kinds of continuing education courses for bilingual teachers that Marylene had attended. "Community of practice," however, was from my vocabulary alone. So, if we consider the slide as a text, we see both my dominant authorship and academic voice and a choice to incorporate elements of my discursive repertoire that I had acquired in my involvement in French/Corsican academic circles. In other words, this slide was slightly different from similar slides I created to talk about the same topic to different audiences. But the slide is also not just a text, it was the result of a literacy event involving Marylene's and my talk around each bullet point. Thus behind the choice of "norms, values, rights and responsibilities" was our discussion of the specific norms, values, rights and responsibilities that she had in mind and wished to foster through the specific cooperative practices we were reviewing together. Similarly, the final bullet was the outcome of a discussion in which we returned to some of the themes I had explored with her in my initial fieldwork, this time focussing more explicitly on the relative weight of language versus other forms of shared practice with respect to notions of shared culture and good citizenship. These hidden literacy events were thus more collaborative than the final product.

The next two slides presented the Freinet pedagogical movement; the first summarising principles outlined in the official website of the international organisation to which the movement had given rise, and the second quoting from one of Freinet's original works.

In the next few slides, we presented material Marylene had developed. This included adaptations of texts she had written for a continuing education presentation in the previous year that outlined the specific learning objectives she associated with the marriage of project-based pedagogy and cooperative learning. The language of these documents is psycho-social and developmental, expressed in terms of competencies to be developed in the individual child. It is an institutional discourse of teaching and learning anchored in the teacher's practice and metapractice. The first of these slides is reproduced below, in Slide 20.2.

This slide was followed by examples of documents that Marylene had used in her classes. These included a contract titled "Knowing How to Do and to Be" that laid out expectations for the evaluation of skills, attitudes and competencies associated with good citizenship and was signed by students, teachers and parents. Excerpts from this document are reproduced in the following slide:

L'école Freinet/ The Freinet School (Jaffe/Menozzi)

Par rapport à l'individu
- il s'exprime
  la créativité
  autonomie et choix
  anti-authoritaire
  raisonnement inductif

Perspective on the individual
Self expression
creativity
autonomy/choice
anti-authoritarian
inductive theory of learning

Par rapport au groupe:
- * apprentissage collaborative
- * organisation démocratique
  droits et responsabilités
- * la Coopérative comme structure
  formelle qui comprend élèves
  et enseignants

*collaborative learning
* democratic structure
*rights and responsibilities
* The Cooperative as a formal
  structure, made up of students
  and teachers

Slide 20.2

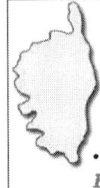

Extracts from C. FREINET "Principes de la pédogogie coopérative"; "Core Pedagogical Principles"

- **Etre plus grand ne signifie pas forcément être au-dessus des autres.**
  Being bigger (grown up) does not mean you are superior to others.
  Les acquisitions ne se font pas comme l'on croit parfois, par l'étude des règles et des lois, mais par l'expérience. Etudier d'abord ces règles et ces lois, en français, en art, en mathématiques, en sciences, c'est placer la charrue devant les boeufs.
  Learning doesn't happen the way we sometimes think, by the study of rules and laws, but by experience. To begin with the study of rules and laws in French, art, math or sciences is to put the cart before the horse.
  Nul - l'enfant pas plus que l'adulte - n'aime être commandé d'autorité.
  No one—and children no more than adults—likes to be ordered around.
  On prépare la démocratie de demain par la démocratie à l'Ecole. Un régime autoritaire à l'Ecole ne saurait être formateur de citoyens démocrates.
  . An authoritarian regime in the school cannot possibly form democratic citizens.

Slide 20.3

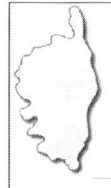

La pédagogie du projet et fonctionnement coopératif
Project-based pedagogy and cooperative practice (Menozzi)

Objectifs spécifiques :	Specific Objectives
¤ **Placer l'enfant au centre de ses apprentissages.**	* place the child at the center of the learning process
¤ Faire de l'enfant l'acteur et l'observateur de son projet d'apprentissage.	* make the child an actor in, and observer of his own learning project
¤ Faire prendre conscience à l'enfant de sa place au sein de la collectivité.	* make the child aware of his/her place in the collectivity
¤ Le rendre capable d'en tenir compte.	* develop his/her abilities to take [this social role] into account

Slide 20.4

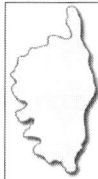

Valutazione CII
Sapè-fà è sapè-esse(Savoir-faire et savoir-être)
◊ Sò capace à manighjà di manera curretta u mo strumentu di travagliu :
mina, penna, pinellu, riga…
(je tiens correctement mon outil de travail :crayon, stylo, pinceau, règle…)
I hold my school instruments correctly : pencils, pens, brushes, rulers.
◊ Sò capace à situà mi in lu quaternu, à nantu à a pagina
(je sais me situer dans le cahier, sur la page).
I am able to situate myself in my notebook and on the written page.
◊Sò capace à rispittà a riga di scrittura, i spazii tra e righe
(je respecte la ligne, l'interligne).
I am able to follow the page rulings and the spaces between the lines.
◊ Sò capace à scrive rispettendu a traccia di e lettare
(je suis capable d'écrire en respectant la trace des lettres).
I am able to trace letters correctly.
◊ Sò capace à frastaglià di manera curretta
(je découpe correctement).
I cut correctly.

Slide 20.5

In the slides discussed so far, we have the co-existence of two independently written framing discourses: a linguistic anthropological one and a pedagogical one. The pedagogical discourse is expressed both as general principles and illustrated in specific classroom examples. On the one hand, the independence of these discourses reflects and legitimates our two different knowledge bases. On the other hand, their juxtaposition in our jointly authored and presented PowerPoint slides indicates the integration of these two vantage points. This integration was made concrete in the next segment of our presentation, which grew out of our joint analysis of a particular video segment we chose to present to the audience. We played the short video segment and presented our audience with the following transcript after explaining the practice: that the children met every week on Monday to discuss past events, raise any social-interactional issues that needed to be resolved, plan out activities for the week and beyond, take stock of ongoing projects and discuss priorities and plans of action for the future.

In this segment, the teacher struggles to get some of the very youngest children (three- to six-year-olds) to talk about something other than behavioral issues in their weekly cooperative meeting. I had noticed this struggle in the data, but hadn't paid much attention to it. I had unconsciously framed it as part of the difficulty of getting very young children to focus on any one topic. In our review of the video and transcript together, however, Marylene identified it as a reflection on the difficulties children of this age have getting beyond the notion of regulating the behavior of others. The teacher's job, she told me, is to respond to this "natural" egocentrism and help them, first, learn to turn their gaze on themselves (which is why they were in a circle) and, then, to view society as a group that does not just self-regulate but also accomplishes shared projects. Looking at the length of time she had spent gently prompting the children to consider things other than classroom rules, she expressed a bit of frustration, but said that this was the difficult work that was needed in order to create the conditions in which a meaningful cooperative project could get off the ground. We used her words to comment on the meaning of this segment to our conference audience.

This was the first time that I had heard her articulate explicitly that cooperative practice was meant to prompt a developmental shift—from the ability to conceive of other-regulation to self-regulation. This added to my understanding and framing of the cooperative approach as an apprenticeship to collective identity, rights and responsibilities, which I relate, in my analyses, to the social and political context of Corsican language revitalisation (reflected in our last slide).

The parallel between the work of cooperation inside the classrooms that Marylene and I were describing and the collaborative work we were engaged in should be obvious to the reader. In fact, I see our developing conversation and its acts of framing and reframing as the kind of joint engagement that can begin to bridge the gap between, or coordinate the developmental/

Sequence 20.1 What Do We Talk about in Cooperative Meetings?

T	Chì si discuta in cuuperativa?	What do we talk about in cooperative meetings?
L	Pisà u ditu	Raise your finger.
T	Ci vole à pisà u ditu per piglià a parolla, ma tandu, quandu tu l'ai a parolla, chì discutemu in cuuperativa? Perchè chì femu riunione di cuuperativa?	You must raise your finger to talk, but once you have the floor, what do we talk about in cooperative meetings? Why do we have cooperative meetings?
L	Perchè luni fate reunione di cuuperativa.	Because Monday you do a cooperative meeting.
T	Melanie.	Melanie.
L	fate reunione di cuper, cuperativu.	You do a coop, a cooperative meeting.
T	Per chì fà? Andria.	To do what? Andria.
A	Per dì e regule di vita.	To say what the rules of life are.
T	Solu per dì e regule di vita?	Only to say what the rules of life are?
A	No. Per, per i denti di l'animali.	No. For animal's teeth.
T	Aspitta, aspitta. Quandu tu dici i denti di l'animali, chì vole dì? (Lisandru, avanza appinuccia, lascia Josselyn tranquillu). Què dinù face parte di cumpurtamenti di cuuperativa, eh? Ci vole à pisa u ditu ma ci vole dinù rispettà l'astru dinò, eh? Iè Morgane?	Wait, wait. When you say, animal's teeth, what does that mean. Lisandru, move forward a bit and leave Josselyn alone. That is also part of cooperative behavior, eh? You have to raise your finger but you also have to respect others, eh? Yes Morgane?
M	*Il faut pas frapper.*	*You must not hit.*
T	Iè ma, ditemi appena	Yes, but tell me
L	*Il faut pas donner des coups de pied.*	*You mustn't kick.*
T	Ripigliemu appinuccia l'affare di a cuuperativa. A cuuperativa ci ghjova à fa u puntu di u nostru cumpurtamentu. Semu d'accordu. Ma un femu, ùn ci hè chè e regule di vita. Un discutemu chè st'affare quì?	Let's revisit a bit what a cooperative is. The cooperative helps us take stock of our behavior. That we are agreed on. But we don't, it isn't just the rules of life. Do we just discuss those things?

Note: In the left-hand column of the transcript above, Corsican is represented in normal typeface and French in italics. These same conventions are used in the English translation in the right-hand column.

cognitive and the socio-cultural frameworks that I mentioned before. And in fact, this joint perspective is where we ended up in our presentation. In our final slide, I reiterated one of the frames I had introduced at the outset: which was the notion that bilingual schooling in Corsica was in many ways oriented towards creating the conditions in which acts of identity—including claims to own and use language—could take place. In the last paragraph (underlined/boldface) Marylene's developmental discourse is incorporated as it relates to our presentation of the process by which pedagogy is linked to the social project.

In sum, this hybrid text represented a productive dialogue between and coordination of different professional discourses. The end product—and our presentation itself, I think—highlighted and legitimated both of our different forms of expertise.

Again, I wish to draw attention to the parallels between the material we described and what we were doing ourselves. The link between pedagogy and the project of Corsican linguistic and cultural citizenship is an experiential one, relying on the development of a shared (democratic) praxis. Our shared praxis was the precondition for finding ways to articulate our two discourses in ways that were stimulating and productive for both of us in our linked but separate professional spheres. In some ways, as Hurtig also points out (2008: 102), the process was an integral part of the product of collaboration.

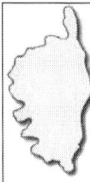

Concluding remarks/slides in the presentation

Relation entre l'approche Freinet sur

   a) la motivation de l'apprenti

   b) les relations entre l'individu et la collectivité dans le contexte actuel sociolinguistique

   c) l'intérêt de l'enseignement bilingue par rapport à la didactique linguistique et les compétences métalinguistiques.

Relationship between the Freinet perspective and

   a) student motivation

   b) the relationship between the individual and the collectivity in the current sociolinguistic context

   c) the benefit of bilingual education with respect to language pedagogy and metalinguistic competencies

Slide 20.6

Concluding slides, cont.

* pour apprendre une langue minoritaire dans un contexte de "language shift"
avancé, il faut un grand effort et une grande motivation du côté de l'individu,
qui doit s'approprier la langue minoritaire sans un grand soutien de la société
autour. Donc, l'enseignement bilingue doit créer des conditions qui puissent
induire cette motivation individuelle, qui puissent persuader l'individu que les
bénéfices personnelles et collectives d'une telle démarche valent l'effort requis
d'apprentissage.

The individual who wishes to learn a minority language in a context of language
shift has to have a high level of motivation in the absence of societal support.
Bilingual education must, therefore, create conditions in which this motivation
may develop. Persuade the individual that there are personal and collective
benefits that make the effort worthwhile.

L'enseignement bilingue s'agit non seulement de renforcer une identité existante,
mais de promouvoir un processus d'identification individuelle avec le corse et
la corsitude et la communauté corse.

**En bas âge, c'est surtout une relation affective avec la maîtresse:
enjeu est de la faire fonctionner à son avantage; après de l'orienter vers
un sens collectif**

Bilingual education is not just about reinforcing an existing identity, but promoting
a process of personal identification with Corsican and corsicanness, and with
the collectivity.

**For very young children, what needs to be done is mobilize their
primary, affective relationship with the teacher in the service of
developing their collective social consciousness.**

Slide 20.7

I alluded earlier to the significance, for the process of selection (of representative data), of us preparing a presentation for an outside audience. This was also a complex representational task on both epistemological and political levels, because the audience included both outsiders (international visitors) and insiders (other Corsican teachers, education administrators and university researchers). As a consequence, our joint presentation involved recontextualising insider knowledge and discourses for outsiders while at the same time responding to the local political context of discourse about Corsican bilingual educational practice. In doing so, we both decided what to say and what not to say, although I don't think we ever made this explicit. I think that this process raises some complicated questions regarding the relationship between our public discursive strategies and positions, our private discussions, and our professional/disciplinary/analytic stances. In general, I would say that our text (the presentation) on cooperative bilingual education underrepresented some of the complexities and dilemmas of practice that we talked about in preparation for the conference, including Marylene's doubts about the fit between cooperative philosophies and Corsican society. Note also that despite my declared reticence to apply linguistic anthropology on behalf of language as an unexamined category, on the last slide, speaking Corsican is embedded as a value in the statement about the "benefits" of bilingualism. There is some ambiguity about my voice in this slide, which can be read as an animation of Corsican values and assumptions, but I think that in the overall context of the presentation I positioned myself as aligned with such statements of value. It is an alignment that I could (and have) expressed in other contexts where I am not speaking with a practitioner, but in those contexts it would be more firmly embedded and framed within a more academic discourse in which my personal politics and ideologies were subject to the same scrutiny as my objects of study. In this presentation, however, I took up a direct, unmitigated stance of alignment with the goals of Corsican bilingual education. In this case, I made myself accountable to some of the imperatives of the social and political context in which Corsican bilingual education is situated, something that Hale identifies as one of the core stances of an activist, as opposed to a critical anthropological approach (2006). I would add that it also illustrates another element of practising applied linguistic (or other) anthropology: being willing to put yourself in a position in which you do not control the discursive context, because these are the conditions in which those who might apply elements of your research have to operate. This was partially true with respect to the framing and unfolding of the presentations during the conference itself; it was even more the case in the discourses framing that conference for the media. Although I do not have time or space to elaborate here, through my participation in the writing of press releases, and in newspaper interviews and radio broadcasts, I was thrust into a world of sound and text bites in which interpretive complexities were lost to basic acts of promotion and validation of minority language education efforts. This discourse was most definitely not mine to control.

CONCLUSIONS: ETHNOGRAPHY, CRITICAL PERSPECTIVES AND OUTCOMES OF APPLIED, COLLABORATIVE LINGUISTIC ANTHROPOLOGY

The first point that I would like to emphasise is a very basic one: that long-term ethnographic engagement is a precondition for the kinds of collaborative relationships and projects that are at the heart of an applied linguistic anthropology. In this perspective, long-term participation is not just the means by which ethnographers come to know and/or are integrated into a particular setting but is also the way that our collaborating practitioners come to know about us and to be interested in engaging with the disciplinary perspectives we bring to the table. Secondly, I want to reiterate a point that I made in the introduction: that a key element of collaborative research is creating a nexus of shared practice and discourse that productively mediates differences between researchers' and practitioners' respective professional Discourses or habituses. I view this mediation *as the fundamental applied goal or outcome* which may (or may not) lead to concrete, language-related products, policies or practices.

In her description of high levels of collaborative practice among teachers and anthropologists in the Hawaiian KEEP program, Jordan writes that "although some common understandings and interpretations certainly develop during the course of interaction and collaboration, these will never be complete" (1985: 116). Similarly, in the terms I am using here, the mediation of different discourses needs to be seen as a site of encounter and negotiation rather than a forced compromise or settlement. The outcomes can thus take a number of shapes and forms. As I hope my discussion of the conference presentation illustrates, this perspective leaves room for collaboratively produced texts in which researcher and practitioner discourses rub up against one another without being completely coordinated or integrated. It also leaves room for a variety of forms of "translation" of linguistic anthropological perspectives into practice or policy. In the KEEP program mentioned above, for example, the research team adopted a principle of "least change," in which ethnographic insights about classroom functioning were used to select, shape and combine practices from within the existing repertoire of professional education (Jordan, 1985: 112). In other words, the application took into account the deep hold of teachers' professional Discourse/habitus. As DePalma and Teague write, there are inevitable tensions between the different discourses and professional systems of accountability within which teachers and research operate (2008: 448). Collaboration in applied linguistic anthropology can thus respond to the "challenge of holding the tension among the various, and perhaps incompatible, perspectives that emerge through research" (Eisenhart, 1999, cited in DePalma and Teague, 2008: 453).

Furthermore, an applied linguistic anthropology that concentrates the focus of researcher and practitioner alike on process, discourse and ideology avoids the pitfalls of viewing language, collective identities and the relationships between them uncritically through essentialising ideological lenses. For example, the text that Marylene and I created together emphasised the link between the way that classrooms structure and scaffold notions and experiences of citizenship, and the role of Corsican language practice in the articulation of Corsican collective membership. Neither language nor citizenship, in this framework, is a fixed entity or target; rather, they are taken as co-constitutive. For Marylene, cooperative practice exemplified the kind of cultural and linguistic citizenship she envisioned in this context of language revitalisation, a perspective she shared with some, but not all Corsicans (and bilingual teachers). Linguistic anthropological approaches to discourse, in this scenario, can do the following: (a) they can provide social actors with access to the underlying terms of their points of consensus or debate, and (b) they can provide analytical tools for making specific connections between social formations and ideologies and forms of talk and interaction. Likewise, these approaches can be used to view our own anthropological discourses as forms of situated social action, and to critically examine the choices that we, and our collaborating partners, make in our representations of language, identity and their relationships. These choices, as Hale points out, engage us in the "contradictory process through which claims in the name of identity politics are made" (2006:114); a process which includes both the deconstruction and reproduction of dominant, essentialising discourses. They may also allow us to recognise the "cultural integrity" (Clifford, 2000) of such hybrid discourses among the people that we study and the academic integrity of occupying multiple and sometimes contradictory roles with respect to the knowledge that we help to produce and circulate.

REFERENCES

Brandt, E. 1988. Applied linguistic anthropology and American Indian language renewal. *Human Organization* 47(4): 322–29.

Clifford, J. 2000. Taking identity politics seriously: "the contradictory stony ground . . ." In *Without Guarantees: In Honor of Stuart Hall*, ed. P. Gilroy, L. Grossberg and A. McRobbie, 94–113. London: Verso.

Clifford, J. and Marcus, G. 1986. *Writing Culture*. Berkeley: University of California Press.

Dementi-Leonard, B. and Gilmore, P. 1999. Language revitalization and identity in social context: a community-based Athabascan language preservation project in interior Alaska. *Anthropology & Education Quarterly* 30(1): 37–55.

DePalma, R. and Teague, L. 2008. A democratic community of practice: unpicking all those words. *Educational Action Research* 16(4): 441–56.

Eisenhart, M. 1999. Reflections on educational intervention in light of postmodernism. *Anthropology & Education Quarterly* 30(4): 462–65.

Goodman, A. 2008. Expanding and engaging anthropologies. *Anthropology News* January: 21–22.

Gottlieb, A. 1995. Beyond the lonely anthropologist: collaboration in research and writing. *American Anthropologist* 97(1): 21–26.

Hale, C. 2006. Activist research vs. cultural critique: indigenous land rights and the contradictions of a politically engaged anthropology. *Cultural Anthropology* 21(1): 96–120.

Hurtig, J. 2008. Community writing, participatory research and an anthropological sensibility. *Anthropology & Education Quarterly* 39(1): 92–106.

Jordan, C. 1985. Translating culture: from ethnographic information to educational program. *Anthropology & Education Quarterly* 16(2): 105–23.

Lassiter, L. 2005. Collaborative ethnography and public anthropology. *Current Anthropology* 46(1): 83–106.

Leap, W. 1988. Indian language renewal. *Human Organization* 47(4): 283–91.

Marcus, G. 2001. From rapport under erasure to theaters of complicity and reflexivity. *Qualitative Inquiry* 7: 519–28.

McCarty, T., Borgoiakova, T., Gilmore, P., Tsainina Lomawaima, K. and Romero, M. E. (eds) 2005. Introduction: indigenous epistemologies and education: self-determination, anthropology and human rights. *Anthropology & Education Quarterly* 36(1): 1–7.

Peacock, J. 2007. Update on the AAA Ad Hoc Commission. *Anthropology News* 48(8): 12–13.

Scollon, R. 2001. *Mediated Discourse: The Nexus of Practice*. New York: Routledge.

Contributors

Jannis Androutsopoulos is Professor of German and Media Linguistics at the University of Hamburg. His research is located at the interface of sociolinguistics and media discourse, and his current interests include mediated multilingualism, style sociolinguistics, language ideologies, linguistic diversity in popular and fictional texts, and computer-mediated discourse. He is editor of special issues on computer-mediated communication in *Journal of Sociolinguistics* (2006) and *Language@internet* (2008).

Mike Baynham is Professor of TESOL at the University of Leeds and co-convenor of the AILA Research Network on Language and Migration. His research interests include literacy studies, narrative and migration. He co-edited with James Collins and Stef Slembrouck *Globalization and Language Contact* (Continuum, 2009).

Adrian Blackledge is Professor of Bilingualism in the School of Education, University of Birmingham and Director of the MOSAIC Centre for Research on Multilingualism. His research interests include the politics of multilingualism, linguistic ethnography, education of linguistic minority students, negotiation of identities in multilingual contexts, and language testing, citizenship, and immigration.

David Block is Professor of Languages in Education at the Institute of Education, University of London. He is interested in dimensions of globalisation and identity and how they relate to relate to language practices.

Florence Bonacina is a Teaching Fellow at the University of Edinburgh. In 2011, she was a post-doctoral research fellow at Edinburgh, funded by the ESRC. Her research interests include language policy and practice in multilingual educational settings, discourse analysis, and ethnography. Recent papers can be found in the *International Journal of Bilingual Education and Bilingualism* and *Language Policy*.

Gabriele Budach is Lecturer in French Linguistics at the University of Southampton. Her research focusses on the study of multilingualism, migration and literacy. Her areas of expertise include socio-cultural perspectives on bilingual education and biliteracy teaching and learning in school-based settings. Her recent work on urban Inuit in Canada is looking at multilingual literacy practices and processes of knowledge construction in the context of transnational migration.

Feliciano Chimbutane is Senior Lecturer of Linguistics at Universidade Eduardo Mondlane, Mozambique. His research interests include languages in education, with focus on classroom practice and the relationship between classroom discourse, day-to-day talk and the wider socio-political order.

Angela Creese is Professor of Educational Linguistics at the School of Education, University of Birmingham and a founding member of the MOSAIC Centre for Research on Multilingualism. Her research involves interactional sociolinguistics and ethnography and covers urban multilingual classrooms, multilingual repertoires and multilingual pedagogies and research methodologies.

Gill Cressey is a Senior Lecturer in Social and Community studies at Coventry University. Her current research is on responding to sensitive 'Race' issues in Higher Education teaching and learning; and an evaluation of educational attempts to prevent violent Far Right extremism in Coventry.

Bethan L. Davies is Lecturer in Linguistics at the University of Leeds. Her current research interests include linguistic politeness and metalinguistic debates, including multimodal analysis of the language ideological debates on the BBC Voices website.

Sheena Gardner a founding member of the MOSAIC Centre for Research on Multilingualism at the University of Birmingham, became Head of Department of English and Languages of Coventry University in 2011. Her research in educational linguistics on classroom discourse and genres of academic writing assumes systemic functional linguistics perspectives, as in *Genres of Assessed Student Writing in Higher Education* (2012, coauthored with H. Nesi, CUP).

Frances Giampapa is Lecturer in Education (TESOL/Applied Linguistics) at the Graduate School of Education, University of Bristol. Her ethnographic research investigates politics of identity, EAL and learning across multilingual educational contexts.

Monica Heller is Professor at the Ontario Institute for Studies in Education, University of Toronto. Her research focusses on the construction of social difference and social inequality in the globalised new economy. Her most recent book is *Paths to Post-Nationalism: A Critical Ethnography of Language and Identity* (2011, Oxford University Press).

Alexandra Jaffe is Professor of Linguistics and Anthropology at California State University, Long Beach. Her research interests include bilingual education on Corsica, minority language revitalisation and language ideologies, language in the media and orthography.

Carla Jonsson is Assistant Professor at the Centre for Research on Bilingualism at Stockholm University, Sweden. She currently works with two ethnographic research projects on bilingualism and multilingualism in education.

Samu Kytölä is currently Junior Researcher at the University of Jyväskylä, Finland. His research areas include English in Finland, multilingualism as a problematic resource, multicultural discourses of football, and the dynamics of internet writing.

Constant Leung is Professor of Educational Linguistics at King's College London. His research areas include additional/second language curriculum development, language assessment, language policy and planning and teacher professional development.

Charmian Kenner is a Lecturer in Educational Studies at Goldsmiths, University of London. Her research focusses on bilingual learning in homes, community settings and schools. Her books include *Becoming Biliterate* (2004, Trentham Books) and *Multilingual Europe* (co-edited with Tina Hickey, 2008, Stylus).

Eleni Mariou is a Teaching Fellow at the University of Edinburgh. She is a sociolinguist and studied for her Ph.D. at the University of Birmingham. Her research interests include language and identity, especially in migrant communities; language ideology, power and discourse; language in education and bilingualism/multilingualism.

Deirdre Martin is a Senior Lecturer, School of Education, University of Birmingham and a founding member of the MOSAIC Centre for Research on Multilingualism. Her research interest is language disabilities and multilingualism, and her major publication is *Language Disabilities in Cultural and Linguistic Diversity* (2009, Multilingual Matters).

Marilyn Martin-Jones is an Emeritus Professor based at the MOSAIC Centre for Research on Multilingualism, University of Birmingham. For over thirty years, she has been involved in research in bilingual and multilingual contexts in England and in Wales. She has a particular interest in the ways in which multilingual literacy practices contribute to the construction of identities, in local lifeworlds and institutional contexts and the ways in which such practices are bound up with local and global relations of power.

Tommaso M. Milani is a Senior Lecturer in Linguistics at the University of the Witwatersrand. His research focus is on language ideology. He has recently published the book *Language Ideologies and Media Discourse* (co-edited with Sally Johnson, 2010, Continuum).

Melissa G. Moyer is Associate Professor of English Linguistics at the Universitat Autònoma de Barcelona. Her current research is concerned with intercultural communication, migration, institutions of the nation-state and emerging forms of social organisation. She dedicates special attention to the link between institutional processes, power and control and how these are linked to multilingual practices in interaction.

Sibonile Mpendukana completed his MA (cum laude) in Linguistics at the University of the Western Cape in a thesis on transformative linguistic landscapes in township spaces. He is currently working on researching local mobile literacies in Cape Town and lecturing on New Literacies.

Sari Pietikäinen is Professor of Discourse Studies at the University of Jyväskylä, Finland. Her research areas include multilingualism in minority language communities, sociolinguistics of peripheral multilingualism, minority language media, multimodal discourse analysis and ethnography.

Mark Sebba is Reader in Sociolinguistics and Language Contact at Lancaster University. His interests are in social aspects of bilingualism, multimodality and the sociolinguistics of orthography.

Christopher Stroud is Professor of Linguistics at the University of the Western Cape and Professor of Bilingualism at Stockholm University. He has worked in the areas of multilingual education and socialisation, the politics of language, ethnographic approaches to literacy, the sociolinguistic development of new (Portuguese) varieties in Mozambique and language ideological debates.

Will Turner is a former journalist. His PhD (Leeds) explores relations between media practice and language ideologies on the BBC Voices website. Particular areas of interest include multimodal discourse analysis and media ethnography.

Li Wei is Professor of Applied Linguistics and Director of Birkbeck Graduate Research School, University of London. His research interests include bilingualism and multilingualism as well as intercultural pragmatics. He is Principal Editor of the *International Journal of Bilingualism* (Sage).

Aizan Yaacob is Senior Lecturer at the Universiti Utara Malaysia. She obtained her PhD at the University of Warwick and her research interests include bilingual and multilingual education, early literacy, English for Young Learners (EYL) and ESL.

Index

A

access, 7, 10, 22, 26, 28, 31, 35, 37, 40, 51, 58, 82, 90, 95, 103–105, 113, 122–123, 128, 133, 151, 181, 198, 201, 210–211, 219, 228, 241–242, 256, 261–262, 265, 269–280, 308–310, 316, 329, 331, 351
Africa(n), 7, 153, 155
African American, 55–58, see also Black American
AAVE, 157
African Caribbean, 134
Africa, North, 40, 51, 120, 187,
Africa, South, 9, 149, 151, 155, 287
African languages, 151, 154–156, 289, 291, see also Changana, Chope, isiXhosa
Afrikaans, 206–207
agency, 2, 11, 20–22, 31, 37, 40, 47–58, 113, 138, 146–150, 159, 164, 168, 170, 175–176, 259, 321
America(n), see African American, Black American, North American
Arabic, 87, 122, 138, 185, 187, 191, 203, 206–207, 219, 243–244
assimilation, 91, 112, 131, 137, 140, 217

B

Bangla, Bangladesh, 84–87, 219
Bengal(i), 64–65, 82–87, 207
bilingualism, 4, 9, 21, 30, 131, 134, 145–146, 179, 182, 256, 259–261, 272, 337, 349
Black American, 134

C

Canada, see French Canadian, Italian Canadian
Catalan, 37, 40, 42–44

children, chapters 5, 10, 14, 16, 17, 19
Changana, 290–300
Chinese, 207, 219, 271
Chope, 290–291
circumstantial activist, 301–303
classroom based research, 12, 79; chapters 13–16
classroom discourse, 65, 76, 85
classroom observations, 82–87, 241–242, 257–267, 321
collaborative research, 170, 221, 307, 324, 350
collaborative photography, 169
community and community contexts, chapters 1, 4, 5, 6, 7, 9, 18
complementary schools, 64–65, 82–84, 91, 219
computer-mediated communication (cmc), 7, 179–180, 197, 212
computer-mediated discourse (cmd), 147, 179, 181, 192
commodification, 8, 9, 28, 35, 36, 150
Cornish, 204–210
Corsican, 287, 334–350
Corsica, 287, 334–355
critical approaches, 1, 68, 145, 308, 335, 350
anthropology,
ethnography, 65, 95–98, 106, 286, 305, 307, 309, 315, 317, 334
methodologies, 96
perspectives, 1, 22, 34, 35, 95, 286, 305, 306, 312
research, 4, 6, 11, 12, 95, 305
sociolinguistics, 22, 34–5
theory, 2
Croatian, 203–204, 207
curriculum, 78, 87, 128, 129, 222–223, 228–238, 241, 289, 320–330, 337

bicultural curriculum development, 320–323

cross-language/cross-subject teaching, 324, 330

culture, language and identity, 26, 28, 32, 56–58, 72–79, 84, 131–133, 135–136, 220, 264–267, 329, 334, see also popular culture

D

dialogic methods, 12, 65, 91–99, 103, 156, 157, 170, 175, 220, 224, 234, 242, 246, 253, 256–267, 293, 300, 303, 320, 323–326, 334, 338, 340, 348

diaries, 101, 169, 220, 257, 263–264, 266–267

diaspora, 5, 63, 65, 68, 70, 72, 77, 98, 131–141

discourse analysis, 3, 12, 19, 145, 146, 163, 167, 169, 179, 180, 181, 188, 192–3

E

epistemology, 1, 2, 4, 180, 319, 335, 336, 349

essentialism, 3, 4, 54, 307, 315, 329, 351–352

ethics, 73, 167, 185, 273, 308–310, 316

ethnography, Introduction
    collaborative ethnography, chapter 19
    critical linguistic ethnography, chapters 6 and 18
    material ethnography, chapter 9
    online ethnography, chapter 11
    school ethnography, chapters 5, 13–17, 19
    sociolinguistic ethnography, chapter 1
    visual ethnography, chapter 10

ethnoscapes, 5

F

Finnish, Finland, 147, 164–168, 175, 179–193

football, 7, 10, 140, 147, 179–192

France, 8, 27, 120, 217, 219, 269–278, 337

French, 8, 21, 58, 68, 120, 152, 204, 207, 217, 219, 269, 271–280, 338–339, 341–343, 347

French Canadian, 8, 9, 11, 21, 24–33

G

Georgia, 10, 63, 67–78

German, 181, 183, 207, 272, 286, 320, 322–330

globalisation, 1, 4, 5, 8, 9, 20, 21, 25, 34, 41, 44, 52, 92, 165

global asymmetries, 9, 22, 63

Greek, 207
    and Pontian Greek 63–64, 67–80
    and Latin, 231–237

H

habitus, 50–52, 150, 287, 334, 337, 350–351

Hebrew, 205

heritage, 8, 64–65, 79–80, 82–84, 88–89, 91–92, 97, 102–104

heteroglossia, 91, 135

Hindi, 138, 201, 203, 207, 209

history, 22, 26–29, 49–58, 64–65, 73, 75, 77, 99, 112, 115, 119, 181, 187, 201, 204–206, 271, 312, 321, 323

I

ideology, 3–4, 19–21, 28, 41–46, 54, 64, 69, 71, 84, 91–92, 189, 271, 276–279, 351

imagined communities, 3

immersion, two-way, 286, 321–323, 329

immigrant/immigration, 6, 27–29, 54, 56–57, 64–65, 75–77, 97, 111–113, 132–133, 137, 187, 339

indigenous/indigenous language/community, 163–164, 165–166, 171, 204, 207, 335

inheritance, 84

internet, 7, 36, 145–147, 180, 182–183, 188, 198, 201, 205, 206, 210–211, see also web

interview, 42, 53, 64, 70–72, 83, 101–104, 120–127, 131–132, 137, 167–170, 193, 220, 241–244, 247, 252–253, 257–258, 260–266, 271–272, 277–278, 290–291, 293, 296, 300–303, 309–314, 340, 350
    ethnographic interview, 285–286, 312
    retrospective interview, 319–331

isiXhosa, 151–160

Italian Canadian, 11, 95–106
Italian, 11, 65–66, 99, 207, 320,
    322–330

K

Kashmir, Mirpuri, 132, 137, 140

L

language and identity, 30, 48, 64,
    68–69, see also culture, lan-
    guage and identity
language industries, 9, see also
    commodification
language policy, 9, 12, 222, 259, 271,
    285
linguistic citizenship, 351
linguistic ethnography, 145, 306, see
    also ethnography
linguistic minority/ minority language,
    3, 4, 21, 29, 30, 31, 63, 65, 68,
    70, 80, 146, 164, 165, 204,
    222–223, 229, 308–309, 316,
    321, 335, 339, 350
local/local communities, chapters 1,
literacy
    adult literacy, 120–1, 126–9
    digital literacies, 7, 8, 145
    early literacy, 245
    literacy events, 247, 258, 264, 343
    Literacy Hour, 244, 246, 251
    literacy practices, 6, 121, 145,
        242–3, 336
    literacy skills, 168
    multilingual literacy, 5, 6, 7, 8,
        137–8, 146, 323
    screen literacy, 7

M

Malay, 219–220, 241–254
mediascapes, 5, 6, 7, 11, 182
Mexican, 55–57
migration, 5–6, 11, 20–21, 27–30, 43,
    54, 56, 68, 77, 92, 113, 131,
    137, 139, 151, 201, 204, 222,
    290, 326, 331
    chain migration, 131, 137, 139
mobile resources, 5, 10, 145, 156, 312
mobility, 5, 6, 9, 28, 29, 31, 34, 44,
    112, 117, 146, 156, 158–9, 164,
    177
mother tongue, 71, 74, 131, 137, 138,
    140, 165, 167, 205, 208, 230,
    248, 291, 311

Mozambique, 285, 288–301
multimodality, 6–7, 9, 55–58, 120,
    145–147, 150–160, 163–176,
    315, 324, 329

N

negotiation of access, 270–280
    negotiation of identities, 64–65,
        chapters 4 and 5
    negotiation of information, 37
    negotiation of meanings, knowledge,
        169, 321
    negotiation of roles, 242
non-Standard English, 92, 184–192,
    291
North America(n), 47–58, 95–106,
    116, 134, 138, 157, 335, 337

O

one-language-one-nation ideology, 4
online ethnography, 180–185

P

Pakistan(i), 86–87, 122, 132–140
pedagogy, 12, 90, 218–220, 222, 237–
    238, 256, 286–287, 320–321,
    326, 341–343, 348
performative sociolinguistics, 119, 128
Polish, 186, 207
political economy, 8, 28, 68–9, 82
popular culture, 4, 28, 56, 83, 88
Portuguese, 207, 271, 285, 289, 291,
    293, 296, 300
poststructuralist approaches, 22, 47–8,
    58, 68–9
    perspectives, 1, 3, 4, 22
    theory, 2, 3
Punjabi, 37, 135

R

repertoire, linguistic/communicative/
    verbal, 6, 65, 68, 71, 79, 83, 94,
    104, 111, 138, 149, 152, 167,
    181, 221, 272, 279, 313, 343,
    351
Russian, 63–64, 67, 71–78, 164

S

Sámi, 146, 163–176
school ethnography, see ethnography
Serbian, 203–204, 207
social inequality, 1, 21, 26, 69, 306,
    307

sociolinguistics of mobile resources, 5
sociolinguistics of/and multilingual-
    ism, 1, 2, 19, 22, 68, 145, 159,
    179
space, chapter 5, part III
Spanish, 40, 42–43, 56–57, 164,
    204–205, 217, 257, 259–260
subjectivity/ies, 1, 47, 50, 53, 57, 58,
    96, 97, 98, 113, 116, 138, 149,
    150, 152, 154, 159, 160
superdiversity, 5, 6
Sweden, Swedish, 164, 183, 220,
    257–268
symbolic power, 2, 66, 69

T
team-teaching, 286, 321–330
technoscapes, 5, 6, 11
text trajectories, 181, 184, 188, 192,
    193
trajectories, 5, 6, 10, 11, 21, 25, 27, 28,
    30, 31, 32, 97, 109, 111, 112,
    113, 117, 121, 125, 126, 127,
    129, 150, 164, 165, 174, 190,
    233, 280, 291, 321, 323 see also
    text trajectories

translation, 9–10, 30, 37, 40, 131–140,
    156, 183, 187–194, 253, 260,
    308, 341–342, 347, 351
tropes, 4, 9
Turkish, Turkey, 63–65, 67, 74, 82, 84,
    87, 88, 89, 122–124, 185–188,
    191, 207

U
Urdu, 137, 138, 201, 203, 207, 209

V
visual ethnography, chapter 10

W
web, 9, 70, 83, 147, 179, 181–183, 193,
    197–201, 205–206, 209–212,
    263, 343, see also internet
Welsh, 207

X
Xhosa, isiXhosa, 151–160

Y
youth, 101–102, 131, 140, 157, chap-
    ters 3, 4, 13, 15